Century's Ebb

Books by John Dos Passos

One Man's Initiation

Rosinante to the Road Again

A Pushcart at the Curb

Streets of Night

Orient Express

In All Countries

Three Plays:

    The Garbage Man

    Airways, Inc.

    Fortune Heights

Journeys Between Wars

The Ground We Stand On

State of the Nation

Tour of Duty

The Prospect Before Us

Head and Heart of Thomas Jefferson

The Theme Is Freedom

The Men Who Made the Nation

Prospects of a Golden Age

The Best of Times

Contemporary Chronicles:

Chosen Country (1)

Three Soldiers (2)

Manhattan Transfer (3)

U.S.A.:

    The 42nd Parallel (4)

    Nineteen Nineteen (5)

    The Big Money (6)

District of Columbia:

    Adventures of a Young Man (7)

    Number One (8)

    The Grand Design (9)

Most Likely to Succeed (10)

The Great Days (11)

Midcentury (12)

Century's Ebb (13)

Letters and Diaries of John Dos Passos (14),
    edited by Townsend Ludington

Century's Ebb

Ebb

The Thirteenth Chronicle

BY JOHN DOS PASSOS

GAMBIT ~ BOSTON

1975

First printing

Copyright © 1975 by Elizabeth H. Dos Passos
All rights reserved including the right to
reproduce this book or parts thereof in any form
Library of Congress Catalog Card Number: 75–920
International Standard Book Number: 0–87645–089–3

Printed in the United States of America

CONTENTS

Part I Century's Ebb

Part II Life's Gymnasium

CONTENTS

Contents

Foreword

JOHN DOS PASSOS finished work on *Century's Ebb* some months before his death in 1970. In the fifties it had occurred to him that the word "novels" did not describe adequately that extraordinary series of books for which he is best known. They are characterized by the uninhibited use of many writing forms: biography, current history, romantic fiction, on-the-spot reporting, historical parallel and even blank verse. They are a series of impressions, complexly interrelated from chapter to chapter and book to book— a single, century-long bolt of cloth miraculously woven on many looms.

Dos Passos chose the phrase *Contemporary Chronicles* to govern them all. Those books that are now the core of his work were then arranged in order, not of their writing but of their happening. Thus *Chosen Country*, not published until 1951, which looks backward to the author's childhood and before, then to his growing up and first marriage, became Chronicle #1; *Three Soldiers*, published in 1921, became #2 and so on. In this sequence, *Century's Ebb*, by any reckoning the concluding volume, is Chronicle #13.

In 1973 Gambit published selections from Dos Passos' letters and diaries under the appropriate but not entirely accurate title, *The Fourteenth Chronicle*. We puzzled long over the timing of its publication. The letters and diaries reveal the author of the *Chronicles* by different means. It seemed to us that Dos Passos' readers had reason to know him as a correspondent and diarist before coming to this concluding book, which in undiminished colors and with all his passionate feeling for the individual's right to thought, dignity, loyalty and love, closes his view of earth's picaresque journey through this century.

Dos Passos himself did not send the manuscript of *Century's*

Ebb to his publishers. He told one of us that he felt the book was done, but that he wanted to go over it, arrange or rearrange, add or delete and consider it as a whole. What he had in mind, or what he was able to do, is now impossible to know. It is evident that one or more fictional sections for the latter part of the book, if they ever existed in any form, were not in the text Dos Passos left, nor is there any record of them. Beyond that it is clear that the time sequences of some of the existing fictional narratives do not always mesh. It may be that Dos Passos thought he followed his characters farther than he did. These things we have, of course, let stand as we have some historical errors whose correction could have been more misleading than the mistakes. Without altering the text, we have changed the order of one or two passages that presupposed knowledge not yet given to the reader and we have adjusted minor infelicities that would have been caught in any final reading.

In these senses and one other, *Century's Ebb* was not completed. No book can be said to be finished until the author has released the last page proof to the printer. He will by then have reviewed his work twice or perhaps three times and, according to his habit of work, almost certainly will have made minor or even major changes. Small questions of fact will be checked, ugly repetitions that damage their first statements will be caught, too much of something will be cut and new detail tooled in. Print, particularly in galley or page proof, does not lose its magic for any writer. Print is a rite of passage in which unexpected qualities suddenly show themselves as in a child first dressed for a grown-up party. This, then, "is not a perfect book," as Henry Seidel Canby wrote in the course of praising *Three Soldiers* in 1921, but as Canby also said, "it cannot be dismissed." But in the broad sense it was a final statement whose edges only are blurred and foxed.

All of us at Gambit knew Dos Passos for many years, and we cannot deny ourselves some reflection on his personal quality and on his work. Although his life may appear long and relatively quiet in retrospect, perhaps more than any other major American writer of his generation except Hemingway he felt impelled to put his body where his pen was, to write of events in which he participated or saw at first hand. He was a man of action without the appearance of it. In the First World War he joined the Norton-Harjes ambulance unit, serving at Verdun and later in Italy. He came to Boston to protest the conviction and execution of Sacco and Vanzetti and was in Harlan County during the coal mine troubles. He reported the Spanish Civil War and, in the Second World War, went to the Pacific to write for *Life* magazine. He loved the places where he lived, particularly Virginia and Cape Cod, but he never could stay long; he was a compulsive, adventurous traveler.

Yet he never forgot his friends. They were everywhere, from all stages of his life. All of them know and have spoken of his sometimes awkward eagerness, his gentleness, constancy and enthusiasm, no matter what literary and political labels were being attached to him. He was not self-regarding any more than he was theoretical or dogmatic. He was not a good hater, except in the abstract. He kept his friends by going to see them and writing them letters.

It is this quality, combined with his power as a writer, that has given the *Chronicles* their sense of immediacy. Dos Passos was insatiably interested. Matters animal, vegetable, mineral and the latest scientific data—he wanted them all and used them continuously. For a writer and a man of action, writing is the supreme action. Thus the *Chronicles* are a continuous engagement with time, as decade by decade it rolled by Dos Passos' camera eye and his recording ear. Each book is of its period, but each is colored by a unifying sympathy for those who suffer misfortune in a world that has inflicted misery in the name of progress.

Like Walt Whitman, Dos Passos respected the herd but chose to celebrate particular, ordinary and unordinary men and women. Explicit in *Century's Ebb,* and implicit through all the *Chronicles,* are Whitman's searching questions about the possibilities for democracy. In his life's work, Dos Passos has embodied what Whitman saw in America's future—a hot, terrible, inspiring, unbelievable jumble of events—our century.

THE PUBLISHERS

Boston
July, 1975

Century's Ebb

PART I
CENTURY'S EBB

I

Strike up for a New World

You, Walt Whitman,
who rose out of fish-shape Paumanok
to go crying, like the spotted hawk,
your barbaric yawp over the roofs,
to utter "the password primeval,"
and strike up for a new world;
what would you say, Walt, here, now, today,
of these States that you loved,
Walt Whitman, what would you say?

     Born of a rundown family on a rundown farm on the high dry
hills of Long Island,
     Walt could well lay claim to the title
     of average man—less than average:
     bottom of the heap—;
     but, from their saltbox at West Hills the Whitmans could see
to the north the silver streak of the Sound already furrowed by
steamboats,
     and to the south on clear days, scallopings of the surf on the
Atlantic beaches—:
     and the old graveyard nearby where lay the graves of farmer
ancestors: Whitmans and Van Velsors, slaveowners and prosperous
men.

Walt's father was no churchgoer but there was a family friendship with Elias Hicks, a Long Island man, the Quaker preacher to
whom the freehearted Hicksites looked for leadership:—

Links to "the big round apple of the world."

Walt was born in the old family farmhouse at West Hills in
1819,

the year the first ship crossed to England under steam.

Monroe was President. Jefferson in Virginia was fighting a last
losing fight for public schools to teach the democratic creed.

Lincoln, in backwoods Kentucky, was a boy of ten.

Farming yielded little on those dry acres: Walt's father
worked as a carpenter, in winter cut cordwood; a dour shiftless man
who never could make a go of things. Biographers have claimed
Walt's mother was as illiterate as Nancy Hanks, but to Walt she was
the paragon of woman's virtues: not his whole life long did he cut
loose from her apronstrings.

When Walt was four the family moved to Brooklyn. The
village was booming. Walt's father had a chance to make a fortune
building houses under contract, but something always went wrong.
Debts. Foreclosures.

Walt's schooling was seven sessions at the public school and
some attendance at Bible classes conducted at Saint Anne's Episcopal Church for the children of the poor.

At eleven he began to earn his living running errands for a
firm of attorneys.

His employers coached him in writing a neat Spencerian hand,
encouraged him to read; set him up to a subscription to a circulating library.

At fourteen his father apprenticed him to the editor of a
Tammany weekly called *The Long Island Patriot* to learn the
printer's trade. Stuffed to the ears with Sir Walter Scott, the boy
early began to contribute "sentimental bits" to the papers he
worked for.

At home, though he adored his mother, he found it hard to
get along with his old man.

Journeyman printer, itinerant journalist, roving schoolteacher
in various Long Island villages.

At nineteen, with his nine-year-old brother George for an assistant, he tried to start a paper of his own, *The Long Islander.*

He campaigned for Van Buren.

Back in New York he worked as editor and compositor. His first publication was a temperance tract.

At the age of twentyseven he began to earn a real salary editing *The Brooklyn Daily Eagle,* carried a cane, wore a frock coat, a silk hat and a flower in his buttonhole;

but, instead of sitting up solemn at his editorial desk he spent his days riding the ferries and buses, never missed a new play at the theatres, roamed the streets, loafed on the wharves,

buddied up to stagedrivers, carmen, jacktars off the ships. Walt didn't drink, steered clear of women, seemed to engage in no sort of dissipation, but at heart he was as shiftless as his old man.

His dissipations were the sights and sounds of New York and Brooklyn:

the unsurpassed situation, rivers and bay, sparkling sea-tides, costly and lofty new buildings, facades of marble and iron, the preponderance of white and blue, flags flying, the endless ships, the tumultuous streets, Broadway, the heavy low musical roar,—

. . . that and the gulls soaring, the twitter of swallows in the sunset, the grace of a wellset young workingman . . .

roughs and little children . . . the young mechanic is closest to me, he knows me well,

The woodman who takes his jug and axe with him shall take me with him all day,

The farmboy ploughing in the field feels good at the sound of my voice . . .

When the owner of *The Brooklyn Eagle* fired Walt for being incorrigibly lazy—Walt claimed it was on account of his "free soil" principles—he took off for New Orleans to write for a sheet called *The Crescent.* For company he took along his young brother Jeff. Walt wrote; Jeff worked as officeboy. In three months they had worn out their welcome. The pair traveled home by steamboat up the Mississippi, by canalboat to Chicago; from there by the lake steamers to Buffalo, rail to Albany, riverboat to Brooklyn.

Walt kept his notes of the trip; at last he was hobnobbing with all the various varied inhabitants of these States.

The vision of the great expanding continent, Walt Whitman's continent, went with him through life.

Back in Brooklyn he edited *The Freeman;* then knocked off for the summer to help in his father's housebuilding and carpentering. He was seriously at work on the poems which were to make up *Leaves of Grass.*

"This is what you shall do," Walt wrote in the preface to the first edition, "love the earth and sun and animals, despise riches, give alms to everyone that asks, stand up for the stupid and crazy, devote your income and labor to others, hate tyrants, argue not concerning God, have patience and indulgence towards the people . . ."

He lived by that creed. He wrote constantly. His earliest writing was crass journalism but gradually his words began to fall into the rhythms that formed him a style.

In 1855, the year his father died, he got up his nerve to publish twelve poems.

"Who is this arrogant young man who proclaims himself the poet of the time?" wrote a critic in the *New York Times,* "who roots like a pig among the rotten garbage of licentious thoughts?"

Ralph Waldo Emerson, a poet himself, took fire. "I greet you," he wrote Whitman, "at the beginning of a great career."

With the successive publications of *Leaves of Grass* Whitman took his stance before the world. In a steel engraving facing "The Song of Myself," there was Walt for all men to see: bearded, a slouch hat on the back of his head, rough trousers, a workman's shirt open at the throat, tramp of the open road, the young man's camerado, the solitary singer of the West.

These were years of prophets and utopias. Robert Owen's New Harmony had set off a spate of communistic communities. Joseph Smith had established a new religion in Fayette, New York. Workingmen's parties, spiritualism, phrenology, labor unions, societies to bring about universal peace, prison reform, woman's suffrage, temperance, the abolition of slavery . . . demands, declarations, protests: a passion to do good stirred the democracy:

"The true nationality of the States," wrote Whitman, looking backwards in *Democratic Vistas* in 1870, "the genuine Union, when we come to a mortal crisis, is and is to be, after all, neither the written law, nor (as is generally supposed) either self-interest or common pecuniary or material objects—but the fervid and tremendous *Idea*."

When "the mortal crisis" comes, Whitman throws himself into the only service he feels fitted for. His evangel of love of man for man he turns into deeds. Half male nurse, half missionary, like some St. Francis strayed from the ages of faith, he tends the wounded and sick. No fear of infection—smallpox, typhus, typhoid, dysentery—no horror of crushed bones, drip of blood, gangrene, maggoty wounds can hold him back.

"My limbs, my veins dilate. My theme is clear at last."

His first visit to the troops was to find his brother George reported wounded in Burnside's unlucky attempt to cross the Rappahannock at Fredericksburg in December of 1862. George, the only member of the Whitman family really competent in practical matters, was a Lieutenant in the 51st New York Volunteers. The wound proved to be merely a gash in the cheek. George was far too busy attending to his troops to listen to Walt's lectures on the manly virtue of "adhesiveness." George was promoted to captain while Walt was bunking in his tent.

Back in Washington Walt wrote comforting letters home to his mother and his brothers and sisters. With no wife or child of his own, his family was all he had to love, his family and the broken soldiers in the putrid wards.

Washington was one great lazarhouse. Public buildings were given over to the wounded and the sick. Not enough beds, not enough doctors, not enough nurses, lack of drugs. Chloroform in short supply. Walt went to work for a pittance copying documents mornings in a paymaster's office. Afternoons he haunted the hospitals, stooping over the crowded cots of the wounded, fetching water, helping as best he could change dressings, "petting and soothing, and sitting by them and feeding them their dinner or supper."

Whitman at fortythree looked prematurely old.

His beard and hair were streaked with white.

He made free of his own money and of contributions he raised from friends to buy fruits and sweet biscuits, stamps and writing paper.

It was a great day when he could distribute a few gallons of ice cream.

He wrote letters home, noted the last requests of the dying, bustled about the wards bringing neglected cases to the attention of physicians. They thought of him as a whiskered old crank who went around kissing the boys goodnight, but many a man who recovered under his care made him happy by declaring it was Walt's attention that had saved his life.

No longer the solitary singer, he had made friends, disciples.

In January 1865, wellwishers wangled him a clerkship in the Indian Bureau. Government jobs were all sinecures in those days. His work must have been considered satisfactory because he was promoted in May. The promotion only lasted a month.

One day in June, Secretary of the Interior Harlan, snooping around the office after hours, found a copy of *Leaves of Grass*, already in its third edition, in Whitman's desk. Horrified, he fired Clerk Whitman, then and there, as the author of an indecent book.

Whitman's friends raised an outcry. By fall he was back in government service, this time in the Attorney General's office. He had formed a firm friendship with John Burroughs who wrote an appreciation of him. A critic protesting his treatment by Secretary Harlan called him "the good gray poet."

Whitman still worked himself sick breathing life into the dying and the maimed. Occasionally on the dusty Washington streets he saw the President drive by in his shabby carriage with a troop of cavalry in his train. He wrote his mother of the sadness he saw in Lincoln's long dark face under the "cylindrical hat." "Mr. Lincoln has done as good as any man could do."

When Lincoln was killed, Walt Whitman poured all the hospital pain, the charnel agony, the courage and the grief into "When Lilacs Last in the Dooryard Bloomed." At last, as he had so wanted, he was the poet who put into words the agony of spirit of the people of these States.

... Then with the knowledge of death as walking one side of me
And the thought of death close walking the other side of me
And I in the middle as with companions, and as holding the hands of companions,
I fled forth to the hiding receiving night that talks not,
Down to the shores of the water, the path by the swamp in the dimness ...

"When Lilacs Last in the Dooryard Bloomed" made Whitman illustrious. Invitations came to read his poems at colleges and before philosophical groups. Emerson talked him up. In England among the Pre-Raphaelites he found passionate supporters. William Michael Rossetti edited a selection of his poems. *Leaves of Grass* went into a fifth and sixth printing. A permanent clerkship was found for him in the Attorney General's office at a salary of $1600 a year.

His verse was more than ever a paeon to America:

As I walk these broad majestic days of peace
I too announce solid things,
Science, ships, politics, cities, factories, are not nothing,
Like a grand procession to music of distant bugles pouring ...
they stand for realities ... years of the modern, years of the unperformed ...

He published prose as well: *Democratic Vistas*. From his sinecure in Washington he let his eye roam over his beloved people. Doubts plagued him. He had dreamed of

Successions of men, Americans, a hundred million,
One generation playing its part and passing on
Another generation playing its part and passing on in its turn
With faces turned sideways or backwards, towards me to listen.

The average man of a land at last only is important. He, in these States, remains immortal owner and boss, deriving good uses somehow, out of any sort of servant in office, even the basest; (certain universal requisites and their settled regularity and protec-

tion being first secured) a nation like ours, in a sort of geological formation state, trying continually new experiments, choosing new delegations, is not served by the best men only, but sometimes more by those that provoke it—by the combats they arouse. Thus national rage, fury, discussions, etc. better than content. Thus, also, the warning signals, invaluable for after times.

Now he heard the warning signals. He dreaded the corruption of his "audience interminable."

Eighteen seventythree was an unhappy year. He had been complaining about "bad spells in the head" in his letters to his mother. In January he suffered a stroke. The hospitals had ruined his health.

That spring he was transferred to the office of the Solicitor of the Treasury. He took sickleave and headed for the Jersey Shore. The seabreeze and the salt spume had always meant health to him. When he reached his brother George's house in Camden he found he could go no further.

His mother was lying there ill. Her death was almost the end of him.

He was dismissed from his clerkship which he'd tried to hold by hiring a substitute. Now he had to scratch hard for a living from the magazines and from lectures.

He stayed for nine years with his brother George, gradually recovering his ability to write and to travel, until he was well enough to visit admirers in New England. On a trip to St. Louis to see his brother Jeff, in spite of his lameness he pushed on to Denver. The following year he took a long jaunt through Canada as far north as the Saguenay River.

He quarreled with George and bought himself his own little shack near the Camden Ferry. His lameness got worse. A group of welloff writers, Mark Twain, Oliver Wendell Holmes and Whittier in the lead, chipped in to buy him a horse and a buggy.

In 1890 he was still lecturing occasionally. He attended a dinner in his honor offered by the citizens of Camden. That winter he was ill of pneumonia. He never really recovered. In March 1892 he died at his house in Camden and was buried in Harleigh cemetery under a tomb of his own designing.

Here, now, today, if you came back to us, Walt Whitman, what would you say?

For the nation still "in a sort of geological formation state, trying continually new experiments, choosing new delegations," what are "the warning signals"?

Singer of occupations: house-building . . .
Blacksmithing, glass-blowing, nail-making, coopering, tin-roofing, shingle-dressing,
Ship-joining, dock-building, fish-curing, the flagging of side-walks by flaggers

Is your "fervid and tremendous *Idea*"
lost in "solid things" . . . "science, ships, politics, cities, factories," in these years of "unprecedented material advancement"?
Are we indeed men worthy of the name, Walt Whitman, in these "years of the modern, years of the unperformed"?

2

Turnpike

Out of the Jersey truckfarms, the cornfields, the green slopes golden with Guernseys; cowbarns sporting a silo the way a church sports a steeple; bright watertanks, one a huge ball rolling through treetops; the toycolored plants of new industries . . .

SCENICRUISER FOR ECONOMY
Go Greyhound

. . . the sixlane highway
   that arches the reedy rivers and skirts the fields of red clover,
   now in whine of windfriction, hiss of tires, valvechatter, grumble of diesels, drone of exhausts,
   plunges under a rampaging bridge,
   sixlane under sixlane.

HORSE TRANSPORTATION

To the right a square brick mansion with curved stone pediments, capped by a glassedin cupola,
   (uncompromising as a tintype of General Ulysses S. Grant, posed on a porch with his family, all in their stiff Sunday best),
   stands up and is gone,
   vanished like the haze of croplands bucolic with summer some long-dead landowner viewed with pleasure from his cupola.

CITIES SERVICE

The turnpike speeds out of yesterday, mudguard to mudguard through sulphuric gusts into tomorrow's horizon:

intertwined tubing that curves round aluminum bottleshapes, distillators, retorts: a plumber's nightmare! Steel pylons supporting hightension powerlines stalk like H. G. Wells' Martians across the industrial plain.

DRIVE SLOW ACCIDENT AHEAD

This was three nights ago. You can still see where the shoulder's gouged. The night had been misty and after midnight the turnpike troopers set the signs putting the speedlimit at thirtyfive instead of sixty. As the fog thickened in the predawn chill, smoke from a smoldering dump reduced visibility to zero.

This is the time when the turnpike roars with produce trucks charging into town to make the early market.

The driver of the first tractortrailer to get into trouble told police afterwards he had already slowed down to thirtyfive when he saw a sign warning of fog ahead. Suddenly he found he couldn't see anything and stepped on his brakes and immediately another tractortrailer, driven by a young man from North Carolina, struck him in the rear. The impact pushed the first tractortrailer about seventyfive feet up the road into a car driven by a New Jersey man.

That car ended up safe in the ditch but the two tractortrailers jackknifed across the traffic lanes. Before anybody could lift a hand ten more tractortrailers and two cars had plowed into the wreckage. Five drivers were killed outright. One died on the way to the hospital and seven men were more or less seriously injured.

The last man to pile up, a man named Gautier from Port Huron, Michigan, who was bringing in a truckload of Great Lakes fish, told a reporter in the hospital he never saw the wreckage before he hit it. All he saw was a fogbank and the brakelights of the truck ahead, and then he crashed. He was lucky to get out of it with minor cuts about the head and hands and was released after treatment. The desk sergeant said it was the worst he'd ever seen. "No cars overturned but the trailers all split open. One was completely buried under wreckage."

The troopers sealed off the turnpike and deflected the traffic to Route 1. Ambulance and rescue squads came in from Elizabeth. It took a fleet of wrecking trucks, bulldozers, a movable crane and a train of flatcars to clear away enough wreckage so that they could remove the dead. It was twelve hours before the turnpike was completely reopened for traffic.

KEEP AWAKE

"Thank you for your patience" on a red ground.

Now there are trucks on every lane:
Suburban Propane
    Mason and Dixon   Flammable
      Liquid Sugar   Red Star Express
        Dog Food   Pigeon Feeds
        U-Haul
          Continental Truckers

Caution Airbrakes. The left arrow points "Home and Fireside"; the right arrow points "Kingdom Come."
Airport. Beyond a row of fatbellied yellow old planes of the Air Reserve, a control tower glistens festive. Across the road wharf buildings, marts, derricks, dance of light on waterways between the straight prows of oceangoing ships.

SERVICE AREA

Then smells of the Jersey salt meadows: sulphur, varnish, a whiff of dead apples, smoldering rags and paper ash, moldy bologna drenched in bay rum, ether . . . obsolete crisco and the strangling stench of burned tires. One good swift reek of a pigpen and always
      exhausts, petroleum essences and, like death immediate and undetectable, carbon monoxide.

Last Gasoline. Through the afternoon haze, beyond the humdrum heights of Weehawken, the buildings of Manhattan rise sunflecked in mirage. Empire State.
    The sun through girderwork stipples the converging lanes of cars that clog an artery cut through the upthrust rock.

Brakes squeak, tires squeal. Pandemonium pours spiraling downward—

(Breathless a lithograph: the old Erie depot, docks and the khakicolored Hudson; seaport smells, tarry ropes, gulls screaming, steamboat whistles, tugs bleating, barges: the North River of my boyhood).

Immediately the traffic is sucked underground into the tranquil routine of the Lincoln tunnel, interminable as officework, tiled like the bathrooms advertised by roadside motels... The even-measured lighting fades into harsh sunlight.

Cops.

New York.

3

1937

The Mississippi River was in full flood that spring. Thousands of acres inundated in Missouri. In Cairo, Illinois, they waited behind bulkheads raised to a height of sixtythree feet.

In Detroit the Governor of Michigan conferred with John L. Lewis in an effort to persuade the sitdown strikers to get out of the automobile plants.

In Washington, D.C., the New Deal was taking root. Franklin Delano Roosevelt, who after defeating Alf Landon by 524 electoral votes to 7 had taken the oath of office for the second time January 20, sent Congress a message requesting legislation to enable him to increase the number of Supreme Court Justices.

The "nine old men" had rejected his National Recovery and Agricultural Adjustment Acts as unconstitutional.

William Howard Taft deplored the message as an effort to intimidate the Court. Hugh Johnson hailed it as a step in the right direction. The New York Stock Exchange responded by heavy selling.

The fall of Málaga to the rebels in the Spanish Civil War made headlines. While one New York Times correspondent, who accompanied General Franco's troops, described "the bloodthirsty Red leaders" as fleeing "without firing a shot" and letting the city fall "like a ripe plum" into Fascist hands, the other New York Times correspondent, with dateline Madrid, extolled "the desperate valor" of the Loyalists who were managing to stave off a pincers movement against the Republican capital. From Madrid came further reports that "leftwing newspapers" were demanding the prosecution of the leaders of a Marxist workers' Party whom they described as Trotskyites and "disguised Fascists who indirectly helped the enemy."

In Madison Square Garden in New York, several thousand supporters waited in vain to hear Leon Trotsky's voice over the phone from Mexico City denounce Stalin and his Moscow trials. Some Stalinist cut the telephone wires.

Germany and Republican Spain were both reported to be in the Chicago market for large purchases of wheat on account of a shortage of food in their respective countries. In Des Moines, Iowa, a young fellow named Bill Heinen who had taken a beating as a real estate operator addressed a meeting of cornbelt farmers to promote a new type of hybrid seedcorn for which he had become the salesman. He was rather proud to announce that hybridizers had been so successful in producing strains immune to the old corn diseases that the federal field station in Illinois had closed its department of corn pathology.

On a grimy February morning in New York City, a middle-aged lawyer named Jay Pignatelli and his wife Lulie read each other snips of these items out of the morning paper as they hurried through their breakfast. Pignatelli wanted to reach his office half an hour early on account of the press of business that day.

4

Eager Beaver—i

Danny DeLong Speaking

With all this publicity and the chance of me going to jail and everything, it looks like the time has come to put down all the little things I can remember so they'll be there when I get hold of a proper ghostwriter to write 'em up. Autobiographies sell like hotcakes. "The Boy Wizard of Wall Street." Don't say it, I know the title's been used a dozen times before. We'll think up a catchy one. You just put down everything I say and try not to blush too much. Next session I'll get hold of a tape recorder so it won't be so embarrassing.

Well, here goes.

Mom used to tell me I was born on Armistice Day 1918. Gave her a bad time on false armistice day but I didn't poke my head out of doors until the real armistice was sealed, signed and delivered. Even then I wasn't taking any rubber nickels.

The DeLongs were a regular American suburban family. Jersey folk. Nobody really knew where the name came from. Grandmother Arnstein was Jewish and I'm pretty sure that most of Dad's people were too. We lived in Montclair but Dad's business was in Newark. He'd come home tired and late and snaffle up his supper and sit in a kind of daze. Mom used to call it his brown study.

We kids were all smart. Anne was the eldest and snooty as hell. Dave was two years ahead of me. He was one of those boys who just always do everything right. He was tall, kind of blond and goodlooking. That was the Nordic streak in the family. He got A's at school and made his letter in basketball and played third base on the ballteam. Me, I was short and dark with long black lashes that gave the girls a fit. The kids started calling me the runt until Dave wouldn't let 'em. Except for tennis, I wasn't too much on athletics, but when I got a little bigger I was manager of all the teams. I managed the teams and Dave played on 'em. They got to making me treasurer of everything because I always could handle the figures.

Mom was all for keeping up with the Joneses if you get what I mean. If she called something oldfashioned that was the end. She and Grandma didn't get along worth a darn. That was how come they had that fight about the ABC blocks. Grandma liked me best of the kids though she tried not to show it. Maybe it was because I was the littlest, I guess. I was a cute little bastard. The girls tell me I'm cute right now. A funny thing to call a grown man.

Well, Grandma was always bringing me little special presents and one day she comes in with a box of ABC blocks. I can't have been four but I can remember it as clearly as if it was yesterday. The letters were embossed in red, blue, green and purple on neat white blocks. They had a gilt edging. I fell in love with them right away. To this day when I'm looking up a name in a phone book just for a flash sometimes I think of the letters of the alphabet as having different colors. It must have been winter because I was sitting on the bear rug in front of the gas logs piling up the blocks and Grandma in her sweet quiet way—she was raised in Vienna—was coaxing me into arranging them in order, when Mom swooped down on us. She was all dressed up and had a lot of lipstick on because she'd just come from a meeting of some woman's club or other or maybe it was the Ethical Culture Society—Mom was great on Ethical Culture in those days.

"Oh Mother," she cried out—Mom has a clear ringing voice—"ABC's are horribly oldfashioned. Danny will learn to read a much better way. Nowadays they learn to recognize whole words." She knelt down beside me with her lips pursed tight and started putting the blocks back in the box. I let out a howl. I knew she was planning to take them away.

Mom got to her feet. "Look what you've done." She yelled at Grandma. "If we take them away now it will give him a complex." For some reason the word stuck in my funny little head. I didn't have any idea what it meant. It was the first time I heard the word but it sure wasn't the last. Of course the minute I saw Mom was the least bit doubtful about taking the blocks away I began to howl all the louder. They must have heard me all around the block. I cried too. I don't know how I did it but when I was that age I used to pump out the tears so that they spouted out of my eyes like a watering pot.

Grandma picked me up and kissed and cuddled me and whispered in my ear, "Oh my poor lamb." There was always something so soft about Grandma's wrinkled cheek and a little whiff of sachet out of her lace blouse, not like Mom's noisy perfumes. "Well the harm's done now." Mom switched out of the room. Her voice trailed off. "Oh why do you have to be so oldfashioned about everything?"

That was how I learned to read, with Grandma's blocks and her funny little old-world picture books she smuggled in when Mom was out. I already knew how to read when I started at the Happy Hour Nursery School. That was as progressive as you could get. A lot of the other kids never did catch on. Even Dave had to take remedial reading. I'd just make out like I was recognizing the words at sight when I was spelling them out d-o-g dog all along. Mom would have called that dishonest. Everything had to be frank and aboveboard with Mom, but when I got into high finance that ability to do one thing while I seemed to be doing something else came in damn handy. Of course some people thought I was too clever at it for my own good. The way it turned out I guess I was.

Now take that word "complex." Mom used it so often. Everybody in our house talked about complexes all the time but I was the only one who ever got anything out of it. I mean with the girls. That all started the summer we spent in a house at Bay Head. It was Depression time. Dad got the house on a bad debt and he had to hold on to it until prices got better. Dad was one of the few businessmen in Newark who wasn't hurt by the Great Depression.

In fact, he made half a million dollars out of it. He saw it coming. By the time the stockmarket crash came he had all his assets in cash. He had it all in Boston banks. He didn't trust any bank in Jersey. Of course there were a lot of accounts he couldn't collect on but he just gathered up the tangible assets like this big old house at Bay Head that he'd been reconditioning for a family that went broke. Mom sure hated it. It was so oldfashioned it wasn't funny. Grandma was real poorly—heart trouble—and we took along our cook, Agnes's daughter, Mary Healy, to wait on her. It was 1933. I was fifteen. Mary was about my age, a nice little girl, kind of homely and dumb, but she had flaming red hair, I dunno why red hair always did something to me.

It was a regular migration. You ought to have seen us crossing South Jersey in two cars and a pickup truck belonging to DeLong's Home Supply that Dad sent along to carry the trunks and some extra furniture. This was years before the Turnpike. There was a real nice beach right near on the bay and Dave and I rented a catboat. When Grandma felt well enough we'd take her down to the beach and Mary would come along and go in swimming with us.

She didn't know how to swim and I said I'd teach her. I'd take her out to where the water was about chestdeep and hold her up by her chin while she practiced the breast stroke. Sometimes a little wave would come and she'd get scared and grab hold of me. It wasn't an unpleasant sensation. I got so I'd put my other hand under her tummy and would kind of feel her up a bit under the bathing suit. She never showed any sign of liking it, but she didn't show any sign of disliking it either. Then she'd go back into shore through the shallow water, half walking and half swimming, and I'd have to take a long swim out to get rid of my hardon before I joined the folks on the beach.

I'd had the old urge real bad for about a year, maybe longer. When Mom discovered I was having wet dreams she insisted I go to see a psychologist. Ever since Anne had her first monthlies Mom had been reading up on Freud and Havelock Ellis and going to lectures so she could give the children proper advice about their sex lives, and then she found this Dr. Ruby. He was a small skimpy man with a wisp of pale beard and yellow eyes. I swear his eyes looked just like a goat's. He gave us all the creeps. It made me want to upchuck the way he talked about masturbation. He seemed disappointed that I didn't. I was crazy to tell him that when the time came I'd get me plenty girls, but all I could say to him was "Yes doctor . . . No doctor." He told Mom he was afraid I was real inhibited and might get a complex that would ruin my life.

I hated that psychology talk at the time, but when I got a little older it turned out to be a hot line with the girls. It even worked on Mary, though I don't believe she understood a word of it. My room was up on the top floor with an oldfashioned bathroom opposite it. Agnes and Mary lived at the end of a long narrow wooden corridor but they had to use the same bathroom, see? because there wasn't any other on the top floor. Well, one day I ran upstairs to change out of my bathing suit for lunch and there was Mary standing stark-naked on her bathing suit that she'd just taken off, in the middle of the bathroom floor with the door open. She must have left that door open on purpose. And the summer light coming in through the window lit up that red flag between her legs. Before I knew what had happened I'd locked the door behind me and was grabbing her to me. "No, no," she said. She wrestled a little but not very much. I kept whispering in her ear that we had to do it now or else we'd get inhibitions or a horrible complex that would ruin our lives.

All she would say was "No, no" but she ended up spreading her legs on the bathmat. I did all right for a virgin. After all, I'd read the books. That's for you, Dr. Ruby, I said to myself as I socked it into her. That doesn't mean it wasn't wonderful and scary too. It's always wonderful and scary. What scared me that time was that when I pulled it out it was all bloody.

Afterwards I was real nice to her and cuddled her up and showed her how to use the douche that by some miracle we found hanging in the bathroom closet. But she didn't bleed much; she said she could fix that with some Kotex. "What'll I tell the priest?" she kept whispering. I grabbed her by the chin and made her look me straight in the eye. "Mary, if you tell him it was me I'll kill you."

"I won't never tell no names."

"Honest to God. Promise. Cross your heart and hope you may die?"

"Cross my heart and hope I may die."

Then she grabbed me and gave me a real sweet kiss on the mouth and I knew I had her hooked.

The bell was ringing for lunch. Mary ran off to her room and I washed myself off in the bathtub and jumped into a pair of duck pants and a shirt and slid into a seat next to Grandma at table on the porch, all quiet and serene, with my hair combed slick like butter wouldn't melt in my mouth.

I sure wasn't quiet and serene that night when I began to think about what I'd done. My first thought was that she'd have a baby and I'd have to marry her. The last thing in the world I wanted to do was marry Agnes Healy's daughter. I got the cold chills so I couldn't sleep. I had to talk to somebody. I went tiptoeing down to Dave's room on the second floor.

Dave was sitting up in bed reading *Red Badge of Courage*. He always was a kind of highbrow reader. The minute I told him, I wished I hadn't. I guess it made him envious. Though he was two years older than me I happened to know that all he'd done was hot petting on the back seat of a car. He'd never properly had a girl naked yet. He couldn't have been less sympathetic. He looked at me like I was dirt and asked did I know I'd committed statutory rape punishable by up to eighteen years imprisonment?

"She really likes me. She swore she wouldn't tell."

"The Catholic priest'll wheedle it out of her the minute he gets her in the confessional. Then the family will blackmail you. Why couldn't you have done it with some girl you could trust? Somebody who was our kind of people?"

I kept saying "Suppose she has a baby."

"Not likely," Dave sniffed. "Don't you know about the sterility of the early teens? You're not old enough." Then he told me to go upstairs and let him go to sleep. What did I think I was doing sitting there jawing all night?

Talking about living a lie. The rest of that summer was horrible. I had to keep loving up Mary to keep her from ratting on me. I was careful to use condoms so there wasn't any more danger of a baby. We always met in the upstairs bathroom. I really did love her when she told me one night that she was having her monthlies quite naturally. But I sure was sick of her. She was the dumbest girl I ever met.

I started talking it up with the parents that the time had come for Dave and me to go to some good boarding school that would get us ready for college. We picked on Taft. In those Depression years the best schools weren't too choosy. They would take anybody who'd pay the fees, and anyway we were both at the top of our classes in highschool. We didn't have to worry about being part Jewish any more because Mom had switched from psychiatry to genealogy. She found an expert who looked up the records and discovered for a pretty fat fee that DeLong was an old Dutch Huguenot name and that we were descended from an original settler at Trenton. Friends had already put Dad up for the Country Club and now he joined the Yacht Club. Anybody who didn't default on dues was mighty popular among the exclusive clubs in South Jersey in those days.

Grandma died that winter and Dad and Mom moved into a real mansion out on Hill Road. They let Agnes go and hired a French couple instead, so when I came home for vacations I didn't have to meet Mary on every stairway and have her look at me in that little way like she owned me that threw me into a cold sweat. My God it was a relief when they went. Sometimes I wonder what she's like now, a fat Irish biddy with a flock of kids, I guess.

But that didn't mean I'd learned how to keep out of trouble. I did try to be careful, but there were some pretty fast girls in the crowd we ran around with. Summers I was working for Dad at Home Supply. Dave worked as a counselor in summer camps but I liked the business. Already I was dreaming about what I'd do when Dad retired. I read all the trade journals and the literature about new types of synthetic shingles and roofing and weatherboarding. Every kind of new material was beginning to come in. Natch I was mad for prefabrication. I'd try to get Dad to stock up for the housing boom that was just around the corner.

Of course Dad didn't believe a word of it. "You hold your horses, Daniel," he'd say. "Your time will come," but I could see it made him happy as hell to have me so interested. He let me have a little back office to keep all my literature in and that office had an outside door and naturally I had the key. Tom McDonald the night watchman and I were just like that, so he wouldn't see a thing when I shuttled some muffled-up dame past the piles of lumber and into the back office.

Days I spent in there learning the building-supply business, and nights, after dances and parties, I learned about girls. All this permissiveness was new then. I'd pull my line about how we must let out our natural urges or else we'd get inhibitions and complexes. You bet I worked out a hotter line than Dr. Ruby. The smart ones just laughed and pulled my ears and made me take 'em home, but most of 'em fell for it. After all, they were human too, and I had my long lashes and my slick black hair and my kind of eager confidential manner. I loved 'em all, I really did, and let's put it this way; they reciprocated.

I was leading the happiest life you can imagine for a kid of nineteen when I met my comeuppance. I'd passed most of my exams for Dartmouth where I was planning to take an engineering course, and everything was hunkydory when I had to take that girl Gladys down to my hideaway. I've always hated girls named Gladys. This one wore glasses and had a sort of pimply complexion. She was a reader. She had read more Freud than I had and Havelock Ellis and that Hindu pornographical treatise. She just laughed when I started my line about obeying that urge and not getting a complex that might end us up in the psychiatric ward. Then I'd quote Whitman, "Oh Furious restrain me not."

That was all kid stuff to Gladys. She had been planning this for some time but couldn't get hold of a boy who would cooperate. I guess I took pity on her. She was so earnest she got me kind of fussed. I got all fouled up with some very tight panties she wore. I couldn't use the French letter and thought, "What the hell, just this once." When I tore her panties she got to yelling and sobbing. It really was hysterics. I was afraid Tom McDonald would think I was killing her. I had to throw a glass of water in her face to make her snap out of it . . . It was the worst mess I'd ever been in in my young life. I didn't think I'd even penetrated her, but what did she do but call me up one day in a soft cuddly voice about a month later and say, "Daniel darling, I'm going to have a baby."

All I could think of saying was "Don't do anything. . . . Give me a chance to think," and then I hung up.

It may all be hysterics, I thought. I'd read about false pregnancies. Even if it was a baby I couldn't see how it could possibly be mine. But how could I prove it wasn't? I didn't like the way she said darling. That showed she had intentions.

This time I really had a fit. It was worse than my fright about Mary. Gladys's people the Dunnaways were not only respectable but they were rich. They were the kind of people who knew how to make things happen. Her grandfather, James P. Dunnaway, was Chairman of the Board of one of the Montclair banks. He had some capital in Dad's firm. I didn't know how much. I could just see the two families putting their heads together and deciding to make the best of a bad business. Not such a bad match after all. Kerist, it gives me the horrors just to think of it.

The way girls were falling for me I knew I could get myself somebody real pretty and attractive. But not till I got out of college. I wanted her smart, too. I didn't care about her being rich. I was planning to make plenty money as soon as I got my feet on the ground. Sure I wanted to marry in due time, but my God not Gladys.

That night I decided I'd better drop out of sight for a while. College would have to wait. This was where Mom's crusades came in. As soon as she got tired of pedigrees she began to go in for causes. Mom had been all worked up for months about the Fascists attacking the Spanish Republic. She worked on committees and addressed envelopes and raised money for the Abraham Lincoln Brigade. If anybody told her they were Reds she'd jump down his throat. What I did was take the train into New York and go to their recruiting center and tell the guy at the desk I was Mom's son and I wanted to go incog to fight Franco's Fascists because if Dad found out about it he'd raise the roof. I explained that Dad was a quiet man but very determined. If he decided he wanted me home he'd get me home if he had to call out a squad of marines to do it. I knew how he felt about what he called Mom's always sticking her nose in other people's business. "Dumb ignorant capitalist," said the man at the desk.

They gave me quite a grilling in the inner office to find out if I was on the level, but finally they turned me over to a jumpy little guy with cigarette stains on his fingers who was a secret Party courier, and he said he could furnish a U. S. passport in somebody else's name. Sure it was valid. Nobody would be any the wiser. The picture didn't look too different from me, particularly when I got my hair clipped off short. Funny coincidence, the name was Donaldson and the initials were just the same as mine: DPD. "But what happened to the guy?" I asked. "He went over in the first contingent. A lot of those boys got killed."

That was the first time I thought about getting killed, but it was too late to back out now. I sailed next day. Third class on the French Line. With the mail that went ashore with the pilot I wrote Dad and Mom that they mustn't be mad at me. Maybe they'd think what I was doing was silly but I thought it was *right*. It would just mean putting off college for a year. We'd lick those Fascists and I'd soon be home, but if they tried to look for me they would never find me because I was traveling under an assumed name.

In France everything was hush, and with my prepschool French I didn't know what was going on most of the time. Everybody we saw was some kind of a secret agent. In Paris a little kraut who always had his glasses crooked took us in charge. He spoke English with a horrible accent. He never took his eyes off us and counted us every few minutes like we were a flock of sheep. He herded us on the train for Perpignan. On the train another guy took over. He was a Frenchman in a beret and only spoke bad German. He made us scatter all through the train so as not to arouse the suspicions of the border police. Then we kept changing trains and there never seemed to be any time to eat. We crossed the border into Spain one night in the pouring rain. We had to go one by one climbing up this slippery trail up in the mountains. We sure were wet and footsore and hungry—I don't believe we had a square meal all the time we were in France—we were just about dead by the time we found the charcoal burners' hut with a blue cross on the door we'd been told to look for on the other side of the pass.

There was a road there. Hardtop, would you believe it? The Spanish comrades turned up with a bus. They couldn't do too much for us: dry clothes and the first square meal I'd had since I landed in Europe. Plenty of wine. Nice clean beds to sleep in. Nice friendly maids and waiters. The place must have been a little mountain resort before the war.

We stayed there a week. We spent our time trying to learn Spanish from the maids and living off the fat of the land. The maids were real young but some of them already had moustaches. Then a responsible came to put us through a training course. We were indoctrinated to beat hell. When we moved down nearer to

Madrid, everybody was all excited about how we had to build cantonments in this village. Nobody knew a thing about the construction business except me, so there I was in charge of the construction detail. We all had rifles to fight off the Fascists if they attacked but actually I was probably the only man who went through the whole bloody business without firing a shot.

I sure did learn about Spanish politics. The carpenters were *Socialistas,* the bricklayers were *Sindicalistas,* the responsibles were *Communistas,* and they all argued every minute about who was doing the most to win the war. That Spanish Civil War wasn't just one civil war; it was two or three different civil wars all going on at the same time.

And there I was with my pigeon Spanish begging and pleading with the guys to get the work done. A fellow named Tony turned up who'd worked in the States and knew a little English. He was a great help. The two of us would argue with them to forget their ideology and pitch in. I truly believe they did it just to please me and Tony. When they did get to work they were terrific. The responsibles were absolutely amazed when they saw the cantonment go up, neat tile roofs and everything. Tile roofs are an awful chore but that was the only kind they knew. Of course there wasn't any plumbing, but people don't worry about plumbing in Spain. Then one day the news started going around the village that the Moros were advancing. I don't know where people went but they sure made themselves scarce.

That was when the arrests began. Somebody turned Tony in for a Fifth Column and they took him out and shot him. Poor Tony, I bet he wished he'd stayed in the States. Then it was Pepe and Pablo, the only guys I had who knew how to lay a cement floor. It broke me all up. I'd gotten fond of the guys. They were some of the nicest simplest honestest people I'd ever known. Good workers, too, once they got started. When they took those boys and shot them I decided I wanted out.

In the middle of all this excitement Don Carp came to town. He was a pasty little thinlipped redheaded guy who'd been a labor-union official back home. When he came around to the cantonment I thought he was a responsible and I went right up to him and said for God's sake do something about these shootings. How could they get any work done if they shot all the good workers? He took me out back of the latrine and whispered in my ear that he'd be lucky if he got out without being shot himself. He'd been working in some office in Madrid and somebody had turned him in for a Trotskyite. He wanted out. I took a chance on his being on the level and said me too, I wanted out in the worst way. We shook hands on it.

We were busy with our little conference when we heard machineguns over the hill: the Fascists were advancing. Don whispered that he had a little Fiat truck hidden in an old quarry outside of town. Luckily it wasn't the side of town the machinegun fire was coming from. We lit out without going back for our duffle or anything.

About here, when I get my ghostwriter, I'll get up a nice little war story about how the Loyalists bravely defended that village against the overwhelming Fascist hordes. I guess they did all right, but to tell the truth I wasn't there to see. Don and I had climbed aboard that truck and headed for Barcelona by the nearest road. The trouble was it was a hell of a long way, and when we measured the gas in the tank with a stick we just had about an inch left. As luck would have it I had travel orders to Barcelona and a requisition to commandeer plumbing materials there. I'd been furnished with it at the Brigade weeks before but they had never been able to find any transportation to go with it.

The gas took us as far as the bridge across the Ebro. That was at the bottom of a sort of junior Grand Canyon. There was a supply station right at the end of the bridge. I could see the big metal drums of gasoline sitting out in a row. But there was a checkpoint too. Orders were to let no troops fleeing from the enemy cross the bridge. Don had some kind of a phony travel order. Mine was all wool and a yard wide. Anyway they stamped them and wrote in *Bueno hasta Barcelona*.

They evidently didn't know about the Fascist offensive just down the line and we sure didn't tell 'em. Everything was peace and smiles. But when we brought up the question of gas the scene changed. Thunderclouds on every face. No gas without special orders from the *Ministerio de la Guerra* in Madrid. We tried to plead but all we got was shrugged shoulders.

Suddenly I got a bright idea. Could I see the responsible, alone, so I could explain *Construir* ... *casas para soldados* International Brigade ... *excusados necesarios* ... *sanitarios*. The sweat was pouring off me as I tried to explain flush toilets—*un regalo de los camaradas americanos.* The responsible was a dumpy little man with a face like a mess of putty. Grubby. He looked like something you would find under a stone. He sat at a desk made of two boards set across gasoline drums in the halflight that came in through the broken tiles on the roof. The boards were piled up with sheets of yellow flimsy, and this egg sat all hunched up with his tunic open, sweating into the flimsy. His little beady eyes twinkled when I said gift from American comrades. Suddenly I pulled a crisp ten-dollar bill out of the wallet in my hip pocket.

He reached for it, smelt of it, read all the writing on it carefully on both sides and slipped it into the inside pocket of his tunic. He spread out the fingers of both hands and pushed them towards me. "Ten litres," he said. *"Nada mas."*

He made out an order and called in one of his ragged orderlies. Ten litres. *El bueno.* A sickly smile crossed his face as I bowed out. You say money's the root of all evil. That little incident convinced me of the power of folding money in this world.

Those ten litres didn't get us to Barcelona but they did get us to a railway station. Our luck was still with us. A train was waiting. Rattletrap cars all jammed with militia. Most of the men were walking wounded: crutches, arms in slings, heads bound up, and that dreary smell of dressing stations, iodoform, clotted blood, stale sweat. Of course there weren't any seats. We propped ourselves in the corner of a corridor. It was an hour before the train started.

"But Don, how can you be sure things will be OK when we get to Barcelona?"

Don looked wise. "Contacts," he said, and gave his head a little toss.

Don's contacts turned out OK. At the station in Barcelona he asked me if I had any more jack. I fished out a couple of dollars and we climbed into the brokendownest little old taxicab and Don had it drive us to a swanky hotel on the Rambla. The driver snatched at the two dollars like they were rubies. He knew good money when he saw it.

At the desk Don asked what number this guy's room is and goes up in the elevator and knocks. When a voice answers he tells me to wait outside. After a while he comes out grinning. "We're all set," he says. "My friend's got an official car of the Generalitat to take him to France in the morning. He'll let us come along." Then he told me to come in and meet the guy. He was a New York lawyer. What he was doing there I never knew.

I'm getting hoarse. I never dictated so long in my life. Just one more thing. It cost me my last crisp ten-dollar bill to get back into France. Don Carp and I went along fine in the Catalonian limousine with this guy who turned out to be some kind of a big shot working on a documentary movie for the Spanish government, free meals and wine and red-carpet treatment all along, but when we got to the border I didn't dare go to the checkpoint. Don had his U. S. passport but the International Brigade had taken mine. They never gave passports back. It was phony anyway. I was scared the immigration officials would ship me back to the Brigade. The guy who fixed me up was the chauffeur of this limousine. While the others were eating supper he took me down to the beach and talked Catalan to a couple of fishermen. They fish at night around there with floating lights. They took me out with them and just quietly landed me in a rocky cove on the French side. I climbed up a path towards the lights of the town until I came to a highroad. I hadn't taken a step on that highroad before a damn gendarme flashed a light in my face and asked for my papers.

I played dumb. No savvy *français*. American tourist out to look at pretty scenery in the moonlight. He kept saying *"papiers, papiers."* I knew what he meant all right but what I did was bring out this other ten-dollar bill. He looked at it with his flashlight, then he shrugged his shoulders, grabbed it up in a grubby paw and just vanished into the night.

Next day I went to the nearest American Consul and told him the whole story. He was a hell of a nice fellow. He loaned me what I needed and when I couldn't send a cable at the post office on account of not having a passport he sent it himself. Next day the folks came across with some dough. I don't know who was more relieved, the parents or little Danny ... well now I'm going to pause for station identification. When I get that ghostwriter we'll really work up my adventures in the Spanish Civil War.... Just put this down: these pages are being dictated to the prettiest little Swedish stenographer in all Copacabana. And after that, asterisks. Plenty of asterisks ... "You wouldn't want to go home with a horrible complex, now would you, Irma?"

5

The Later Life and Deplorable Opinions of Jay Pignatelli—i

The Documentary

The Pignatellis had finished their grapefruit. Lulie got up to pour the coffee. She liked to pour the coffee and the hot milk at the same time out of two whitemetal pots the way she had seen waiters do it in Madrid. Then she dropped back into her chair, took a sip, and let out one of her little shrieks.

"Jay Pignatelli, you ought to be ashamed."

Jay laughed. "At least I made a clean breast."

"I should think that you would have learned by this time, most beloved Modesto," she said, choosing her words carefully, "that nothing does more harm than doing good."

Jay couldn't help feeling a tiny bit nettled. She saw it on his face and leaned towards him. "Who's your loving girl?"

"You are."

He kissed her. He couldn't have gotten mad at her anyway, not with the crinkle of green in her eyes and the comical expression of her mouth. She was absolutely adorable.

"It's all those fine Spaniards. Don't they deserve a break?"

Trying to find words to explain why he had to go he sat eating his eggs and bacon and staring out through the French windows at the pile of snow rotting between tubs of dead boxbushes that had ornamented the terrace beyond during some summer long past.

"There was just no way of backing out. I was the one who suggested this damn documentary. When Annie put up the money ...my lord, I didn't know poor Joe Sylvester had all that money...."

"Most of it came from Annie's Quaker grandfather," interrupted Lulie.

"Now they all insist that I'm the one to set the thing up with the Spanish Republicans."

"On account of being such good friends with Ramón?"

"Exactly."

Lulie gave a little shudder. "I know Ramón had to stay. He's a Spanish patriot. It's his country. But I do wish his wife and children were safe at home in Princeton, New Jersey."

"Ramón's a sensible fellow. He'll make out."

Lulie collected the cups and plates on a tray.

"The dogooders are getting so spiteful these days," she was saying. "That woman who called me up from your committee almost chewed my ear off about the wrong people trying to take over.... I told her you wouldn't let them and there wasn't anything I could do anyway. I was just an ignorant little white Protestant American, so she hung up."

Jay went into the bathroom to tie his necktie in front of the glass. Lulie ran after him and hung on his arm.

"Maybe we could bring them home with us.... I know Amparo won't leave Ramón if there's any danger, but the little ones ... after you have arranged about the film." She tugged at him pleadingly. "I'd just love to have Paco and little Lou for a couple of months. They are cute as bugs' ears.... I guess it's because I haven't been clever enough to have any of my own."

He stroked her hair for a moment. Then he reached for his jacket. "I've got to go on downtown. I'll be late. I've got to see George Elbert."

"I was going to say give him my love.... But I'm so mad at him for walking out on Madeline I could beat him with a stick."

Jay had planned to invite George Elbert Warner downtown to lunch, but the only satisfaction he got from calling the Warner suite at the old Berkeley Hotel was a gravelly voice he did not recognize saying "Mr. Warner does not wish to be disturbed." Around noon he had to break off the logical process of his argument in the Joppa case, and after hurriedly scratching a yellow pad full of notes to help him pick it up again when he got back, to nerve himself for another subway ride.

Things at the Berkeley turned out worse than he had expected. George Elbert was deep in his divorce so there was no woman around to keep order. His parlor was piled confusedly with books and newspapers, guns, cases of fishingrods, and even half-unpacked dufflebags from the last safari he had taken with Madeline. A stuffed sailfish stuck its bill out from the excelsior of a packingcase beside a number of rolled-up leopard skins. Galley sheets that represented George Elbert's latest book dangled from the top of the bookcase, held down by a tray containing a water pitcher, some glasses and a bottle of Jack Daniels (black label). The hippopotamus foot that served for a wastebasket was stacked with empty bottles.

Jay discovered right away that the voice that had affected him so unpleasantly over the telephone came from a sallow slender blackhaired man with the skin so dark around the eyes he looked as if he had a couple of shiners. He was perched on the back of the sofa with a glass in his hand. When George Elbert introduced him to Jay as "Cookie my sparring partner" a reptile glaze came over his eyes. His only mark of recognition was a stifled belch.

George Elbert was sober but he was in a nasty temper. Walking as he often did with a slight limp, he hauled his big bulk across the room until his chin almost touched Jay's. "What about this Dutch bloke?"

"Everything says Dirk de Jager is the best documentary film man since Eisenstein."

George Elbert stepped back and went into his shadowboxing routine. Jay, who as an officer of the court and a wearer of steel-rimmed spectacles made it a point never to engage in fisticuffs with anybody, smiled at him blandly. "How about lunch?" he asked.

"Not goin' to eat any... got to watch my weight. Algy called. He'll meet us at 52 West 52nd later. Let's go down and check on these blokes... Cookie, you police the joint." George barked back over his shoulder as he strode out the door.

CENTURY'S EBB

Jay had to skip to keep step with him down the hall. "Cookie's a wonderful guy," George Elbert spluttered in Jay's ear as they waited for the elevator. "Don't you go making hasty judgments about him. The only Brooklyn boy who ever made a name as a bullfighter. He's not at his best today.... Bad luck in Hialeah.... It's not the money. But it hurts him to play the wrong horse.... You damn Commies look down your nose at everybody."

Going down in the cab Jay fell over himself trying to explain —though he really didn't need to, he knew George Elbert knew better—that he wasn't a Commie any more than a rabbit, and neither were the Spanish Republicans.

George Elbert wasn't listening. He complained of a sore throat and kept poking his neck with his finger to see if it was swollen. Then he started humming. The most aggravating thing about George Elbert was a way he had of humming while you were trying to talk to him.

The office was at the top of a long flight of gritty stairs in an old loft building in the West Twenties. He had the feeling he'd been there before. He couldn't remember when. Dingylooking men and women and a few pastyfaced boys poring over newspapers, mimeographed material, typewritten sheets at two long tables. When he opened the groundglass door, they all turned their heads. Gimlet eyes glared accusation. Holier than thou. The Kentucky miners' strike, the Finklestein case, the Sabatini trial: he'd seen them all before. Everything he'd been telling George Elbert coming down in the cab was a goddamn lie.

He must be dreaming. The girl standing beside the mimeograph machine was Hedda Gelber. How could she look exactly the same after so many years? Jay made a step towards her. Then he caught himself. She was staring into his face without a sign of recognition. Had he really changed so, or was it some other woman?

Jay felt as if his feet were frozen to the floor. It was the sort of feeling he'd had in nightmares. He'd forgotten about George Elbert or why they had come. A skinny little towheaded officeboy was dancing attendance. "Is it really Mister Warner? I recognized you from the pitchers."

The boy was leading them to another groundglass door at the far end of the room. Before he knocked on it he had managed to ingratiate himself with George Elbert to the point of getting an autograph scribbled on a scratch pad. After ushering them in he hung in the doorway trying to catch every word the great man said.

Ben Feldman jumped up from behind his desk and pumped their hands. He always seemed a pleasant fellow, with his freshlooking white skin and wavy black hair. "This is a redletter day. Please be seated. . . . All right, Junior, close the door behind you. The poor little guy," he explained with his disarming grin, "is trying to get us to send him to Spain. Of course we can't; he must be all of thirteen. . . . So he just works for nothing as an officeboy."

Jay hadn't noticed a small sawed-off fellow huddled on a chair in the back of the room. "Don, come and meet the celebrity." Ben beckoned him to the desk. "Mr. Warner, this is another recruit in the struggle against war and Fascism. . . . This is Don Carp who was recruiting for us out in Wisconsin, and now he's recruited himself. Off for Spain tomorrow."

Don Carp had a face full of freckles and red stubbly hair. He couldn't seem to find anything to say so he just stood there with his shoulders pulled back and his belly sucked in. "Like so many thousands Don is ready to give his life in the struggle against war and Fascism. . . . Thanks, Don," said Ben in his most velvet tones. "We'll have your papers in about a half an hour."

Don gave them the clenched fist salute, to which George Elbert and Jay were clumsy in responding, and followed the officeboy out of the groundglass door.

Ben talked on glibly. He knew all about the Popular Historians project, more than Jay did himself, Jay thought ruefully, even though he had the incorporation papers in his pocket at that very moment. Ben was enthusiastic about the idea of a documentary film. The best possible propaganda. His organization would cooperate in every possible way. Their contacts in France had already been notified. The next courier they sent would check with them again. It was a little tricky getting across the border because the French government was party to the Non-Intervention Committee.

Ben pursed his lips. He produced two typewritten slips from his desk drawer and handed one to George and another to Jay. "These will be your contacts in Paris. . . . You'll notice that they are to two different people but there is a reason for that. They are both important Frenchmen and they will arrange your transportation to Valencia. There you'll find your government contacts." He added in a whisper that they must be careful not to let the addresses fall into the wrong hands.

Jay said it just happened that one of his best friends was working for the Republican government. He was a professor of Romance Languages at Princeton and knew the United States and would understand exactly what they wanted to do. Ramón Echevarria. The name didn't seem to mean anything to Ben.

George Elbert was beginning to hum; so Jay decided it was time they went back uptown. It was on the tip of his tongue to ask Ben if that really was Hedda Gelber he had seen standing by the mimeograph machine. A casual enough question; but somehow—again he felt caught in a nightmare—he couldn't quite get his tongue to phrase the words.

As he left he told Ben they were on their way to the incorporation meeting of Popular Historians, and Ben cried out "Good enough" in his mechanically cheery way. Going out Jay caught himself looking furtively around the outer office to see if Hedda Gelber or the woman who looked like Hedda Gelber were still there. She had gone.

On the way down the steps he whispered to George Elbert that he hadn't told Ben Feldman where they were meeting. "He'd have written us off as a bunch of damn capitalists."

"I like that guy," George Elbert exploded. "He's like a good Jesuit. Thing about fanatics is you know where you stand with 'em. They don't have to change their minds every fifteen minutes."

If there was one place in town Jay hated it was 52 West 52nd, but George Elbert insisted it was "good neutral ground" for a meeting, so they had arranged with the owner of the joint, Dick Hammersmith, whom George Elbert had been extolling as an honest crook, to fix them up a private room upstairs. The plainclothes doorman, a relic of speakeasy days, whose deadpan Jay usually found so disagreeable, flashed a smile when he caught sight of George Elbert. As Jay's feet sank into the deep carpets of the dim red interior, he nerved himself against the downthenose looks of the drinkers at the tables. Not too different from the stares that had raked him from the Party members at the recruiting office, he told himself with a tingle of amusement. "Insiders are all alike," he exclaimed outloud to George Elbert.

George Elbert's answer was to start humming.

Jay didn't have time to explain what he meant because right away they were in the midst of Popular Historians. Handshakes. Claps on the back. Reminiscent kidding. Smiles breaking into laughter. Redheaded Algy McGurk as usual looked several years younger than when anybody had last seen him. Anne Sylvester, with her straight brows and lovely skin, was still attractive, though she had put on a terrible lot of weight. Ed Harrington wore his pin-striped suit and that look of spiteful innocence on his thin lips. Art Unger seemed to have faded. His white hair was untidier than ever. His true blue eyes had gotten a bit bleary. He was complaining that Lily O'Dwyer was late as usual.

But she wasn't. After a little search they found her in an alcove crying into a Tom Collins. It was Lily's way, Art cried out. She would deliver one of her famous wisecracks looking up in your face with her eyes full of tears, batting her lashes that always had big gobs of mascara on them. Art kept saying "My dear, you are irresistible."

At that point one of the doormen came up and whispered in George Elbert's ear. "Bring him in," George Elbert shouted, "he's the most important man here." Dirk de Jager joined them. He was grinning. "They thought I was a suspicious character."

"It's just that you looked too damn young, Dirk. Why do you have to look so goddamn young?" said George Elbert.

With his shock of wavy black hair above blue eyes and smooth cheeks, Dirk de Jager did look like a highschool boy playing hookey.

"Then," he said, "I'm afraid I must apologize twice. Once for being late and twice for feigned adolescence which I assure you is quite misleading."

The ladies looked at him lovingly. "Isn't he the sweetest thing?" Lily whispered to Art Unger.

They trooped upstairs and arranged themselves around a long table in a private room. Jay pulled his papers out of his inside pocket. "My position at the head of the table," he declared as soon as he could get the company quiet, "is strictly pro tem; I'm merely your lawyer.... First I'd like to report that Mr. Hammersmith is graciously allowing us to use this room, free, gratis and without payment. He says it is his contribution to the cause."

Jay read over the articles of incorporation as a nonprofit institution under the laws of the State of New York and suggested that since she was putting up most of the money, Anne Sylvester should be president.

Art got very red in the face and said "Hum . . . what about the check Lily sent in out of her first royalties?" Lily dabbed her eyes in her damp little handkerchief and said that was just a fleabite compared to what Annie was putting up. Annie got all flustered and said she couldn't think of being president. Jay was her lawyer and Jay must handle everything. Jay promptly nominated Algernon McGurk. Algy was prevailed upon. Algy was a bonny man, Jay was telling himself. After that the meeting flowed along smoothly. Ed Harrington, who was already the treasurer of the Save Loyalist Spain Committee, was made secretary-treasurer. Art Unger, maybe a little too eagerly, accepted the office of vice-president. The rest of them would be listed as directors.

When Jay vacated his seat to let Algy take over, he slipped into the hall to telephone Lulie.

"Not a hitch," he announced.

"Why should there be?" asked Lulie. "Isn't everybody getting a free ride?"

"Several of us will be eating dinner here," Jay continued severely. "Why don't you come on up?"

Lulie emitted a sort of mew and Jay could imagine what a face she made, but she said she would come.

When Jay slid back into a seat at the table, George Elbert was going strong. He was circulating a bottle of Jack Daniels. Dirk, who was no drinker, sat opposite him spinning an empty glass.

"Faces," George was declaiming, "what we want is faces. Faces of old peasants working in the fields, of muledrivers and tavern-keepers, vineyard workers turned into infantrymen. Faces in combat. The man at the machinegun. The man who has just pressed the spring on a grenade. The face of the man who's just been hit in the belly with a dumdum bullet."

"It's just going to be awful," blubbered Lily O'Dwyer.

"We've got to puncture the terrible complacency of the ordinary American," declared Algy in his preacher's voice.

"That," said Dirk in a dry didactic tone, "is the business of the documentary."

Everybody started talking at once. The meeting broke up.

Jay found Lulie sitting on a sort of mourner's bench in the vestibule downstairs. Beside her sat Cookie, all spruced up, tall and lean in a black suit that made him look like an undertaker's mute. Next to him a frozenfaced blonde in a striking orange dress. As soon as Jay heard her name he knew who she was.

When he introduced them Hilda Glendower and Lulie looked at each other strangely.

"I'm sure you don't remember where we met," Hilda said to Lulie in an icy voice.

"I certainly do," said Lulie. "It was Geology 4 and my how I hated it."

Jay could see that Lulie hadn't liked her then and wasn't going to like her now.

They found George in the bar. He hardly noticed them because he was so busy telling Algy about how the first time he was in New York he'd inadvertently laid a gangster's moll in that very private dining room where they'd held the meeting.

"Inadvertently, I said. Inadvertently is the key word. I didn't know who the hell she was, just a nice plump Italian girl sitting on the stairs with that look in her eye. . . . It turned out she was Legs Diamond's girl. . . . It's a good thing I'm not much of a one to hang around New York."

"Georgy, we'll protect you," cried Lulie.

"Well, if it isn't the Lady of the Lake!" George Elbert burst out laughing. All at once he climbed off his high horse. "The Lady of the Lake and Don Modesto her faithful squire. Doe," he said, addressing Hilda, "meet the only girl I ever really loved."

"We've already met," said Hilda with ice in her voice.

"Old college chums," chimed in Lulie.

During dinner George Elbert had eyes only for Hilda whom he kept addressing as Doe. For her benefit he told the story Jay and Lulie had heard before of his African safari. It was still funny. He did his imitation of a hyena wounded by a rifle shot and told his oft-repeated yarn about how he tried to stalk a black leopard until he found that the black leopard was stalking him. Jay and Lulie tried to act as if they hadn't heard it before but Hilda and Cookie and Anne Sylvester sat there goggleeyed. It was still a good story, particularly the part about the leopard hiding out on a branch of a tree above the tent and glaring down at George Elbert. George Elbert managed to look like a leopard when he told it. Of course in the end George Elbert shot the leopard just in the nick or else he wouldn't have been there to tell the tale.

Dinner took hours. When George Elbert ordered the third brandy, Annie said it was time she went home to Columbia Heights. Lulie jumped at that. She cried out that they were going downtown anyway. They would drive her home. Any excuse to cross Brooklyn Bridge on a fine moonlight night.

Jay and Lulie were childishly happy when they found themselves alone in the cab together after leaving Annie at the big old brownstone Sylvester house. Though they couldn't see it much on account of the lights, there really was a full moon shining in the wintry sky.

"Remind you of anything?" asked Lulie snuggling up to him.

"I had the funniest experience this afternoon . . . at the Brigade recruiting office . . . you know the déjà vu sensation? Well it was just like unreeling some film you've seen before. I told you about that Commie girl I used to know in Chicago before we were married. There she was looking exactly the way she used to ten years ago. Then when I came out she was gone. Do you suppose it was some kind of hallucination?"

Lulie let out a shriek. "I'd have scratched her eyes out."

They laughed. They were both still laughing when the cab pulled up to the curb in front of their place.

Jay and Lulie had just begun packing their suitcases when the phone rang. Annie was saying please come right over to lunch. Ugo was there and insisted on seeing Jay before they sailed. They must come right away because Ugo was teaching Ella to make a spaghetti napolitano and that couldn't wait. Lulie said she couldn't see how they could but they would, so they hauled on their galoshes and raincoats and went sludging out through the slush of a late snowstorm to the subway.

Ugo was Annie's boyfriend. Ugo Salvatore was a tall selfsatisfied man with some of the chill selfpossession of a croupier at Monte Carlo, a journalist from Milan who had made a name for himself with a witty series of articles, widely translated into English and

French, on the dilemmas of the League of Nations. He had slid out of Italy with the blackshirts at his heels on account of his opposition to Mussolini and had turned up in New York as correspondent for some Swiss newspapers. Jay and Lulie suspected that Anne Sylvester paid his bills. They were both devoted to Annie and were developing a grudging sort of affection for Ugo.

Ugo opened the front door. He wore a green baize apron over his business suit. He gave them each a hug and hung their wet coats round the base of the art nouveau bronze nymph in the hall. The air of the house was heavy with garlic and olive oil and the smell of sizzling tomato sauce.

Ugo ushered them into Annie's oldfashioned Victorian dining room. The loaves of Italian bread and the provolone cheeses stacked amid Chianti bottles in the middle of the long table looked incongruous under the crystal chandelier.

Annie in a red velvet dress sat brighteyed at the head of the table. "Isn't this fun?" she cried. "The best thing about Ugo's cooking is it smells so good."

"Ella's cooking, my dear."

Ella, Annie's little hunchback mulatto maid who had been with her ever since anybody could remember, arrived from the kitchen holding the spaghetti up above her head in a blue polkadotted pottery bowl. "Howdy Miss Lulie, Mr. Jay.... I sure do hope it's goin' to suit." She gave Ugo a puckish look as she set down the bowl. They could see she wasn't any too fond of Mr. Ugo.

Ugo poured them each a glass of Chianti and sat down.

"Jay," he said in his precise copybook English, "you must not take Lulie to Spain . . . to Paris yes but to Spain no."

"I wanna go where he goes." Lulie put on a mock whimper.

"We have idealist Italians fighting the Fascisti there. News comes through the exiles' underground. The news is not good."

He settled down to filling his face with spaghetti. The spaghetti was delicious. "Ella is an apt pupil," said Ugo as he reached for another helping. "Now, Ella, the scallopini before they get cold." Ella scuttled into the kitchen.

"Ugo likes his vittles so much," said Lulie. She gave one of her little laughing shrieks. "He can turn a ham sandwich into a Roman orgy."

Ugo gave Lulie a tolerant smile. Then he wiped his mouth

and turned to Jay. "You read my article, 'La Guerre Triangulaire' in the *Journal de Genève?*"

Jay's mouth was too slippery with spaghetti to answer. He and Lulie both nodded enthusiastically.

"There I broke the story, as you say in America. The Spanish Civil War has become a triangular war. On the one side Franco helped by Hitler and my dear friend Benito Mussolini"—he slithered the name out as he pronounced it so that it sounded like a snake. "On the Republican side there appears to be a split between the government in Valencia—fast being infiltrated by Sta*leen*'s Communists—and the working-class Parties, anarchists, syndicalists centered in Catalonia. Mr. Sta*leen* enthusiastically supports the Republic but most of his enthusiasm is directed toward the Spanish gold reserve. The British and the French and that great lover of mankind, Franklin Delano Roosevelt, have delivered the Republic over to him with their stupid Non-Intervention Committee. Result: only the Soviet Union will furnish them arms. They give up their gold reserves to buy arms and with every shipment of arms comes a commissar."

"But Ugo, there aren't any Communists in the government," said Jay firmly. "We met almost everybody who's anything in the present government the summer we were in Spain with the Echevarrias. Lulie, remember the *limonada socialista?*"

Lulie nodded brighteyed.

"We even met a few Communist leaders. Remember the little guy at the Ateneo with inflamed eyelids who looked so much like a rat? He admitted the Party didn't have popular support."

"That was two years ago; politics change in two years," said Ugo. He struck himself on the forehead with the flat of his hand: "*Dio mio,* why can't the Americans understand international politics? The entire Western world in this case refuses to understand that the Russians play for keeps. Sta*leen*'s particular political style is: everybody must be his slave or get his throat cut. Very simple. Sta*leen* loves three things. He loves himself, he loves gold and he loves power. He has the Spanish gold in his pocket; now he wants Spanish power."

Jay felt his face getting red. "The Spanish people won't stand for it. We know the Spanish people fairly well."

Ugo poured another round of Chianti. He raised his glass to each of them with a disarming smile.

"The American people are blockheads, if you excuse my saying so, that is most of them, but let us talk for a moment about nice kind liberal wellinformed American people like Mrs. Annie Sylvester and Mr. Algernon McGurk and Mr. Jay Pignatelli. You form an organization to make propaganda for the Spanish Republic. Very good. But why in the name of all the saints and martyrs do you pick a director who is a Party member?"

"Who is?"

"De Jager."

"Ugo, I've known hundreds of Party members," said Jay, "and I don't think this boy fits the specifications. His people are Dutch Catholics."

"He is an excellent documentary film director. He'll make good propaganda, but for the Communists," said Ugo quietly. "His camera man, Anselmo Ghiberti, himself a Party man, told me so. Among anti-Fascist refugees we talk freely."

"That's what I meant, Don Modesto," Lulie whispered to Jay, "about dogooding. . . ."

Before Jay could think up an answer Annie broke in soothingly in her warm contralto voice: "Ugo, you are always right, at least almost always . . . but maybe just this one time it won't come out the way you say. . . . I'm betting on Jay that it won't."

Ugo reached for Annie's hand and kissed it romantically. "Never argue with a woman," he whispered. "Particularly with a beautiful woman. But a nice sweet girl like Lulie, she must not go to Spain. It is not safe."

When they finally managed to drag themselves and their bags aboard the *Queen Mary,* Jay and Lulie were so dog-tired they flopped right down in their bunks. They heard the deep throbbing whistles of departure with profound satisfaction. They were too weary to go up on deck for a last look at New York harbor. The shaking of the screws pushing the great ship through the water was a lullaby. "Thank heaven we don't know one soul on board," mumbled Lulie. "Wake me up when we get to Cherbourg."

Next morning they were sitting happily side by side on the

lower bunk, eating their breakfasts off a tray, and drinking in the surge and swish of broken water on the chillybriny breeze that poured in through the porthole, when the steward brought them a note on ship's stationery. Somebody with rather immature handwriting was inviting them for a drink in the bar. It was signed California Jones.

"An old flame?" asked Lulie. There was a green twinkle in her eye.

Jay blushed and shook his head.

A dim outline was taking shape in his memory of a tall gushing girl at a benefit cocktail party in connection with some case he had handled for free. "We called her the American Beauty. . . . When I was a child there was a vogue for American Beauty roses on very long stems. She was some kind of a sculptress on a very long stem."

When they found California Jones in the bar she had a rosebud mouth and rolling brown eyes under a shock of dark hair, all on a very long stem. She talked in bunches. They must think she was awfully fresh—every now and then she emphasized a word so that it stood out as if in electric lights—to send a note like that, but she'd followed the Pignatelli career from way back when she was a mere babe in Los Angeles during the Sabbatini case. One of her first successful portrait heads was of old Sabbatini. She did it from newspaper photographs. She'd seen a release about Popular Historians. She thought it was wonderful. "I believe in the Spanish Republic."

When the steward came they each ordered dry port. California Jones giggled that port always was her morning drink. She added that everybody called her Calla, like the lily. She had a high rippling laugh. She hoped they would call her Calla.

Calla must have noticed that Jay wasn't listening very carefully, because she raised her voice.

"Mr. Pignatelli, have you read the first-class passenger list?"

"Why on earth should I?"

"What we plan to do," Lulie declared firmly, "is sleep, sleep all the way to Cherbourg."

Calla insisted that she always read the passenger lists, all of them. That's how she found the Pignatellis were on board and so was our ambassador to the court of St. James. . . .

"One of my most unfavorite people," Lulie interrupted.

Calla rattled on without paying attention ... "And all his family and Arthur Brent and John Haines Bentley. But the most important passenger"—her brown eyes beamed like searchlights into their faces—"one of the most important men in the United States of America—isn't on the passenger list at all.... The columnists call him the Adviser of Presidents. He's the one man in the world who could bring real influence to bear on the Spanish situation, not only in America but in England.... If we could talk him into it."

She paused a moment for breath. Then she added in a husky whisper: "It just happens that we are friends."

She must have caught something in Jay's face, because with a toss of her chin she said "No inferences please," then she let out a rippling laugh. "He likes to imagine he's my uncle. Sometimes I think he's all the world's uncle."

"The plan I'm working on," she addressed herself to Lulie now in a woman-to-woman confidential tone, "is to bring the two of them together for a long quiet talk about the Spanish situation. It would do more good."

She rubbed in the word "good" so that they could hardly stand it.

They mustn't get her wrong, she hurried to explain, he wasn't a man you could influence, but he was so openminded. Deliberate too; he never made a move unless he knew it would work. That was the secret of his marvelous success.

Calla beamed into each of their faces. All she wanted was their permission to bring the matter up with him. All she would say was that she'd met old friends who were wellinformed on Spain. He would do the rest; he was a tireless seeker for information.

"My dear," she beamed on Lulie, "he'll fall for you like a ton of bricks. He likes them petite. I don't know what he sees in me." Her lips pursed coyly. "Maybe it's just the artist he sees." She let out another soprano ripple. "When you talk to him you mustn't forget that he's quite deaf. I'll see that he wears his hearing aid.... Well, *hasta la vista*. I'm going to meet him now."

"But who?" asked Jay and Lulie in unison.

"Bernard M. Baruch. ... I thought you knew."

She was so preoccupied with her mission that she forgot to pay for the drinks.

The next morning when Calla ushered them into the walnut-paneled salon of a suite on the top deck, Jay was amazed how much Berny Baruch looked like a picture of him sitting on a park bench that appeared so often in the newspapers. Though it was indoors he wore the same darkishgreen tweed cap and smoked the wellknown brier pipe. He was wearing his hearing aid. Just as Calla had said, there was an avuncular kindliness about his throaty southern drawl.

It was obvious that the great man was fond of the ladies. A special smile crossed his face when he caught sight of Lulie. Jay could see at once how taken he was by the green of her eyes and the auburn glint of her hair and the comical expression of her mouth. Words flashed unspoken on a screen inside Jay's head: Not for you, Mr. Baruch.

The chief flaw in their interview, to Jay's way of thinking, was that they were not alone. A gnomish little steelyhaired man who sat deep in a leather chair smoking another brier pipe was introduced as Mr. Arthur Brent of the *New York Times*. Ponderous redfaced John Haines Bentley of the Associated Press sat in another. He smoked a cigar. They both had the relaxed air of men come to spend the morning with an old crony.

California Jones seemed a different woman: a mere slip of a girl. She hardly said a word. She tiptoed around with a demure smile on her lips, helping the blankfaced gentleman's gentleman pass around the eleven o'clock cups of hot bouillon.

Jay sipped his bouillon. He was casting about for the words he needed to present his case. "Go right ahead, Jay," coaxed Calla. "You are among friends. It won't do the least bit of harm to let Mr. Brent and Mr. Bentley in on what you have to say. It's publicity we've all been working for ... to have the truth come out." She turned her beaming gaze on Berny Baruch's long furrowed countenance. "Just imagine ... one of our most brilliant young liberal attorneys, and shy."

Jay blushed. Berny Baruch, showing himself to be a kind man indeed, leaned towards him with a receptive smile. The faces of the two newspapermen took on a woebegone expression. They were sure they had heard it all before. He could see them buttoning up their ears.

Jay launched into his brief. It wasn't too late to turn the tide of the Spanish Civil War. Madrid was holding firm. The rest depended on liberals outside of Spain as much as on the Spaniards. More than anything else it was the Non-Intervention Committee that was strangling the Spanish Republic. By refusing to furnish arms to the legally elected government, the French and British and Americans were letting the Communists appear as the only defenders of European democracy. If the Fascists were allowed to win in Spain it would be the signal for fresh aggressions by Mussolini and Hitler.

That was why a group of writers in New York was promoting a documentary film as the opening wedge of a campaign to convince the American people that the Spanish Civil War was their war. George Elbert Warner had already left for Madrid to work on the continuity.

Brent and Bentley sat up in their chairs when they heard the name.

"Hasn't he gotten himself killed yet?" cried Brent. "He's been the perpetual war correspondent as long as I can remember."

"And when he's not dodging shells in brush wars, he's out tracking dangerous wild animals," groaned Bentley. "I don't see what he gets out of it."

"Some darned good English prose," said Jay.

"I'm an oldfashioned man," drawled Berny Baruch, "and no literateur. What I've read seemed a little hectic to me.... But I suppose he's highly regarded by the young men."

"The first young man we have to convince, Mr. Baruch, is the very subtle gentleman who occupies the White House."

They all laughed at that. Jay felt he'd made a point.

Berny Baruch unfolded himself gradually out of his chair until he rose to his full six-feet-two, and suggested that there was just time for a constitutional before lunch.

"The trouble with Pignatelli and me is we're idealists," he drawled. He put his arm round Jay's shoulders for a moment. "We need the opinion of a practical man.... The most practical man in the world happens to be right on this boat. We are going to have lunch with Joe Kennedy. Why don't we take our friends along?"

While the gentleman's gentleman called up the ambassador's quarters to find out if he could accommodate three more guests, the party walked up and down the boat deck in the sharp wind. Berny Baruch took one of the girls on each arm and skipped about like a two-year-old with his long muffler trailing behind him. Jay and the two journalists followed more sedately in their wake.

"Being a fresh air fiend dates Berny Baruch," Brent was saying in his dry nutcracker voice. "The mania came in with T. R."

The ambassador's suite was twice as large as Baruch's. Jay and Lulie found themselves pressed with little Brent into a corner of a sort of lounge. Stewards were circulating cocktails. The place smelt of carnations and cigarette smoke and expensive furs. There were many young people. Brent whispered that most of the crowd were family, children, in-laws, although two of the boys were away at college. Caviar canapés were being rushed about on silver trays, but the press was so dense neither Jay nor Lulie managed to latch hold of one.

Joe Kennedy turned out to be a plainfaced man with a sharp cold eye behind steelrimmed spectacles. He'd never lost the flat South Boston accent. The moment he put in an appearance everybody was herded into the private dining saloon. There was so much heavy banter up and down the long table Jay had no chance to exchange a word with the ambassador. Kennedy's Down East intonation stood out against Baruch's South Carolina drawl. In the midst of it the ambassador called down the table to his sons: "Boys, don't forget it's Friday."

Waiters had to come scurrying back while orders were changed from steaks and chops to filet of sole.

It wasn't until after the meal that Jay found himself meeting the ambassador over the coffee. Berny Baruch had evidently filled him in on the Spanish project. "Not a bad notion," he said. As he talked his eyes carefully scrutinized Jay's face. "You've got a good name in George Elbert Warner ... my boys read everything he writes. If you could get hold of a pretty señorita and a good plot ... but keep away from politics. If there's anything people hate in motion pictures it's politics."

Jay asked mildly how the British seemed to be sizing up the Spanish situation.

"The City, thinking of British investments, tends to consider Franco the lesser evil. Enthusiasts whoop it up for the Loyalists in the Cocoa press but nobody reads them. I have a secretary of course who reads them all. The question they never have been able to answer to my satisfaction is the incompetence of the Spanish Republicans. If they'd been on the ball they wouldn't have let the army revolt get started in the first place or have allowed the anarchists and Communists to shock the civilized world by burning churches and murdering nuns."

"But aren't most of those stories just propaganda?"

"If only a quarter of them are true it's bad enough."

The ambassador turned away. When Jay moved towards a table to set down his empty coffee cup he heard him saying to Baruch, "Berny, I'm a loyal Catholic but I'm also the father of sons. I'm appalled by any outcry that increases the danger of war."

"Even in a righteous cause?"

"We learned about righteous causes in 1917–18."

People were drifting away. While Jay and Lulie were looking for someone to say "Thank you, good-by" to, a young man in a dark suit came up to Jay with a card in his hand. "Mr. Pignatelli, the ambassador asked me to give you this card. You know he has motion-picture interests. He says when your picture is ready to be sure to consult Mr. Pirelli at his New York office."

Calla came swooping down on them. "You see. Isn't it wonderful? I told you I could be a help. Now you must promise to come to my show."

"Of course, if we get to London," they shouted in unison.

They ran around the boat deck taking deep breaths. A slaty sky was clamped down over the green Atlantic. There was a beginning of whitecaps.

"Well," panted Lulie, "I never saw a neater job of passing the buck. Mr. Baruch is an old duck."

"No hits, no runs, no errors," grumbled Jay.

A sudden spat of icy rain drove them below. It took them a long time, wandering through the great ship's creaking corridors, to find their way back down to Tourist Class and the quiet of their close little cabin. Bad weather must be forecast because the steward had bolted up their porthole.

It had been a long first day in Paris. Jay was tired to the bone. His feet were wet from slogging through the Parisian drizzle. As he opened the door of his hotel room he caught a comforting whiff of Lulie amid the emanations of furniture polish and mildewed draperies that evoked every Paris hotel he had ever stayed in. The lights were on. Lulie lay asleep with her glasses slipped down her nose, her book on her chest. The parquet floor creaked as he stepped towards her. She woke with a start and stared at him out of blinking blind eyes. "Tell everything, Modesto," she mumbled. "I'll wake up as you go on."

"Lulie, I'm too sleepy. . . . It was like groping through a can of worms." He tore off his clothes, slipped into his chilly pajamas and slid into the big bed beside her. He pulled her slender body to him and fell into deep warm oblivion.

When they woke up the first thing Lulie said was "Modesto, tell about the worms."

The room was dank but an unexpected streak of rusty sunlight glowed through the ancient lace curtains.

It was an odd room in a grubby old hotel that they both loved. The room, higher than it was wide, had been constructed some time in the distant past by partitioning off one end of a huge seventeenth-century salon. The original walls were still covered with threadbare crimson damask. The corner of an ornate stone cornice towered overhead. Their bed faced a blocked-up fireplace with a magnificent mantel supported by stone cupids strenuously elevating a gilt escutcheon. The tall frenchwindow, draped with lace and stained velvet, opened on a balcony that looked down on ranks of toy trees set in the yellow gravel of one of the colonnaded inner courts of the Palais Royale.

The radiator was cold but at least there was hot water in the triangular bathroom with a superannuated tub that Lulie claimed must have been the very tub Marat was assassinated in. Of course the reason Marat stayed so long in that tub was that it was the only way you could keep warm.

Jay hurried through his bathing and shaving. While they ate their croissants and drank their sour *café au lait* huddled in the blankets and coverlets off the bed, Lulie kept whining that she wanted to hear about the worms, until at last, striding up and down and flapping his arms to get the circulation going, Jay started to

talk: "First worm: *le camarade Aristide Chenier,* Communist Deputy. Went to see him in a sort of notary's office on the Rue Mon-
taine Sainte Genevieve, the street that always makes us think of
François Villon. A small shiny baldheaded man with a shiny black
moustache. Smell of soap. Looks like he was all made of celluloid.
Affected me unpleasantly though he was friendly enough. He has
arranged for my passage tomorrow with a truck driver—*un homme
de confiance vous comprenez*—from Perpignan to Valencia. I'll go
down on the night train—*huit heures dix*—tonight. There's all
sorts of monkey business about getting across the Spanish border on
account of the Non-Intervention Committee. The fact that I have a
duly visaed American passport doesn't mean a thing.... If it
weren't for the queasy feeling that his main interest in the Spanish
Civil War was drumming up votes of the *braves ouvriers* in his
Parisian *arrondissement,* I'd be more sympathetic. Another thing
.. You know the way people suddenly let the cat out of the bag
when you least expect it... I got the impression that he had a
financial interest in the cargo of that truck I'm going down with
and that he wants me to ride on it for the protection of my
American passport. I may be doing him an injustice."

"Modesto, what you really mean is that he's a double-dealing
coundrel," cried Lulie letting out one of her little shrieks.

Jay burst out laughing: "Not quite as bad as that. He took me
out to Clichy to meet his constituents in the workers' clubs and then
to the Chamber of Deputies. He got me a pass to the press gallery.
In fact, he couldn't have been nicer. Who should I run into but
Bentley, our Bentley, on the *Queen Mary.* Anyway Bentley must
have thought I was on the trail of a story because he took me out to
Foyot's for an exorbitant lunch and then made me go with him to
interview a contact ... turned out to be the damnedest Fascist you
ever saw.... At that, you would have liked Dubois better than the
comrade.... I guess he's one of Georgy's honest crooks.... Bentley
wanted to get a story about gunrunning across the border but
nothing doing. Dubois is about my age or a little younger and he
runs the family furniture-moving business. Said right away that
what France needed was an Adolf Hitler. He believes in workers'
syndicates properly run and good wages and all that, but he claims
this lashing up of class hatreds has to stop.... Communist provoca-
tions. He says his profits were so slim he couldn't buy a new car he

really needed last summer.... He didn't speak any English so Bentley kept pressing me to ask him about gunrunning until finally he burst out laughing and said all right, if Bentley promised not to publish the story he would admit he had used a few idle trucks—business was slack—to take a number of boxes marked pianos across the border. His rightist connections were very useful in these matters. The machineguns came from Krupp's if you can believe it.... We came away throughly confused." Jay let out a laugh.

"Bentley was sore as a boil about not being able to use the story. Then he insisted on going to a salon on that great big old square near the Invalides.... I didn't know they still had salons. ... A funny little hunched-up woman all covered with jet named Mme. de Montpensier, like in Dumas ... or in a chapter that Marcel Proust never lived to write. She's an American, by the way, but she's lived in France so long she's forgotten her English ... the strangest doddering people, old and young ... nothing to drink but lukewarm tea out of magnificent Sèvres china ... the bitter hate they felt for the French working people and the Spanish Republicans.... They were misinformed about everything. A goaty little man with a beard was telling a horror story about how the Reds were shipping masterpieces by Goya and Greco out of Spain to sell them. You know Paco Fuentes who runs the Prado. He's a man of absolutely crystalline honesty. He's putting on a traveling exhibition to get some of his masterpieces out of harm's way and to raise money for the Spanish hospitals. What could be more legitimate? You could feel the hatred like something slimy and writhing all about you. It really was a can of worms.... After that we had some food and went back to the Palais Bourbon to hear Léon Blum make his great speech.... He's really a clever parliamentarian. The opposition didn't have a chance.... All about turning the Popular Front into a National Front.... Funny to hear a Socialist wave the old tricolor, but it worked. It was after midnight when he started ... That's why I got home so late."

"Well, Modesto, we've got twelve hours." Lulie's voice started forlorn but ended up cheerful. "It's a sunny day. Let's do something perfectly delightful. How about going out and walking in the woods at St. Germain?"

6

Towards 1984

George Orwell led a rough life: "a bloody life a good deal of the time."

Born in Bengal in 1903 he was christened Eric Arthur Blair.

His father was a minor official of the Opium Department of the Indian Civil Service. His mother was the daughter of a teak merchant in Burma. The family traditions were all of careers in the East Indies.

When his father retired, the Blairs, in an afterglow of Victorian gentility, set up housekeeping in a seacoast town. Eric Blair grew up hating their shabby genteel world with a poisonous hatred.

Being his father's son, he had to go through the mill that trained young gentlemen to serve the empire.

His parents must have skimped to send him to board at St. Cyprian's at Eastbourne on the South Coast. It was an expensive school. Among his schoolmates were Cecil Beaton and Cyril Connolly, bright boys both; Eric Blair made a name for himself as the schoolboy poet, but he had less spending money than any of them. The masters never let him forget that he was one of the poorest boys there.

The outbreak of war in 1914 stirred the boy with patriotic zeal. He composed a poem (he was all of eleven years old) called "Awaken Young Men of England," which was published in the *Henley and South Oxfordshire Standard*. Two years later when

Kitchener's ship was torpedoed by the Germans, a poem on the great drillmaster's death was set as an exercise for the boys. Eric's was considered the best and duly printed in the local paper.

His head was full of rhymes. He tried a full-length comedy in the style of Aristophanes. He circulated burlesque verses among his classmates. Cyril Connolly wrote of him at this time that "he alone among the boys was an intellectual, not a parrot, for he thought for himself, read Shaw and Samuel Butler, and rejected, not only St. Cyprian's, but the war, the Empire, Kipling, Sussex and character."

He never got over being a good student. In 1917 he won a scholarship to Eton. As king's scholar he wrote satirical verses, edited a school magazine. He was remembered as a loner. Connolly, who was at Eton at the same time, described him as being "tall, pale, with flaccid cheeks, large spatulate fingers and a supercilious voice." His nickname was Cynicus.

Whether it was lack of funds or family tradition or glimmering childhood memories of India, instead of finishing his schooling at one of the universities he enlisted in the Indian Imperial Police. He served in Burma.

He hated the life of a sahib as much as he'd hated genteel poverty in England. In Burma he "saw the dirty work of Empire at close quarters. The wretched prisoners huddled in the stinking cages of the lockups, the gray cowed faces of the long-term convicts, the scarred buttocks of the men who had been flogged with bamboos—all these oppressed me with an intolerable sense of guilt. . . . I was young and ill-educated and I had to think out my problems in the utter silence that is imposed on every Englishman in the East."

He didn't even know, he wrote years later, that the British Empire was dying. He was tortured by the bitter anti-European feelings of the natives, the sneering yellow faces of the young Burmese, the scorn of fledgling Buddhist priests who seemed "to have nothing better to do than stand on streetcorners and jeer at Europeans. . . . All I know was that I was stuck between my hatred of the Empire I served and the evil-spirited little beasts who tried to make my job impossible."

At the end of five years he decided that the sooner he chucked his job the better. In the fall of 1927, after a leave with his parents in Cornwall, he sent in his resignation.

The time had come to strip off the middle-class trappings. He was determined to throw in his lot with the underdog. In Burma, language, race, position had kept him from exchanging an honest word with a coolie. At home the coolie spoke English even if he did drop his aitches. As a boy he'd had a yen for the tramp's life. He took a cheap room in Notting Hill in the western part of London. It was a depression period. Unemployment. He wanted to live the way working men lived but it was hard enough to get any kind of work.

For several years he tramped, slept in dosshouses, washed dishes, picked hops, made a pretense of living the life of the lowest of the low.

He wanted to sink to the bottom. He would get drunk and try taunting the police to throw him in jail, but the police were quite civil to him (perhaps it was his aitches). He couldn't help but be civil in return. He never quite made a jail sentence.

In the spring of 1928 he moved to Paris—must have had a little saved-up money left; Parisian poverty was more picturesque. He took a cheap room in the Rue du Pot de Fer. Montparnasse. He wrote articles protesting against the grinding underside of capitalist civilization. He was a flaming Socialist. The topdog moneymakers were the root of all evil: give the underdog a chance to run the world.

Henri Barbusse's *Le Monde* published in French translation his exposé of the silent censorship of the British press and his reflections on beggars and British tramps. He wrote constantly: short stories, a ballade, two novels; all ended in the wastebasket. Winters were cold on the Rue du Pot de Fer. He fell ill with pneumonia and was treated in a charity hospital.

Back in England he lived off and on with his parents in Suffolk, with relatives in London. He wrote reviews and articles. They didn't bring in enough to cover the cheapest board and lodging. He tried other ways of making a living. He tutored schoolboys, wrote boys' stories for juvenile magazines. In the winter of 1933, Victor Gollancz, a leftish publisher who followed the Party line at a safe distance, finally brought out *Down and Out in Paris and London* which he'd been having the author tinker with for years.

Eric Blair decided to sign it George Orwell. Why? So as not to hurt his aging parents' feelings? To negate his old bourgeois identity? These were the days when every bourgeois intellectual tried to imagine himself a proletarian sprung up spontaneously out of the gutter.

He couldn't stand living off his family; he signed up fulltime to teach in a boys' school. During the summer holiday he wrote *Burmese Days* into which he packed all the bitterness of his service in the East.

George Orwell had an agent now. Proletarian novels were the rage in avant-garde circles. His first book was published by Harpers in New York as well as in London. Neither edition sold, but the dogged truthtelling of his very personal narrative brought readers, even some notice in the press. These were the days when the leftwing critics were waiting, as for a second coming, for "the great proletarian novel."

Gollancz blew hot and cold over *Burmese Days*—a sticky subject. Harpers published it in New York. Meanwhile Orwell was down with another bout of "pneumonia." When he came out of the hospital he gave up teaching for good and took a job in a second-hand bookstore. In his free time he was struggling with an elaborate spoof on the lower-middle class: *Keep the Aspidistra Flying*.

Work in a bookstore convinced him he hated books: "The sweet smell of decaying paper appeals to me no longer." Ever after he associated books with dust and paranoic customers and dead bluebottle flies.

Gollancz gave him a small advance to write a book about the plight of the British miner, employed and unemployed. To write about miners he had to live with them. He spent two months in the Black Country and told what he saw. *The Road to Wigan Pier* caused pain in trade-union circles.

The spring before he had become friends with Eileen O'Shaughnessy, "the nicest person I've met for a long time." In spite of his desperate slumming, he was not the man to marry out of his class. Eileen was the daughter of a Collector of Customs and working for her master's degree in psychology at University College in London.

Orwell had published three novels and a swarm of book reviews, article after article in the literary weeklies, but he still barely earned his keep. He didn't even have the cash to buy a ring. Eileen took him as he was.

Orwell had come to hate living in the city. He leased a cottage in the quiet village of Wallington in Hertfordshire. There was a shop attached where the former owner had sold groceries, knick-nacks, candies out of jars, family remedies, aspirin. The place was known as The Stores. Orwell thought it offered a small income. At least they'd have a roof over their heads. There was a gardenplot where they could grow potatoes, cabbage, Brussels sprouts. He had bought chickens and goats. He owned a golden retriever named Marx.

They had barely settled to this country life they both enjoyed when Loyalist Spain's call for help against the Fascist uprising stirred the crusader in Orwell. Since he had had military experience in the Officers' Training Corps and in the Burmese constabulary he convinced himself it was his duty to offer his services to the working people defending Socialism in Spain. Like his radical friends in London he saw the war all white and all black: the good Socialist Republicans fighting the bad bloodthirsty Fascists.

As soon as he'd finished the last chapter of his book on the miners he went off to Barcelona and enlisted. His political friends in London belonged mostly to the Independent Labor Party so it was inevitable that he should sign up with the ILP's opposite number in Catalonia.

POUM, the Workers' Party of Marxist Unification, led by a wellmeaning intellectual named Andrés Nin, was trying to unite the Spanish people against the encroaching Communists as well as the Fascists. Nin aimed for a workers' Republic. In Catalonia POUM had enough adherents to put a sizable army in the field. Orwell didn't care by whose side he fought so long as they were shooting at Fascists.

He joined the ragged battalions on the escarpments overlooking Huesca in Aragon. The winter was bitterly cold. The troops suffered more from frostbite than enemy action. He was delighted by the simple fraternal Socialism of his Spanish comrades, but appalled by their lack of the most elementary organization. No discipline. Only the vaguest overall command. Not enough rifles. Few machineguns, scanty ammunition. No warm clothing. Not enough blankets. The only thing they didn't lack was food . . . and bravery.

When the ILP contingent arrived Orwell was transferred to it as a Corporal. The Aragon Front was so quiet that when Eileen arrived in Barcelona to serve as secretary to the ILP liaison officer she was allowed to visit her husband for a couple of days. She found Orwell fuming. He'd come to Spain to kill Fascists, but their lines were so far away he hardly ever got one within range. In April he took a leave to Barcelona. His intention was to join the International Brigade. He was vaguely aware that they were Communist controlled, but their reputation was of an efficient fighting force. On the Madrid Front he would see action. If he lived through he'd go home and write about it.

When he piled off the troop train in Barcelona, thinking only of a hot bath and a good meal and of sleeping with Eileen in a comfortable bed at the Hotel Continental, he was flabbergasted to hear rifle fire up and down the Ramblas. Who was fighting whom?

As he prepared to help his fellow POUMists defend a strong point over a restaurant, the story unfolded. Since the resignation of Largo Caballero's Socialist government, the Communists were running wild in the Junta for Defense. Stalin in Moscow was purging supposed Trotsky adherents. His agents in Spain had orders to identify Trotskyites whether or not. The nearest thing was the POUM, which with the Anarcho-Syndicalists stood in the way of a Communist takeover: all in the pay of the Fascists, trumpeted the government newspapers. The crack Assault Guards were sent into Barcelona to disarm the population. The POUMists and the anarchist labor unions were resisting as best they could.

Three days in Barcelona taught Orwell more about revolutionary politics than three months in the lines. There he had seen everything through a rosy haze of Socialist brotherhood. His poor knowledge of Spanish, his ignorance of the complicated chess game Stalin was playing in the Kremlin had kept him from any forewarning of the events that master of history was preparing behind the scenes. No longer could he see the Civil War all white and all black.

The fighting in Barcelona petered out in an uneasy truce. Orwell was promoted to Second Lieutenant. Berating himself for a blockhead, he went back to the Aragon Front. The Loyalist attempt to take Huesca fizzled for lack of artillery. Now the Fascists took advantage of all the disunity in the Republican rear to stage a minor offensive. Orwell was shot through the throat by a sniper. By a miracle the bullet missed the artery and the spine and merely damaged the vocal chords. Speechless he was sent to a hospital. From the hospital he wrote his old schoolmate Cyril Connolly that at last he really believed in Socialism. . . . "I never did before." He was thinking of the comradely Socialism of the front lines. By June he was well enough to go back to his outfit for his discharge papers. It was time he went home to get his throat properly treated.

At headquarters everything was in uproar. The POUM had been declared illegal by the Valencia government. The Assault Guards and Communist secret agents were tracking down every POUMist they could find. Nin had been arrested; later he was shot in his cell.

Orwell and his friends were on the run. Back in Barcelona he didn't dare be seen at the Hotel Continental. The hotelkeepers were turning in any POUMists they found. The old owning bourgeoisie was uniting in unholy alliance with the Communists to exterminate the working-class revolutionaries. By a series of dodges he met up with Eileen. It delighted him to find she was treating the whole thing as a lark.

A friendly British consul helped smuggle the Orwells across the border. Like so many others they found Perpignan their city of refuge. By early July they were back at the cottage in Wallington.

Wallington was delightful though the garden was grown up with weeds. They had made friends of their neighbors the summer before. But in leftwing London faces were grim. From Barcelona Orwell had written Gollancz that the stuff about Spain published in the English press was "the most appalling lies. . . . I hope I shall get a chance to publish the truth about what I've seen."

Gollancz took fright. The left intellectuals were following the Party line. There had been no Communist takeover, merely a suppression of disloyal elements. POUMists, Syndicalists, in short any groups or individuals who opposed the Communist program, were in Franco's pay. Liberals wagged their heads sagely over the Fifth Column. Gollancz declared, before a word of it was written, that he had no intention of publishing Orwell's book on the Civil War. The *New Statesman and Nation,* where he'd been welcome before, turned down his reviews. Acquaintances cut him on the street. In his old haunts Orwell found himself a pariah.

He never flinched. He'd tell the truth if it killed him. "I hold the outmoded opinion that in the long run it does not pay to tell lies."

Again the old treadmill of want. He was working day and night to finish *Homage to Catalonia*. His agent found him a better publisher than Gollancz. The old English spirit of fair play was asserting itself. He found friends in unexpected quarters. Non-political magazines invited him to write for them. In the spring of 1938 he fell ill. This time those recurrent bouts with pneumonia were definitely diagnosed as tuberculosis. The following fall a fellow novelist sent him anonymously a check for three hundred pounds so that he could spend the winter abroad.

The European war, that seemed to him inevitable since the defeat of Republican Spain, was already looming. When the tension snapped with the first hostilities on September 3, 1939, he tried to enlist. Every service barred him for his lungs. In the end he had to content himself with the Home Guards. Eileen got a job with the Censorship Bureau. Wartime travel to Hertfordshire became so difficult they had to move to London. In 1940 both Orwells went to work for BBC. At last they had salaries they could rely on.

Orwell's reputation was becoming established. He edited bookpages, wrote columns of his own: controversial was the critics' word for him. When the Party line was in the doghouse during the Hitler-Stalin pact, even Gollancz plucked up his courage to publish a volume of essays: *Inside the Whale*.

Orwell's mind was shaking loose from Socialist dogma. He began to see history whole: "What is obviously happening," he wrote in his offhand way, "is the breakup of laissez-faire capitalism and of the liberal-Christian culture. Until recently the implications of this were not foreseen because it was generally imagined that Socialism could preserve and even enlarge the atmosphere of liberalism. It is now beginning to be realized how false this idea was. Almost certainly we are now moving into an age of totalitarian dictatorships—an age in which freedom of thought will be at first a deadly sin and later on a meaningless abstraction."

Nineteen fortyfour opened auspiciously. The British-American alliance was winning the war. Orwell was making enough to live in a certain comfort. He'd resigned from BBC to become literary editor of the far leftist *Tribune*. Eileen stopped working to take care of a baby they adopted whom they named Richard Horatio

Blair. They had a nice flat in Maida Vale (Orwell had overcome his repugnance for the lower-middle class). His writing brought in a fair living.

Orwell was never the lucky one. They'd barely established the baby in Maida Vale when the flat was bombed and they were homeless again.

All this while Orwell was at work on *Animal Farm*. He thought he had found his pulpit. In writing humorous fantasy perhaps he could say what he wanted without having people blow up in his face. He couldn't have been more mistaken. As Britain's brave ally, Communist Russia was in the good books again. It wasn't cricket to spoof the Soviet Union. Three publishers turned the book down in a hurry. A whole summer went by before Secker and Warburg reluctantly decided to bring out *Animal Farm*.

Nineteen fortyfive was the worst year of his life. While he was in Cologne covering the aftermath of war for the *Observer*, Eileen died suddenly under an anesthetic administered for a minor operation. Orwell's friends expected him to give up the baby. No, he said doggedly, he'd raise the boy himself.

When *Animal Farm* came out in the fall, to the amazement of its British publishers, it caught on. American troops had saved Britain; now the American market saved *Animal Farm*. The Book-of-the-Month Club. The American edition sold half a million copies. Translation followed into every conceivable language. Acclaim. For Orwell in this black time it meant release from strangling poverty.

He and Eileen had talked off and on of some day setting themselves up on an island in the Hebrides. Now he could lease a small estate known as Barnhill on Jura and keep up a London flat besides. Friends found a young man to farm the land for him. Meanwhile he had become friendly with Sonia Brownell, Cyril Connolly's editorial assistant on *Horizon*.

All their lives he and Connolly had kept up an offhand sort of friendship. Connolly was delighted to print Orwell's stories in his magazine. Sonia helped Orwell revise his writing, corrected proofs, ran errands for him, treated him with loving care.

He was admittedly an invalid. Tuberculosis was gaining on him. He spent more and more time in bed. Relapses took him to hospitals. All the while he stuck with ferocious tenacity to the novel he was writing. *1984* was a bitter parable of the totalitarian world he saw developing out of German Nazism, Russian Communism and the decay of the spirit of liberty in Britain. With a satirical flair that had not appeared in English letters since Samuel Butler and Swift, he depicted the world he'd long imagined "where freedom of thought would be considered a deadly sin." He fought off his illness until he finished the book, and typed the whole manuscript himself at Barnhill. The winter of 1949 he was so weak he couldn't go out of doors. He let himself be taken to a sanatorium in Gloucestershire.

That June *1984* was published in London and New York. It was a frightening book. The British hemmed and hawed but the American public still enjoyed a good scare. Again the Book-of-the-Month Club. An English classic overnight. Big Brother, double think, thought crime, telescreen. . . . Orwell poured a cascade of new terms into the language.

Orwell was dying but consumptives always hope. He was in University College Hospital in London when he married Sonia Brownell. They were talking brightly of moving him to a sanatorium in the Alps. It was too late. Within a few weeks he was dead.

7

The Later Life and Deplorable Opinions of Jay Pignatelli—ii

The Trouble with Causes

Lulie," Jay wrote when he arrived in Perpignan next morning, "I'm drinking my coffee under a budding planetree in the sun and I miss you most hellishly. It was wonderful to go to sleep in the Paris drizzle and to wake up in the *midi*. The sunlight's violetcolored and everything smells of figs and dust and rancid olive oil. This is called the Café des Etrangers and it sure is. There are miscellaneous Spaniards. Thuggishlooking men in dusty *boinas* talk Catalan at the next table. Beyond them the people might be Poles. Half the jokers sitting at the tables have that hangman's jaw I associate with plainclothesmen. There are just too many people sitting around for so early in the morning. A blueeyed squarehead, his closecropped noggin very sunburned under the tow hair, just gave me a kind of secret-service stare as he went by. It is smuggling? What the hell are they all up to?"

A beefyfaced heavyset man plunked himself down suddenly in the chair beside Jay. Jay looked up from his writing with a start. The man muttered Café Continental à midi and was gone. Jay went on with his letter:

"That was my *homme de confiance*. He must have been told

what I look like because he slipped into the chair beside me, whispered "Café Continental à midi," poked his fingers towards his mouth in the eating gesture and was gone before I could say *Bonjour*. He was a redfaced man about fifty, I should say. Looks like a solid citizen. Now I'll take this to the post office and mail it before any of these characters with X-ray eyes start reading over my shoulder. While my *homme de confiance* was there you could just see their ears stretching to try to hear what he said.... So much love, Jay."

The Café Continental turns out to be Loyalist country. It is the local bus station; bustle of country people and baskets and boxes and trussed-up fowls and sacks of potatoes. In a room behind the bar, brownfaced Spaniards in blue denims cluster round a map of the peninsula where little flags indicate the fighting fronts. Grubby fingers show Jay the spot in the mountains where the Loyalists gave the Italians a bad time a few days before. With an air of proprietorship a skinny young waiter with an eyebrow moustache points out the long lines in Aragon where the POUM and the anarchists hold the Fascists at bay. An arrow indicates the new Fascist offensive.

A heavy hand on his shoulder draws Jay away from the map. It is the *homme de confiance*. He beckons Jay into a corner of the room and demands in a gruff whisper to see the letter of *le camarade Aristide*. Jay produces it. The man must know the handwriting because instantly he smiles. Dimples appear in his weatherbeaten cheeks. He growls into Jay's ear that his name is Marcel. "*C'est l'heure de l'apéro.*"

While they sip their vermouth-cassis at a table outside, Marcel explains carefully in one-syllable words, as one would to a child, that monsieur must be careful to retain his documentation. Over there—he points with his thumb over his shoulder to indicate the direction of the frontier—they shoot you first and investigate afterwards. Even he, Marcel Vilain, *membre du parti depuis les premiers jours,* was almost *fusillé*. Several trips back some fifth columnist stole his papers while he was asleep in Gerona. The guards were just about to march him to the nearest wall when a French comrade—*un responsable*—turned up who knew who he was. "They all apologized but if I'd been dead their apologies wouldn't have been much consolation to my old woman, now would they? . . . *C'est comme ça les espagnols.*"

Marcel's truck is shiny new. While he is filling up with *essence* another new truck appears driven by a lanky strawhaired man whom Marcel declares was a sailor with the French fleet that mutinied in the Black Sea. They are going in convoy. Grind of gears. Backfires. They are off down a white road that runs straight through an avenue of planetrees towards the mountains. The Pyrenees begin to rise up ahead purple and huge under a stack of billowing clouds. "Rain," says Marcel.

Marcel, who feels no pain after all that wine, immediately starts in on the story of his life. He is thirtyseven years old. Jay had figured he was fifty. Born in Le Havre. Left an orphan, went to sea at fourteen. *Dans la marine* during *la grande guerre. Pas rigolo.* Three times torpedoed. *Réformé.* Worked as an upholsterer in a furniture factory until he lost two fingers in an industrial accident. It was the raw deal they gave him on worker's compensation that turned him to the Communists . . . and the need for peace. *L'union des travailleurs fera la paix du monde.* He took up truckdriving. A man can drive a truck whether he has all his fingers or not. . . . But he had to go to work to organize the truckdrivers' syndicate and get blacklisted by the employers, *les salauds,* so here he is driving for the Spaniards and, like a good pacifist, helping them make war, making good money at it too. . . .

Then all at once in a totally different tone of voice he begins to tell Jay about how he and his old woman raise Hartz Mountain canaries. His heavy features relax. The innocent dimples come back into the weathered cheeks. They have two blackbirds and a nightingale, too. The neighbors bring him their sick birds to doctor. What you do is hold the bird in the palm of your hand and give it a couple of drops of cognac and cayenne pepper with an eyedropper, diluted with water, of course. You have to be very careful not to frighten them when you open their little beaks.

Marcel's chatter is interrupted by a patrol of the *Guarde Mobile.* Men with rifles halt the trucks on a bridge. Packing cases have to be opened, manifests checked. It would have gone on forever if the rain hadn't started to come down so hard the guards lost interest and let the two trucks go on. He will phone Cerbère, the sergeant calls after them threateningly; the control will examine them at the border.

At the border the busybody agents of the special control give the trucks a thorough going over. They bluster and fuss. Jay gets a hunch they are working for handouts. While the drivers argue Jay sits on a bench in the bus station writing Lulie about Marcel and his Hartz Mountain canaries. He knows that will amuse her. As the rain has stopped he roams around the gray town overlooking a gray bay with a forlorn shingle beach until he finds the *Bureau de Poste.* Before he closes his letter he adds: "across the mountains I suspect that mail won't go through. Don't be worried if you don't hear until I'm back on French soil."

Back at the customs post he finds that Marcel's truck, which is loaded with field telephones and dyemaking machinery, will be allowed to pass but that *le copain,* the lanky sailorman, will have to wait until someone in authority makes up his mind as to whether or not the rules of the Non-Intervention Committee prohibit gasmasks.

Marcel cranks up in high good humor. The road is empty. As soon as they cross into Spain, brokendown trucks and smashed cars begin to appear in the ditches of the wide highway, winding between the mountains and the sea. Whenever they approach one of these wrecks Marcel slows down, examines it carefully and exclaims *Imbéciles.* Such a waste. The dirty anarchists don't know how to take care of machinery. *C'est comme ça les espagnols.*

By the time they reach Gerona it is pitch black and raining hard. Only an occasional blue light shows. A sign on the wall of the hotel lobby announces that the place has been expropriated by the CNT—the Syndicalist workers' organization, Marcel explains—but the only sign of revolution is that all the walls have been recently repainted an even battleship gray. The elevator is running. The bed has clean sheets. The dining room is still open. After the standard fourcourse meal of Spanish hotels they turn in.

Next morning it takes Marcel five hours to find the man he needs to give him an order for gasoline, in spite of his having all his papers neatly arranged in a *serviette* and his knowing all the ropes.

While Marcel suffers Jay amuses himself walking around the town. Now he is glad he didn't bring Lulie. It would have hurt her to see how much damage vandals have done to the magnificent

Catalan Gothic cathedral. Wartime posters are plastered over the carvings.

One thing she would have liked. Jay sits down on a bench and pencils the beginning of a letter in his notebook: "Poor Gerona. Battered but still full of ancient dignity. The shopwindows are all taped for protection against the blast of General Franco's bombs, but people have worked the paper tape into ornamental designs. A spider in the middle of a web is very popular. There are elaborate monograms of the Socialist UGT and the anarchist CNT linked by rays and squares and complicated interlaced triangles. Art will out."

When Marcel emerges from the transport office triumphantly waving a packet of *Laissez-passers* and orders for gasoline, he is so red in the face Jay's afraid he'll have a stroke. Under his breath in a whining monotone he curses the anarchist committees, the Socialist committees, the Generalitat of Catalonia and Spaniards in general.

"My truck and cargo are consigned to the Ministry of War in Valencia but nobody will recognize my authority. What can you do with people like that? ... Imbeciles. Idiots. They'll never win the war unless we others the Communists take over."

They drive through Barcelona without stopping. Marcel just waves his pass at the sentries. He is in a blue funk for fear some anarchist committee will try to requisition his truck. As they argue their way past roadblocks Jay tells himself again it is a good thing he didn't bring Lulie. Those browneyed boys in tattered uniforms have the look of being careless with their triggerfingers.

Darkness comes down before they reach Sitges. Marcel has been burning up the road to reach a place where he knows he can get a good French meal. The restaurant is brightly lit though the town is dark. The bar is full of militia and internationals from the Aragon front, all buzzing, like flies on a bit of spoiled meat, around the big sexy blackeyed woman who runs the joint. You can tell from her lingo and the aroma of garlic that she's from Marseilles. It is obvious that she approves of Marcel. Drinks are on the house. Double entendre. Slaps on the buttocks. She manages to jostle them both with her big hips as she ushers them into a pretty little whitetiled dining room to eat their supper.

There are eaters at another table. Five rosyfaced young men in militia uniforms, singing and laughing and carrying on high. It's only when they get up to go that Jay notices something odd about them. They go hopping around a pile of crutches in the corner. Each one of them has lost a leg.

Not a bed to be had in Sitges so they press on. Marcel whispers that if he'd been alone, he'd have had a bed . . . with the *patronne*. He bursts out laughing. Never mind. *"Au retour."*

It's a night of flaming moonlight. On the Mediterranean breeze Jay catches a first whiff of orangeblossoms. Distant hills, beaches, palms in the village squares. Jay begins to feel the way he used to feel years ago in the *grande guerre*. The adventuring tingle. Even in those days when he was a dedicated pacifist he'd dimly realized that the most treacherous thing about war was that it was fun.

They drive clear to Tortosa before they find a vacant room. The east is already aglow. The tiled domes of the churches are beginning to show blue. Cocks are crowing. As Jay leans over the lavabo of his square whitewashed room he tells himself "Tomorrow Valencia."

He's tired but not sleepy. His eyes burn. He sits down on the edge of the bed under the dim electric bulb that dangles from the ceiling and adds to his penciled letter to Lulie:

"Darling, driving down the coast road in the magnificent moonlight—the smell of the orangeblossoms made me want you so much—I kept thinking of another moonlight night walking around Segovia with Ramón and the poet and those two painters. Remember, we drank beer spiked with lemon ice and you got sleepy and went back to the *Three Sirens* to bed. We walked down the hill to look up at the aqueduct from below. The moon was so bright I could make out the peachcolor of the stone carving. The poplars in the valley really showed green. I'd never seen moonlight bring out color before. Somehow I got started trying to explain to my Spanish friends that one reason wars were so hard to stop was because in a curious way wars were fun. Trying to say it in Spanish didn't make it any easier. They all cried me down but it was pleasant arguing with them. Without animus. It wasn't like back home when people think you're a yellow dog if you bring up some proposition they don't agree with."

72

Jay slips the notebook in the pocket of his jacket, switches off the light and slides in between the sheets. Not tomorrow; today will be Valencia. They'll make it in three hours even if the road is crowded. As he closes his eyes he gets a clear flash like a snapshot of Ramón's long tobaccocolored face with its thin eagle beak, and Amparo's black eyes under her straight brows, and the little jet beads of the children's eyes. How all their tongues will rattle.

Valencia that afternoon turns out to be full of sun and noise and dust. Recruits are drilling in the squares in tasseled militia caps. Long lines of dustcaked trucks encumber the streets. Before going on to deliver his truck and its cargo at the Ministry of War, Marcel lets Jay off at the hostel for foreign visitors. Jay grabs his bag and jumps down from the cab. They part with reluctance. They have become friends. *A bientôt, mon vieux:* growls Marcel.

It is a handsome old palacelike building with colored glass round the great brassbound doors. Jay suspects it was some kind of a seminary before the war. In the black and whitetiled hall he finds some sort of superannuated professor seated at a desk—a gray goateed tired man. Señor Pignatelli has been expected. A room is ready. But when Jay asks if anyone knows the whereabouts of Ramón Echevarria the only response is a blank stare. Following the professor's shuffling steps to his room, the spirits drain out of him. He feels incapable of deciding what to do next. He stretches out on the cot and falls asleep. When Jay wakes it is dark. He looks at his watch: eight o'clock. He must do something. Fast. He throws water on his face and hurries out to the desk. A different professor is in charge. After a good deal of urging this professor finds Jay an old man who walks with a limp to show him the way to the Ministry of Information. The streets are blacked out, only an occasional blue light in a doorway. The old man walks desperately slow.

Soldiers and girls. Low voices, nudges in the dark. Everybody young, amorous, eyes seeking out eyes, lips seeking lips: it is like the Paris boulevards in the *grande guerre*. Jay feels old and a stranger as he shuffles after the old man.

It is black as pitch under the portal of a huge stone building. After sending his name in Jay waits in the dim anteroom while a string of men with briefcases, some in uniform, some in denims or black business suits, file in through a pair of green baize doors. Every time the doors swing open a shaft of brilliant white light streams out from the room beyond.

After what seems hours Jay decides to barge in. A young man with a pale moon face looks up in surprise from a desk piled with papers. "Why Mr. Pignatelli," he exclaims in clipped Oxford English, "haven't you seen the Minister yet?" His tone makes Jay feel he himself is somehow to blame for the delay. Making clucking noises the young man darts off through a little door behind his desk.

He pops back in an instant. "Mr. Pignatelli," he intones, "I am really distressed, the Minister will be distressed. He has been called away on a matter of supreme importance. . . . Tomorrow, dear Mr. Pignatelli, if you will be so kind as to accept an invitation to lunch with the Minister, a car will call for you at the Casa de la Cultura at twelve noon."

The young man's speech is so formal Jay can almost see an engraved invitation held up before his eyes.

The young man grabs his hand and keeps shaking it as he escorts him across the room. "Lunch," he murmurs in a confidential tone into Jay's ear, "will be at the *Grao de Valencia*, a little affair for the foreign correspondents. . . . Meanwhile you must understand that we greet your project with enthusiasm. Mr. Warner and Mr. de Jager are already at work, with cameramen, porters, assistants, two automobiles for transportation, filming the defense of Madrid."

Under the dark portal the young man lets go Jay's hand. "Alfredo Posada," he gives his name with a stiff little bow, "at your orders. . . . I believe you know the name—weren't you a friend of my brother Juanito—you'll find him Chief of Police in Madrid."

"Of course I knew him. He was a law student," says Jay.

They shake hands again.

"Hasta la vista," says Posada.

The paella is as good as ever at the glassed-in restaurant overlooking the beach and the harbor entrance. Jay remembers with a pang that the last time he sat there was with Lulie and all the Monohans on that wonderful sailing trip down the Spanish coast five years before. The rice and shrimps are the same, the bread is the same, the wine is almost as good, but Jay keeps having a feeling that he can't swallow. A prime case of jitters. All morning he has tried to work up a conversation with various inmates of the Casa de la Cultura. Nobody will talk about anything. Now don't get the creeps, he tells himself. There's an expression in people's faces he's seen before. He remembers his crazy expedition to Constantinople and Tiflis after he got out of the army. Tiflis was where he saw that expression on people's faces. Red army. Military Communism. U.S.S.R. Terror: the word spells itself out etched in red behind his eyes.

The plump and popeyed florid little man beside him seems to on cutlery and glassware, the white cotton gloves on the waiters; all affect him unpleasantly.

The plump and popeyed florid little man beside him seems to feel no qualms. It's a free meal; he shows every sign of enjoying it. He turns to Jay with his mouth full, introduces himself as André Marron of the *Petit Parisien* and urges Jay not to neglect the lobster. He drinks down his glass every time it is filled. Throwing back his head to take a deep breath he exclaims, "*C'est bath quand même.*"

A lugubrious Swede on the other side of Jay puts away his wine more silently but just as greedily. Around the table sits a Swiss, a couple of Danes, two Britishers who address their whispers to each other, and a Hollander. There is a chatter of excitement when someone points out a cruiser hull down on the horizon. French or British? The Non-Intervention Patrol.

Meanwhile, so close they could almost touch it, a gray-painted steamer eases its way into the harbor between the jetties. A blockade runner? In broad daylight. How could that happen? the journalists ask each other.

"A Mexican!" André shows all his gold teeth in a laugh. "All the blockade runners are Mexicans." He shrugs monumentally and beckons to the waiter to bring him more paella. The bottles go spinning from glass to glass. The party grows noisy. The Scandinavians are raising their glasses and looking each other in the eye and crying skoal.

At the end of the table the Minister of Information, Juan Hernández del Río, presides with a subtly contemptuous smile on his face. There is something about his smile that rubs Jay against the grain. Jay remembered meeting Hernández a number of times at the Ateneo on summer trips through Madrid years ago when he was a leading journalist among the liberals. Jay never liked him much. Before the luncheon Hernández was so hemmed in by questioners Jay had only a moment to shake his hand before sitting down. They agreed to meet after the meal.

When Hernández is introduced, after a good deal of tapping on glasses to get the attention of the polyglot journalists, Jay pricks up his ears. Hernández has always worn a kind of bridgework behind his front teeth that gives him a curious whistling diction. He speaks in Spanish. As one journalist to another ... "Amigos, all we want is the truth. The Loyalist government has nothing to hide. It was the Fascists who started the aggression. We represent the people of Spain who have sprung with such courage to the defense of legality and the Republican constitution." Then, after apology for his accent, *comme une vache espagnole*—that brought a laugh— he repeats the speech in French. He makes a good impresson; applause.

When the luncheon breaks up Jay has difficulty in intercepting the Minister. "I'll only detain you for a moment," Jay says when he catches up with Hernández as he is about to bolt out the door.

"Indeed, indeed, we must see much of each other," whistles Hernández in his British English. "If it weren't for this dog's life of a public official."

"Shouldn't we confer about the film?"

"Everything is going smoothly.... Just ask what you want and you shall have it. Arrangements are already made for a car to Madrid when you want to join Warner.... My secretary will call on you tomorrow."

"Tell me, Don Juan, where can I find Ramón? ... I'm sure you know him ... Echevarria.... It seemed to us in New York he would be just the man to act as a sort of liaison officer."

Hernández del Río has a long pale horse face. His high forehead is a little freckled where it meets the receding line of curly reddish hair. For a moment the muscles of his face seem to freeze. Beads of sweat appear among the freckles. "Ah yes yes, the Princeton professor.... We'll have to get in touch with him a little later." Hernández shakes Jay's hand hard. "Begging your pardon ... the official life. . . . You can take my word for it, your friend is quite all right."

Hemmed in by a bevy of attendants the Minister vanishes out the door.

Jay's tablemate of the *Petit Parisien* is waiting for him. They have agreed it will be more interesting to walk back into town than to be transported in the official limousine.

When Jay goes to the checkroom to get his hat his fingers brush against a slip of paper under the sweatband. He glances at it thinking perhaps it is a check number. On the paper is written in pencil in a neat Spanish hand: *dirección de la señora Amparo Foz de Echevarria, Fonseca 25, Valencia*. Jay folds it and tucks it in his wallet. Who the devil put it in his hat? No chance to ask a question of the hatcheck girl. She is besieged. Jay's Frenchman is waiting. On the edge of breaking out in gooseflesh Jay follows him out into the seabreeze and the sunlight.

It is hard for Jay to pay attention to André's newspaperman's gossip as they walk through the dusty avenue of palms, screeching and jangling with the traffic of the port, that leads back into the city. As soon as they reach the first shady square on the edge of town Jay excuses himself, jumps into a *tartana* and reads off the address to the driver.

Calle Fonseca lies in a slummy part of town. Blocks of tall old stone houses are squeezed tightly in together. The slatternly woman in the *porteria* at number 25 can't seem to understand Jay's Spanish. At first she denies in the local dialect that anybody named Echevarria lives there. Eventually Jay gets it out of her that a Doña Amparo *con dos niños* lives in the fourth floor back.

The stairs are wellgrimed. Jay knocks on the door. For a long time there is no answer. At last there is the click of a key turning in the lock. The door opens a crack. It is Amparo.

"Hay," she whispers, *"qué maravilla!"*

She opens the door just wide enough to let him in; then locks and bolts it behind him. The room has the stuffy shutin smell of a room where a family has eaten and slept and lived for too long. Amparo lets herself drop on one of the two cots in the center of the floor. Under her abundant rusty black hair her face is so drawn it looks like a skull.

"Hay, what do you know?"—she never did learn to pronounce his name except in the Spanish way. "You can speak freely. The children are at school."

"I don't know anything. I just got here last night."

"Ramón was arrested five days ago. They told me he was being taken away for questioning."

Amparo was never a demonstrative woman. Now she speaks quietly with her hands clenched on her knees and her eyes on the floor.

"What possible reason could they have?"

Haltingly she explains what little she knows of Ramón's work for the government. Jay feels a consoling sense of competence come over him. He's been in this position so often before. Attorney for the defense. The more he feels himself the lawyer the less he suffers as a friend. He snatches at the hope that his professional air may give Amparo a little courage. He starts jotting down her answers to his questions in his notebook.

She really knows nothing. First Ramón acted as a cultural attaché with the Ministry of Information. Then in recent months he was engaged in secret negotiations at the Ministry of War. He knew a little Russian; could it have been with the Russians? Ramón kept saying he wasn't free to tell what he was doing, not even to his wife. He turned off her questions with his usual sarcastic sayings, but she could see he was worried and harassed. And then suddenly one night the knock on the door, soldiers in uniform tramping on the stairs and he was gone.

"Could he have made enemies? He was pretty freespoken."

"Not recently. You wouldn't have known him. He became quite careful how he talked."

"Is there anything else, anything they could have against him?"

"Who do we mean by 'they'?" asks Amparo.

"I wish I knew."

"His brother Gil, you know," continues Amparo, "is in Franco's army and there's a cousin, another Gil . . . Gil Palacios . . . who is a conservative politician. I don't think Ramón has seen either of them since his father died eight years ago. They never did get along."

"It's ridiculous. There must be some way of appealing to the process of law."

Amparo looks at Jay as if he's lost his mind. "Law!" she mutters. "You don't know the Spain of today."

There is a scuffling of children's feet on the stairs. Amparo unlocks the door. Before she opens Jay whispers hurriedly in her ear, "You must not worry. . . . Hernández knows something. He was evasive but he assured me Ramón was all right. . . . I'll see him tomorrow and get something definite out of him. I'll get hold of a lawyer. We'll get him out."

Paco and Lou burst into the room. They are both much bigger than Jay remembered them. Instead of running up to him and throwing their arms about him as they usually did they stand still in the middle of the floor staring down at their feet.

"Don't you remember your Uncle Jay?" They nod two tousled brown heads. Amparo suddenly bursts out crying and runs off into the back of the room.

"I'll be back," Jay calls to her as he starts down the stairs.

"Darling," Jay writes in his notebook, "there is something absolutely horrible about the atmosphere of Valencia. Of course I went right over to the Ministry. The Minister had left for Madrid an hour before and taken his secretary—you know 'utterly English' I told you about—along with him. Nobody there seemed to know who I was or who Ramón was. I had to bring out all my documentation. Losing contact with the higherups gives you a damn funny feeling in a situation like this. Luckily there's somebody I used to know in Madrid who might be helpful. Years ago I used to go climbing in the Guadarrama with 'utterly English's' brother who by some strange chance is now Chief of Police. Do you notice I'm not putting down anybody's name anymore? It isn't that I really expect them—whoever 'they' are—to steal my notebook; it's something about the atmosphere.

"The *Petit Parisien* man is a *débrouillard*. From all accounts there's nothing to eat in Madrid or along the road so he's out rustling up chocolate and sardines and stuff. He likes his vittles. He's managed to get a *Hispano-Suiza* out of the Ministry and we are starting for Madrid first thing in the morning. I've got to get some kind of news for our friend's family, or she'll lose her mind. Of course she has her friends working too, but nobody can find out anything. The President of the Republic is in Madrid. I think I can get to him. What I hope to do is somehow to get our friend out of the country. I've picked up hints at the Casa de la Cultura that there have been such cases before. I get the feeling that some people know a great deal more than I do about this business."

The road west leads them out of the city through blooming orange groves and then winds up into a tumult of tawny hills. The hilltop villages are ancient and stony. The sky is lazuli blue. Jay can't help feeling the exhilaration of new landscapes. He keeps himself distracted trying to explain to André, who has never been in Spain before, the ways of the Spaniards.

The chauffeur is a goodnatured oliveskinned fellow named Antonio. When, near noon, André begins to clamor for an apéritif, Antonio takes up the search with enthusiasm. Finally in a shuttered-up *parador* in a tiny stone village overshadowed by a great buttressed church, he uncovers a bottle of homemade vermouth. They drink it in the sun under a budding grape arbor at an old stone table stained blue with copper sulphate. *"Buvable,"* declares André.

When they inquire about lunch, the hunched innkeeper whose gray hair, over a withered apple of a face, is cut bowlshape like Sancho Panza's, leads them into a plastered room almost filled by a long table. Giggling village girls serve them fried eggs cooked with tomatoes and tender little steaks with potatoes fried in olive oil. There are stone pitchers of a dark heady wine.

They hardly get a chance to swallow before army officers, truckdrivers, militiamen, officials with briefcases come bustling into the room. Everybody gets fed. Nothing upsets the good nature of the waitresses. As soon as one eater has finished another takes his chair. *"Epatant,"* exclaims André.

When they discover a pastryshop selling spongecake flavored with almond in a tiny back street, the rolypoly journalist is in the seventh heaven. So is Antonio. "Look!" he exclaims, "and the Fascists try to tell you we are starving."

It is dusk before they reach Madrid. Clouds of dust driving through the steely twilight. Ever since Alcalá de Henares—where Cervantes once lived, Jay reminds his Frenchman—the highway has been full of military trucks, troops marching, horsedrawn field kitchens. Some of the soldiers wear illfitting tin hats of French make with a keel down the center. The rest wear the metal mushrooms the Germans used in the *grande guerre*. In front of the terracotta-trimmed bullring at the edge of the city, recruits are drilling, eager schoolboys in denims and workingmen's blouses, using broomsticks instead of rifles in the manual of arms. No lights in the streets. Everything is black when they drive up to the Hotel Florida in the Plaza de Callao. The minute Antonio switches off his motor they hear the ratatat of machineguns coming from the edge of the city. Distant rifleshots tinkle in the tense dark. *"Merde alors,"* cries André. *"C'est le front."*

The first man Jay sees when he shoves his bag through the heavy curtains that keep the light from seeping out of the hotel lobby, is Cookie, Cookie sprucely dressed in tight-fitting black. His eyes have the same look of heavy weather about them they had in New York.

"George Elbert has been expecting you all day," Cookie says rather deferentially. Then he addresses the elderly room clerk in surprisingly good Spanish: "Señor Pignatelli must have a room on the fifth floor. He is associated with Señores Varner and de Jager."

Cookie takes the key and hefts Jay's bag. To Jay's surprise the elevator works. "Cookie, you seem to be the acting bellhop," he says laughing.

"Jack of all trades, master of none. *No hay toros,* so I bum around with George Elbert." He waits while Jay settles his hat and coat in his room and immediately leads the way to what he describes as the royal suite.

"How much grub did you bring?" is the first thing George Elbert asks. George Elbert hasn't shaved that morning. He lies propped up on the bed with a glass of wine in his hand and a blanket over his legs.

Jay has to admit he didn't bring anything.

"Then how do you expect to eat? ... Doe," George Elbert calls over his shoulder, "he hasn't brought a goddamn thing."

When Hilda Glendower strides out of the adjoining room wearing an oversize silver fox stole, Jay has to admit she's a handsome woman. It becomes immediately clear that she doesn't like Jay any better than he likes her. "We might have known," she says. She gives him a steely look from under her pale blonde brows and with a little shudder tightens the stole round her shoulders. "I'm still chilly." She speaks to George Elbert as if there were nobody else in the room. "Madrid's the coldest place in the world."

George Elbert sits up bundled in the blanket on the edge of the bed.

"Isn't that something?" he points to the stole. "Doe wangled that off the boys in the Fifteenth Brigade."

"George, I didn't want to take it. You told me I had to."

"We filmed a little attack they made," George Elbert explains. "You ought to see Doe under fire. Never bats an eyelash. . . . Cookie, pour Jay out some of that Valdepeñas. We'll drink if we can't eat."

"Well," says Jay lifting his glass, "here's to the happy pair."

Hilda gives him one of her absentminded smiles.

"Have you seen the Posadas?" asks Jay.

"Sure. See 'em all the time. . . . What are you looking so worried about Jay?" George Elbert gets to his feet and stares him in the face. "The Fascists don't shell the hotel until morning. Even then his gunners are aiming at the Telefonica. Damn poor shots. If they aimed at us I'd feel better."

"I'm not worried about that."

"If it's your professor bloke's disappearance, think nothing of it. . . . People disappear every day." George Elbert makes a fluttering gesture with the fingers of one hand. . . . "Cookie, what the hell's happened to Dirk? See if you can find him, will you?"

As soon as Cookie is out of the door George Elbert stamps across the room in his stocking feet and shouts in Jay's ear, "Don't put your damn mouth to this Echevarria business . . . not even before Cookie. Cookie's the rightest guy in the world, but he might get potted some night. The Fifth Column is everywhere. Just suppose your professor took a powder and joined the other side."

"That could not be," Jay cries out. "I've known the man for years. He's absolutely straight. Nobody forced him to give up a perfectly good job to come over to help his country."

Hilda's voice comes like a blast of cold air. "People have different ideas about how to help their country." She sits at the dressing table filing her fingernails. "Your inquiries have already caused us embarrassment," she adds without looking up.

Deep in Jay's head is the memory of Amparo and the children huddled in that stuffy room in Valencia. He hears again Amparo's broken voice: "You don't know the Spain of today."

A knock, the door opens, and Dirk is shaking Jay's hand with his pleasant small-boy smiles all over his face. "It goes better than I'd hoped. I can't wait to have you see the first reels. We'll have rushes in Paris. The Brigade, the government, everyone is cooperating splendidly . . . but it will cost more money than we figured. Jay," he bursts out laughing, "the first thing you'll have to do is go home and raise some more money."

"Have a heart," cried George Elbert in his most jovial tone, "let him stay long enough to get the feel of Madrid under siege. It is the greatest thing ever. I've got to take him up to the lines. The University City is the spookiest place I've ever seen."

Cookie pours out wine all around. George Elbert keeps shouting that they'd better drink up strong so that they can face the stink of the food at the Gran Via.

The dinner, when they all troop over to the other hotel, with Cookie leading the way through the pitchblack streets, turns out as bad as George said it would be. The restaurant is a cellar with a vaulted ceiling that had been a cabaret before the war. The air smells of scorched milk. The soup, though watery, is passable, but the ham that follows must be moldy because nobody can eat it except Cookie. "Cookie can eat anything," George Elbert declares proudly. The bread is stale but edible. Jay makes his supper on bread and sausage. The wine has run out but the single waiter, who still wears a worn tuxedo, produces excellent Fundador brandy.

"This is the foreign journalists' dining room. They run it this way," says George Elbert, "to keep foreigners from eating up all the grub that ought to feed the *madrileños.* . . . Out at the brigades the food is great."

A steakfaced Englishman, who has eaten somewhere else, joins them over their brandy. George Elbert introduces him as Sir Wilfred Tottenham, "you know, the great biologist."

Sir Wilfred has large blue bloodshot eyes, a clipped gray moustache and a dogmatic manner. He seems obsessed with Franco's Fifth Column. Jay is getting weary listening to a long list of arrests and suspicions when a voice behind him that sounds vaguely familiar exclaims "Hay, *que tal?*"

Jay jumps to his feet. It is Juan Posada. Juanito's face has shrunk to the bones and lost the ruddy look it had years ago in their mountaineer days. His skin is waxen but his eyes are the same sharp black.

They shake hands vigorously. Right away Jay feels that here is one old friend who is really glad to see him. "Remember, Juanito, how you explained the Spanish civil code climbing up la Maliciosa?" Juanito laughs wryly. "That was in another century," he says.

"There will be other problems of law that I shall want explained." Jay pronounces his words slowly.

Juanito presses the air down with the flat of his hand in a gesture of silence. He looks Jay straight in the eye. "Later, as much as you want."

Late that night Jay gets back to his room at the Hotel Florida. "It's 2:00 A.M.," he scribbles to Lulie in his notebook, "and I bet you're tucked into bed in the chilly old *hôtel de Beaujolais*.... It's just as chilly in Madrid, though down in Valencia it was balmy spring.... I've been all evening over in the Chief of Police's office in the Telefonica. That American baroque skyscraper built by the International Tel and Tel is still the center of the communications network for Madrid and the whole Madrid Front. In spite of the fact that the Fascists shell it daily, with the result that the building looks as if it had smallpox, everybody who is anybody has an office there. The elevators run. The bathrooms work. There's an extraordinary bustle there. I could even discover traces of efficiency. That's where the press censors operate and the dispatches go out. My friend the C of P—he's an extraordinary fellow—took me all over it. I knew him that summer vacation from lawschool when I was doing paper on Spanish civil law. We used to go walking with a gang of fellows every weekend to various places in the Guadarrama. That's when I learned what little I know about Spaniards. I liked him then and I like him now. He's the only person I've met in Madrid who doesn't seem scared to death. He says he doesn't know anything about our friend's case and I believe him, but he's going to find out. He added something rather alarming about 'uncontrollables.' I get the notion that certain events the government

84

doesn't want to be held responsible for are blamed on uncontrollables. For the family anything will be better than this horrible uncertainty."

Jay wakes up next morning with a funny tight feeling in his throat. Dreaming? Something remembered from years ago? Then a shriek getting louder and louder ending in a sharp bang and a rattle of dislodged tiles and the tinkle of smashed glass. Jay's eyes are open. The sky through the window is an indigo gray. Another whine and a louder bang. This is now. These are incoming shells from a small caliber gun.

The last one bursts so close the sharp almond smell of high explosive drifts in through the open window. From somewhere comes the yelping of a hurt dog. Jay gets up and closes the window. He is shivering. He decides to shave and dress. No hot water. He shaves with cold. He gives himself a sort of birdbath and rubs down with a towel. Nothing has hit the hotel yet. By the time he has tied his necktie he feels quite calm again. The electric light is on. The water runs. Nothing like shaving for the morale. He runs his fingers over his smooth chin and then holds them up in front of the mirror. No they aren't shaking.

After he's slipped into jacket and pants Jay opens his door. The hall is full of scampering, lingerie, disheveled heads. The door of the room next door pops open and who should appear but the jolly little curlyhaired waiter who brings the morning coffee. He has his arm around a half-sniveling half-giggling young woman. Jay starts down the hall. André stands gesticulating in his bathrobe in excited conversation with another Frenchman in striped pajamas, whom he introduces as Saint-Exupéry, *"le grand Saint-Exupéry."* This is all *emmerdant,* André is explaining; he'd had enough of this sort of thing in the *grande guerre.* Saint-Exupéry seems to be in high spirits. He has just arrived by plane from l'Algérie and he has a box of *pamplemousses.* Assorted journalists stick touseled heads out of doors. With a magnificent gesture Saint-Exupéry begins distributing his grapefruit.

Meanwhile a lady novelist from Iowa appears completely dressed and announces that she is making coffee on an electric plate. Everybody crowds into her room and drinks her coffee in the hotel glasses along with scorched toast and Saint-Exupéry's grapefruit. People chatter their heads off until the place sounds like an aviary at the zoo. By his debonair manner Saint-Exupéry has changed the whole scene into something out of a fairytale.

The shelling stops as suddenly as it began. No sound has come from the Warner suite. Jay decides he'll slip back to his room for a little more sleep. On the way he passes the curlyhaired waiter now consoling a totally different young woman. Only this time he is ushering her into her room instead of out of it.

Everything is quiet; a slight rumble of traffic comes from the street. The cosy midmorning smell of sizzling olive oil rises from the kitchen downstairs.

"How did you like Franco's alarmclock?" Juanito asks when he calls for Jay around noon. He adds that the only casualty today at the Plaza de Callao was a poor old newsvendor. "The Fascists are mad. What good can it possibly do them to vent their spite on a poor old man?"

The back seat of Juanito's car is occupied by three stonyfaced plainclothesmen. As he waves Jay into a front seat Juanito whispers that he thinks Jay may find it interesting to visit the Hotel Windsor. They may tell him something there . . . if he asks no questions.

"What's the Hotel Windsor?" asks Jay.

"You'll see."

The Hotel Windsor, on a quiet dead end near the Prado, looks from the outside like the sort of shabby genteel hotel that retired English couples who couldn't afford to live at home used to patronize on the continent. The military cars parked in a row outside seem out of place there under the peppertrees. As soon as he and Juanito step into the lobby Jay is struck by something even more incongruous. The place has been stripped of its fittings. A man in an illfitting gray suit with a pistol in a black holster on his hip jumps up from a bench by the door. As soon as he recognizes Juanito Posada he slumps back into his seat.

Behind the desk two stocky men at a table are talking what is undoubtedly Russian. They wear baggy gray suits like the man at the door. One of them rises and squares his shoulders in a thoroughly military manner. He faces them with a suspicious glint in the small pebbles he has for eyes. Juanito asks in Spanish for *el Viejo*. He's hardly spoken before an obsequious old Spaniard who might once have been the hotel doorman comes out of a little door in back. Juanito addresses him as *tu*. In Madrid everybody calls everybody else *tu*. They fall into a rapid conversation which Jay can't quite overhear.

Juanito turns away smiling. His manner has a cheerful dash that even brings the ghost of a grin to the face of the Russian noncom behind the desk. "Hay," he says, "I must leave you here. You will find old acquaintances.... You will come to the house tomorrow with the Warners. They know the address.... My brother will be there and perhaps Hernández del Río."

Jay is ushered into a bare little room with a deal table and two chairs that remind him of rooms in state penitentiaries where he has waited to interview some imprisoned client.

A trim little woman opens the door and sits down briskly in the chair opposite him. No doubt about it this time. It is Hedda Gelber. Close to, she looks much older. Her features are the same but a mass of tiny wrinkles have spread from the crowsfeet in the corners of her eyes around her cheeks to her mouth. She still carries herself like a woman who feels she has looks.

"Hedda, what on earth are you doing here?"

"Party business, of course."

Jay immediately launches into his story. Did the Party have anything to do with the arrest of Ramón Echevarria? If so what was he charged with?

"The attorney for the defense," exclaims Hedda in a sneering tone. "Jay, you haven't changed a bit. I thought you might have grown up in all these years."

Jay argues on. He tries to appeal to her sense of justice, to fair play. Bourgeois notions. He knows he is floundering. Everything he says sounds glib and stale. He is stuttering like a schoolboy who has forgotten his lesson.

Hedda leans back in her chair looking at him with an expression of amused condescension as if he were a clown at the circus.

"You social Fascists would be funny if you weren't so dangerous," she says slowly and deliberately. "Our business is to help the Spanish workers win a war against a gang of reactionary sadists. Have you come over here to help us or to help the Fascists?"

"Hedda, you ought to know me well enough from the old days. . . ."

"All too well," Hedda breaks in savagely. "I thought you might have learned about the class struggle in all these years."

"The class struggle hasn't a damn thing to do with it. . . . This is plain right and wrong. How can I prove the man's innocence if I don't know the charges?"

Hedda rises to her full five-feet-four. She is frowning. She is going to cut the interview short.

"The best thing you can do, Jay, is work out a budget with de Jager and go home and raise some money." Her voice has its old dogmatic tone. "Even our friends from the east," she lets her voice drop to a whisper—"are enthusiastic about the film. One of the responsibles told me a documentary filmed by de Jager and narrated by George Elbert Warner would be worth a truckload of machineguns. I give you credit where credit is due . . . but raising a fuss about an indiscreet Spanish professor! . . . You ought to have better sense. This is a war to the death."

She turns her back on him and trots out of the room without shaking hands.

When he reaches the hotel after a long walk through forlorn stone streets, he finds Dirk and George Elbert waiting with a battered red touring car to take him out on location.

"Everybody is getting suspiciously attentive," Jay writes Lulie from the hotel the next afternoon. "Yesterday George Elbert and Dirk drove me out to the village on the Tagus where they are filming the venture of a village collective, to install pumping machinery for irrigating a tract of land for truck gardens. Before they had to import all their onions and tomatoes and cabbage. Now they hope to grow their own and sell the surplus on the Madrid market. All the village land used to be owned by ten families, I suppose the descendants of the *hidalgos* whose escutcheons still ornament the portals of the old fallendown houses on the square. The Fascist rebellion was the signal for a general rising against the landowners. Those who escaped being shot fled to Franco. Now the village is being run by the Socialist *Casa del Pueblo,* with subdued opposition from the Syndicalist local of the CNT. The Socialists whisper that the Syndicalists all wear the swastika under their shirts. I guess they say the same of the Socialists.

"Anyway, the president of the *Casa del Pueblo* took over as mayor. He seems to be an energetic fellow. Deeds of ownership are annulled. Housing redistributed according to the size of the family. Everybody paid five *pesetas* a day for every day they work, women and boys three fifty. Since the main capital of the village lies in the stock of the three or four expropriated wineries, everybody who works gets a liter of wine a day and some firewood. After the next wine harvest they hope to raise wages to seven *pesetas*. Five is a real sacrifice for the masons and carpenters who work on the pumping station because they used to make seven. . . . And then this morning who should turn up at the Hotel Florida but Alfredo Posada in a snappylooking convertible to drive me out to a fiesta one of the Brigades is putting on somewhere near the Escorial. When I asked him if he had any news of our friend he shook his head. His brother would find out something. I mustn't worry. We were alone in the car. He was wearing a captain's uniform. He told me what the war meant to him. He's a professional pianist. He'd been living in Paris, composing a little music that he said wasn't any too good, occasionally giving a recital. The Posadas are a rich man's sons. Unsatisfactory. The egoistic life of a dilettante—When the rebellion broke out he put himself at the orders of the Communist Party and was given charge of an arms depot of all things. To his amazement he discovered he had the organizing mind. . . . He was on loan now to the Ministry of Information on account of his knowledge of languages, the *beau monde* and that sort of thing. He hated it; he'd much rather be with the army, but in wartime orders were orders. His utterly English accent made it all sound rather quaint. I certainly liked him better than I had in Valencia.

"Incidentally, though I still love the poor devils of Spaniards, I find the foreigners mixed up in this business thoroughly detestable. There's a Mexican painter swaggering around Madrid with an automatic on each hip who is something to frighten crows with. Murder just comes natural to so many people. Georgy isn't showing his prettiest side either. As soon as I reached town he walked me out the Paseo de Rosales to show me the front lines. The damned English scientist came along. The *paseo* is in full view of the enemy lines across the Manzanares. As we started to walk out to examine their gun emplacements through Georgy's fieldglasses, a nice little guy, a corporal, pops up out of a trench and says please not to walk out in the open like that, we'll draw enemy fire.

" 'Who's chickenshit?' cries Georgy.

" 'Not me,' says the Englishman, his face taking on the red and purple hues of the hind end of a baboon. The silly bastards walk arm in arm the length of the *paseo*. I took the corporal's hint and followed along behind a line of busted-up private houses that used to be the finest places to live in Madrid. When I met the precious pair at the other end they were puffed up like turkey gobblers. I pointed out that it was lunchtime. The Fascists, being Spaniards, would finish their *almuerzo* before they started to fire. I was right. As we were working our way back in the shelter of the smashed-up houses, all hell broke loose. I hate to think how many good guys lost their lives through that piece of bravado.

"The fiesta out at the Fifteenth Brigade broke my heart. I'll tell about it when I see you. Personnel *très intéressant*. Many really moving speeches. Good food produced by a French chef. The steak was tough: it must have been walking around that morning, but it was garnished with a *sauce béarnaise* worthy of Foyot. Just as we were leaving who should arrive but two gypsylooking women with wide straw hats perched on top of their shawls; the sun was hot that afternoon. When they took their hats off it was Niña de las Peñas and Pastora Imperio. Remember how Pastora danced last time we were in Madrid and *la niña's canto hondo?* Remember the expression of contained anguish on Pastora's face—under those straight black brows—when she danced? Unamuno's Tragic Sentiment of Life. She wore just that expression when she handed *la niña* a glass of sugared water. 'For her throat. . . . It is she who will sing,' she said. You ought to have heard the roar that went up when they arrived. The sight of them sure did hearten the troops."

It is dark when Alfredo drives Jay back into Madrid. He suggests that if Jay don't mind skipping supper, they better go straight to Juanito's apartment. A fine new apartment house with a great deal of fancy ironwork in the lobby. The elevator is not running so they walk up five marble flights. Juanito hasn't arrived yet but a couple of girls in spangled skirts seem to be waiting for him. They have the roving eye. Tiredlooking men lounge in the anteroom. The salon is immense with crystal chandeliers, an Aubusson carpet and tall windows opening on balconies.

A dark little Andalusian butler wearing white cotton gloves

appears and brings them Scotch and soda. The Scotch is excellent. With their second Scotch the butler produces a tray of torpedo-shaped rolls stuffed with ham. "Alfredo, this is high life," says Jay.

Alfredo nods apologetically. Then he sits down at the grand piano and begins to play a Chopin nocturne, well Jay thinks. To avoid talking to the uniformed men and the plainly but snappily dressed women who keep drifting into the room, Jay slips out onto the balcony. He has slumped back into a mood of desperate anxiety. He stares glumly out over the desert of tiled roofs and distant domes and spires faintly visible in the starlight. From the salon comes a whiff of Scotch whisky and ham and fresh bread, cultivated voices, low laughter, all against the background of Chopin's rippling trills. The talk grows louder. Jay can hear Hernández's voice, the curious way the words whistle through his bridgework. Then George Elbert's rickety Spanish and Hilda's dry laugh.

"I brought you another Scotch." It is Juanito's voice speaking English behind him. Jay gives a start. He turns sharply. He didn't see Juanito come out on the balcony. "Nice view isn't it?"

Jay doesn't answer.

"The man has been shot," says Juanito in his curt English.

"But what was the reason? There must have been a reason."

Juanito shrugs. "Who knows?" he says in Spanish. "Hay, we are living through terrible times. To overcome them we have to be terrible ourselves."

Jay can find nothing to say. Through the open window come the tinkling rhythms of another nocturne. The brilliant finale is followed by a burst of applause.

"Why has nobody told his wife?" Jay asks.

"Hay," Juanito continues in Spanish, addressing him as *tu* in a tone that is almost pleading, "you know this is not my fault. In spite of this life I'm not more inhuman than when I was a dedicated student of the law, a boy, if you'll remember, of somewhat extreme sensibility.... How do I do it? *Juerga*. Continual orgy ... Whiskey, women, gypsies, the most indecent whores."

"Juanito, I don't hold you responsible," Jay pronounced his words with difficulty.

"I will see to it his wife and children are not molested ... I promise ... but from now on ... silence."

Juanito puts two fingers to his lips in a melodramatic gesture, lets them drop, and swaggers into the crowded salon. "Pepe," he calls. "Where is that scoundrel? We need more whiskey."

Jay finds himself face to face with Hernández.

"Hay, *hola que tal?*" The expression on the bony countenance is impossibly genial. It is as much as Jay can do to keep from hitting him in the face. Before Hernández has a chance to extend a hand, Jay makes a stiff little bow, says "Good night, Mr. Minister" and slips through a group of new arrivals out onto the marble stairs. He stumbles down the five dim flights and out into the black streets.

Jay's last days in Madrid were a nightmare. He felt a heart-broken admiration for the ordinary people, the carters, the boot-blacks, the old women who sold bowls of *café con leche* in little stands at the streetcorners, the bakers who still turned out fresh bread every morning, the waiters at the hotel, the haggard militia-men in the trenches round University City.

"I'd never understood what the words 'besieged city' meant," he wrote Lulie in one of the letters he kept in his notebook. "The people have a quiet heroic splendor about them. Their dignity contrasts wildly with the sadism of war's hangers-on and the steel fanaticism of the Communist apparatus. But the people have become mere pawns. The Party has climbed into the shell of the Republic and is eating it up the way a starfish eats up an oyster.

"That fiesta I told you about was to celebrate the incorporation of the old International Brigade in the People's Army. My impression is that the People's Army is completely under Communist control. A weatherbeaten Russian general with a shaved head who goes under the name of General Walter showed himself at the fiesta for the first time.

"Fat puffy old Republican General Miaja is reduced to a figurehead. Wherever Miaja went there was Walter right beside him. The Russian general's aide-de-camp is a strutting little popinjay in an overtailored green uniform with a shiny new mapcase over his shoulder. He scared me out of a year's growth. Moved in jerks like a robot. The New Soviet Man.

"Russian headquarters in Madrid, and Party headquarters too—I had a bad quarter of an hour with Hedda Gelber there—are in an old shabby genteel hotel with an English name back of the

Prado. Sitting in the lobby the sense of brutally effective organization seeped through the walls like the hum of the dynamos in a power station.

"The way things are going the fiesta was heartbreaking, the cheers, the marching troops, the Hymn of Riego, the speeches by youthful commanders who had been carpenters or stevedores or blacksmiths in private life. Of course the leadership of the Republic troops had been pathetically amateurish. Russian and Communist discipline has improved the organization, but at what cost!" As he writes the words, he can see as vividly as if he had been there himself, Ramón's bloody body crumpling against a flaky wall. "The Defense Junta," he added, "is moving against the independent armies run by the POUM and the CNT. Everything is working out exactly as Ugo Salvatore predicted."

Jay felt that the least he could do for the Echevarrias was to get a death certificate out of the government so that Amparo could collect on Ramón's American insurance. Everybody he went to see in Madrid passed the buck to Valencia: he must apply at the seat of government.

Madrid had been bad. Valencia was worse. At least in Madrid the danger from shot and shell made the adrenalin flow. In Valencia fear took a different shape. Nameless terror. "Irresponsibles" were taking people out and shooting them every day. Who was directing the irresponsibles? Nobody dared ask.

His first agonizing duty was to tell Amparo. He climbed the grimy stairs in a cold sweat. He didn't need to tell Amparo. She already knew. The children were out. She was sitting with bowed head on one of the tumbled cots like a woman of stone, her handsome brown hands hung limp between her knees. Jay tried to interest her in the problems of Ramón's insurance and of taking the children back to America. He couldn't get her to look up at him. The ambassador was a good friend of his, said Jay coaxingly. He would certainly be helpful. She let out a dry laugh: "Meester Bowers is a very nice gentleman, but what can he do from Biarritz?" The thought of the impotence of Mr. Bowers seemed to amuse her.

She broke out again into that same laugh when he showed her the certificate: Death by misadventure. It had taken a last painful interview with Hernández. They both behaved with a sort of poisonous cordiality, though Jay knew that Hernández hated him and that he hated Hernández. Suddenly Hernández brought the certificate out of his desk drawer. It had been there all along. "So they admit," was all Amparo would say, "the men of the Republic, that they are cowards and fools."

After the funk of Valencia, Barcelona seemed alive and cheerful. In Barcelona he at last met a man he could talk to.

This was a gangling Englishman with his arm in a sling. He was wearing a threadbare uniform. A squashed overseas cap on the side of his head nestled in abundant wavy black hair. His long face, with deep lines in the cheeks, was distinguished by a pair of exceptionally fine dark eyes. They had a farsighted look, like a seaman's eyes. When Jay breezed into the hotel, after arranging for his transportation to Perpignan with the friendly Catalans of the Generalitat, the Englishman lurched out of a wicker chair in the vestibule. He evidently knew who Jay was, because he advanced smiling with a hand outstretched. Right away Jay took a liking to him. He had a bloody-but-unbowed air that was almost a swagger.

"Things I've heard," the Englishman said in a low voice, "lead me to believe that you are one of the few who understand what's going on."

"I'm sure you've heard no good," said Jay laughing.

They settled in two chairs in a corner. The Englishman uttered his name in a low voice. Jay scribbled it on a corner of his notebook and promptly forgot it.

Jay never forgot the Englishman. An extraordinary sense of relaxation came over him when he realized he was talking to an honest man. All these weeks since he'd landed in that horrid Casa de la Cultura in Valencia he hadn't dared talk frankly to anyone. At first he was afraid of saying something that would endanger his chances of smuggling Ramón out of the country and afterwards he was afraid some misinterpreted word of his might lessen Amparo's chances of getting out with the children. He found himself, almost against his will, pouring out the sorry tale of his misadventures.

The Englishman suggested that they move to a table in a corner of the bar, still empty because it was barely eleven o'clock. They ordered the substitute vermouth that was the only drink available at the time.

94

"You've been up with the POUM," Jay suddenly changed the subject. "What was all the shooting about in the Ramblas?"

"We're not sure. In this situation one can't be sure of anything. . . . The Civil Guard seems to be trying to disarm the working-class armies. That includes me and our I.L.P. boys." The Englishman grinned broadly.

"The uniforms I saw were Assault Guards," said Jay.

"I wouldn't know which was which. The Russians have their thumb on whoever it is. . . . It is pathetic," the Englishman went on to say, "the confidence the Russians have in their terror. They are purging Trotskyites in Moscow and Leningrad, so they have to find Trotskyites to purge in Spain. Since there don't happen to be any Trotskyites they pick on the independent working-class Parties. It's our hard luck. It has all happened very fast. Besides an infected finger. . . ." He twiddled the fingers of his hand under the bandage. "I got this leave to enlist in the International Brigade. Not enough action on the Aragon Front. Damn fine people and surprisingly good food but we are all dying of boredom up there, to say nothing of the cold. When I got here I found the Brigade taken over lock stock and barrel by the C.P."

"That's what I saw happening," said Jay quietly.

"It's this bloody Non-Intervention Committee that is the root of all evil."

"Stalin furnishes the Republic with arms but the Terror goes with them," whispered Jay. "The Terror alienates the working-class Parties and the middle-class moderates. A perfect recipe for a Fascist victory."

"Isn't alienate rather a euphemism?" said the Englishman, with his very special grin.

"I guess liquidate is the proper term."

"A Fascist victory," said the Englishman, "and it won't be the last."

"Half the people I talked to in Paris were secretly rooting for Hitler."

"When I came down here I thought Barcelona was secure or else I wouldn't have let my wife come down. Now I'm trying to get her to go home. . . . Do you see any hope at all?"

Jay shook his head.

Each of them was taking a gloomy satisfaction in agreeing

with what the other man said. By the time another I.L.P. man, a husky young towhead just arrived from the Aragon Front, interrupted them, they had become firm friends. "What's new?" they both asked.

"Nothing's new, just every day things get a little bit worse. Less ammunition, less bandages."

All three slumped into silence.

Jay felt that the Englishmen wanted to talk privately. He got to his feet briskly, shook hands and went up to his room. He felt better than he had felt in days.

"After Valencia," Jay wrote Lulie from Perpignan, "Barcelona was almost pleasant. Red carpet for yr humble servant. President Companys' secretary turned out to have read an article of mine published in some law review years back about Spanish judicial procedures. So the Generalitat of Catalunya made a fuss over poor yours truly. It turned out damned convenient. They put a limousine at my disposal to take me to the French border. The secretary—a hell of a nice fellow—was a frantic cooperator ... so we had to visit every fishing and farming cooperative between Barcelona and Port Bou. Don Carp almost lost his mind. Why Carp? Lulie, you may well ask. I thought Carp was a down-the-line dyed-in-the-wool Party member, but it turned out the poor guy had associated with some splinter in Wisconsin. He was trying to do his stunt with the Brigade when somebody turned him in for a Trotskyite and he had to run for his life. He appeared in my room in the hotel in Barcelona in the middle of the night with a Lincoln Brigadier who was also on the lam. I split my covers with them so that they could sleep on the floor. Poor Don was in a lather of fright but he behaved pretty well. I introduced the pair of them to my Catalan friends as my private secretaries and took them along in the limousine. I never saw a more relieved man than Don was when we squeezed past those hardfaced French border guards at Cerbère.

"Though I don't think I was ever in any personal danger, it sure is a relief to be back on French soil and able to mail you my little packet of letters. I might as well come out with it. I hate to write it down. It makes it a *fait accompli*. Ramón is dead. The Commies have taken over the Republic. The story being circulated is that he was shot by 'uncontrollables' who overheard him talking indiscreetly in a café. The Republican officials from Hernández del Río down fell into a blue funk whenever I mentioned his name. Indiscretion hell. The indiscretion of being a Spanish patriot for Christsake. My suspicion is, though in the atmosphere of terror there is no way of getting confirmation of anything, that he knew too much about the negotiations between the government and the Russians. Ramón was pretty proficient in Russian if you remember. He may have been called in as an interpreter. He may have protested against the takeover as any honest man would. My only achievement in all this business was the sorry one of getting a death certificate out of the government."

He'd hardly mailed the letter when he wrote out a telegram: TAKE TRAIN BLEU TO ANTIBES . . . MEET AT THE MONOHANS WILL WIRE THEM WE'RE COMING.

He had to see Lulie right away. He had to have a couple of days to think before he met the documentary film people in Paris.

It turned out that he had plenty of time to think during the long roundabout train trip through Cette and Marseilles. Instead of thinking he slept. When he reached the Monohans' by cab from the station, Lulie was already there. Charles and Ada were putting them up in a little stucco house they called the Bastide at the end of the garden. With the tact they were famous for among their friends they didn't ask Jay a single question about the Civil War. They acted as if he had come back from a pleasure trip.

The Bastide was delightful. There was no sound but the bees buzzing through the heliotrope in the bed around the house. The rough tang of a row of tomato plants mingled with the scent of the heliotrope. The sun glowed in a sky so blue it seemed almost violet.

Jay and Lulie lolled out of the window side by side with their elbows on the cool tiles of the sill. It was a delight to feel her slender body against his, to inhale the special fragrance of her hair.

"Modesto," she said, "it must have been horrible."

"The worst thing is the waste, the waste of all this courage and effort . . . all this reckless disregard of life, our own and the next man's. . . . At least—" he turned to her with a grin—"I met a man who agreed with me."

"Who was that?"

"It was an Independent Labor Party man. One minute, I put his name down. . . ." He rummaged in his pockets for his notebook. "Can't find it."

Charles Monohan was hailing them from the other end of the vegetable garden: "Want to go swimming?"

They swam in the chilly silky Mediterranean brine. They scampered about the beach with the Monohans' towheaded children in the warm Mediterranean sun. They got the sherry up their noses just a tiny bit. Charles drove everybody back to the villa in his red touring car with the top down. Then he played Debussy's *La Mer* on the phonograph while they ate lunch of omelet and tomatoes provençal and asparagus hollandaise all right out of the garden washed down with a sharp little wine of Cassis. Then, lapped in the warm security of Charles and Ada Monohan's affectionate understanding, Jay and Lulie strolled back slowly to the Bastide.

Lulie was yawning. "Modesto, I'm so sleepy. . . . In Paris I kept waking up with a start and remembering that those nasty Fascists were taking potshots at you."

"Just for one day," said Jay, "I'm not going to think."

After an hour's sleep he woke up with a start. Through his head resounded Juanito's curt voice "The man has been shot" and the sound of Alfredo's nimble fingers trilling through the Chopin nocturne. He felt fuzzy from the wine and the lunch. He ducked his head in a basin of water muttering "God, I hate naps."

"But Jay, what are you going to do?" Lulie was asking again as soon as he opened his eyes.

"Well," he drawled in answer, "there's no point in resigning from Popular Historians until I get back home."

Jay couldn't help feeling pleased when George Elbert appeared unexpectedly at the station in Paris to see them off on the boat train. Lulie whispered that this was an attention the great man usually reserved for magazine editors and Hollywood agents. They were both still fond of the old ruffian. Georgy's manner chilled their pleasure fast. His face was a thundercloud.

The Pignatellis had arrived a little late. The porter was trundling their bags along in a hurry. Lulie and Jay and George

Elbert had to half run to keep up with him along the crowded platform.

"What I want to know, Jay, is what are you going to do about this business?" George Elbert snapped his words out like cracks of a whip.

"I'll tell the truth as I see it. Right now I've got to straighten out my ideas. You people are trying to believe it is one isolated instance. It isn't."

"In wartime . . ." growled George Elbert.

"George," chirped Lulie sharply, "Jay knows all about that."

Jay caught his breath when the porter stopped at a second-class carriage. Lulie with the tickets in her hand scampered aboard to show him where to put their bags.

Jay and George Elbert were left facing each other on the station platform. The glass trainshed overhead was dark with beating rain. Jay had to shout to be heard above the hiss of escaping steam from a locomotive on the next track.

"The question I keep putting to myself," said Jay trying for a mild, reassuring tone, "is what's the use of fighting a war for civil liberties, if you destroy civil liberties in the process?"

"Civil liberties shit," said George Elbert. "Are you with us or are you against us?"

Jay caught himself shrugging like a Frenchman.

George Elbert, his brow black as an old fighting bull's, pulled back a fist as if to hit him.

From down the platform came the trainman's little horn *"En voiture Messieurs 'Dames"*.

George Elbert's nostrils were distended. Breathing hard he let his fists drop to his sides. "I'll tell you one thing, Mr. Jay Pignatelli. I don't care how good a law practice you have, or liberal reputation or what the hell. These people know how to turn you into a back number. I've seen them do it. What they did once they can do again."

The train started to move. Jay swung up on the steps of the coach. George Elbert turned and went off down the platform without looking back.

PART II
LIFE'S GYMNASIUM

I

This American World

From his sinecure in Washington, Walt Whitman let his eye roam over his beloved people:

"I will not gloss over the appalling dangers of universal suffrage," he wrote in *Democratic Vistas*. ". . . the battle advancing, retreating, between democracy's convictions, aspirations and the people's crudeness, vice, caprices . . . with unprecedented materialistic advancement—society in these States is canker'd, crude, superstitious and rotten . . . the most important vertebra to State or man, seems to me either entirely lacking or seriously enfeebled or ungrown. . . . Never was there more hollowness of heart . . . the underlying principles of the States not generally believed (for all their hectic glow and these melodramatic screamings) nor is humanity itself believed in. . . . Coming down to what is of the only real importance, Personalities, and examining minutely, we question, we ask: Are these indeed men worthy of the name? Are these athletes? Are these perfect women? Are these the crops of fine youths and majestic old persons?"

"We sail a dangerous sea of seething currents, cross and undercurrents, vortices all so dark and untried; and whither shall we turn?" Walt Whitman in 1862 was already writing. "How long it takes," he exclaimed, "to make this American world see that it is in itself the final authority and reliance.... For you too, as for all lands, the struggle, the traitor, the wily person in office, scrofulous wealth, the surfeit of property, the demonism of greed, the hell of passion, the decay of faith, the long postponement, the fossil-like lethargy, the ceaseless need of revolutions, prophets, thunderstorms, deaths, births, new projections and invigorations of ideas and men."

"...We believe the ulterior object of political and all other government (having of course provided for the police, the safety of life, property, and for the basic statute and common law and their administration, always first in order) to be among the rest not only to rule, to repress disorder, etc., but to develop, to open up to cultivation, to encourage the possibilities of all beneficent and manly outcroppage, and that aspiration for independence and the pride and self-respect latent in all characters ..."

"... Political democracy," he added in a burst of optimism, "as it exists and practically works in America, with all its threatening evils, supplies a training school for making first class men. It is life's gymnasium."

2

1939

Gone were the glories of the Hundred Days, when Franklin D. Roosevelt could pose in the Blue Room in the White House as the savior of the banking system, the rescuer of farmers crushed under top-heavy mortgages, when NRA was at least doing the job of giving Americans the first statistical picture of the complications of their industry, when WPA fed the hungry, encouraged art, employed thousands of amateur dogooders to staff its hastily improvised platoons, and F. D. R.'s persuasive voice was soothing uprooted Americans to sleep with the gentle wizardry of his fireside chats.

Business was sluggish. In spite of continual pump-priming recovery was still, as discredited Herbert Hoover had seen it in 1932, "just around the corner." Big industry was plagued by strikes. John L. Lewis was taking full advantage of the Wagner Act to build himself an empire in the CIO.

Except for happy officeholders, experiencing for the first time the intoxication of power in the burgeoning Washington bureaucracy, the nation was restless. The Republicans were at last getting up their nerve to launch a presidential candidate. Wendell Willkie, who was to prove the first to sound the great "Me too" which was to destroy the usefulness of the Republicans as the defenders of traditional ways, dutifully prepared himself for his campaign by exhausting flights around several continents. He came back laden with the portentous truism that we lived in one world.

This turned out unfortunately true.

All hell was breaking out in Europe. Hitler had already reoccupied the Rhineland. Mussolini had long since proved the paralysis of the League of Nations by running wild in Ethiopia. In France, Léon Blum's Popular Front had proved a fizzle; Czechoslovakia was next on Hitler's timetable for European conquest. In August 1939, the Hitler-Stalin pact prepared the way for the partition of Poland which made a second war inevitable. The unanswered question was when it would begin.

Meanwhile in Washington, F. D. R. played his cards close to his chest. He didn't dare work too fast for fear of running ahead of public opinion somewhat tinged with America First. His every energy was bent towards winning an unprecedented third term.

3

The Big Thicket

After an hour's cruising over the dim spring greens of East Texas, the pilot brought his plane in for a roughish landing on a barely visible airstrip and burst out of his cabin: "Sorry folks, ignition went out on me. . . . We are grounded as of right here and now."

On the concrete, the passengers crowd around him.

"A pickup plane, how soon?"

He shrugs and points to the waiting room. Pilot and copilot make themselves scarce.

The sign on the clapboard waiting room says: Tyler, Texas.

As the passengers line up to pick out their baggage, all they can see is a vaguely undulant green plain with small stands of pine topping the higher hills. The sky overhead is densely blue, dappled with neat pinkytipped clouds. Miraculous flying weather.

Inside the elderly man behind the desk is lost on the telephone. "How long will we have to wait for a pickup?" the passengers ask. He shakes his head. "Can't tell."

Somebody reads off the billboard: "Next scheduled flight four fifteen."

This passenger had to be in Nacogdoches for a two o'clock lecture date.

"How about a taxiplane?"

The elderly man points out the window to another shack some

fifty yards away. The passenger trudges over with his bag. In the taxiservice shack there's another elderly man. The passenger explains his predicament. "Sure, I'll take you right to Nacogdoches." They settle on a price.

As soon as they are strapped into the twoseater, the elderly man starts talking: "Ever heard of the Big Thicket? Odd that the last frontier to quiet down should be in the Eastern part of the state. . . ." As the motor roars in climbing his voice is drowned out. He goes on calmly. . . . "Born and raised here, sixty years old. Family settled in the Big Thicket before the Mexican War . . . in the days of General Wilkinson . . . old scoundrel but knew how to keep out of trouble. . . . Wouldn't think to look at me I was part Indian would you? . . . not only part Indian but part English from the Lost Colony. . . ."

"What's that?" the passenger shouts to make his voice heard over the motor.

"Roanoke Island people," the elderly pilot goes on in an even tone, "mixed with the Indians. . . ." The motor drowns out the name of the tribe. . . . "Indians moved south and west when the Tarheels invaded their hunting grounds. My people came with them . . . story came down in the family. . . . See those lakes?"

There are three blue lakes to the eastward.

"That's where the Big Thicket begins . . . at least it did in the old days . . . my folks . . ."

As he reached what the passenger suspected was the most interesting part of the tale, the motor drowned out his voice completely. There was something about a grandmother, an attack on an Indian village, a woman walking twentytwo miles through the woods with her baby strapped to her back to escape a burning village. Was it his grandmother or was it an Indian woman two hundred years ago?

Already they were circling the rustic airstrip at Nacogdoches.

Once on the ground there was no time for questions. As soon as the passenger had his bag out, the elderly pilot waved his hand and gunned his motor for a start back to Tyler.

The passenger had to turn his attention to a group of men walking across the field to welcome him.

Next day when he spoke of getting plane connections to Houston to connect with an afternoon flight, he was told that a forestry student had particularly asked to be allowed to drive him there. After breakfast he waited at the curb outside his lodgings with his suitcase beside him. On the dot a car drove up.

He'd been afraid it would be a longhaired weirdy who wanted to be told how to write successful novels. Instead it was a broadshouldered young man with closecropped light hair and lively gray eyes. Known as Sandy naturally. They shook hands and the passenger climbed in.

Sandy started talking right away: "You are probably wondering why I wanted so bad to give you a lift. Well, the way you talked yesterday you sounded like a guy who'd give me advice." He had just a trace of the local drawl. "About my life naturally.... I'm twentyfour. What else interests you at that age?"

As soon as they left town the road plunged into pinewoods ... no towns or villages ... an occasional unpainted shack. Outside of one dilapidated filling station the skin of a giant red fox was tacked on the wall.

Sandy grinned. "You've heard of the Big Thicket?"

The passenger nodded, laughing at the recollection of yesterday's frustrated conversation.

"Well, these fine stands of pine are still full of deer and bobcat and possum and coon ... it would be a great life here if you liked to hunt, but I don't particularly ... what I like is studying, passing courses, getting degrees so that I can pick out the best jobs. What most people hate. Sounds real peculiar in this day and age.... I guess it's because my people were so darned illiterate...." He smiled happily. "I really am an example of what public education can do for a man in this country if he'll take advantage of the opportunities. I was raised on the worst little poor white street in Houston. Family of four. My Dad walked out on us when I was eight. Mom had to do everything, but she always spoke up when her sisters tried to talk Dad down ... naturally irresponsible. 'Just a backwoodsman from way down in the Big Thicket,' she would say. 'Never learned to read and write.'

"I get mad at these darned demonstrators. If a man wants to study and work, it's fantastic the opportunities that are offered him in this country. Looking back it seems to me I was given all the breaks. The usual story. Paper route when I was eight. All sorts of little jobs, but mostly with people who were kindly and helpful. Nice teachers in gradeschool. Utter strangers would give me a step up when I needed it. Scholarships in college and now I'm working for my master's in Forest Ecology at East Texas State, which is one of the best schools of forestry in the country. I'm no millionaire but I own a car all paid for.... Mom brought us kids up never to buy anything until we had the cash in our hand.... It was getting so deep in debt drove Dad to leave home.... And I can scrape up a little cash to help Mom from time to time.... Sounds like I was talking myself up too big, but honest to God, it makes me feel right 'umble."

"Then what are you worried about?"

"I'm getting to that." He paused. He was blushing. "I've been dating two girls and I don't know which one of them I ought to marry. Don't misunderstand me, they are both darn nice girls, that's the trouble. One of them comes from a family just like mine but she's gotten along just the way I have. She's studying to be a teacher right here in Houston. The other is quite welloff but she's Mexican, she's from a Mexican family that moved to Brownsville a generation ago. I met her when I had a summer job there, one of those extension jobs to teach poor Mexican families to take care of themselves. I'd picked up a little Mexican. Of course she spoke perfect English, honor student in highschool and all that. She worked on the same project. Her family treated me like a son."

"My mother used to say that marriages came off better when both parties had the same family background."

"Suppose, like me, you don't have any family background. I'm on my own. Sometimes I think I ought to just toss a coin."

They were penetrating the outskirts of Houston.

Sandy pointed out developments, industrial parks, new white concrete and aluminum factory buildings sparkling in the sun.... "You've heard about Colonel Hoffbein. He bought up all this land and developed it. Of course he's made millions but look what he's done for Houston. At school they try to tell me he's just an old robber baron born out of his time, but how else can you build up a city without somebody taking a risk? The bigger the risk the bigger the profit. He must have put a whole lot of it into the Vistadome. I just don't know how many millions of dollars that cost. Now you can't tell me that isn't a good thing for Houston."

At the airport the passenger checked his bag and confirmed his reservation. Three hours to wait. Sandy suggested they would just have time to take a look at the Vistadome. The visit took an hour. The passenger set Sandy up to a hasty snack in the coffeeshop and they set out.

The passenger was all ready to laugh off Colonel Hoffbein's enterprise but when he got to look at it he couldn't help but be impressed. Visitors were taken through in flocks by pleasantvoiced girl guides. The engineering was a marvel. The vast dome covered a fullsized baseball field supported by an intricate spiderweb of girderwork. It was surrounded by countless tiers of red plush and green upholstered seats. The glass roof had proved too glary. The light was throttled down by some sort of screening. The immensity of the place was tempered by the balance and proportion of the engineering work so that it seemed to the casual eye hardly larger than an ordinary auditorium.

Off the colosseum there were suites for entertaining, club rooms, banquet rooms, lounges and bars which the passenger found more hideous as they became more elaborate. He didn't let on to Sandy who seemed as pleased as if he had designed the whole thing himself.

A good half of the tourists that day were Mexican. Their group was being ushered into the expensive boxes each with an ornate suite behind it for eating and drinking. On the last phase of the visit, the passenger noticed that Sandy had slipped away to join a Mexican family group just ahead. There was a stout tobacco-colored gentleman in a black felt hat who sported a buff vest with brass buttons. There were old ladies in black with silk shawls, several redfaced men with carefully buttoned gray shirts but no ties, major domo types, a couple of skittishlooking teenagers dressed for riding and a pleasantlooking girl with brown skin and eyes that shone under delicately arched eyebrows and glossy black hair.

Immediately the passenger decided that must be the Mexican girl.

Sandy didn't introduce any of them but in a little while he rejoined his passenger and steered him down the ramps and out to where his car was parked. "What a coincidence," he said. "Looks like destiny. They are all up here on a visit," he added jubilantly.

When he dropped his passenger off at the airport, he squeezed his hand warmly.

"This has meant a lot to me . . . I'm going to have dinner with her tonight. . . . I guess it is destiny."

4

American Philosophy, 1859–1952

When the University of Paris conferred an honorary degree on John Dewey in 1930, he was described in the citation as "the most profound and complete expression of the American genius."

The Frenchmen were right, tragically right.

John Dewey was the layman's philosopher. He embodied the American virtues, tolerance, altruism, sympathy with the poor and oppressed, impatience with dogmatism, but as the philosopher of democracy, he failed us in the hour of need.

John Dewey was a Vermonter. His people were Vermont farmers. Both his parents were raised on the farm.

His father, A. S. Dewey, moved into Burlington as a young man to take advantage of the sudden growth of that country village into a lumbering town. He set up a grocery that did well and in middle life he married Lucina Rich.

The Riches could lay some claim to prominence. Grandfather Rich had served five terms in Congress. Lucina's father was a member of the General Assembly.

John was the third child. He could barely toddle when his family was broken up. As soon as President Lincoln called for volunteers at the onset of the Civil War, A. S. Dewey put his grocery up for sale and joined the First Vermont Cavalry as quartermaster.

Lucina Dewey moved to northern Virginia to be near her husband. For the children everything was at loose ends. Johnny was eight before the family was peacefully settled again in shady little brick Burlington overlooking Lake Champlain. When he resigned from the Army, A. S. Dewey bought an interest in a cigar store. That suited him to a T. He was popular as a storekeeper. Some of his popularity stemmed from his genial deadpan manner, and his hesitancy—he stuttered—about asking people to pay their bills. He was a jokester in a lame sort of way: he put up a sign: HAMS AND CIGARS SMOKED AND UNSMOKED.

In school Johnny turned out a conscientious worker. Without getting really top marks, he polished off gradeschool and highschool in short order. He was still under the thumb of his mother's evangelical pietism. In spite of his father's whimsies, the Deweys were rigid Congregationalists. No sports on Sunday.

Hard work was part of the farm family ethics: each boy was expected to keep his end up. Johnny worked a paper route to bring a little extra cash into the family till. The summer he was fourteen he earned six dollars a week tallying lumber.

He was ready for college at fifteen. The University of Vermont, right in Burlington, was acquiring a reputation as a center of transcendentalist philosophy. He didn't care much for Greek and Latin but he was carried away by the discovery that there was such a thing in the world as abstract thinking.

He dutifully joined the church at sixteen but he had to admit he didn't feel any of the ecstasies of conversion. He was as bashful about religion as he was about girls.

John Dewey's early ecstasies were all sparked by the intellectual excitement of the problems of the day. It was in college that he first read the English periodicals. They opened up vistas beyond the lake and the Green Mountains and the selfcontained Vermont towns, of what Whitman used to call "the big round apple of the world."

The *Fortnightly Review* and *The Nineteenth Century* were all atingle with the Darwinian controversy. *The Origin of Species* came out the year John Dewey was born. The controversy had raged through all the years when he was growing up. Now Thomas

Huxley led the palladins of evolution against the fundamentalist worthies backed up against "the impregnable rock" of Holy Writ.

Young John Dewey followed the paper warfare with gusto. By senior year he had decided that his business was to reconcile Darwinian biology with Christian ethics. He graduated second in his class with the highest mark the college had ever awarded in philosophy.

When people asked him what he wanted to be he would answer bashfully: a philosopher.

The profession of philosopher hardly existed in America. In the colleges philosophy was mostly taught by retired clergymen steeped in the ancient tongues; in their spare time they debated, with much reference to scripture, the virtues of transcendentalism over positivism or intuitivism or instrumentalism: and now the controversy, daily more vituperative, over Darwin's evolution. Young Dewey had to explain: No, he wasn't studying for the ministry. He wanted to be a lay philosopher.

John Dewey's father had never been a moneymaker. After he sold his cigar business, his income was scanty. The boys would each have to hoe his own row.

A cousin was principal of a high school in Oil City, Pennsylvania. The Deweys induced her to find young John a job. She engaged him to teach Greek, Latin, Science and Mathematics at forty dollars a month.

In his spare time he read philosophical German.

Oil City was in the flush of the first petroleum boom. Brokers who ate at his boardinghouse tried to get him to buy some Standard Oil stock. Not interested. Petroleum discoveries meant little compared with the discovery of the theory of evolution. He was torn between enthusiasm for biological science and the pain it cost him to turn his back on Holy Writ. He used to tell people he had undergone a mystical experience at Oil City. He never could explain what it was. Fifty years or more later he tried to tell Max Eastman what he meant:

"What the hell are you worrying about? Everything that is here is here and you can just lie back on it. . . . I've never had any doubts since then, nor any beliefs. To me faith means not worrying. . . . I claim I've got religion and I got it that night at Oil City."

In John Dewey's conversation, as in his father's jokes, it was the unsaid that counted.

He was unhappy teaching public school. He was still younger than many of his pupils. He shifted to the Charlotte Academy near Burlington. There he found himself hopelessly inadequate. He couldn't keep the young people in order. His mind was full of two articles he was preparing for a learned review published in St. Louis: "The Metaphysical Assumptions of Materialism" and "The Pantheism of Spinoza."

He struggled through a term at Charlotte and then decided on postgraduate work. Johns Hopkins had just started a German-style graduate university in Baltimore. Like Veblen, Dewey was turned down when he applied for a scholarship. He borrowed five hundred dollars from an aunt and enrolled anyway for a Ph.D.

At Johns Hopkins he fell in love with Hegel. Hegel seemed the remedy for the dichotomy of his thinking always torn between experimental biology and Christian ethics. The Hegelian logic was so rigid you could tilt it sideways or turn it upside down if need be.

Fortified by a Ph.D. and armed with the dialectic, John Dewey was ready to accept a teaching job at the University of Michigan. Ann Arbor he found congenial. He had known President Angell when he was at Vermont. The head of the Philosophy Department was George Sylvester Morris who had initiated him at Hopkins into the Hegelian mysteries.

Most congenial of all was a stocky opinionated young woman named Alice Chipman who ate at the same boardinghouse and was a fellowmember of the Philosophical Society. Left orphans, Alice and her sister were brought up in an adjoining town by their grandfather Frederick Riggs. Riggs was a nonconformist from the word go. He had traveled and prospected in the West. He was a friend of the Indians, an honorary member of the Chippewa tribe, and in the war an avowed Copperhead. He trained his granddaughters in his independent ways. Alice emerged from a Baptist seminary a woman's suffragist, and a passionate righter of wrongs.

Since she wanted to finish her college course and neither she nor John Dewey had any money, they had to wait until Dewey was promoted to Assistant Professor to get married.

A boy was born. Dewey accepted a professorship at the University of Minnesota at four thousand a year. When his dear friend

Morris died, he took his place as head of the Philosophy Department at Michigan. Another child, a girl, had been born in Minneapolis. A third infant appeared after they had settled into a large and comfortable house in Ann Arbor. John Dewey's parents came to live with them there. More mouths to feed, to say nothing of another baby on the way.

In spite of the complaint of some students that they never knew exactly what he meant, enrollment in his courses kept increasing. He was such a disarming man.

He and his wife were never too pinched with money worries to invite students to the house. His students found him absent-mindedly goodnatured, vaguely humorous: he had a way of giving young people the impression that he was meeting them on their own terms, gently probing their minds for notions he might find useful himself: the Socratic method. If Walt Whitman was democracy's poet, John Dewey was democracy's philosopher.

Since his friend Morris's death, the dialectic was loosening its hold. Pragmatism was the philosophy for Americans. William James's brilliant investigations of the vagaries of the human mind brought pragmatism home to every alert reader. Science was shouldering out the absolute. As God faded in John Dewey's mind, Democracy took his place. "The next religious prophet who will have a permanent, a real influence on men's lives," Dewey told a group of seminary students, "will be the man who succeeds in pointing out the religious meaning of democracy, the ultimate religious value to be found in the flow of life itself." Nobody stood up to ask him what that meant. In those days, Americans young and old piously took democracy for granted. Walt Whitman knew better.

He left the Congregational Church behind when he moved from Ann Arbor to the new and handsomely endowed University of Chicago. Chicago was in its moment of glory. Railroad center, hog-butchering center, meat-packing center, intellectual center. Rich Chicagoans were pouring out their money for social projects. Their university must outshine every other university in the country. With John D. Rockefeller furnishing a lion's share of the funds and President William Rainey Harper beating the bushes for brains, in the four years since its foundation Chicago had attracted a galaxy of talents. There was Chamberlin in astronomy, Michelson in physics,

Jacques Loeb in biology, Veblen in political economy, Shorey in Greek, Breasted in Egyptology.

John Dewey was invited to head the combined Departments of Philosophy, Psychology and Education. He insisted on five thousand a year and plenty of time for a sabbatical abroad.

Instrumentalism became the scheme of Dewey's thinking after he had sloughed off Hegel and Holy Writ. Thought and philosophy were instruments men used to seek practical ends. Life was an experimental laboratory. Truth was a continual becoming, daily adapted to human needs.

His first enterprise after settling the family in Chicago was the establishment of a laboratory school. From dealing with his own children he had deduced that education could be fun. "Learn by doing." For his own use he hedged the notion around with the intuitions of his old Vermont horse sense: even after he'd ceased attending church his children had to go to Bible school and to services on Sundays.

Alice Chipman Dewey was a doer. She idolized her husband. She had considerable executive ability. She was driven by impatient zeal. She didn't care whose toes she stepped on. She snatched ideas out of her husband's mouth before he had completed their outline.

John Dewey never finished with a notion. He would knead an idea for years like a potter working a lump of clay: often he didn't seem to know whether the lump he was working on would turn out a cup or a saucer.

In his wife's hands his tentative suggestion that children might learn by doing became a battle axe.

The school was immediately the center of controversy. Nationwide, people vociferously took sides. The Deweys became friends with Jane Addams and the Hull House group. While perfecting education why not perfect society too? Chicago was full of ardent ladies who felt it was their duty to perfect society right now, today.

The sounds of battle reached the ears of the university trustees. Particularly, John D. Rockefeller became alarmed. He suspected that all this social service would end in an attack on the Standard Oil Company.

In those days if you stepped on the toes of a trustee, the college president cried ouch. President Harper began to feel that the world was hearing too much of John Dewey. His radical theories were too much in the press. By a series of bureaucratic maneuverings, he got Professor Dewey into a corner: he would either have to see his wife forced out as principal of the Dewey School or resign from the university. He resigned.

John Dewey's influence was at its peak. When William James came to Chicago after reading Dewey's "Studies in Logical Theory," he saluted him as pragmatism's first founder. John Dewey bashfully returned the compliment. Later in quiet conversation, they agreed that Charles S. Pierce, the logician whose reputation James was nursing into fame but whom Dewey had underestimated at Hopkins, deserved a share of the honor.

Almost immediately Dewey was offered the chair of philosophy at Columbia. For a little quiet after all the ruckus the Deweys took the family to Europe. The brightest of their boys, Gordon, caught typhoid in Ireland and died of it. Alice Dewey never recovered from the blow. It was a grisly repetition of what had happened before when diphtheria had carried off little Morris during a vacation trip to Italy.

All at once she had nothing to live for. Nothing in New York replaced the excitement of running the school and social service in Chicago. She became bitter, frustrated, sarcastic, nagging. Arteriosclerosis made the situation worse. At times she seemed hardly sane. According to Max Eastman, during her last years only a saint could have lived with her.

When "principle" was involved, she could be relied on.

One of the first ordeals the Deweys underwent after settling in New York was the Maxim Gorki scandal. After the collapse of the uprising in 1905, Gorki came to America to collect funds for the Russian revolutionaries. With him he brought his longtime companion Madame Andreeva. Possibly tipped off by Czarist agents, the press raised an outcry against these foreign freelovers come to destroy the sanctity of the American home. Hotels closed their doors. Literary hostesses wouldn't receive them. Even Mark Twain turned his back. John Dewey offered them a room in his hideously noisy apartment full of children at Broadway and 56th Street.

The newspapers turned on him: the Columbia trustees were at the point of pulling the chair out from under their new Professor of Philosophy. Mrs. Dewey was quoted as saying: "I would rather starve and see my children starve than see John sacrifice his principles."

What were John Dewey's principles? He had formulated his political notions many years before: "Democracy is not in reality what it is in name until it is industrial as well as civil and political." What did this mean? Plants run by workers' councils? Workers representation on the boards of directors of the great corporations? Still no incisive description of how political democracy might actually work in daily life.

American philosophy remained a thing of words; words that might have tentative value today, but tomorrow? The great philosophers of history have tended to cast an occasional uneasy eye on the future of their notions.

"The hungry sheep look up and are not fed," wrote John Milton.

To say that John Dewey's writing was infelicitous is an understatement. Slow as cold molasses, his prose engulfs a topic rather than illuminating it. Max Eastman, who admired him exceedingly, claimed that in the thirtysix books and eight hundred or more pamphlets and articles he published during his life, it was impossible to find a single quotable sentence.

Slogans were taking the place of thought. "Industrial democracy" was a fashionable slogan in those days. Dewey supported indiscriminately every political movement which seemed headed in that direction, T. R.'s Bull Moose faction in 1912 and La Follette's Progressives in 1924. He allowed himself to be listed as president of the People's Lobby, backed the League for Industrial Democracy and the League for Independent Political Action, ancestors of Henry Wallace's Progressives and the New Left of the Sixties. Almost without intending it, he became one of the founders of twentieth century liberalism.

Max Eastman, who studied logic under John Dewey during his early years at Columbia, remembered him in his middle forties as still a young man with abundant lank hair that looked as if it had been brushed with a towel, and a not-too-well-trimmed moustache. His luminous dark eyes reminded Eastman of portraits of Robert Louis Stevenson. He often looked as if he had dressed in the dark. His neckties would hang loose from the collar. One pantleg might be caught up in a garter, or there would be a rip in his coatsleeve.

He would walk briskly into the classroom and suddenly sag all of a heap into the chair behind his desk, fix his eyes on the crack between the wall and the ceiling and start talking slowly with long pauses. Thinking aloud. He seemed to be extemporizing his philosophy as he went along.

When someone asked a question everything changed. Vivid eyes would focus on the student's face and his sympathetic questions would draw out his philosophical improvisations that the student didn't know he was capable of. He was an intensely kind man.

Under the untidy outward semblance, his students respected his inner dignity. They felt protective towards him. They would worry for fear he would be run over when they saw him shambling along the sidewalk with his eyes in the air, as abstracted as a Hindu fakir, a saint in a way, a man reaching for some formulation he never could quite attain.

Honors left him unchanged. He was elected president of the American Philosophical Association, to the National Academy of Science and the American Philosophical Society. Johns Hopkins invited him for a special course of lectures.

The Vermont farmer was never very far from the surface. When he moved the family out to Long Island for country air, he actually made a small plot pay selling vegetables and eggs. He worked the children, but when they were in school he thought nothing of walking around with a basket himself to deliver a dozen eggs to some customer. His little farm was in Huntington not far from West Hills where Walt Whitman was born. John Dewey felt a kinship with Walt.

Max Eastman held it against him that he never would read Karl Marx, "the only other man on the left who backed a political program with a system of philosophy." Dewey's philosophy failed Max Eastman, as Marx's did, in his hour of need. When out of decent human kindness he repudiated the furies of Marxism, all he had left was a vague benevolence.

Woodrow Wilson's declaration of war on Germany found Dewey President of the American Association of University Professors which he had helped found. Max Eastman and Randolph Bourne and the young radicals of the Masses group, who wanted to keep us out of war, were thoroughly shocked when Dewey came out for President Wilson against the Hun. He even wrote some nasty things about German philosophers.

To Max Eastman's surprise, he emerged from the war hysterics openminded about the Bolshevik revolution. Meanwhile, his fame had spread among America's Allies. He lectured at the Imperial University in Tokyo. Sun Yat Sen's followers invited him to Peking and Nanking. Mustapha Kemal asked him to Ankara to reorganize the Turkish system of education. The revolutionary government in Mexico asked his advice about rural schools. The Institut de France made him a corresponding member.

Lecture fees, royalties from books piled up. He received an endowment from the Carnegie Foundation. For the first time, he could put financial worries behind him.

All sorts of people were willing to pay his fare overseas for all sorts of purposes. In 1926, Albert C. Barnes, become fantastically rich from the patenting of Argyrol, induced Dewey to make the rounds of the European dealers with him while he was collecting paintings for his museum in Philadelphia. Testy old Barnes, who hardly got along with anybody, treated John Dewey with respect.

Alice Chipman Dewey died in 1927. The following year Dewey accepted an invitation from Lunachársky, Minister of Education since Lenin's day, to survey the schools in the Soviet Union. Lunachársky, like Dewey, was a nineteenth-century progressive. The child-centered school, learn by doing and the other slogans of Dewey's followers appealed to him immensely. Everywhere Dewey went, he found the Russians sympathetic. It was a period of interregnum. The good effects of the N.E.P. had not worn off. The persecution of Trotsky's followers had hardly begun. Stalin was yet to show his fist. Americans and American engineering were popular. There was nothing factitious about the Russian enthusiasm for education. John Dewey came home delighted. Here was industrial democracy in the making, educational democracy: political democracy would follow.

Stalin had other ideas. When he discovered that the boys and girls weren't learning to read and write and were picking up doubts about Marxist theory to boot, he tossed out progressive education and Lunachársky with it. Back to the tried and true. Russian education was reorganized along lines which had proved successful in France and Germany for three hundred years.

It wasn't till nine years later, when at seventyeight John Dewey accepted the job of Chairman of the Commission of Inquiry into the Charges Made Against Leon Trotsky in the Moscow Trials, that he met Marxism head on. He behaved like a courageous and fairminded citizen, but it was too late for him to draw the philosophic inferences.

The son and daughter-in-law he lived with had begged him not to go to Mexico City where the inquest was to be held. He was too old. "I'll enjoy the trip," was his reply.

It turned out that he was the only American member of the Commission who kept his health.

The Party line Communists claimed he was senile. A faction of the liberal press, for lack of ideas of their own, echoed the Party line.

Dewey confounded them by publishing his *Logic: The Theory of Inquiry,* which may turn out to be his most lasting book.

He went on writing. At eightyseven, he remarried. He died in New York aged ninetytwo.

"The most profound and complete expression of the American genius."

As the twentieth century advanced, the American genius rose to paramount heights in the organization of technology, but philosophy in the true sense languished. Nobody propounded a scheme for living to replace the disintegrating ethos of Protestant Christianity. No one had the wit to imagine a political philosophy vivid enough to rescue "democracy" from the self-serving incantations of the politicians. Young men looked in vain for the deeprooted substance of belief they needed to face death and disaster. American thought was left, as Whitman put it a hundred years before, "a dangerous sea of seething currents, cross and counter currents, all so dark and untried; and whither shall we turn?"

Pragmatism, experimentalism, instrumentalism dribbled away into the doctrine that anything goes.

John Dewey was a virtuous man. It was enough to see him in extreme old age sitting over his papers in the sun at Key West to write him down as a virtuous man, one of "the crop of majestic old persons" Walt Whitman foresaw as avatars of his democracy. He could have existed only in America.

In spite of the involved academic sentences when you talked to him, he fitted somehow into the traditional pattern of the homespun thinker cogitating over a crackerbarrel in a Vermont country store.

The failure of Dewey's thinking hardly stemmed from its homespun quality. Academic formulations had taken the place of the horse sense that comes from a knowledge of men. Dewey's notions dissolved and lost outline in the minds of his followers. The American genius was fed on sugarpap when what was needed was wormwood and gall.

In the universities and teachers' colleges where Dewey's ideas had most influence, the old optimistic pragmatism developed into a weird cult of failure. It wasn't long before his disciples had turned his thinking upside down, the way Marx did Hegel's, and were using it as a tool to dismantle the very traditions of civilization they were supposed to be imparting to their students.

So many of Dewey's followers were educationists, teachers and the teachers of teachers. In *Experience and Education,* his teachers' handbook, Dewey had enumerated his goals: "Self-expression and the cultivation of individuality instead of the imposition of tasks from above; free activity instead of external discipline; the acquisition of knowledge, instead of by rote, by relating it to the world of today" (not the teacher's world but the child's world) . . . . On the same page, he warned somewhat ambiguously that there was "always the danger in a new movement that, in rejecting the aims and methods of that which it would supplant, it may develop its principles negatively rather than positively and constructively."

Negatively with a vengeance. The educationists made a clean sweep. Discipline went into discard with the classics. History didn't apply. Social studies must take its place. Literature was last season's bestsellers. Languages were too difficult. Teaching was not subject but method. No matter if the children no longer learned to read and write; method was a value in itself.

The educationists grew arrogant. They were out to reform the world. Individualism must go. Collectivism was the coming thing.

"Progressive" teaching became like Islam an unassailable

dogma. One of its energumens at Teachers' College at Columbia declared "that the teachers should deliberately reach for power and then make the most of their conquest." He called on the progressiveminded teachers of the country to unite in a powerful organization, "militantly devoted to the building of a better social order and to the defense of its members against the ignorance of the masses and the malevolence of the privileged."

Teaching had become a vested interest. Teachers' organizations subsidized lobbies in Washington and every state capital. Critics, like Admiral Rickover who pointed out that American education by fostering mediocrity instead of talent, by offering no challenge to the young to stretch their capacities to the utmost, was doing young people a disservice, found a swarm of hornets round their heads.

In education John Dewey was the apostle of experiment, learn by doing. His followers made experiment their dogma. When their experiments didn't work, they ignored the results. Failure became their vested interest.

5

The True Believers—i

Paul Edwards was elected president of his class at Shelbyville High junior year. He was a minister's son and an only son.
At seventeen he stood six feet in his socks, was skinny and gangling
with a mop of sandy hair over a fresh complexion somewhat marred
by pimples. The teachers explained his success by his earnest blue
eyes and his way of going all out for everything he did.

His father, the Reverend Paul C. Edwards, usually known as
Dr. Edwards, because he was the only preacher in town who could
add a D.D. to his name, was rector of St. Andrews Episcopal
Church. St. Andrews was a small white frame building, carpenter
Gothic in style. There weren't many Episcopalians among Shelbyville's twelve thousand or so people and a good many of them
neglected their religious duties, so the congregation was small.

Dr. Edwards was small, too, a slight brownskinned man with
brown eyes and a closecropped white beard. He wore a Phi Beta
Kappa key and was reputed to have been a brilliant student of
Semitic languages in college and at the seminary. His sermons were
delivered in the same modest unassuming tone he used in reading
the Book of Common Prayer. Some of the parishioners complained
that his sermons were too abstruse. He had a way of referring to
archaeological discoveries in places with unpronounceable names
which confirmed or illuminated the Old Testament stories. Others,
led by the ladies of the Book Club, insisted that Dr. Edwards'

sermons were an education in themselves. On the whole, his parishioners were proud of him. Doc Niles, the pharmacist, an outspoken
cynic in most matters, used to wonder out loud why a man of the
caliber of Dr. Edwards could have let himself get stranded out in
the sticks. When his auditors bridled at this slurring description of
their hometown, Niles would cry out, "Well, if Shelbyville ain't the
sticks, you tell me what is."

Paul's mother was quite different. She was blonde and blousy
with bulging blue eyes. People wondered what had brought them
together. She was fifteen years younger than her husband and much
more outgoing. She taught English in the gradeschool, conducted
Bible classes, gave lessons in embroidery, coached the annual highschool play and even found time to put on a Christmas pageant for
little tots at the small settlement house across the railroad tracks
where the ladies of the Shelbyville Woman's Club tried to encourage good citizenship and the ambition to rise in the world among
the children of the deserving poor. Ruth Edwards had a finger in
every uplift movement in town. The ladies remarked that Paul took
more after his mother than he did after Dr. Edwards.

Virginia Morris was secretary of the junior class. She and Paul
had been close for years but junior year they started to go steady.
She was a cute quiet girl with brown hair pulled back over her ears,
the daughter of a grain and feed merchant who had a small elevator
down near the railroad station and a large Tudorstyle home on
Forest Avenue. Paul and Ginny, as everybody called her, were, one
or the other of them, at the top of every course they took. Between
them they accumulated so many A's there were hardly any left for
the rest of the class. Nobody really could get mad at them, because
Ginny was so mousy and cute with melting brown eyes and a little
look as if she might burst out crying any minute; and Paul had that
enthusiastic manner, and a sandy cowlick that kept flipping over his
eyes. Of all the honors group, Paul and Ginny were the only ones
who made a point of helping the dumber kids with their lessons.

Unlike most mothers with only sons, Mrs. Edwards never tried
to get between Paul and his girlfriend. Mrs. Edwards was far too
busy with her social work. Dr. Edwards treated Ginny like his
daughter from the first time Paul brought her to the rectory. Mr.
Morris gave them both jobs the summer before their senior year.
Paul worked in the mill and Ginny worked in the office. When they

walked home together, Ginny sometimes teased him about looking like a clown in the circus all powdered up with flour and dust from the mill. He'd pull his hand away from hers and declare that he'd washed his face as hard as he could in the sink. "But I like you that way, Paul," she'd say, sidling up to him a little. He'd edge away and walk faster with his eyes straight ahead. A wish was forming, so far down inside her that it never quite clothed itself in words, that Paul would love her up sometimes, the way the other boys did their girls.

They were so busy the fall of senior year, they hardly had time to eat or sleep. Mrs. Edwards had decided to do something really artistic in the theatrical line and put on *Romeo and Juliet*. Of course, son Paul had to play Romeo to Ginny's Juliet. When they rehearsed the love scenes in private, Ginny would get to giggling so she couldn't recite her lines, but Paul, though he blushed a great deal, took it all dead seriously. He was beginning to see visions of himself as a Shakespearean actor declaiming "To be or not to be" to applauding houses in some New York theatre.

"If it was anybody but you, Paul, I wouldn't do it," Ginny whispered in her little tearful voice as they waited quaking in the wings the night of the dress rehearsal. "Me, too," said Paul gruffly.

The performance was a riot. Some of the minor people forgot their lines and Friar Lawrence's whiskers came unglued, but on the whole, it passed off very well. The boys really went for each other in the dueling scenes. The principal, Mr. Poindexter, got so fearful that blood might really be shed that he kept whispering: "Careful now, boys," from behind one of the flats. The ladies all agreed that Paul and Ginny were the stars. "They played it so sincerely . . . they must really be in love."

After the play came the Christmas dance. Paul used up his allowance for the rest of the year hiring a tuck and buying Ginny a corsage of teeny little pink roses. Ginny was so pretty in the same pale yellow dress she'd worn as Juliet his head began to spin whenever he looked at her. He might be shy with Ginny but he sure did appreciate her. Paul wasn't much of a dancer, but that night they whirled through every dance as if they were three feet above the dance floor.

Afterwards, as he walked her home to the Morrises', they had one of their heart-to-heart talks. They decided they'd both apply for scholarships at Ephesus—she'd major in psychology and he'd major in sociology—but how were they going to wait those long four years to get married? Paul was so nervous when he kissed her good night all he did was give her a little peck in the corner of the mouth.

He hurried home and, telling his parents his feet hurt him, rushed upstairs and tore off his tuxedo. Just that little kiss had excited him so he had to take three cold showers before he quieted himself down. He'd avoided self abuse all his life: he wasn't going to start it now that the sweetest girl in the world was willing to marry him. He spent most of the night padding back and forth in his bare feet between his bed and the window. He was a whirlpool of feelings. Part of him was happy and part of him was miserable.

Next day the razzing began. Everybody called him Romeo. Bunches of little boys would follow him home after school jeering Romeo from behind hedges and bushes. When he caught one of them and spanked him, it quieted them down a little, but for weeks mocking howls of Romeo greeted him whenever he went out on the street.

Paul always remembered that he first heard of the bank failures the day of the big basketball game with Mansfield. He wasn't expecting to play, but he had to be on hand as a substitute. He had hurried home to do his homework, grab an early supper and be back at school in time for practice.

His mother met him at the door. She kissed him. "Paul, your father wants to see you in his study. He's worried about something."

"But Mom, I haven't got time."

"Go right in there now and get it over with. . . . He hasn't told me what it is yet." She put her hand on his shoulder and pushed him gently down the hall.

His heart was pounding. Suppose Dad wanted him to break it off with Ginny.

His father sat at his desk between two lamps with green glass shades. He was beating the ashes out of his pipe into an ashtray. Paul hated that smell of stale pipe tobacco. That was probably why he never wanted to smoke. The study seemed stifling. The big dark books round the walls edged in on him from every side.

"Paul."

"Yes, Dad."

"Sit down, Paul."

His father didn't seem to know where to begin. He packed some fresh tobacco into his pipe. Paul was in a cold sweat. He could tell by his father's face that something terrible had happened. It couldn't be something wrong with Mom. He'd just seen her alive and healthy in the hall.

"Paul, a man has to face many things in his life." This was how Dad always started his lectures. Paul began to feel easier. "A Christian must face ill fortune with the same equanimity that he accepts success. . . . You've certainly heard of the rash of bank closings all over the country."

Paul hadn't. He'd been too busy with his studies and the play and the basketball season to listen to the radio.

"Hannibal Jones has just told me that none of the branches of Farmers Central of Ohio will open tomorrow morning. I had been accumulating a small sum, about two thousand dollars, for your college education. . . . Well, since I've been counseling my parishioners—you probably heard me last Sunday from the pulpit—not to add to the panic by drawing out their accounts, I couldn't very well draw ours out."

Paul tossed the damp hair off his forehead. "I was afraid it was something I'd done."

They both burst out laughing. It wasn't often Paul felt really at home with his father. This was one of the times.

"Son, you've been a pleasure to your mother and me ever since you came out of the cradle."

"Dad"—the words tumbled out helterskelter—"you did just right. It's just what I would have done."

Dr. Edwards explained carefully that the closing of the bank was not Hannibal Jones's fault. If there had been mismanagement it was in the central office. Hannibal was going to a meeting of all the branch managers in Columbus tomorrow. They would pool their resources. After a period of reorganization, Farmers Central would resume payments. There was something about his father's voice that made Paul feel he didn't quite believe what he was saying.

"Ginny and me," said Paul getting to his feet. "We sure do want to go to college. . . . We'll work something out."

"Ginny and I," said his father firmly.

Paul grinned.

His father went on in a more relaxed tone: "Whatever happens we'll have this roof over our heads. The church funds, limited as they are, are not involved. I shall continue to receive my stipend, or part of it."

"Dad, I'm going out to get some air."

"Don't be late for supper."

"I'll be right back."

Out in the hall Paul started to whistle. He pulled on his overcoat and stuck his feet into his arctics: outside it was snowing. Though early in the afternoon, it was already almost dark. He headed straight for Ginny's house. There was a light in her window. He whistled. "Ginny." A little dark head stuck out. "It's Paul." In a minute, she came out of the front door wearing her mother's big fur coat which was much too large for her.

"Paul, I'd ask you in but everybody's so upset. I can't get mother to stop crying. Sis has locked herself in her room and I don't know where Buddy is. The Morris Feed and Milling Company may be going into receivership. It's all so sudden. I've never seen my father like this. I'm afraid he's going to have a heart attack. He says his customers haven't paid their bills for three months and the farmers are shouting for their money. And now with the bank closing, he won't even be able to pay the help."

Paul grabbed her and hugged her through the fur coat. For a minute he felt strong and competent and grown up. "We'll work our way through college. Two can live cheaper than one."

That February 16 was a black day for Shelbyville. People had been telling each other that their farm supply economy would outlast the Depression. Not too many farm mortgages. Thrifty people who were accustomed to keeping a little cash on hand. The closing of Farmers Central hit them like a tornado. Everybody blamed Wall Street.

Dr. Edwards took it all so casually his wife said he was being perverse. He wrote a series of sermons on the Christian virtues. The virtue of poverty, he said, had been too much neglected in the Middle West. He even claimed that for the church it was a prosperous time. Parishioners appeared whose faces hadn't been seen for years. People put less money in the plate, but farmers began bringing contributions in kind. They would leave milk and eggs and butter at the kitchen door before service.

Mrs. Edwards took advantage of their contributions when she set up a soupkitchen at the settlement house. The farmers seemed quite happy to contribute foodstuffs they couldn't find buyers for. The ladies from the Women's Club served a hot meal every afternoon for two hours. Anyone who came was served and no questions asked. The only rule was children first.

"Now this," said Paul who had taken to laying down the law to Ginny on social matters, "is how society ought to be set up. From each according to his ability, to each according to his need."

Paul had begun to take a passionate interest in current affairs. Franklin D. Roosevelt was inaugurated President March 4. Paul's blood tingled when he listened to the inaugural address over the radio. He read in the papers about "sound" banks reopening all over the state, but the doors of Farmers Central remained obstinately closed. Paul began to feel that the interests were discriminating against him personally. Wall Street was ganging up to keep him from getting a college education. By the time his eighteenth birthday came around, he had decided that Socialism was the only answer.

Senior year he did so much outside reading his marks suffered. He read everything Socialistic he could find in the public library: Henry George and *Looking Backward* and Jack London and Upton Sinclair. He even tried Daniel deLeon and Karl Marx. That spring he spent the money he made mowing lawns sending away for cheap Socialist paperbacks published by Haldeman-Julius.

Ginny, who was a slower reader, toiled along behind him. She already knew how to type. Now she was preparing for earning her living by taking courses in stenography and shorthand.

At supper he'd argue with his father. "But, Dad, these writers all prophesied capitalism was going to collapse. Well, it has."

"Paul," said his father in his carefully articulated patient voice, "don't close your mind."

"But, Dad," Paul's voice broke, "I'm opening it . . . to new ideas."

He confided in Ginny that he was afraid Dad was losing his grip. "Studying all these Semitic texts gets between him and the real world."

It was Dr. Edwards who suggested he ought to read Bernard Shaw. "He's a Socialist, too, but he's more amusing than the others." Paul read *Captain Brassbound's Conversion* and decided he wanted to be a playwright.

Graduation was a dismal function. The boys and girls were facing a bleak future. Paul was valedictorian. He fought over every word of his speech with Mr. Poindexter. "But, Paul, it's too controversial." Finally, he consented to leave out any reference to Socialism. He tried to turn it into a eulogy of the New Deal. That looked like Socialism to him. Mr. Poindexter thought it was all right to praise the New Deal, but he mustn't describe the New Deal measures as Socialistic, and maybe he'd better not mention President Roosevelt. Shelbyville was full of oldtime Republicans who grew apoplectic at the mere sound of his name.

Ginny patiently typed out each new version and listened sympathetically to Paul's curses and groans. Finally, Paul delivered his speech. It was a hot day. The gymnasium was an oven. He sweated like a horse. He thought he'd done badly, but people applauded. He was the center of a whirl of congratulations. Walking home with his diploma under his arm, he decided he might have a career as a public speaker.

He was wild for the New Deal. Right at home he had an example of the New Deal in action. Mom's soupkitchen had been taken over by a government organization under the Federal Emergency Relief Act. Now she got a salary for managing it, and the work was done by relief clients. She even found a job for Ginny in the office. Paul was engaged at fifteen dollars a week to ride around on his bicycle getting up a census of hardship cases.

When the Morrises lost their house to the mortgageholder, Ginny came to live at the rectory. The families agreed it was all right for the young people to be formally engaged but that they were much too young to get married. For next fall they decided Ephesus would be too expensive. They signed up for courses in education at the Linwood County Normal School; which could be reached in thirtyfive minutes on the interurban trolley.

After a year of Normal School, Paul decided the last thing he wanted to do was teach school. He wasn't learning a damn thing, and he told Ginny he couldn't stand it a day longer. Ginny, who loved little children, wanted to stay to finish her course in the lower grades. It turned out that Dad's friend, Hannibal Jones, who had resigned when Farmers Central tried to get its depositors to consent to a settlement of twenty cents on the dollar, now was in the Finance Department at Ford Motors in Detroit. Dad wrote him, and one fine winter morning with a recommendation to the Personnel Department in his pocket, Paul set out for Detroit. Ginny, who so often looked as if she was going to cry, really did cry this time. Waving out at her through the blurred glass of the window, Paul had trouble to keep from blubbering right there in the crowded daycoach.

Paul used to say later that these months at Ford's were his real college education. He started as a sweeper, and since he had no more mechanical ability than a rabbit, ended up as timekeeper. Timekeepers weren't popular, but Paul was developing a knack for getting along with people. The run-of-the-mill automobile workers, who didn't seem to have an idea in their heads beyond getting drunk and chasing skirts every weekend, thought he was an odd fish but admitted he was on the level. The men he enjoyed talking to were serious fellows, foreigners mostly, who had ideas about how the world ought to be run. They were all Socialists. They gave him the impression that all thoughtful members of the working class agreed with his ideas. Capitalism was collapsing. It was iniquitous anyway: production for use must take the place of production for profit.

The assembly line—the belt they called it in those days—made an incredible racket. It was dusty and greasy and horrible. At first, Paul's head swam trying to follow the hundreds of different operations at the various work stations, but he couldn't help feeling a sort of personal satisfaction at the sight of the cars taking shape as they moved along. It was the weird lull that came when there was stoppage for some breakdown that was frightening. He kept a notebook in his pocket to jot down things people said. He was planning to write a play about the assembly line. He'd start with men talking during a stoppage.

As soon as he'd saved his first hundred dollars, he wrote the admissions office at Ephesus asking what his chances were of getting into a drama course as a special student. For a while, all he got was booklets. When he sent in his highschool record, a personal letter came back from a gentleman named Earl Washburn Hovey who said he directed the Ephesus theatre workshop. Mr. Hovey was interested. He thought working in industry was a great experience. He'd see what he could arrange.

Paul sent Mr. Hovey's letters to Ginny, marked please return. Every day of his life, no matter how tired he was when he got back to the Amberson House, the grim YMCA-like "club" where he boarded, he scratched off a little note to Ginny. Nights when he didn't find one of hers waiting for him in the mailrack were gloomy indeed.

Ginny was teaching first grade at an elementary school in Shelbyville. She was all steamed up about a new method of teaching reading she had learned at the Normal School. Miss Howell, the principal, was letting her try it out. "Look, Say" they called it. She just loved teaching little children. They were so responsive. The idea was not to bother with ABC's but to let them get the sense of the word as it appeared on the page. She wrote that the children loved it, too.

That fall, Paul arranged to take a weekend off and to go home for Thanksgiving. Paul was so happy when Dad and Mom and Ginny met him getting off the evening train that he hugged and kissed them all indiscriminately. They said he had grown. They were all amazed by his appetite. After all those months of eating horrible meals at the Amberson House, he just couldn't seem to get enough of Mom's good food.

That Thanksgiving of 1936 was notable in a number of ways. Ginny had been old enough to vote for Franklin D. Roosevelt on Election Day but Paul hadn't. His birthday came ten days later. Now they were both free white and twentyone, and he and Ginny were damn well going to get married. After breakfast he followed Ginny upstairs to her room with Mr. Hovey's latest letter. After she'd made the bed up, they sat down side by side very close on the edge of it. He smoothed the letter out on his lap so they could both read. No doubt about it. Mr. Hovey was arranging to have him admitted as a special student. The college would make no objection if he brought his wife along. The new term started in February.

"Oh, Paul," she rubbed her head hard against his neck, "it's been so long."

Then in her little tearful voice, she began whispering fast in his ear. Dr. Edwards was being mean to her. He wouldn't stop teasing her about how she taught reading. He was just hipped on the subject. Paul would see.

Paul found himself kissing her, kissing her with his arm about her slim little shoulders. It was the first time in his life he'd kissed a girl properly. He was pulling her to him, closer, closer.

"Children," Mom's voice rang in bell-like tones from the foot of the stairs, "you've got callers."

Dad held forth all through their Thanksgiving dinner. Paul was just as glad because it put off the evil moment when he and Ginny would have to tell him that they weren't going to be married in a church; it was against their principles.

"I thought it might interest you both—though poor Ginny feels I've been rubbing it in a little too hard—to know about the recent discoveries in Syria and Palestine that have for the first time brought the history of our alphabet to light. This isn't dry-as-dust information dug out of an encyclopedia. The discoveries were made during the last ten years. . . . All we knew before was the rough outlines. We suspected that the alphabet as we have it came down to us from the Phoenicians through the Greeks to the Romans. Now we have chapter and verse. It was only seven years ago, the year of the stockmarket crash, that Shaeffer's work at Byblos disclosed a hitherto unknown culture: Ugaritic, which seems to have been a sort of middleman culture between East and West. The people of Ugarit adapted the cuneiform to develop twentyseven phonemes. A phoneme is a sign which represents a sound. This was in the fourteenth century B.C. Up to then in cuneiform, which had approached a syllabic system, and in Egyptian hieroglyphics, a sign usually stood for a thing or an idea. That's the system which our reading reformers who consider themselves so modern are trying to inflict on our children. They are three thousand years out of date."

He paused while he piled some more turkey and stuffing on Paul's plate. "Go on, Dad, it's all new to me. . . . One of the advantages of growing up is that one can disagree with one's parents without getting mad at them." Even to Paul that remark sounded stuffy as he heard himself saying it.

"The sarcophagus at Byblos was first discovered in 1923. It was made for a certain Ahiram, a high priest. First it was dated too early and then too late. The inscription was thought to be linear Phoenician. Shaeffer nailed it down as Ugaritic.... 'Only one sign represented each phoneme noted,' I'm quoting. 'This act of abstraction and simplification, absent from all other syllabic systems, created the alphabet.' "

Paul and Ginny on opposite sides of the table were thinking the same thing: What on earth could the system of writing of the early Syrians have to do with the education of children today?

Dr. Edwards went on as if he had read their minds. "What you children's education has not prepared you for is the fact that the human mind is indivisible. The shape of the brain has hardly changed at all since the earliest skulls of the cavemen. The alphabet is as cogent to the children of today as it was three thousand years ago when its invention unlocked the secrecy of inscriptions.... To my way of thinking, the development of a simple alphabet out of the basic Ugaritic, which we now understand to have been the writing of the entire Syria Palestine region for several hundred years—with old Phoenician and Hebrew and proto-Arabic and Aramaic branching off at various periods—is one of the primary achievements of the human mind. What it meant was that writing and reading, which had been the prerogatives of the priestly caste, were thrown open to everybody who was willing to learn a few simple symbols. To give up the alphabet in the year 1936, and that's what these alleged reading reforms amount to, is to break the thread which held together the culture our forefathers handed down to us from earliest times. And our little Ginny, whom we all love so, when she keeps children from learning their ABC's, is an unconscious accomplice in a crime against the human race."

Ginny let out a stifled squawk and ran out of the room with the tears streaming down her face.

"Paul, you go after her and bring her back," said Ruth Edwards. "Tell her we've got the best mince pie she ever tasted.... We mustn't all get morbid on Thanksgiving Day."

"Ruth, I guess they think I'm as superannuated as Ahiram the high priest. I shouldn't have spoken so harshly to Ginny. But it's a subject on which I feel strongly."

Ginny came back with her face washed and her hair combed, looking prim and collected. Paul followed with his big hands on her shoulders. He couldn't help giving his father a disapproving look as he sat down.

"Ginny, dear," said Dr. Edwards in a low voice, "I didn't mean to hurt your feelings. . . . I was scolding you as the representative of a whole generation of silly schoolteachers, not you personally."

"Now I know," said Ginny in an icy voice, "what it's like to be excommunicated with bell, book and candle."

"What Dad doesn't understand," said Ruth Edwards soothingly, "is that young people like to try new things."

Paul and Ginny were married in Detroit by a little Jewish notary public with a waxed moustache. Since the license had been issued in Shelbyville, Ohio, they had to go through a lot of hokus-pokus. The notary said it would cost them fifty dollars to get a license predated at City Hall. Giving up that fifty dollars, after all the trouble Paul had taken to save it, was like losing an arm, but the landlady they had rented a room from said she wouldn't let them have the room unless they showed her their marriage license.

Ginny tried to kid about it: "Remember how you used to say two could live cheaper than one?"

The room was horrible. The closet smelt of cockroach powder and they were afraid there would be bedbugs in the bed. Paul had dreamed so often of undressing Ginny he didn't have any trouble there, but he tried to wear a safety because they'd decided they just couldn't have a baby until Paul had finished his play and things didn't go well at all.

"Paul," said Ginny in a little frightened voice, "you don't think we've waited too long?"

"No," whispered Paul, "It's just that when it's real, it's all different." He was almost sobbing.

Ginny was frankly crying. They went to sleep in each other's arms.

She was still asleep when he had to get up to go to work. When he came back, he had under his arm a fat red volume called *The Complete Sexology.* One of the boys at Ford's had recommended it.

The parents were heartbroken when Paul wrote that he couldn't go home for Christmas. Paul said he was going to work through every holiday till the time came for them to leave for Boiling Springs. He had to make up for that extra fifty he'd had to spend on the marriage license.

When they finally left for Boiling Springs on the bus, Paul had a cashier's check for eight hundred and seventyfive dollars in his pocket from the bank where he had been depositing his paychecks.

There was snow on the ground. It was a shining winter day. After they left the factories and slagheaps of Toledo, the sky became blue. They were driving through farming country like the country around Shelbyville. The shadows on frame houses and the ruts in the roads had a lilac tint.

They both were bubbling over with the beauty of the country in winter by the time they dragged their traps off the bus at Boiling Springs. It was late afternoon. They managed to find the college registration office before it closed. A nice girl with bobbed blonde hair found them a place to board like winking. The second landlady she called up had a room for them. She wrote the address down on a scratchpad and with it the number of Mr. Hovey's office in the Arts Building.

The streets were full of cheerfullooking young people on skis or snowshoes and ruddyfaced children with flexible flyers. There were bobsleds and toboggans stacked on the porches of what they guessed were fraternity houses. "Working at Ford's," said Paul, "I'd almost forgotten about winter sports."

The landlady was a primlooking whitehaired woman. "Oh, I'd much rather have a married couple," she said. "Girls are so much neater than boys."

The room was clean, the sheets were clean. The bathroom down the hall just sparkled. The place was marvelously quiet. There was a nice view out of their window onto a snowy lawn and a grove of birch trees.

Next day it took Paul all morning and several phonecalls before he could corner Earl Washburn Hovey in his office. Mr. Hovey was rather a shock. He was a cherubic pinkfaced man with almondshaped gray eyes and slightly grizzled hair. His small pink hands emerged from large starched cuffs held together by complicated silver links. He yawned several times while they were talking. It took him the longest time to remember their correspondence.

When he finally did remember, he seemed convinced that Paul had been working for General Motors. It took some time to explain to him that Paul was actually registered for his workshop.

In class next day Mr. Hovey was much better. There were about a dozen girls and a dozen men ranging in age from a beaming freshman to a middleaged Englishman with walrus whiskers who had actually acted in Music Hall. Mr. Hovey immediately fastened his long gray eyes on Paul.

"Ladies and gentlemen, let me introduce Mr. Paul Edwards. Mr. Edwards can be described as a hornyhanded son of toil. He's been working on the assemblyline at Chrysler Motors and believes he can turn his experiences into a play. It is up to us to help him in every way we can. What the American theatre needs more than anything else is direct experience with life."

Paul had brought along his first act.

"Just read the lines and describe the characters," said Mr. Hovey, "in a slow even voice that we can understand. Don't try to act it out."

Mr. Hovey really could tell the difference between a line that fell flat and a line that had a lift to it. Though he'd redpenciled page after page, Paul went home to Ginny feeling that the outline of the play was still there. Ginny had good news, too. The secretary of one of the deans had just been taken ill, and she had been asked to substitute for her temporarily.

They sat up late that night retyping the first act, so late that the landlady came to ask them to stop. Paul would read the new lines and Ginny would type them. It wasn't until they were in bed long after midnight that Ginny whispered to Paul that she'd been to see a woman gynecologist who had understood immediately what their predicament was. She had put in a pessary.

Paul winced. "Doesn't it hurt?" he asked.

"I can't feel it."

He tore off his pajamas and grabbed her by the shoulders. Everything worked just right. This was the first time they'd been really happy together in bed.

They came to look back on these years at Boiling Springs as the happiest time in their lives. Paul was awarded a special scholarship to finish this play. As the polishing proceeded Mr. Hovey became more and more critical; but the girls in the workshop, who seemed to have more of a bead on Mr. Hovey than the boys, said it was because he thought the play really had possibilities.

"The fact of the matter is, Paul," said Helga Davison, who wore black bangs and spangly earrings and prided herself on being a plain speaker, "that the prof has a crush on you. You'd better watch out."

Paul named the play *The Assemblyline*. The whole workshop declared that it was ready for a producer by spring vacation in 1938. The Englishman, Darby Wills, who had been working inconclusively for the last five years on an epic of the Midlands, which bore far too much resemblance to the *Machine-Stormers*, declared in a sepulchral voice that it was the most powerful indictment of capitalist exploitation he had ever read. Paul's and Ginny's heads were in the clouds. Fame and fortune loomed.

One day after class, Mr. Hovey beckoned Paul to his desk in that peremptory way he had. "I have an invitation for you. There's a man in New York I want you to meet . . . an old friend who dates back to college years: Maurice Silverstone. At present writing, I think he's the best dramatic agent in New York. You come with me for a few days to New York in spring vacation and we'll stand over him and see that he reads your play."

Paul looked doubtful.

"What are you worried about? Cost too high?"

"That's my trouble," said Paul.

"Maybe I can do something about that," said Mr. Hovey. He showed his small pearly teeth as he smiled up into Paul's face. "It won't be my money, so you won't have to be grateful, but I keep a small revolving fund that various wellwishers contribute to, for just these contingencies. The fund will handle theatre tickets, hotel, meals, everything. All you'll need is cigarette money."

"I don't smoke."

"Neither do I," said Mr. Hovey. "Is it a deal?"

Paul begged off deciding until the next meeting of the workshop. That night he told Ginny he didn't want to go without her. She said nonsense, it was a great opportunity. Anyway, it would cost too much if she went. She had to stay. A permanent job might open up in the dean's office when his other secretary left to get married.

Paul said the idea of all that time with Mr. Hovey kind of gave him gooseflesh, but he guessed he'd go.

Mr. Hovey turned out to know his way around New York. He bought the theatre tickets, ordered the meals, made the train and hotel reservations. All Paul had to do was listen to Mr. Hovey talk. He never stopped. He told about playwrights and actors he'd known. Some of the things were so interesting Paul asked if he might take notes.

That amused Mr. Hovey. "Paul, you make me feel like Socrates, corrupting the youth." Occasionally, he'd try to get Paul to take a drink. "Not right now, thank you," Paul would always answer. According to his teetotaler notions, Mr. Hovey was drinking far more than was good for him.

Paul had hardly ever been to the theatre in his life. They went to plays, matinee and evening, till his head spun. It was miserable not having Ginny along. She remembered things so much better than he did. Every day Mr. Hovey talked about the appointment he was making with Maurice Silverstone, but somehow it kept being postponed. He already had *The Assemblyline* on his desk.

The night they went to see Maurice Evans in *Richard II,* Mr. Hovey talked all the way back to the hotel at Tudor City about the nuances of characterization. He considered the play one of Shakespeare's greatest, a preview of *Hamlet* in a way. Paul went to bed mightily impressed.

He was just falling asleep when he heard a tapping on the door. It was Mr. Hovey in brocaded bathrobe and slippers to match. He had a highball in his hand.

"I can't sleep," he said in a peremptory tone . . . "I've got to talk." He installed himself in the only armchair. "Paul, if you want my opinion, it's a goddamn bore having you never drink. . . . It's easier to talk to a drinking man."

Paul didn't know what to say.

"I know you are happily married and all that, but haven't you ever thought of a little adventure with somebody of your own sex?"

Paul was flabbergasted. He shook his head. Almost unconsciously, he started buttoning his pajamas up to the throat.

"Don't worry, I'm not going to try to rape you, though I probably could. . . . Look at it this way. Though he has a wife and four children, Maurice is somewhat ambidextrous. The play is on his desk right now. He would be much more interested if you let his emotions become involved. We have an appointment with him for five this afternoon. I know he'll fall for you like a ton of bricks, the way I have."

Paul felt as if he was choking. He wanted to let out a roar. Instead, he strode into the bathroom and locked the door behind him. His mind was working fast. By some miracle his suitcase was in the bathroom closet. He put on his clothes, packed his toilet things in the suitcase, unlocked the door and in two strides was snatching up his hat and overcoat that hung on a chair.

Hovey had gulped down his highball. He was really drunk now... "And I thought you would be coming out stark naked like Nero covered with unguents."

Paul didn't even look at him. He slammed the door, went down in the elevator and out onto the street. It was a good thing the night clerk didn't see him because he wouldn't have had enough money to pay for the room. Mr. Hovey had paid for theatres and meals, but he'd let Paul handle the taxicabs and they cost plenty.

It was a cold March night with a cruel wind out of the northwest. Paul went to the waiting room of the Grand Central Station and sat down to see how much he had in his wallet. While he was counting his money, a rather decentlooking young man in a tightly buttoned-up raincoat sidled up to him and began to make propositions. Paul jumped to his feet and walked off into the almost empty station. Frowsty women with mops and buckets were sloshing water over the marble floor. "What's wrong with me?" Paul was asking himself. "Have I suddenly gotten to look like a pansy?"

When the pawnshops opened on Sixth Avenue, he went into the most reliablelooking place he could find and pawned the gold watch his mother and father had given him on his twentyfirst birthday. It was the only thing of value he had. That gave him just enough for a bus ticket to Boiling Springs.

It was the gloomiest bus trip he'd ever taken. He kept dozing off and waking up with a start to face the horrible consciousness of failure. It was seven in the morning when he reached the new kitchenette apartment they lived in that year. He ran up the stairs and opened the door with his latchkey.

Ginny, warm and cozy with sleep, tore herself out of bed and threw herself in his arms. Holding her to him suddenly he had that wonderful feeling again of being strong and competent and grown up.

"The trouble with us, Ginny, is we're too goddamn naïve." Since working at Ford's he'd taken to using foul language when he felt like it. "Cook me some breakfast, darling, all I've had since I left New York was a cup of coffee and four doughnuts."

While Ginny squeezed orange juice, made coffee and toast, fried bacon and eggs, he strode back and forth in the embrasure to the kitchenette, trying to put the whole business in perspective.

"But how can a man of Earl Hovey's breeding, intelligence—he knows more about the theatre, ancient and modern, than any man I ever met—I learned a whole lot going around to the plays with him—but how can a man like that be so fundamentally rotten inside as to make anybody, even the foulest little punk he picked up in the gutter, a proposition like that? And Dad tells me to be patient with the capitalist system. Franklin D. Roosevelt is helping it reform itself. That's what Dad says. You can't reform what is fundamentally rotten. The bankers steal your money. A man tries to do a little something for social justice and the degenerates in positions of power wreck his chances for a New York production."

Ginny started to giggle. Paul blushed. "That's what they did." She pushed a plate of bacon and eggs under his nose and he started eating.

Ginny had been waiting to get him eating before she tried to get in a word. "It's partly my fault, Paul. You didn't really want to go. I just can't get mad at the poor devil for feeling that way about you. That's how I feel. Maybe it's the cowlick."

"But, Ginny, you're a girl . . . you're my wife," said Paul with his mouth full of toast. He drank down some coffee. "I don't think I was ever so hungry in my life. Maybe I'd better get a crew cut."

"The first thing we've got to do," said Ginny, "is send that pawnshop a check to get your watch out of hock before the interest eats us up."

"I don't know what else I could have done. I'd have had to beat the little guy up to get rid of him. I didn't want to do that after he'd been kind to me."

By the time spring vacation came to an end, they had decided

Paul ought to go to the workshop as if nothing had happened. After the seminar, Mr. Hovey beckoned Paul to his desk. He looked up at him without the slightest expression on his face. "Maurice Silverstone doesn't think your play is Broadway material," he said dryly, "but he thinks it might have a chance at one of the WPA theatres. Do you want him to try something out? Of course, there won't be any money in it."

"Maybe I'll sit on it for a while and try oneacts for the rest of the term," Paul heard himself saying.

"Good enough," said Mr. Hovey. "This particular scholarship," he added with a shade of acid in his voice, "is, as I'm sure you've been told, never renewable."

Paul walked thoughtfully home across the campus towards his apartment. He sure would like to spend another year at Boiling Springs. Ginny was fixed up with a job. If he could only get something to tide him over.... On the spur of the moment, he went to see Professor Heinz at the School of Journalism.

Professor Karl Heinz was an erstwhile editor of the *Milwaukee Sentinel.* A slight blond potbellied man, even after he shaved off his moustache he looked like Hitler. This resemblance gave him infinite pain, particularly as hostile tongues in the Modern Language Department were accusing him of being an America Firster, and that, as everybody knew, was the nearest thing to a Nazi. Professor Heinz greeted Paul Edwards warmly. Earl Hovey had boasted about the brilliant play one of the youngest of his students had written about the sitdown strikes in Detroit, too radical for the New York producers. Heinz knew all about his visitor.

Paul explained in a hurry what his problem was. The scholarship he'd written the play on was running out. The money his parents had saved to put him through college had gone down the drain when the banks closed. He was married; they might have children.... "I know only too well," interrupted Professor Heinz. "I have four and another on the way.... We ought to find some way of getting you college credits for the work you've been doing which I understand has really been brilliant." He started thumbing through the Ephesus catalogue.

"If it can be arranged," said Paul, tactfully, "I'd like to take advantage of your courses at the School of Journalism, Professor."

They were interrupted by a cheery voice shouting in the hall outside, "Heinz, you old isolationist, where are you hiding your-self?"

Heinz hurried to open the door. He was wincing at the epithet. "Quiet, Grover, somebody might believe you."

Grover Wilson had brickcolored hair, slightly curly, tumbling over a broad prognathous face. Goodfellowship oozed all over him. He slapped Professor Heinz on the back. "What did you do with your moustache, Karl? Is this one of your students?"

"Paul, meet Grover Wilson. He was a member of the President's Brain Trust during the Hundred Days."

"Fired for insubordination," said Grover Wilson making a face.

"What are you doing, Grover, out here in the heartland? I thought Washington was your beat."

"I'm bound for Detroit. I stopped off for the pleasure of eating lunch with you. . . . Paul," said Grover in an aside, "I don't need to tell you that under this modest exterior, Karl Heinz is one of the best-informed journalists in the whole Middlewest. Karl, I've signed up to do a series of articles—middle of the road, strictly nonparti-san, acceptable to General Motors as to John L. Lewis—about the automobile worker . . . North American Newspaper Alliance . . . you know the way I make these rash commitments. I need somebody who knows his way around Detroit. . . . I want to get the workers' story."

Professor Heinz got to his feet with some solemnity. "That young man sitting beside my desk . . ."

"Looking like butter wouldn't melt in his mouth," inter-rupted Grover Wilson.

"He worked two years at Ford's, or was it three, Paul?"

Paul's mouth dried up he was so excited. "Two," he said huskily.

"And he's written a play about it that Earl Hovey says is one of the most brilliant things that ever went through his work-shop. . . . Of course, the producers won't touch it because it takes the side of the workers."

"Well, Karl, this is a coincidence. . . . Suppose we all three eat lunch together. Is there still that German joint with the draft beer?"

Heinz turned fiery red. "I'm ashamed to admit it, but I've

stopped going to the Heidelberg because there are people on the Ephesus faculty trying to get me fired on account of being German . . . and I'm the third generation of my family in Milwaukee."

"And the most Socialist of Social Democrats," roared Grover Wilson. He grabbed Paul by the flap of his jacket. "Paul, listen to me. I've known this man for fifteen years, since the early days of the Sacco-Vanzetti case. . . . He's like driven snow. There's not a deceitful bone in his body."

"Just to prove you wrong," said Karl Heinz grinning, "I'll tell you what we'll do. We'll go to my house and eat at the kitchen table. My wife's out playing bridge and the kids are in school. They have a send-out service. I'll order a growler of beer and sauerbraten and fixings, and we'll be able to talk without having all those faculty snoopers listening in on what we're saying."

Paul was walking on air. By the time their three-hour luncheon was broken up by the arrival of Mrs. Heinz and the kids, he could go home to tell Ginny he'd been hired by a prominent journalist to act as leg man for him in Detroit while he wrote a series of articles. The pay was seventyfive dollars a week. Ginny could hardly believe him so he said it twice over.

"Paul, you've got what it takes."

"I guess it's a case of striking while the iron is hot. It wouldn't have happened if Professor Heinz weren't such an extremely nice guy. He's going to arrange with the workshop to give me a leave of absence for two weeks to collect new material for a oneact."

As it turned out, Paul not only collected the material but he wrote the articles. When he called Mr. Wilson at the Springs House by phone next morning, Mr. Wilson sounded pretty blurry. He apologized for having mislaid his copy of Paul's play. Just on his way to bed, he met an old friend walking along the hotel corridor with a bottle of whiskey under his arm. He told Paul to come around to the hotel about noon. They'd take a cab to Dayton and catch an afternoon plane for Detroit.

Grover Wilson found a lot more friends in Detroit, some male and some female. Paul lost him for three days in the Belle Isle Hotel. He kept making appointments and breaking them. The only thing he was punctual about, thank God, was writing Paul checks for his salary and expenses. Paul went around meticulously checking on every man he had known at Ford's. Some had disappeared without a trace. Some still held the same jobs. Others had been promoted to foreman or were working as organizers for the CIO. He even managed to arrange an interview with the Reuther brothers. He certainly thought Mr. Wilson would turn out for that. He did, but he was too drunk to make sense. Since neither of the Reuther boys drank, they didn't give him a very cordial reception. Soon after that, Paul, with the help of a couple of local journalists, poured him on the plane to Washington.

Paul went back to Boiling Springs to write up his material. Ginny typed it out nights when she got home from work. Grover Wilson seemed to have sobered up under the influence of his wife and family. Every morning he called Paul long distance and told him what to play up and what to play down and what to revise in each article. Paul mailed him an installment every day.

Drunk or sober, Grover Wilson turned out to be a remarkably decent fellow. After the third of the series, he added Paul's name to the byline. When the last article was ready, he wired Paul the funds to fly it himself personally to Washington.

Grover and Dotty Wilson put him up in their attic floor in a picturesque little frame house at the back of a garden in Georgetown. By the end of the week, he was able to phone Ginny. She must beg off from the dean's office and pack up and come. The Wilsons would put them up till they found an apartment. She'd love Dotty Wilson. Nicest woman in the world. He had a job in the Department of Labor. Grover had arranged it. Grover knew everybody by their first name from Eleanor Roosevelt on down. He had all kinds of people—Senators, Representatives, Supreme Court Justices—at his house every evening.

Waiting for the train to come in, Paul reminded himself that they'd never had a honeymoon. "This is our Washington honeymoon," he told Ginny. It was May. There were still flowering trees in bloom. They'd never seen any place more beautiful. In Georgetown, mocking birds were singing among the sapgreen leaves.

If he'd ever had a doubt about how Ginny would get on with the big names, there was no reason for it. She sat at dinner looking mousy and cute with that heartbroken look on her face. Everybody was crazy about her. After dinner they crept upstairs to their little room. A smell of honeysuckle came in from the garden. From downstairs they could hear the clink of ice in glasses, loud voices in argument. "Listen to 'em," whispered Paul. "Ginny, those two weeks in Detroit convinced me that the man who doesn't drink has an immense advantage over the man who does. Guy Stephenson, he's my boss, he doesn't drink either. He's on the right side. It's going to be wonderful to work for something you believe in."

When he started to make love to her, he felt it had been years since she'd been in his arms. "Do you think we'd better?" she whispered. "I haven't anything. You know."

"Suppose we did have a baby ... I'd love it ... You'd love it. We'd love it."

Long after, when they lay quiet side by side on the narrow bed, Paul said, "That fellow, Guy Stephenson, he made an impression on me. We must try to arrange to meet him tomorrow. The last thing you'd expect from a government official—he recited a little verse:

For we must build Jerusalem
In England's green and pleasant land."

6

Bogey

At an earlier time the American people might have lent a sympathetic ear to Joe McCarthy:

> poorboy makes good.
> In the nineteen fifties
> the bellwethers of opinion
> could see no good in him at all.

They smudged up his image into a bogey to frighten young intellectuals with; the fear of McCarthyism became a drug that paralyzed the reasoning faculty of generations of college graduates.

How did such a bogey come to be?

Joseph Raymond McCarthy was the fifth child of a dirtpoor farm family struggling for a living on some scrabbly land known as the Irish Settlement in an out-of-the-way Wisconsin township. They were Catholics. All around were more prosperous German, Dutch and Scandinavian farmers, mostly of the Lutheran persuasion.

Joe was an irrepressible youth.

At fourteen he left school to strike out on his own.

He rented an acre from his father for a chicken farm. Within a couple of years, he owned a string of chickenhouses he'd built himself and two thousand hens, five times as many broilers, and a secondhand truck to market his produce with. He was doing fine when he was laid low by World War I influenza. While he was laid up, the boys he hired neglected his fowls, a cold snap carried off his broilers. He told his mother he was through with farming.

As soon as he could get on his feet, he piled his few possessions into his truck and drove off to the nearest town.

In Manaway, he talked himself into a job managing a chain-store. He was a strapping oaf of nineteen with a Hibernian gift of gab. He so enjoyed talking politics with his customers he was always late closing up the store. He decided he had to have more schooling. He enrolled in the local highschool, where most of the kids were six or seven years younger than he. It took application, but he had a retentive memory and a frantic desire to make his way.

The principal let him take all the shortcuts.

As soon as he graduated, he enrolled at Marquette University in Milwaukee. The Jesuits were exacting teachers. First, he tried engineering. Since that wasn't his meat, he switched to law.

He worked his way: dishwasher, short-order cook, truckdriver, construction worker.

For athletics, he chose boxing. He was game, but he couldn't learn the style. He'd charge in with his fists flying and fight till he dropped.

He was in his middle twenties before he caught up on his education. He passed the bar exam and hung out his shingle at Waupaca.

Cases came slowly, but he made himself popular with the Lion's Club and the Junior Chamber of Commerce: a softspoken black Irishman with dark eyes and hairy hands, a friendly fellow, lonesome without a crowd. For him the law was an invitation to politics. He ran for District Attorney as a Democrat and lost. At thirtyone, he ran for Circuit Judge on the Republican ticket. He won.

He was a popular judge in rural Wisconsin. He worked hard, cleaned up a long backlog of cases. He was no legal scholar, but he dealt out a rough sort of justice. Moving around the state when the judges switched benches, he filled his notebook with the names and addresses of people which might be useful politically. He had a good memory for faces. He remembered their wives and children, too.

Right after Pearl Harbor, though as a judge he was exempt from the draft, he volunteered for active service in the Marines.

The Marines suited Joe McCarthy and Joe McCarthy suited the Marines.

He was sworn in as First Lieutenant at Quantico, and shipped right out to the Pacific Islands. He served as intelligence officer in the air arm and pinch-hit as a gunner when there was need. For his activities in the Solomons, he earned a personal citation from Admiral Nimitz. Personal citations from Admiral Nimitz were not so easy to come by.

"Acting as aerial photographer in addition to his regular duties," the citation read, "he obtained excellent photographs of enemy gun positions despite intense anti-aircraft fire. Although suffering from a severe leg injury, he refused to be hospitalized and continued to carry out his duties as intelligence officer in a highly efficient manner."

On Munda he staged a wild party long famous in the far Pacific.

There, too, he made friends with John F. Kennedy, then a Navy Lieutenant who had lost his PT boat and saved the crew under spectacular circumstances. All McCarthy knew about Lieutenant Kennedy was that his old man was ambassador to England. The friendship was to prove useful. He was invited to Hyannis Port and played touch football with the Kennedy tribe: when he ran for the Senate, Joe Kennedy contributed to his campaigns.

While the war was still on, McCarthy's political backers in Wisconsin called him home to run for United States Senator in the Republican primary. A man in uniform with a good combat record was hot stuff at the polls. He took a thirty-day leave and barnstormed the state.

He failed to unseat Senator Wiley, but he built up such a following that when he was mustered out of the Marines, he was ready to take on the incumbent La Follette.

The La Follette family had dominated Wisconsin politics for half a century. "Young Bob" during the twenty odd years he served in the Senate had reflected great credit on his state. He was independent, industrious, public spirited, with a profound knowledge of world affairs. His position seemed so unassailable that he went on quietly working in his Washington office and only came home for the last two weeks of the campaign.

Young McCarthy rampaged through the state. He accused La Follette of being too much interested in raising Congressional salaries, jeered at him as an isolationist and denounced him as a warprofiteer because he had a share in a Milwaukee radio station.

When the returns came in, it wasn't the rural vote that McCarthy had been shouting for that carried the day; it was Milwaukee.

Labor unions were powerful in Milwaukee.

At that moment, many of the CIO unions were infiltrated with Communists. The Communists were out to get Bob La Follette because he wouldn't be duped by their propaganda and had pointed out in speeches in the Senate that the Russians were appropriating a dangerously large share of the booty after World War II. The labor precincts in Milwaukee carried the state, by a five-thousand-vote margin for McCarthy.

In December 1946, Joe McCarthy, junior Senator from Wisconsin, installed himself in the Senate Office Building. The Republicans had carried Congress.

Harry S. Truman was in the White House, presiding over the pellmell demobilization of the victorious forces that had swept the globe. As Secretary of Defense, Forrestal was wearing his life out trying to unify the armed services.

In the Kremlin, Joseph Stalin, having probed Roosevelt and found him wanting and heard Harry Truman play the Missouri Waltz at Potsdam, and having carefully placed his agents around them, was manipulating the innumerable strategic levers which were to turn the Russian disaster into a Communist victory.

Joe McCarthy marked time during his first years in the Senate. He was no thinker. He hardly had the education to evaluate the complicated issues paraded before him in the Senate debates. He needed a stiff course of reading: he was impatient of reading.

Ignorance, like sodapop, is one of democracy's indulgences. We Americans wallow in it. His assumptions of ignorance had served him well in toppling the pretensions of learned and thoughtful "Young Bob" La Follette.

He had accomplished an astonishing political overturn. He was ambitious: where do we go from here?

It's hard to tell when McCarthy picked Communists in government for his pet cause. Back in 1946 Winston Churchill had sounded the warning against Communist imperialism when he launched the phrase "iron curtain" at Fulton, Missouri.

Alarmed by the Republican wave that helped sweep McCarthy into the Senate, Harry Truman had revised his views about genial Joe Stalin. In 1947 he asked Congress for military aid to the Greeks and the Turks, sore beset by Communist infiltrators. In 1948 he established the Marshall plan. Meanwhile, the House Committee on Un-American Activities was uncovering evidence of a swarm of Communist agents planted in the Washington bureaucracies.

Investigating Communists was a dangerous business. They fought back in very devious ways. Martin Dies had been driven out of politics. Another Chairman of the House Committee, J. Parnell Thomas, was sent to jail for accepting salary kickbacks from his staff.

The country was split on the question of uncovering Communist conspirators: the majority was apathetic but the liberals were becoming increasingly hysterical in their cries of "witch hunt" as each new secret agent was unmasked.

They were building up a bank of hate.

The climax came with the conviction of Alger Hiss for perjury on January 21, 1950.

Every liberal in the country felt part of him was going to jail with Alger Hiss.

Fear, revulsion, possibly stifled feelings of guilt built up into frantic affirmation: Alger Hiss is innocent. Anybody who thought differently was a scoundrel. The press was divided. The liberals controlled a good half of it. The liberals were massing for a counterattack.

Roy Cohn, McCarthy's devoted chief counsel, described the Wisconsin Senator as shopping around for a cause as coolly as a man picking out a new automobile. It wasn't as simple as that. Plain oldfashioned patriotism had sent him out to risk his life with the Marines. Plain oldfashioned patriotism had a lot to do with his taking up the anti-Communist cause.

According to Roy Cohn, it was around Thanksgiving of 1949 that Joe McCarthy "bought the package."

The package was a two-year-old report by the FBI on Soviet

espionage which had lain neglected in the files of the Pentagon and been swallowed up without a ripple by the Department of State. Three members of intelligence services whose names have gone unreported brought the document to Senator McCarthy's office. McCarthy was the fourth Republican Senator they talked to: the others made excuses. A politician who messed with Communism tended to get his fingers burned.

McCarthy took the report home and read it after supper.

He couldn't stop reading.

He'd heard some of these things before but now he found them arranged in an orderly sequence: the theft of the atomic formulae by the Rosenbergs and Klaus Fuchs; the seriocomic incident by which Harry Dexter White, risen to the post of Assistant Secretary of the Treasury under gullible Henry Morgenthau, furnished the Russians with the American currency plates off which they diligently printed occupation currency to pay their expenses in Germany, with the result that the American taxpayer was out two hundred and twentyfive million dollars. The little sadist in the Kremlin must have had a good laugh at that one.

McCarthy was fascinated.

He went to bed and woke up with a start. "After a couple of hours sleep," he told Cohn, "I got dressed and went to the office. I had made up my mind. I was going to take it on. It was fantastic, unbelievable. Take any spy story you ever read, any movie about international intrigue, and this was more startling."

Some six weeks later, he launched his trial balloon. In a speech to a group of Republican ladies in Wheeling, West Virginia, he read a letter written four years before by the then Secretary of State, James F. Byrnes, which reported that of two hundred and eightyfour alleged Communists working for the government, seventynine had been fired. McCarthy interpreted this to mean that two hundred and four Communists still worked for the State Department.

When the investigating fury first began, President Truman had issued a Presidential order prohibiting any officer of the government from turning over loyalty records of U. S. employees to anyone outside of the Executive Department, including Congressional Committees.

McCarthy demanded that this order be rescinded.

The Wheeling speech fell flat at first, but by the time he reached Denver on his way to Salt Lake City, where he was to deliver another, newspapermen swarmed about his plane. The story was going big. McCarthy dramatically offered to read the list of the two hundred and four Communists over the phone to Dean Acheson. Acheson wouldn't play. The State Department issued a flat denial. President Truman refused to budge.

In 1952 McCarthy was easily re-elected in the Eisenhower landslide. He played up the Red menace in his campaign. Now he had seniority. He found himself Chairman of the Senate Committee on Government Operations. It was his prerogative to staff the Subcommittee on Investigations.

Joe Kennedy must have thought that McCarthy was a coming man because he insisted that his son, Bobby, fresh out of lawschool, be made Chief Counsel of McCarthy's Committee. Joe Kennedy had made campaign contributions and he was no man to forget the law of tit for tat.

This demand, re-echoed in no uncertain terms over the long-distance telephone, threw McCarthy's arrangements into disarray. On the advice of George Sokolsky, a sober and reliable journalist wellversed in the Communist story, he had already picked a young man from the New York District Attorney's office.

Roy Cohn was the son of a Tammany judge. He was bright—some figured too bright for his own good. At twentyfive, he had chalked up an extraordinary record as assistant to several prosecutors in Communist cases. He was an indefatigable worker with an incisive mind, dedicated to his task. At the same time, he was arrogant and vain with a taste for flashy clothes and flashy cars and flashy blondes: he had a genius for rubbing people the wrong way.

Joe McCarthy was a stubborn man. As soon as he made a friend, he stuck by him. He was immediately impressed by Roy Cohn's brains: at the same time, he didn't want to disappoint Ambassador Kennedy, who'd been good to him. He made Roy Cohn Chief Counsel and Robert Kennedy General Counsel, an arrangement which pleased nobody.

The early investigations by the McCarthy Committee were well received in Congress. An important security risk was uncovered in the most sensitive department of the Government Printing Office.

The man was fired, and Senator Dirksen introduced corrective legislation. At the same time, Communists were found smuggling reports to the Soviet Union on defense work in General Electric plants. The sorry tale of Harry Dexter White and the currency plates was the subject of a special paper, which the Senator hoped would impel all the free-world governments to tighten their security arrangements. Mr. White could not be called to testify because, when subpoenaed for an earlier investigation, he had conveniently died of a heart attack.

The Korean War, which many good citizens felt could have been avoided by more skillful diplomacy, had the voters' teeth on edge. The prophets sensed a Republican groundswell. In the fall, Senator McCarthy campaigned against Millard Tydings of Maryland whom he accused of doing a whitewash job on Owen Lattimore. Tydings was defeated. He took on Benton of Connecticut. Softness towards Communism was rat poison to the voters. But when emboldened by Republican gains in the Senate that automatically made him Chairman of his Committee, he delivered himself of a long speech denouncing the whole career of George Catlett Marshall; it was too much even for his friends. General Marshall was the sacredest of sacred cows left over from World War II. Certain unsolved mysteries about his behavior the day of Pearl Harbor were forever to remain unmentionable. The upper echelons of the Army were seized with an inextinguishable hatred for the Senator from Wisconsin.

The opposition remained latent and disorganized until the appointment of J. B. Matthews as Chief Investigator offered an opening for a charivari. J. B. Matthews, a retired Methodist minister, had earned the hatred of the liberals for his energetic work for the House Committee on Un-American Activities during the war years.

McCarthy doesn't seem to have known that Matthews had recently delivered himself of an article for *The American Mercury* in which he claimed that Protestant clergymen made up the largest group in the United States supporting the Communist apparatus. McCarthy was an unlucky man, or maybe it was that fatal lack of style that made him such a poor boxer in college. Nobody paid any attention to the rest of the article where Matthews described these ministers as innocent dupes and figured that anyway they only amounted to about two percent of the American clergy. The protest rose shrill. An insult to the clergy. Matthews handed in his resignation, but McCarthy already had the hornets around his head.

A group of McCarthy haters in the White House decided that this was a good time to pull the rug out from under him. They knew that Matthews was about to resign. While they drafted an angry statement for President Eisenhower to sign against "generalized and irresponsible attacks," they got friends in New York to stimulate a telegram of protest to the President from the National Conference of Christians and Jews. As soon as the telegram arrived, the President's statement was rushed to the Capitol and reached the Senate a short time before the announcement of Matthews' resignation. As the press carried the story, Matthews' resignation was the result of a Presidential reprimand.

Even with the McCarthy Committee somewhat discredited by these events, it took all the king's horses and all the king's men in the White House to head him off from investigating the CIA.

Robert Kennedy had been working on a report on the astonishing growth of trade between America's European Allies and Communist China, America's bitterest enemy in the Far East. The report was duly presented to the Senate and duly smothered by influences from the White House and State Department.

The political fortunes of the Kennedy clan were on the rise. In 1952, the Eisenhower year, John F. Kennedy, a declared Democrat, had taken the Massachusetts Senate seat away from Henry Cabot Lodge. A few months after young Kennedy took his place in the Senate, brother Bobby resigned as General Counsel for the McCarthy Committee. His pretext was that he wanted to take up private practice. Actually, he couldn't get along with Roy Cohn.

In the summer of 1953, McCarthy and his Committee were subjected to fresh obloquy. McCarthy had discovered that American libraries and reading rooms abroad were stocked with an unconscionable number of Communist books. He dispatched Roy Cohn to Europe to get chapter and verse. Cohn took a young friend along with him, a Californian named G. David Schine. Schine, whose head was full of naïve ideas about countering Communist propaganda with Democratic propaganda overseas, had joined the Committee as a consultant in the early days. To an unprejudiced observer, it would have seemed rational that it was foolish to spend American money to promote Communist causes; but to the press, this was bookburning à la Hitler. American and European newspapers vied with each other in vituperative clamor against the "bookburners." By that time, McCarthy and his doings were as safe a subject as the maneating shark for a selfrighteous editorial. The facts as usual were lost in the hubbub.

That fall McCarthy's private life, which had been an affair of stormy liaisons and heavy drinking, approached an even keel. He married Jean Kerr, who had been his secretary, a handsome and intelligent young woman, whom even his enemies had to respect. Their honeymoon was interrupted by the sudden irruption of the Peress case.

A middleaged Long Island dentist named Irving M. Peress was inducted into the Army under the Doctors' Draft Act. In applying for a reserve commission, which was his due, he refused to answer three sections of the questionnaire attached to the loyalty oath. In each case he pleaded the Fifth Amendment. Dr. Peress was a conscientious Communist and while in the Army continued to organize and propagandize as best he could for the Party. Mysterious forces watched over his career. Originally destined for the Far East, he somehow managed to remain at Camp Kilmer in New Jersey. He petitioned for promotion to Major.

Meanwhile, some officers in G2 came upon Peress's questionnaire. They were shocked. Getting no results through the mesh of Army red tape, one of them tipped off the McCarthy Committee. The commanding officer at Fort Monmouth, who tried to cooperate with the inquiry, was ordered to Walter Reed Hospital for a checkup and given a disability discharge. Dr. Peress's promotion went through in jig time.

McCarthy decided this was pay dirt. The FBI for years had been warning the Army about Communist infiltration into the secret radar laboratories at Fort Monmouth. Somewhat prematurely, the Senator announced to the press that he'd uncovered an important spy ring. He liked to blow his own horn as much as the next man.

When he subpoenaed Major Peress, all he could get out of him was reiterated pleadings of the Fifth Amendment. Four days after he appeared before the Committee, Major Peress received an honorable discharge at Camp Kilmer.

Confusing. McCarthy was a simpleminded man. He couldn't understand why the Army authorities, instead of helping smoke the rascals out, were doing everything they could to cover their tracks.

The confusion was compounded by a fresh move of the McCarthy haters. In response, it was claimed, to a letter from Drew Pearson, David Schine's draft board in California revised his classification, which had been 4F. He was ordered to Fort Dix for induction. Roy Cohn was indignant. Dave Schine must at least be given a commission and allowed to wind up the work he had undertaken for the Committee. Cohn began to throw his weight around. McCarthy backed him up. Between them, they pulled all the strings at the command of Congressmen seeking Commissions for their friends. Usually such Commissions were granted as routine procedure. Schine remained a buck private.

Brigadier General Ralph Zwicker was now in command at Fort Monmouth. After hearing testimony in New York to the effect that Dr. Peress was a fairly important functionary in the Communist machine, McCarthy invited General Zwicker to testify. The General proved almost as unsatisfactory a witness as Irving Peress. Later he admitted he'd been overcautious and "perhaps on the defensive." The interrogation degenerated into a long drawnout wrangle. McCarthy lost his temper and shouted at the General that he ought to be removed from his command.

For the brass hats in the Pentagon, these were fighting words. Beyond and above the normal protective obfuscations of the Army bureaucracy, the old esprit de corps was aroused. Communists were a dim threat. Senator McCarthy was the enemy at the gates.

On Capitol Hill, political considerations were taking over. The whole House and many Senators were facing the voters that fall. In spite, or perhaps because, of the outcry in the liberal press, McCarthy had a national following. Catholics in Massachusetts, American Legion people, Veterans of Foreign Wars felt he said things they wanted to hear said. He had already been instrumental in the defeat of liberal Senator Millard Tydings of Maryland. The liberal wing of the Republican Party was entrenched in the White House. They dreaded a conservative upsurge in 1954 as much as the

Democrats did. McCarthy had stung the Democrats to fury by labeling them the Party of Treason.

An informal conspiracy built up in the Senate to put Joe McCarthy in his place. Republican Senators on the Committee began to join the Democrats in critical remarks. The plan was to make Roy Cohn the scapegoat. He had stepped on plenty of corns. The pretext was his trying to pressure the Army into giving Dave Schine a Commission. They hadn't counted on McCarthy's ferocious loyalty. He stood by his subordinates.

McCarthy found the tables turned on him. From investigator he became the investigated. A new Special Committee was formed inside the Committee on Government Operations. Its purpose was to investigate the Army's complaints against McCarthy's proceedings. Senator Karl E. Mundt of South Dakota, a fairminded man, took the chair.

The Army would be represented by an eminent Massachusetts lawyer named Joseph N. Welch. Senator Dirksen on a trip to Tennessee uncovered a shaggy mountaineer lawyer, with a successful practice, named Ray H. Jenkins whom he invited to represent the Special Committee. Roy Cohn convinced Senator McCarthy that he was quite capable of taking care of their interests. This showed poor judgment; Roy Cohn was a brilliant young man, but too much involved to serve as attorney in this case.

The hearings became a TV spectacular. For thirtysix days, Generals, Senators, Legislative Assistants put on a performance to rival the World Series. The public watched fascinated, in bars, movie theatres, restaurants, clubs, department stores. When out of reach of TV, people listened in on the radio. The sale of TV sets skyrocketed.

The lawyers stole the show. Joe Welch and Ray Jenkins became heroes of a soap opera. Even Roy Cohn had his following. Robert T. Stevens, the Secretary of the Army, a well-intentioned gentleman who meant no harm to anybody, ended by appearing a perfect damn fool. Joe McCarthy kept charging out of his corner like a baited bull. He knew the truth was on his side, but he became more and more exasperated at not being able to bring it to the surface in this welter of nonsequiturs and legal doubletalk. Accusations and counteraccusations. The most picayune hairsplitting confused any rational issue at every possible point.

When McCarthy produced a copy of a letter of J. Edgar Hoover's warning of subversives at Fort Monmouth, which had been furnished him by the intelligence officer who first involved him in the Peress case, Lawyer Welch deftly put him in the wrong. Who gave him the letter? Naturally, McCarthy refused to tell, so there he was triumphantly exposed in the position of an accused Communist taking the Fifth. For the press, it became The Purloined Letter.

Before the hearings had gone on a week, Senator Dirksen began to maneuver to choke them off. It was obvious to any reasonable man that they were doing nobody any good. President Eisenhower helped throttle them down when he published an order forbidding Defense Department personnel from testifying about private conferences or telephone calls within the Executive Department. He huffily told a group of Senators who protested that the White House staff was under no obligation to the Legislative Branch.

Lawyer Welch held the center of the stage until the final curtain. He had made a backstairs agreement with Roy Cohn that if the McCarthy forces laid off a young attorney in his office who was discovered to have been a member for a short time of the Communist Lawyers' Guild, Welch would lay off Cohn's draft status about which he claimed to know dark things. Cohn agreed, but McCarthy got so mad under Welch's goading that he forgot about the agreement and accused him of harboring subversives in his own law firm.

Welch made a tragic scene. He called down the wrath of heaven on the Senator's head for having ruined the career of a promising young attorney. He laid it on so there was hardly a dry eye in the Caucus Room. He so savored the pathetic scene that at the close of the hearing, he wept real tears in front of the reporters and photographers waiting in the marble corridor outside. The TV people were so taken with his histrionic ability that they offered him the part of a judge in a forthcoming drama. He accepted with alacrity.

For the press, the destruction of this young lawyer's career was the peak of McCarthy's iniquity. Nobody mentioned the fact that the inconsequential little tale had appeared, with a photograph of the victim, in the *New York Times* two months before.

The verdict was as unsatisfactory as the hearings. Voting on simple Party lines, the Republican majority cleared the Senator of all charges while the Democrats held the Chairman and his Counsel guilty of "inexcusable actions."

Roy Cohn resigned as Chief Counsel and went home to New York.

McCarthy's enemies had more potent measures in reserve. The day the Army hearings closed, a new Committee started proceedings on a resolution introduced by Senator Ralph E. Flanders of Vermont.

They were bound they would give McCarthy no time to catch his breath. He was accused of abusing General Zwicker and of making "contemptuous, contumacious and denunciatory remarks" about other Committees of the Senate. He hired Edward Bennett Williams as his lawyer in this action. These proceedings were not televised. Senator Watkins, a strict Mormon from Utah, who presided, said with perhaps unconscious humor, "Let's get off the front pages and back among the obituaries."

The motion of condemnation passed. All the Democrats were for it, plus Senator Morse of Oregon, then listed as an Independent. The Republicans split in half: twentytwo in favor, twentytwo against censure.

Partly as a result of this guerrilla warfare between conservative and liberal Republicans, the Democrats carried Congress in the fall elections. Senator McClellan of Arkansas, the greatest investigator of them all, took over as Chairman of the Committee on Government Operations.

McCarthy lived on in coventry. Senators pointedly walked out of the chamber when he rose to speak. He was left out of White House receptions. The press neglected to notice his most carefully prepared addresses. From headlinemaker extraordinary, he became the un-Senator.

The frustration destroyed him. He could never quite understand why the molders of opinion should let loose their rage on him instead of on the Communist malefactors. Back home in the heartland, nobody had ever thought it wrong to make the eagle scream. It was as if Horatius at the bridge should be set upon by his own troops while he was hacking and hewing at the Etruscans.

He'd always been a drinking man. Now there was something

wrong with his liver. He drank more and more. The doctors warned him. His friends tell that he had some months of happiness when he and Jeanie adopted a little girl. He doted on the baby. Suddenly, it was life as he might have lived it. It was too late. His liver got the best of him. He died May 2, 1957.

Perhaps the oddest thing about McCarthy's career was that the Senate which had repudiated him gave him the rare honor of a funeral service in the Senate chamber. It was as if the Senators were trying to make up to the poor corpse all the agony they had visited on the living man. An Air Force plane flew the casket out to Appleton, Wisconsin, where he was buried between his father and his mother.

The bogey persists. For fear of McCarthyism, it is a brave man indeed who dares think straight about the dangers his country faces in a Communist-dominated world.

7

The Later Life and Deplorable Opinions of Jay Pignatelli—iii

Thought Crime

For the Pignatellis, it was a letdown to find themselves back on the same old *Queen Mary*. Jay was jumpy to get to his office. He was regretting the wasted weeks. The trip over had been fun. Now it was like a movie run backwards. No comic meetings with California Jones, no sorties into the great world of the Kennedys and Berny Baruch.

It was a roughish crossing with head winds. The tourist-class passengers kept to their cabins so that mornings Lulie and Jay had the writing room to themselves. Jay sat at a desk filling sheets of yellow legal cap with the report he had to present to Popular Historians. To operate effectively through these cross currents, they had to know exactly what was going on. He covered page after page with his scratchy writing. He knew that any report he turned in would be in the hands of the Communists by the next morning, so he named no names. He left out any mention of the Echevarria case. Too dangerous for the Echevarrias. How could be explain the situation to people who had no knowledge of Spanish politics without naming names?

Jay began to think of his position in courtroom terms. "How

do you know this is true?" "People I trusted told me so . . . I could tell by the way people behaved." "Well, just who?" "I can't name names. . . ." A fat chance he'd have on the witness stand.

Suddenly, he found himself on his feet making a speech to Lulie in the empty writing room as if she were a public meeting.

"What we've got to explain to people back home is that the collapse of the Spanish Republic is a warning. We've got to pay attention to that warning. The American republic is in as great danger as the Spanish Republic. The Russian revolution, instead of being a sudden flareup like the French, is a long-term proposition that will engulf the whole world and the whole century. The Bolsheviks invented a brand new technique for exercising power over mankind. I had suspicions before, but I had to see it working in Madrid and Barcelona to understand the power of terror, continual scientifically implemented terror. Kerensky and Largo Caballero, by their wellintentioned flounderings, prepared the way for that power. Franklin D. Roosevelt belongs to the same breed. The New Deal is preparing the way for a Socialist society. To make Socialism work, it has to be implemented by force. Force means dictatorship. That's Communism.

"The bloodshed in Spain is just a preliminary workout for Hitler and Mussolini and Stalin. Between them, they will soon divide Europe between Communism and Nazi-Fascism which is Communism's mirror image.

"England is already half-perverted. It's going to be up to us in America. Franklin D. Roosevelt's fireside talks are not going to be much help in keeping civilization from going down the drain."

Lulie looked up from her book with her eyes full of affection: "Modesto, it's a large order."

"Somebody has to have the brains and the guts to find a formula. . . . Some way of applying the principles of the founding fathers to modern industrial society."

Jay settled back at his desk, tore up half his pages and started over. A strangling sense of impotence came over him. He dropped his pen and sat staring out of the salt-smeared window at the heaving gray sea. Soon after noon, he bundled his pad into his briefcase, jammed his notebook down in his pocket and cried out, "Lulie, the sun's over the yardarm."

Lulie had spent the morning curled up on a settee reading

War and Peace. She claimed Tolstoy was the best cure for political frustration. She walked towards Jay yawning with her book in one hand and her glasses in the other: "Modesto, why can't you just settle down and enjoy the trip?" she asked teasingly.

"Well, you've been asking me what I learned in Spain. I had to tell you."

They started walking down the companionway towards their cabin on the lower deck. She chattered brightly about how she always loved being on a boat, any boat.

"I'd be much more depressed if it weren't for certain people being along." He pulled her to him as they walked down the long vibrating white corridor towards their cabin. She nuzzled up under his chin. "Very affectionate people," she whispered.

Their cabin was stuffy and dark. Jay opened the porthole. They both took deep breaths of mid-Atlantic air. "Otherwise," he spluttered as he dabbled his face in the washbasin, "I'd be mighty near to dropping myself over the stern some dark night."

Lulie gave one of her little shrieks. "Over my dead body," she said. She tickled him in the ribs and got him laughing. Then she stood on tiptoe in front of the other washbasin to look in the mirror while she penciled a fine line of lipstick on her lips.

"Auntie used to say there were some things too serious to take seriously. . . ."

"It's a damn sight easier telling people what they want to hear."

"Saint Paul was a great man for telling people what they didn't want to hear. He called it kicking against the pricks."

Jay burst out laughing: "Lulie, I always thought you hated Saint Paul."

"I do," declared Lulie, "but he comes in handy sometimes."

Jay locked the door behind them and started striding along the corridor towards the companionway. Lulie ran after him.

On the brassbound steps she plucked at his arm: "Saint Paul said something else. Didn't he say: 'All things work together for good for them that love God'?"

The bar was heartbreaking. Fustylooking passengers without an idea of what to do with themselves sat staring into their drinks while a dispirited string orchestra dawdled through superannuated tunes like "My Bonnie Lies Over the Ocean" and "The Old Oaken

Bucket." While they waited for their pink gins, Jay sat in a glum trance tapping on the tabletop with his fingers.

Lulie tried to snap him out of it. "What I thank God for, Modesto, morning and night on my knees like a little child," she said in a singsong little voice, "is that those savages didn't lean you up against a wall and shoot you like they did Ramón. . . . I'm so happy and relieved, I just can't be in the dumps. Maybe it's mean of me, but I can't."

When the steward came, Jay made it a double one. Lulie couldn't drink all hers so Jay drank it. He was just feeling the glow when Lulie said in that funny little singsong voice she sometimes put on, "If we sit here any longer, I'm going to scream."

"Go ahead. . . . I'll scream louder."

Jay signed the chit and they joined the trickle of people headed towards the dining saloon.

"Let's not get the screaming-meemies," he whispered as he steered her towards their table with his hands on her shoulders. He let his lips touch the tip of one pink ear.

"Not here!" she whispered. "As it is, people think we are bride and groom. . . . One lady told me so."

Their dining-room steward was a Liverpool limey who enjoyed telling long gruesome tales of torpedoings during the Great War. "Seventeen days in a hopen boat with water ration down to a gill per man and pullin' bleedin' straws for who would be et. . . ."

Somehow the steward's tales whetted Jay's appetite: he ordered a mixed grill and a bottle of stout. Even Lulie ordered sweetbreads on toast with her hot tea with lemon in it. "Thank you, Sir and Madam," said the steward as he swept away the menu cards. He turned back towards the table as he left and ponderously winked one eye. "There'll never be hanother one, I'll wager you that," he said as if giving them a tip on a racehorse. "People are more sensible now."

After he'd gone, Jay let out a groan: "I sure wish he was right."

In the Gulf Stream the weather turned balmy and calm. They swam every day in the pool. The hours passed faster and faster. Before he had a chance to put finishing touches on his report, Jay found himself staring out of the writing-room window at the red lightship that marked Ambrose Channel. They had hardly closed their bags before they found themselves trooping down to the Health Officer. They had so little baggage, Customs took no time at all. Nobody met them. Nobody knew they were coming. They had the feeling of sliding into New York down a chute.

Long before they were in a frame of mind to face the city, they found themselves rattling in a cab along a crosstown street. It was a soggy May afternoon. A hot southerly wind blew dust and papers past brownstone steps, over ranks of ashcans standing amid spilled garbage. Brick and concrete walls defaced with lettered boards rose towards cornices and skysigns that teetered against a gritty blue sky. "Lord," cried Lulie, "I feel as if we've been away a thousand years."

It wasn't until they dragged their bags into the entry of their two-flights-up apartment and smelt the familiar musty smell of the converted Stuyvesant Square mansion that they felt at home. Jay went to the telephone to tell his secretary at the office that he was back in town. Lulie hurried into the kitchen to see what their food situation was for dinner that night.

While Jay went down to the office to go through his mail and to have his report typed, Lulie went shopping on Second Avenue. Lulie had stowed her provender in the refrigerator and pantry and was just filling the icebucket for drinks when Jay turned up with Larry Raisen in tow.

Larry was the senior partner in Jay's law firm: Raisen, James, Bradshaw and Pignatelli. Larry and Jay had been friends since Jay was a junior in college and Larry was in third year law. A passion for French history and maybe for French wine brought them together in spite of the disparity in age. Now in his fifties, Larry had become a trim precise little man with a silver edging to his black hair. He had a way of cocking his head to one side when he was thinking so that his long sharp nose and black eyes surrounded by greedy little wrinkles gave him the intent look of a bird about to gobble up a worm.

"To be perfectly frank, Jay," he was saying as Lulie bustled into the living room with the icebucket and cheerfully clinking glasses on a tray, "what business is it of yours anyway?"

He jumped up from his chair before Jay did and ceremoniously took the tray out of Lulie's hands. He set it down on the coffeetable before him and gave Lulie a quick peck on the cheek before letting himself sink back into the Pignatellis' only over-stuffed armchair.

"Young lady, it is certainly a relief"—there was a Harvard drawl to his speech that somewhat belied the sharp shyster look in his eyes—"to have you two back in one piece.... From what Jay's been telling me the practice of law in Republican Spain is not without its hazards."

Jay apologized for bringing out bourbon when he knew Larry liked Scotch. No time to stock the cellarette. Larry took out a pair of blackrimmed noseglasses and quizzically inspected the bottle. "Not the best bourbon either."

The glasses and his cocked head gave him the look of an unusually intelligent talking crow.

"It's not the brand," he rhymed, "it's the friendly hand."

He looked up at Lulie with a twinkling eye as he held out his glass for Jay to fill.

"Lulie," he drawled, "Jay and I have been friends for a quarter of a century and more. I love him like a brother. What I have been trying to say coming up in the cab is: make no hasty statements. Particularly, don't put anything in writing. You know: *publico ergo damnatus.*"

"The trouble is," said Jay, "I might get into a spot where I had to tell the whole story."

"Save your historical improvisations for that book you are going to write some day." Larry yawned and stretched and got suddenly to his feet. "Now, Jay, if you will remember back a few years you will recall that I played a small but not insignificant part in getting you out of a certain hornets' nest in Chicago."

Before Jay could answer, Larry turned pleadingly to Lulie. "Lulie, hornets' nests have a fatal attraction for your husband.... Please help me keep his nose out of this one."

Jay started to pour another drink. Lulie said no and divided her bourbon between the two men.

All at once Larry slapped himself on the forehead. "Good heavens, I was forgetting the little woman." He hurried out to the wall phone in the hall.

Jay and Lulie had trouble to keep from laughing. The only thing not neat and precise in Larry Raisen's life was his relations with women. Ever since he had divorced Rachel, his first wife who came from an orthodox Jewish family and whom they had both loved, he couldn't seem to manage to stay married. The alimony he paid amounted to a fortune. Twice he'd asked Jay to be best man and assured all his friends that this was forever. Last time it had taken a year of psychoanalysis of both parties by his friend, Dr. Tybalt, before they could arrange an amicable divorce. Neither Jay nor Lulie had met the fourth Mrs. Raisen.

"Well," Larry came back rubbing his hands, "it's all arranged. Nora will get the cook to put a couple more chops on the fire. We'll pick up a cab and go on up there."

He waved off Lulie's objecton that she'd just brought in food for dinner. "No, tonight you must dine with us and meet Nora. . . . She's the loveliest little girl, eventempered, conciliatory. . . . You'll see." A broad smile made his face look more birdlike than ever. "Lulie, you go powder your nose. This will give me a chance to scold Jay. I'll scold him in the cab . . . and all through dinner, too, if I feel like it."

Nora turned out to be cute and blonde and dimplefaced, a Gretchen in blue satin. They were waited on by a sourfaced French couple in the empire-style apartment Larry had furnished on Park Avenue to celebrate his new marriage. The double English lamb chops were excellent. Larry brought out a firstrate bottle of Beaujolais and did most of the talking. His theme was that a lawyer must be politically neutral. "Larry's an old dear," said Jay when he handed Lulie into a cab to go home, "but I'm going to turn in that report just the same."

Next day was Friday. By the time his report was typed, it was too late to reach anybody on the telephone. He tried Anne Sylvester on the Cape. The first thing she asked him was: had Ugo been right? "He certainly was," said Jay. "I was afraid he would be. It's terrible having Ugo always right. It makes him so conceited."

She begged Jay to put Lulie in the car and come right on out, but he explained that he had to spend the weekend catching up at the office.

"Well, Ugo and I will come down on Monday. You'll need us. Don't shoot till you see the whites of their eyes."

It was Monday before Jay caught up with Ed Manchester in his little office on East 42nd Street where he handled the paperwork of several committees defending Loyalist Spain. Ed's attitude, as usual, was cool and ironic. First thing, he spread out a radiogram on the desk before Jay from George Elbert on the *Ile de France:* ARRIVING TUESDAY WITH DIRK AND MAGNIFICENT COMPLETED FILM ISSUE NO STATEMENTS BEFORE WE ARRIVE. WARNER

"Well, Jay," said Ed spreading the typed report over the radiogram, "I can pretty well guess what you have to say without reading it. . . . Don Carp gave an interview to a London newspaper and his story, somewhat garbled, appeared in the *New York World.*"

Ed handed Jay the clipping.

Jay burst out laughing. "I helped smuggle him out of Catalonia. . . . Poor little guy. He's obviously trying to tell the truth."

"But where does that leave us?" Ed asked bitterly.

"So far as I'm concerned, I've done what I could, free gratis and without charge. Nobody owes me anything. I don't owe anybody anything . . . except Annie—she paid the round trip. Drop my name from the letterhead as counsel. I really oughtn't to have been there in the first place."

Ed groaned. "That'll mean buying new stationery. Here I've been trying to keep the overhead down."

They sat silent staring at each other across the desk. The clangor of the morning traffic poured deafeningly into the room through the open window. Ed got up to close the window.

"Well, here's my position as of now." Ed spoke slowly and deliberately as he turned back from the window. "If the film is halfway decent, I'm for going ahead with it . . . even if it is a little trimmed up with Marxism."

"That's all right by me. You won't have any trouble finding new counsel. Phil Hyman was sour as a pickle when I took over the job."

Ed tapped on his desk pad with a cigarette. "Have one?"

"No thanks . . . but please eliminate my name as of now." Jay got to his feet. "I promise you I won't give any interviews. . . . In fact, I need to button up my face until I've thought this business over."

"It's a deal," said Ed.

They shook hands on it.

Jay walked out of the office feeling like Christian when the pack fell off his back. He hurried through Grand Central Station to the subway. Already his mind was full of the Joppa case that had lain all these weeks untended on his desk.

The *Ile de France* docked next day in time for George Elbert to make the afternoon papers. Reporters interviewed him eagerly in the smoking room as the liner steamed up the bay. He was described as tanned and healthy and quaffing champagne with Hilda Glendower who talked charmingly about the excitement of the war and the beauty of de Jager's film. Mr. Warner declared that the Loyalist position was not hopeless but admitted it was difficult, particularly since the collapse of the Aragon Front. He talked darkly of the Fifth Column and of Franco's success in buying leaders of so-called working-class Parties who had come out in opposition to the Loyalist government. Certainly he was going back as soon as he could. He'd come home merely to help launch the film and to raise money for sorely needed ambulances.

Jay read all this by the jerkily blinking lights of the subway express on his way home from the office. He found Lulie looking strangely flustered. "I keep pinching myself to make sure it isn't a nightmare," she said. "California Jones just called up. She crossed with Georgy and his Doe. She gave me the worst tonguelashing I ever heard. If she'd been in the room, I'd have scratched her eyes out. She seemed to think it was all my fault you'd accepted a retainer from the Fascists. I tried to tell her you hadn't even seen any Fascists except at the other end of a telescope, but she wouldn't pay the slightest attention. So I hung up."

Jay tried to laugh it off. "Lulie, you know she is a little cracked. Somebody has gotten hold of her and filled her up with a lot of mahula."

Half through supper, the telephone rang. It was California Jones. "Mr. Jay Pignatelli," she shouted so that the receiver jangled in his ears, "I couldn't rest until I called you to tell you what I thought of you. . . . After I let you sweettalk me into introducing you to my prominent friends, you turn out a louse."

"If you'd just stop yelling over the phone, we could talk

reasonably," said Jay as calmly as he could. "You're yelling so I can't hear half of what you're saying."

"You dirty snake!" She went on shrieking and cursing. Jay hung up.

An hour later, while they were washing the dishes, the phone rang again. Jay dried his hands with a tea towel and answered after he had let it ring a good long time. "You can't get away from me that easy, Mr. Jay Pignatelli. Hilda and George Elbert told me the whole story. She's a lamb. We were inseparable during the whole crossing. He tried to take your side because you used to be a friend of his, but he couldn't on account of the facts." Every now and then, she would emphasize a word in that funny way she had. Jay couldn't help an amused smile as he listened to her.

She wasn't going to let him sabotage that marvelous documentary Dirk and George Elbert had risked their lives to shoot. All the artist in her revolted at the thought. Dirk was a lamb, one of the most charming young men she'd ever met. Bernard Baruch would be revolted when he heard about Jay's attitude. Just because she was a modest sculptor with bohemian ways, he mustn't think she had run out of highplaced friends. Right now she had a call in for the First Lady. She and Hilda were going to arrange a showing at the White House.

"More power to you," said Jay soothingly. "Good night." When the phone rang again, he did not answer.

A week later the *New York Times* dedicated a column and a half to a meeting of the Second Writers' Congress at Carnegie Hall with Earl Browder as Master of Ceremonies. An ad announced that the meeting had been rededicated at the last moment to the Spanish Republican cause. George Elbert Warner and Dirk de Jager were billed as headliners. The directors of Popular Historians sat on the platform. The *Times* reporter wrote enthusiastically of the down-to-earth sincerity of George Elbert Warner's speech. Mr. Warner declared that the men of the International Brigade were the bravest men in the world. The only thing that kept them from cleaning up the Fascists was the dastardly Fifth Column. He read in a choked voice a list of his friends who had given their lives for the defense of Madrid and asked the tensely emotional audience that filled every seat to stand silent for two minutes in their memory. Silence, followed by frantic applause. Calls for an encore. "More. More." But George Elbert had already left the hall. The *Times* man described it as a moment of great emotion.

Next morning Jay and Lulie found three scurrilous letters in their mail. While Lulie was alone in the apartment, the phone kept ringing. Mostly women, all abusive. Some of them obscene. Her head was spinning so she decided to go over to Annie's in Brooklyn to get away from them.

Annie was an old brick. Her deep warm voice in the quiet overfurnished room made everything seem comfortable and secure. She got Ella to make Lulie a pot of tea and some microscopic watercress sandwiches and tucked her away in the guest room for a nap.

It was six o'clock before Lulie woke up. For a minute she couldn't remember where she was until she tiptoed to the window and looked out through the closed Venetian blinds at the dock-buildings and the steamboat funnels and the sparkling harbor with its tugboats and carferries and the tall buildings of lower Manhattan standing up creamy beyond. She washed her face and went to find Annie.

"I slept like a log," she said. "I guess it was seeing all the hatred and malignity there is lying around loose in the world . . . it fair gave me the jeebies."

"Let's not talk about it," said Annie with a shudder. "I called Jay and Ed Manchester and asked them to come over to dinner so all you need to do is stay right here. Ugo will be along after a while. Meanwhile, let me feed you some little sips of whiskey."

"Don't need 'em, Annie, I'm all braced up."

Ed arrived first. He had all the news. George Elbert was going to show the film at the White House. Hilda Glendower had arranged it. She turned out to be an old buddy of Mrs. R's. That woman knew everybody.

Jay and Ugo came in together. They had met in the subway station. The afternoon had been hot. They sank into the deep chairs of Annie's living room and waited for Ella to bring in glasses full of ice for the drinks. Annie poured at her teatable.

"Well," said Ed Manchester, "the Commies have got the bit in their teeth and are running away with the show."

"Just as Ugo predicted," said Jay.

"What I didn't predict," said Ugo, "was that they'd lose the war in Spain and win it in America."

"But did any of the gang read my little report?" asked Jay.

"I read it. Annie read it," Ed replied in his meticulous way. "Art Unger read it. So far as I can discover, nobody else took the trouble to turn over the first page. . . . Art wants you to write up the whole story for *Tomorrow's Commonwealth*. Then he's going to get somebody to rebut it from the government side."

"Would there be any harm in that?" asked Jay hotly. "They can't keep a lid on the truth forever."

"You'd be surprised," said Ed.

Ella was making signals from the dining room. For some time they had been sniffing the aroma of sizzling beef. They ranged themselves round the table. Ugo sat at the head sharpening his carving knife. "Meanwhile, you might as well know," said Ed coolly as he unfolded his napkin, "that I am seeking other employment. . . . The situation of secretary for Popular Historians is too damned ambiguous. Working for the C.P.U.S.A. was not among my plans."

Annie told Jay to fill the wineglasses as Ugo was busy spreading a slab of rare roast beef on each plate.

Annie moistened her lips with the wine and said in a hurried girlish voice that came on when she was excited, "Joe Hilton says I can't give away any more money this year anyway. Dirk has been after me for funds for promotion, but I wrote him a little note saying I'd done all I could and would like my name dropped. After all this publicity, they can get a lot of richer people than I am." She patted Jay's hand that was beside hers on the table. Her brown eyes looked a little tearful. "Still, I'm glad I did it."

"No regrets," echoed Ugo as he tucked the napkin under his chin. Suddenly, he threw out his arms. *"Dio mio,* what can I do to teach Americans the art of politics, revolutionary, municipal, any kind of politics. When there's no need you make big excitement. When you should fight, you resign so as not to hurt feelings. Jay doesn't dare speak out for fear that they'll shoot his friends in Spain. . . . They'll probably shoot them anyway. . . . I love you all very much, particularly my beautiful Annie." He picked up her hand and kissed it reverently. "But when you deal with Communists, why do you arrange it so that it is so easy for them to beat you?"

He drank a gulp of wine and started spearing the fried zucchini around the edge of his plate with his fork.

It wasn't until mid-June after the newspapers had reported the outlawing of the POUM and the arrest of Andreas Nin that Jay turned his report over to Art Unger for publication. Jay had implemented it with as many names, times and places as he dared. The rebuttal was by someone who merely signed himself A Friend of the Republic. Art captioned the articles: Two Views of the Spanish Tragedy.

The rebuttal contained every distortion that had appeared in the Spanish press since the resignation of Largo Caballero. It contained a summary, which could only have come from someone with connections in the military junta, of the case against Andreas Nin. Without mentioning Jay by name, the author managed to implicate him with other unnamed "individuals" involved in Fifth Column activity "who found it necessary to leave Spain with somewhat comic precipitation on learning of the arrest of some of their associates."

"Why, Jay," cried out Lulie when she read it, "he's going after you with a meataxe. . . . I wish I had him here. I'd scratch his eyes out."

Soon after the issue appeared on the stands, Jay got an unexpected letter from Jed Morris, an old friend who was making a handsome living as a screenwriter in Hollywood:

"Jay, I bet you never expected to hear from me after our rather unceremonious parting five years ago. . . . I'm not writing to say I told you so (though I really am) but merely to point out that if you would straighten out your thinking you wouldn't find yourself on the wrong side of the fence all the time. It's never too late to straighten out and join the progressive forces of history. Remember the three-months argument all those years ago? Every day I had you nearly convinced but the next day I had to convince you all over again. . . . Warner and his documentary—it's really thoroughly amateurish—have been quite a success raising money for Spanish ambulances among the people who count out here. California Jones is a shriek. I'm certainly going to put her in a play. She hisses like a snake if your name is mentioned. I didn't let on I'd ever heard of you. She got a lot of Big Names penned up in her studio and wouldn't let them out until they coughed up a grand each. She talked their ear off and made them look at that boring sculpture till they thought any price was a bargain to get the hell out. I kind of miss our arguments. For crissake get wise, Jay.

P.S. Please tear up this letter right away."

One hot July day, Jay got down to his office at nine thirty to find Larry Raisen pacing up and down in it. It was surprising because except on court days, Larry never appeared downtown till ten fifteen. He had a redeyed sleepless look.

"Why, Larry, what's wrong?" Jay himself was feeling particularly suntanned and hearty after a four-day weekend spent sailing and swimming with Lulie on the salt pond back of Anne Sylvester's cottage on the Cape. "Didn't you get away over the Fourth?"

"Get away, shucks. I spent all last night sitting up with Dr. Tybalt over your article. He is convinced that you are the victim of a profound psychological disturbance."

"Never felt healthier in my life, Larry."

"You know as well as I do, Dr. Tybalt was not talking of physical health. He thinks he can help you rid yourself of certain delusions that are likely to interfere with your career and with your usefulness in this office. He says your entire report is the expression of a manic depressive psychosis. He's got it all marked up with red and blue pencil.

"You know the firm is inaugurating one of the most comprehensive health insurance schemes in this country. Why not extend it to include mental health? ... I've made an appointment for you with Dr. Tybalt at 3:30 P.M. You know how much he's done for me.... Nora and I are just like that"—he rubbed his two fingers together—"since she began her analysis."

Jay got to laughing.

"I don't see anything·to laugh about," said Larry.

"Larry, if I didn't laugh, I'd be crying. I'll go up to see what he has to say, but I can't promise to undergo psychoanalysis ... not for anybody. I think I'm right, Larry. Can't you understand? I have to tell the truth as I see it."

Larry made clucking noises as he collected some papers off

Jay's desk to take into his own office. "Call me tonight and tell me what he has to say."

Dr. Horatio Tybalt's office was on the ground floor of an old Park Avenue apartment house. An intenselooking secretary with mascaraed lashes, black hair and big jingly earrings that clinked when she got to her feet greeted Jay enthusiastically. "Mr. Jay Pignatelli, Dr. Tybalt will receive you immediately."

Dr. Tybalt was a roundfaced thickset man with tangled gray hair and protruding blue eyes that looked Jay up and down as he advanced from his desk with the springy step and bent knees of an athletic coach. He reminded Jay of a disagreeable Mr. Glover who had coached boxing and wrestling at a much-detested boarding school he had once attended. Jay wondered whether Dr. Tybalt was planning to take a poke at him; but instead he asked a question in a withering tone: "When did you last have homosexual relations with this man who was shot?"

Jay stood still and folded his arms. He felt his face and neck turn red. He was considerably taller than Dr. Tybalt. He waited a few seconds to get control of his voice. "Dr. Tybalt, that question is not only impertinent but silly."

Dr. Tybalt's round face broke into a smile. He pushed out a blunt pudgy hand. Jay noticed that his arms were extraordinarily short. "That's my way, brusque and to the point.... Bam bam bam. Mustn't mind me. Oh, come ahead, shake hands.... I may be barking up the wrong tree. Quickest way of getting an answer was to catch you offguard. I observed you carefully. My guess now is that we'll have to reduce the homosexual factor to below fifty percent which is plain humdrum normal." He pronounced the word "normal" with evident disgust. "These compulsive delusions inevitably stem from an erotic root. We may have to look for it among the ladies. Maybe you were in love with the man's wife and are building a world of fantasy to cover your guilty feelings on account of having wished his death." He plunked down in the chair behind his desk and started playing with an ivory papercutter. "Please sit down, Mr. Pignatelli. Take it easy."

Jay was deciding to find it all amusing. He must remember every detail. How Lulie would roar when he told her about it.

He managed a smile: "Why are you so certain that I'm suffering from a delusion?"

"A lot of people who seem to know more about the situation in Spain than you do seem to hold contradictory opinions. . . . Take George Warner for an example. His opinions as to what has happened politically differ markedly from yours and so do the opinions of most of the others."

"Did it ever occur to you that you might have the story backwards, Dr. Tybalt?"

Dr. Tybalt paid no attention. "George Elbert Warner," he was saying dreamily, "there's a fellow I'd like to psychoanalyze . . . the universal extrovert."

Dr. Tybalt rubbed his little hands together and let out a low chuckling laugh. "He needs it as badly as you do but for different reasons."

"Wait a minute, Dr. Tybalt; you haven't convinced me that I need your services."

"Man, my dear fellow, is a herd animal. Whenever anyone holds opinions in violent conflict with the opinions of his fellows, it is wise to analyze the subconscious roots of these opinions so as to forestall the growth of the ineradicable complexes upon which the delusions of insanity are based. Our work is prophylactic. We can't cure paranoia but often we can avert it."

"I understand the patient has to be willing," said Jay.

"Since I have a considerable background from my examination of our mutual friend, Larry, I'm going to be able to give you a great deal of help. I'm sure you don't know what an important part you played in the development of his libido as a young law student. You were young, irresponsible, poetic. He was a hardworking grind bent on making the Law Review. He had a collegiate crush on you for years."

"That's a lot of guff," said Jay flushing again. "I found him an amusing man to talk to because he knew so much about the Code Napoleon and French society under the *Directoire*. Later, after I got out of law school, I became more and more interested in the development of Roman Law in France and Spain. That's the sort of thing we used to talk about. We were congenial, that's all."

"The great dictators and tyrants of the world have always polarized young men's erotic reveries."

"I don't think either of us had ever heard of the Marquis de Sade, if that's what you are thinking of . . . we were congenial, that's all. We still are. We both liked the food at a little French restaurant in downtown Boston . . . I can't even remember its name."

"Memory," Dr. Tybalt's face took on the expression of a man producing a royal flush at poker, "is a ruthless censor."

"Dr. Tybalt," Jay got to his feet, "it's fun to reminisce about college days, but I can't take up your time under false pretenses. I have no intention of undergoing psychoanalysis."

"It's your decision, Jay," said Dr. Tybalt in a genial voice. "Perhaps we can induce our friend Larry to bring us together socially." They parted on surprisingly good terms.

Jay and Lulie laughed about Jay's psychoanalysis over their beforedinner drinks that night, but Larry didn't seem to think the matter was funny at all when Jay next ran into him at the office. For some time a feeling of strain had been building up with his partners. Jay had never been on really intimate terms with Cadwalader James or Ben Bradshaw, but now they seemed actively to avoid him except when they met to discuss some case or other in the conference room.

The tensions came to a head when they all got back to the office after Labor Day 1939. The papers were full of Hitler's invasion of Poland. Business was depressed. The three senior partners had suffered losses on the stockmarket. Collections on bills for legal services were slow and spotty. The Joppa case they had all put in so much work on was stalled by the adverse decision of an appellate court. Jay got the feeling that his partners were blaming him for everything that went wrong.

After an hour of dreary wrangling about the Joppa case, Cadwalader James suddenly came out with the proposition that maybe the time had come to reorganize the firm. New blood needed. He suggested that Roy Stanley be taken on as junior partner. "Maybe there are some among us who feel the time has come to start up on their own."

Larry had been hopping nervously in and out of his chair like a crow in a cage. Cadwalader James with his high shoulders, high-domed forehead and lowslung jaw suddenly looked to Jay like a pelican. Wasn't there a little of the marabout stork about the crinkled reddish skin around Ben Bradshaw's eyes? It had become clear to Jay that this whole scene had been rehearsed. He felt far away from all of it. They were trying to get him to resign. He was so busy trying to make his partners look like birds in a cartoon that he missed several cues. They were pressing him to speak. When they came to another meaningful pause, Jay cried out louder than he had intended, "Well, suppose I drop out."

They were all sweating. They mopped their foreheads with relief. Right away they became embarrassingly cordial. When they began to discuss the division of that year's profits, they couldn't have been more accommodating. Larry became positively affectionate.

He asked Jay to share his cab uptown: "Jay, I know you understand how painful this has been for me. When I invited you into the firm seven years ago, you were just the kind of redeyed radical that was fashionable at the time . . . the Hundred Days . . . the New Deal etcetera etcetera, but now . . . I don't know what to say. Do you realize that Cad James and I have been receiving two or three poison-pen letters a week? . . . It's been costing us business. The Garment Workers for an example . . . they used to turn over about half their legal troubles to us. . . . Now they are retaining Phil Hyman. I know you can't help the way you are . . . always ready to bleed and die for a principle. . . . I admire you for it. You'll be better off running your own shop. You're a loner, that's what you are, a loner."

When they reached Stuyvesant Square, Larry almost tearfully sent his love to Lulie. "And give my best to Nora," said Jay in a coldly formal tone. He didn't ask Larry to come up.

When Lulie heard the story, she hugged and kissed him and said, "In the end, you'll be better off without those old stickinthemuds." Three weeks later when the newspaper headlines announced the Hitler-Stalin pact for the partition of Poland, Jay gave himself the satisfaction of mailing a thick wad of clippings to Lawrence Raisen, Attorney at Law, 14 Maiden Lane.

8

One World

Wendell Willkie
rose into the political sky
a rocket out of the Midwest,
blazed into glory
at the Republican National Convention
in Philadelphia in 1940
and after four loud years faded into oblivion.

Wendell Willkie was a large untidy man, with untidy black hair and a head full of large untidy ideas. A congenital promoter, he lived in a whirlwind, always losing the only copy of the speech he was about to deliver or his briefcase or his keys. He never had a hat. He carried no watch. He made friends fast and lost them even faster.

He was the son of a hardworking, hardthinking German couple from Elwood, Indiana. The father established the Elwood High School and the Elwood Public Library. While working as superintendent of Schools, he studied law. The mother was one of the first women lawyers in the state. Together they established the firm of Willkie and Willkie.

When Wendell took his law degree at the University of Indiana, his father wanted him to join the firm; but he didn't get along too well with his mother.

He dreamed of politics.

Woodrow Wilson was his idol. The day Woodrow Wilson declared war, Wendell Willkie enlisted as a private. By the time the war was over, he'd married just the right girl and spent a short time overseas in the artillery. He was discharged as First Lieutenant in March 1919 and the following year took a job in Harvey Firestone's legal department in Akron, Ohio.

Akron was booming. Wendell Willkie boomed with the rubber boom.

He was an enthusiastic Democrat. With his eye on a political future, he never turned down an invitation to speak. He defended truckdrivers and workingmen as well as big corporations. He threw himself into the battle against the Ku Klux Klan. He was elected a delegate to the Democratic National Convention in 1924.

There he met Bernard Capen Cobb, a New Englander with a keen nose for bright young men and almost supernatural skill in stitching together vast corporate enterprises. Being in the course of assembling a consortium of utility companies into Commonwealth and Southern, he induced the thirty-year-old Willkie to join his legal team.

When Cobb retired nine years later, he put Willkie in as President of Commonwealth and Southern.

It was in 1933. Franklin D. Roosevelt had just taken office. The dogooders were in control; the New Deal; the Hundred Days; the White House Brain Trust was storming the battlements of the "malefactors of great wealth."

For six years, in behalf of Commonwealth and Southern, and the utility business in general, Wendell Willkie fought the New Deal.

In court and out, he excoriated the Tennessee Valley Authority as a government monopoly. He ended by extorting an enormous price from the government for various utility properties he had to let go.

In 1939, with Hitler threatening the freedom of all the world as his tanks rampaged through Europe, friends began whispering to Willkie that he might prove the man of the hour. Immediately, the presidency of Commonwealth and Southern seemed stale and profitless.

Wendell Willkie discovered rather suddenly that he was not a Democrat but a Republican.

Success had come easy. He had found himself at thirtyseven sitting at a Wall Street desk, heading, at an enormous salary, one of the largest corporations in the country. Now he was called to save free enterprise and constitutional government.

Brain Trusters disenchanted by Franklin D.'s obsession with personal power flocked to Wendell Willkie. They were opposed to a third term and to the totalitarian facets that began to appear in the burgeoning bureaucracy; they deplored welfare; they asked why, after four years of pump priming, prosperity was still around the corner.

These became Wendell Willkie's slogans. Amid enormous popular excitement, he was nominated on the sixth ballot in Philadelphia to be the candidate of a resurrected Republican Party.

The voters had high hopes but he remained the amateur. He couldn't abide the humdrum of political organization. His campaign train covered an unprecedented thirty thousand miles. Crowds whooping and hollering met him at every whistlestop. The cheers went to his head: he began to consider himself unbeatable. He turned his back on wellmeaning critics.

In spite of committing every blunder on the political calendar, he stacked up twentytwo million votes. Franklin D. ran scared, but he won his third term.

When the campaign was over, Wendell Willkie found he no longer got a lift out of the moneygrubbing affairs of Commonwealth and Southern. He had to remain in the public eye. The Democrats were content with the spoils of victory, but the Republicans were torn in two by the vendetta between isolationists and internationalists.

In January 1941, Willkie took his stand with the internationalists. He announced himself in favor of lend-lease. Franklin D., trying to unite the country behind him in the face of Hitler's war of extermination against Britain, asked Cordell Hull to bring the defeated candidate to the White House.

The two primadonnas got along.

Franklin D. was still in full possession of his faculties. He immediately saw the advantage of harnessing the defeated candidate to his chariot and sent Willkie off as his representative on an "inspection trip" to England.

Willkie was delighted. The headlines again. He never stopped talking. Newsmen swarmed about him wherever he went. He'd hardly got through the VIP routine, lunch with Winston Churchill, visits to the ruined shrines of Coventry and Birmingham, playing darts with soldiers on leave in an English pub for the camera, before a cable from Cordell Hull brought him back to America.

Franklin D. wanted him to testify before a Senatorial Committee.

Juan Trippe flew him home on a new route he was investigating for Pan-American. The clipper stopped for a night in the quiet waters between some islands off Portuguese Guinea. Taken to visit a local chieftain, Willkie showed his usual lack of tact. There was a convention in those parts that daughters must not be mentioned except in a proposal of marriage. After brashly asking the chief how it felt to have twentyseven wives, he remarked in his breezy way that he'd seen one of them and her daughter bathing in the river. The chief took this to mean Willkie wanted to take the young woman to wife.

Bright and early next morning a canoe approached the clipper. In the bow sat the daughter demurely dressed in white. It was explained that her price was twelve silver dollars. A member of the crew dished out the twelve dollars but declared that Mr. Willkie's bride would have to wait for the next trip. No room on this plane. The clipper took off.

Somehow the press wasn't alerted on that story.

Fresh from England, Willkie began to style himself the leader of the Loyal Opposition. At the Capitol, crowds stormed the Caucus Room where the hearing was to be held. Willkie had left his notes in his hotel room. Everybody had to wait around until they were fetched. In spite of that and the sharp questions of the isolationist Senators, who quoted his own speeches against him, the hearing was a great personal success.

Next he came to the rescue of Franklin D.'s draft bill, which, having squeaked through the House, was suffering hard sledding in the Senate. The isolationists accused Willkie and Roosevelt of conspiring to send American boys to be slaughtered overseas.

In a speech in Pittsburgh, Willkie came out for the use of convoys to protect American shipping. Two days later the Committee to Defend America by Aiding the Allies endorsed his stand. Willkie was riding high. A series of public opinion polls proved that people were with him. Hardly knowing what he was doing, he had created a bipartisan foreign policy.

Pearl Harbor put a quietus on the debate between isolationists and internationalists. The very success of his Loyal Opposition left Willkie at loose ends.

Running for the Presidency had become an obsession. He missed the newsmen swarming about him. Franklin D. had a mania for sending out personal emissaries independent of the State Department. The two men had luncheon conferences fairly frequently.

In spite of their admiration for the pluck the British showed in the battle of Britain, they shared an outdated suspicion of the worldwide empire on which the sun alas had set forever. The moment Hitler invaded the Soviet Union they classed Stalin's despotism among the "peaceloving" nations.

Between them, they cooked up the plan of Willkie's tour: "Around the world in fortyseven days." Franklin D. sponsored him as his personal representative and furnished an Air Force bomber nicknamed the *Gulliver*. Willkie jumped at the opportunity to hit the headlines once more.

He had become extremely arrogant. He managed to insult every American diplomat who tried to be civil to him on the trip. The Russians could hardly conceal their amazement at his antics. In Kuibyshev, the wartime capital, in an effort to show his enthusiasm for the leading lady in a ballet which was put on especially for him, he climbed out of his box onto the stage holding out a bedraggled bunch of flowers, tripped on an electric light wire, floundered into her arms and kissed her. The audience sat frozen.

In Moscow he astonished the Russians even more by telling the leadership he wanted to be shown everything, but that he was ready to promise that if he noticed anything he didn't like he wouldn't mention it. Though in his book he claimed to have been given free access, what he saw was the usual VIP tour of spruced-up model farms, Potemkin villages and showcase apartments.

Like Franklin D. at Teheran, he expressed great satisfaction from an interview with Stalin, that good kind old man.

In China he saw even less. He had trouble with interpreters. Street demonstrations were rigged by the Kuo Min Tang. Whenever American diplomats met his plane in an effort to be helpful, he brushed them off. He didn't want information. He wanted newsmen. This was a publicity trip to din in America's ears the need to spend spend spend, and to impress all and sundry with the country-boy charm of Wendell Willkie.

One World. The book sold two million copies, but neither Willkie nor whoever did the hard work of writing cared to remember
    that this one world was split in the middle
    by the life-and-death struggle between Marxist fanaticism
    and the head-in-the-sand business-as-usual mentality of the
    capitalist countries.
    It was Wendell Willkie who first lulled gullible Americans
    with the doctrine that the way to get along with the Russians
was not to oppose them:
    this became a cornerstone of the nonpartisan foreign policy.

Back home in his New York law office, he kept himself busy defending the motion-picture industry from charges of conspiracy to bring America into the war, brought by isolationist Senators. The movie men in those dim days found patriotism paid. They were so pleased with Wendell Willkie's performance they elected him Chairman of the Board of Twentieth Century-Fox.

Then, working the other side of the street, Willkie represented a Communist functionary named Schneiderman and induced the Supreme Court to overrule a lower-court decision to revoke his citizenship. Don't stir distrust of Russia was his theme.

Not long after, he admitted his disillusionment with Stalin when a *Pravda* editorial slapped him down for mentioning in a speech that the Baltic countries might have some right of self determination, too.

He was still the Presidential candidate but nothing he could say would restore the confidence of the Republican precinct workers. Though he campaigned desperately for the nomination in 1944, he was snowed under in the Wisconsin primary.

Campaigns, speeches, hurly-burly, bustle, the daily struggle to hit the headlines wore him out. Wisconsin shook his self confidence. Maybe he should have been a newspaper publisher all along.

After a halfhearted effort to buy the *Chicago Daily News,* he went back to New York ill and discouraged. In four short years the sudden glory had faded. He developed a virulent streptococcic infection in his throat. After a series of heart attacks, he died October 8, 1944, in Lenox Hill Hospital. He was fiftytwo. He was buried quietly in Rushville, Indiana, where he had kept up a residence so that no voter would forget he was a country boy at heart.

9

Eager Beaver—ii

Danny DeLong Speaking

Here I am talking into a tape recorder. Life story: part two. I miss that pretty Swedish girl. Well, where was I? Home. Funny thing, none of the family asked me where I'd been or anything, except Mom, and she talked in whispers when there wasn't anybody else in the house. Mom didn't seem so keen about causes as she used to be. Now it was all the Garden Club and the Women's Club and the Public Library Board. She put her arms around me and whispered I was a hero to her even if other people didn't look at it that way. She was afraid I'd be branded as a Communist and it would ruin my life. . . . "As if it hadn't been hard enough living down your father's past."

What the devil did she mean by that, I kept asking myself. To tell the truth, I just didn't have the nerve to ask either of them. Dad would just barely speak to me. Anne was engaged to Clyde Vansant, a Harvard senior Dave had brought home from college one weekend. Dad and Mom were in a tizzy. The Vansants were in the chips all right. The local paper called him a Westchester County socialite, but I didn't think he had much above the ears. Still, we got to be pretty good friends in the years to come. Anyway, Dad was all set on the marriage for business reasons and he was scared it would upset the applecart if it came out I was a Red. Of course, I wasn't, not after that experience, but how could I explain it to them?

I was still a little nervous about being seen around Montclair. Suppose I ran into Gladys. It turned out I didn't need to be. She'd been in trouble with a couple of other guys and her folks had sent her to a sanitarium, under a psychiatrist's care. That was the first time I heard the word "nympho."

Anne and Dave treated me like I was dirt. Anne was on a purple cloud about getting engaged, and Dave was so stuck up about being a sophomore at Harvard you couldn't get near him. So though I'd been awful homesick for the folks when I was overseas, I felt kind of relieved when Dad packed me off to a flooring factory down in North Carolina to learn the building-supply business. From the ground up. Dad had to laugh when he made that crack. Even when he laughed, he kept that sourpuss look. All at once it made me feel kind of cozy with him, and to tell the truth, I've felt that way ever since. Kinda wanted to ask him what mother meant when she said he'd had to live something down. I felt it would kind of make us closer admitting we both had something in our past. You know how teenagers dramatize things. But Dad was a hard man to buddy up to. I just didn't have the nerve.

I went to work as a common laborer at the Acme Roofing and Flooring Company. Had to learn how to sweep the floors before I learned how to lay them. I didn't have any friends in Charlotte, so I used to go around to the YMCA to do a little boxing. I'd boxed bantamweight in prepschool, but now I was nearly up to lightweight. Got me all tired out so I didn't worry too much about girls after I went to bed.

In the middle of winter, I went home to Montclair and went to tutoring school to work off a couple of conditions I had before I could enter Dartmouth next fall. Anne and her husband were honeymooning on the Riviera. Dave never left Cambridge where he was going out for the crew, so Dad and Mom were quite glad to have me home again. I've always been a companionable little guy.

Dad did a funny thing. He calls me in his office one day about closing time and gives me the telephone number of a call girl. He'd noticed I'd been getting jumpy and he didn't want me getting any more respectable girls in trouble. He seemed to know all about Gladys. I was surprised he'd been watching me so carefully. I acted huffy and said I didn't believe in any double standard of morals, but I did use that number.

The girl's name, I mean the name she went under, turned out to be Gwendolyn. Polish Catholic. Never would tell me her real name. I guess she must have been ten years older than me. She was a professional all right. She smoked too much, but she didn't drink. What do you suppose we talked about when we went to bed? Mathematics. When she found I was interested in math, she would never lay off pumping me. I'd had a darn good teacher in school, Dr. Chalk, we used to call him. It was Dr. Chalk got me interested in the theory of probabilities. Willard Gibbs and all that sort of stuff. Of course, Gwendolyn didn't really know much about higher mathematics. She'd barely had a gradeschool education, but she had this hunch that the theory of probabilities could be applied to beat the stock market. Of course, she never let on how much she had, but the way she talked about General Motors and Standard Oil and Christiana Corporation made me think she must have a tidy little portfolio. I couldn't afford to go out with her often. Fifty dollars a night is pretty steep for a boy who's making seventyfive a week. She was the coldest, calculatingest little woman I ever met. I'd work myself into a sweat without ever getting her to bat an eyelash. Chalk it up to experience, I'd say. Going out with her sure didn't do me any harm. It made me appreciate real nice women more. And then it got me thinking: suppose you could apply some theory of probabilities to the stock market. It was Gwendolyn that started me studying high finance. The last time I saw her she was evidently sitting pretty. "One more killing like that, Danny," she said, "and I won't have to sleep with anybody except guys I like."

"How would I stack up?" I gave her that blueeyed look right in the eyes.

"If you weren't such a conceited little squirt," she began, but she did love me up a little special that night. I guess she was afraid she might fall for me because I never could get another date out of her.

I liked Dartmouth fine. The guys were rough and tough and out-of-doorsy. But I couldn't keep my mind on the courses. Except math. I went right on getting A's through every course they had. It's all or nothing in math. No middle ground. You are right or you're wrong. I like that; but I couldn't keep my mind on the rest of the curriculum. I went in for sports in a big way. I guess it was being teased for a sheeny runt when I was little that made me so competitive. When Dave made the Harvard crew, I had to even things up by getting two letters at Dartmouth: swimming and boxing. Then I really did put it over on old Dave, who was a good sound student but no flash of lightning, by making the chess team and table tennis. Lord how Dave and Anne used to kid me about being a pingpong player.

It was the competition I liked in games. Later I got all wrapped up in the mathematical theory. Boxing and swimming made me so tired at night I didn't fret too much about not having a regular girl. It was the technical side of sport that interested me more than the rough and tumble. I even tried out for quarterback but I never could quite make the varsity, a little too light. All these sports took it out of me. Then I put in a lot of time and thought playing the stock market with Dad's allowance. I didn't lose too much. It was good practice. What I lost on stocks I won back at poker. I was the champion poker player of my frat house.

All in all, Pearl Harbor was a liberation. I was just on the edge of flunking out in spite of my A's in math. Too much sitting up late, too much poker. The dean thought I was too smart for my own good and even my fraternity brothers were getting tired of me cleaning them of their folding money every weekend. I'd worn out my welcome at college.

I was just turned twentythree and I thought the world was my oyster. I was sick and tired of lectures and athletic coaches and peptalks in the locker room. I'd been in the ROTC and the first enlistment center I went to I was accepted for training in the Navy Air Force. After six months at Appalachicola, I thought I was a pretty good flyer. I was crazy for combat but they came along with one of those aptitude tests and my math scored so high they decided my place was in G2. So when I got my commission, they shipped me out to CINCPAC and there I was in Honolulu for the whole bloody war. I did get to fly a few reconnaissance missions in connection with amphibious landing studies. I came back from one of them with a small piece of Japanese flak embedded in my rear end. That earned me a promotion and a battle scar. By the time I got out of the hospital, the war in Europe was over and suddenly I found I might be allowed to resign my commission. Dad had been bombarding Washington with pleas about how much he needed me for important war work at home. And Dad sure could pull his weight at the Navy Department. He'd gotten to be one of their prime contractors.

When Lieutenant DeLong went back to Montclair, things sure had changed at the old homestead. Though Dad claimed he lost money on every war contract, he was several times a millionaire. Besides the house on Hill Street and a beach cottage at Bay Head, the parents had furnished an apartment in the Waldorf Towers in New York.

All I could think of was how much I wanted to get married. I'd first met Delphine at a get-together for young officers in San Diego while I was still in training. Then when I was laid up in the Naval hospital on Oahu what did she do but turn up as a Gray Lady. She explained that she was the niece of Rear Admiral Saunders, retired, but back on duty for duration, and that her mother who was his sister was divorced from her father who was a lawyer in New York. Her father's name was Nathan. Her mother kept house for the Admiral who was a widower.

Girls were so scarce out in the Pacific almost any old hag looked attractive to us, but Delphine was a charmer. She had a long slender neck and shoulders under black shingled hair and eyes just as blue as mine. First thing I thought was if we had kids, they'll be sure to have blue eyes.

Just the second time I saw her, I decided she was the girl I wanted to marry. When I got to taking her out—or at least she took me out because I was still hobbling around on a crutch and couldn't drive a car—we both kinda took it for granted. I never believed in wasting time in preliminaries. At first she wanted me to stay in the Navy. Everybody was Navy in her mother's family. I told her no, I had better prospects at home. All the time the poor devils in the ETO were advancing on Berlin after the Battle of the Bulge, Delphine was driving me round the beautiful island of Oahu on the Admiral's gasoline.

What a place to get engaged. The nights were full of sweet-smelling flowers and those weird mountains stuck up everywhere, and waterfalls in the moonlight. What I liked particularly about Delphine was she'd been around so much. She was a little older than me but that didn't faze me. She spoke French and read books and knew all the latest about plays and poetry and art. She was the first girl I had ever met who was really interested in what a guy wanted to do. When I let drop a remark about math, she dredged up a copy of Hogben's *Mathematics for the Millions* out of some bookstore. If you ever saw a pair of happy little lovebirds, it was Delphine and me.

That was really a happy two weeks. The war was ending in Europe and the Japs were on the ropes in the Philippines, and I was being sent home on convalescent leave with the prospect of getting out of the service. To tell the truth, I was just as ready as the next man to skip the invasion of Japan everybody was gritting their teeth over.

And Dad really did need me at home. His business had grown so fast he couldn't keep up with it. Dave was over in Germany in military government. He didn't want to go into the business anyway; he wanted to study law. Mom kept writing about how gray and worn Dad looked. Poor Dad just didn't have any relaxations. He didn't even play golf.

Even before I stopped walking with a cane, I was back in Dad's office. Right away I saw that he was trying to run a two- or three-million-dollar business like a corner hardware store. I'd seen enough of large-scale procurement out in the Pacific to see that Home Supply had to expand if we weren't going to choke to death on too many contracts. It costs money to make money. I kept telling Dad we were horribly undercapitalized; every department was understaffed. Ever since the Depression Dad had borrowed little piddling sums at high rates from the Massasoit Trust in Boston, but they were too darned conservative. Building supplies wasn't their kind of investment anyway.

I kept telling Dad about how Acme Roofing and Flooring ran their business down in Charlotte. It took six months, but in the end we reorganized the whole financial structure. We put a couple of bright young local bankers on the Board of Directors and retired the old fogies Dad kept around mostly because he liked to play gin rummy with them Saturday nights. The Vansant family came in with a big chunk of dough. We changed the name from stuffy old Home Supply to Northern Millwork Corporation. We were ready to go places.

The chief problem was how Dad and I could keep a control

ling interest. For several years I handled the Personnel Department myself. As young guys came out of the services for one reason or another, I scooped them up. I was particularly keen for guys out of the Seabees or Army Engineers. These guys were raring to go, after all the years they'd lost going rock happy on some Pacific island. Several of them were finishing up college in their spare time.

All this time I was wanting to get married in the worst way. Woman trouble was a continual ache. When Delphine came home, she insisted on taking a job in a New York advertising agency. I kept telling her she didn't need to do it. I was already making fifty thousand a year outside of my share in the business. But she said she wanted the experience so that she might be useful to me in later life. In private, we lived as man and wife. I was crazy about her, just lived for the two or three hours a week we managed to be together. I smelled Delphine, tasted Delphine, felt Delphine under my skin all day long. But she had developed a contrary streak. Maybe it was that I was too busy to keep courting her every minute. I found out since that you never can stop courting women if you want to keep them. I was working eighteen hours a day in the business and kept having to make trips to check on construction and supply jobs. She kept putting off the wedding. She was damned if she'd have the wedding until her uncle could give her away. Her father was right there in New York, senior partner in one of the big law firms, but she was on the outs with him. At the time of the divorce, she'd stuck by her mother and the brothers had stuck by their Dad.

She had an apartment of her own in the East Sixties and one night when I was taking her out to the San Marino for dinner, she suddenly grabbed my hand and whispered that she was pregnant. I was ready to jump for joy. "Now we'll damn well have to get married . . . let's order up a bottle of champagne."

That contrary look came into her face. "No, not now," she kept saying. She seemed to be going cold on me. She was shaking. I drank a lot of wine and made a big noise about the food and did everything I could to bring her out of it but nothing seemed to work. She wouldn't eat or drink and kept shaking and shuddering as if she had a chill. Afterwards we went to her apartment like we always did, but she wouldn't let me touch her. Her hands were icy cold. She had me almost crying. "Later but not now," was all she'd say.

Next morning I had to fly out to Seattle to look over a bachelor officers' quarters we were building at the Bremerton Navy Base across Puget Sound. I made a big splash out there with the procurement officers on account of me being Navy myself and engaged to Admiral Saunders' niece. That night when I was undressing to go to bed at the hotel, it came to me all at once that the thing to do as soon as Delphine and I got married was to form a new corporation especially for Navy contracts and make Delphine's uncle, who was seventy years old and about to retire for keeps, Chairman of the Board. Delphine had patched things up a little with her Dad, George Randolph Nathan, since she'd been back in New York. She said he had accumulated so much dough as senior partner of his law firm he didn't know where to invest it. It looked like he might settle some of it on her as a wedding present.

Straightening things out over at Bremerton took me about two weeks. There had been a strike. The plumbers were raising hell. Labor leaders had to be paid off. All sorts of grisly details. I'd been writing Delphine every day but hadn't had a word from her. That had me worried, but not too worried because she never was a very good correspondent. So all the long flight back—it sure was a long flight with the old prop planes in those days—I kept myself happy planning out that new corporation. I guess it was when we stopped in Chicago that the stewardess came aboard with a mimeographed sheet: Atomic bombs had been dropped on Hiroshima and Nagasaki. So that was what the bombing crews had been so hush-hush about. The age of the mushroom cloud began that August day.

It gave me the creeps like everybody else. I didn't like it either when I didn't get any answer at Delphine's apartment but it didn't worry me too much. It wasn't until I got to the office next morning that I found a message: Please come to Room 794, New York Hospital. I called right away but couldn't get anybody but a nurse who said Miss Nathan was recovering nicely but wasn't allowed to speak on the phone. I rushed over there in a cab. Delphine was deadpale. Her eyes looked bigger and bluer than ever in her dead white face.

It took us a while to get that damn nosy nurse out of the room. Then she told me. She'd gone to some lousy quack for an abortion. An infection had set in. She'd nearly died. In the end they had had to remove her ovaries. Now she was recovering. "Don't hate me, Dan," she whispered. "I love you more than ever."

That shook me worse than anything that ever happened in my life. A voice kept saying in my head: "She killed my child." It was too late not to go ahead with the marriage now, and besides, most of me was still crazy about her but way down inside I never forgave her.

We were married at the Hotel Gotham ballroom on Fifth Avenue. They kinda combined the services. It all seemed unreal to me—like watching a scene in a play. Mom was a bit subdued by the rush of high society around the Admiral and the Nathans. Dad never said anything anyway. It got the biggest writeup of any wedding the *New York Times* covered that fall.

So much happened about that time it's hard to tell it straight. I resigned from Northern Millwork because Dad wouldn't raise the measly six thousand dollars he was paying me as Personnel Director. I figured it was demeaning for me to accept a sum like that. It would make damn poor publicity if it should get out. At the wedding reception, while everybody else was sopping up the champagne and caviar—I like to eat and drink as much as the next man, but I like business better—I was lining up support for the Delphic Supply Company. Naming it after Delphine went over big with her folks.

Mr. Nathan had a young man in his office taking care of the legal end so I figured we could take a month's honeymoon in Europe. Delphine and I had to have a little time alone together to straighten out our private lives. Instead of the Depression the pundits had all prophesied when the war ended, we seemed to be in for a mild boom, particularly in the building trades. Even so, Delphine and I both thought I ought to wait a little. I didn't want to make any move before I knew how the cat was going to jump.

They were still flying the old clippers from Miami to Lisbon. Great big old comfortable flying boats. We really enjoyed that flight. We stayed awhile in Estoril with the crowned heads in exile, then we moved on to the South of France. We took a villa out on the Cap d'Antibes for a month. France was just barely recovering. The Marshall plan wasn't on yet, but Monte Carlo had been going strong all through the war. I liked that casino: the lights, the chandeliers, the liveries, the worried faces of international VIP's. I hit a winning streak. I was thirty years old but I still looked about twenty, so before I knew what had happened I was the boy wonder of roulette. The people who run Monte Carlo really know publicity. They build up any story like that to attract the other suckers. My exploits got into the Paris *Herald Tribune* and were picked up by the New York press. Every story they printed had me a little younger.

The payoff came when some old coffeecolored Hindu potentate with a turban and an Oxford accent congratulated Delphine on being the mother of such a lucky gambler. That wasn't the kind of story we wanted to get started. We wanted to be boy and girl like Scott Fitzgerald and his wife. Delphine knew how to wear clothes, but I'd been buying her a lot of jewelry that made her look older. We went up to Paris to see if her dressmaker couldn't dress her a little younger. On that same trip we found out about adopting war orphans. Adopting war orphans was all the rage. We learned the procedure at the American consulate. Old Eastman the Kodak man was collecting all the orphans he could handle at a big house on the Riviera he called le Chateau des Enfants. We ended by adopting a little three-year-old boy and two-year-old girl. They came from the North of France somewhere. Their people were all dead. They both had blue eyes.

André and Jeanette were something I never regretted. I didn't regret buying that villa either. It was the place we'd been renting. The cost was so insignificant in dollars we just couldn't let it go. It took a team of French attorneys about a year to clear the title according to French law. That cost more than the property did. We'd no sooner bought the place than we had to go home. We made quite a show when we got off the *Ile de France* in New York with two French nurses and a French couple to man a nice new apartment we bought sight unseen on upper Fifth Avenue. The camera men came scampering. There was a guy I knew slightly covering arrivals for the *World-Telegram*. I gave him just a hint of this new enterprise, and gave him just enough about a plan I had in the back of my head to assemble a corporation that would handle every sort of supply for the building trades; of course, he got it wrong and said all out of one warehouse which couldn't have been possible, but it was enough to make some of the Wall Street boys prick up their ears.

Delphine and I lived together tolerably happily for about ten years. We were genuinely interested in bringing the kids up right and they turned out fine. They were the first ones I thought of when all this tragedy came up. How will it affect them? But I'm getting ahead of my story. I was being so damn successful in everything I did we couldn't help be happy. She taught me how to enjoy art and artists. Delphine dressed well, she entertained well. She even got so she could wear a lot of diamonds without getting that hard look. Everybody thought we were the most devoted and fortunate couple, but it got to be just an act. Underneath we were drifting apart. We were scared of being alone together. Wherever we were, we kept the house full of guests.

Meanwhile, Dad and I made up. He'd been really miffed when I left his firm, but I'd gotten things so wellorganized the outfit ran itself. You can do anything in the world on a rising market. When our sales at Delphic passed the quarter-million mark, I talked Dad into buying all Delphine's and my Delphic stock at par. I'd organized our company so that it would not be competitive with Northern Millwork. We handled swimming pools, patio materials, quarry tile, all sorts of items coming into demand as suburban families spread out into the affluent world of the Fifties. Dad saw the advantage right away. Dad was a mighty shrewd operator but he was hampered by his early training in running things on a shoe-string. After all, he'd built the business up from a little hardware store he and his two older brothers ran somewhere out in the Flatbush section of Brooklyn. But now he was beginning to under-stand my dream of putting together a building-supply business that would furnish every item the modern builder needed. Except cement. We weren't ready to take on the cement people, not those tough hombres. Not yet. And prefabrication. I wanted to be ready for it when it came. But Dad said it never would come. The unions would never allow it.

The romance had gone out of my life with Delphine, but I was still romantic about Acme Roofing and Flooring. It was a tightly held family corporation, the McGinnises, a bunch of clan-nish old North Carolina tarheels, but the stock was on the big board. Their position was vulnerable.

Five mortal years I worked on that deal. Entertaining was a great help. For elbowroom Delphine and I rented a big house on the shore near South Norwalk. We sure threw some parties. That was all we enjoyed doing together any more, throwing parties. Delphine specialized in getting in the classy element, the yachting set and folks like that. We already had as many art lovers as we could handle. We entertained them at the apartment in town. We'd come to admit that Dad's and Mom's friends in Montclair were just plain common. Delphine was great in corralling French counts and Englishwomen of title.

I worked on the Wall Street boys. I'd gotten really cozy with a lot of young guys in the big brokerage firms. Used to play poker with them in the club car going out to South Norwalk every evening. Then I'd ask them over to the house with their wives some night when we'd hired a big-name band to play by the swimming pool. I didn't try to get them to do anything for me until I had 'em eating out of my hand. Then I had them buying little blocks of Acme stock for me in their own names every time the market slipped a little. I had to be careful not to alarm those damn suspicious tarheels. Then in the spring of 1955 I was ready to show my face. I took advantage of a nationwide slackening of construction to ride a bear market for a few weeks. Selling short. With all my private operatives working for me, we managed to beat down Acme Roofing and Flooring about ten points. Then I started buying in my own name.

By that time I was running out of collateral. Dad had made me Executive Director of Northern Millwork and I got a good friend of mine, Hale Watkins, in as Treasurer. Hale just thought I was the boy wonder and could do no wrong. Hale wrote me out some pretty big checks to buy Acme stock—of course in the company's name. It was risky, but I knew that Acme was so damn sound its stock couldn't go any lower. With each rise we put a few thousand dollars back in the till. Dad never noticed a thing. Overextended in every direction. For ten days I was on pins and needles until things began to click. Acme stock got back its old bounce.

Then I called up Tim McGinnis and suggested we have a little conference. I and a number of friends held about forty percent of the stock. Anne's husband, Clyde Vansant, had bought in heavily on his own. I never saw a more frustrated man than Tim

McGinnis, but he and his brothers decided to be good sports and roll with the punch. We figured time wasn't ripe for a merger, but we sketched out ways our two companies could quietly cooperate without getting in wrong with the SEC or any other Federal watchdog. The last thing we wanted was to have the Attorney General of the United States on our necks.

Rumors of a merger lashed up the speculators. My operatives began buying on their own and that helped boost the stock. Those guys began to think I was the Second Coming. The happiest day of my life was when they invited Dad in to become Chairman of the Board of Acme Roofing and Flooring. Selden C. DeLong, sixtyseven years old, sitting up there as the boss of the works. That was when he learned what kind of a son he had. Even the McGinnises began to claim me for the boy wonder. Was I riding high?

Tape recorder seems to have stopped. Rewind for new reel. I guess that'll do for now. If you press that button that says erase, it's like death. I never thought of that before. The great eraser. I was mighty close to it the first few days down here in Rio. All I had to do was point that pistol and squeeze the trigger to erase the record and leave it blank.

IO

The Later Life and Deplorable Opinions of
Jay Pignatelli—iv
Export Democracy

Several months after Pearl Harbor, walking into his office one fine spring morning, Jay was greeted by his secretary with "Mr. Lawrence Raisen on the phone." Elsie Husek, who had been with him down at Maiden Lane, let a discreet note of triumph seep into her voice.

It was pleasant to hear Larry's drawl again. Jay had always been fond of the old thing. "I've just been promoted to Colonel in the Judge-Advocate Corps...." Jay burst out laughing. "Don't laugh, it's a serious business," Larry said severely. "I've got a commission for you if you can come right away.... Catch the first train."

Business hadn't been too good since Jay had set up his own shop. It didn't take him long to decide he'd better see what Larry had to offer. He called Lulie to explain he wouldn't be back till tomorrow, snatched up a briefcase full of papers to work on, and took a cab to the Pennsylvania Station.

He found Larry in one of the temporary buildings hastily thrown up along the Mall, a full chicken Colonel in an office packed with Captains and Majors in new uniforms with fresh-minted insignia.

"Bless you, Jay," said Larry, jumping to his feet with hand outstretched, "long time no see."

Jay was grinning broadly. "But, Larry, I thought you'd read me out of the party."

"This is a different ball game," said Larry with one of his birdlike glances that amounted to a wink. "Let's step across the street for a second. There's no privacy here."

Jay followed Larry down the corridor. He had trouble keeping his face straight as he watched the little man strut along ramrod stiff, birdbeak and beady eyes almost lost under the massive khaki headgear. He was solemnly saluting his way through a press of lesser officers.

Crossing Constitution Avenue, Larry took Jay's arm. "Why do you always laugh at me, Jay? You always did."

"Don't mind me, Larry. It's a nervous habit."

"How's your lovely Lulie?"

"Fine." For the moment Jay couldn't think of Larry's present wife's name. "How's your pretty little partner?"

"That's another story. . . . I shan't have time to explain. Dr. Tybalt has gone into the service." As they got into a cross street leading up to Pennsylvania Avenue, Larry relaxed a little. "This military courtesy gets me down."

As soon as they had slid into a table in a dark corner of O'Donnell's, Larry began to talk. "I'm supposed to help train these guys for service overseas. But, Jay, they don't know anything, not anything." Larry's voice rose to a squeak. "I bet we've got every unsuccessful attorney from every hick town between the Ohio River and the Rocky Mountains. The smart ones have good practices and manage to stay out. I don't see how these guys ever got through their bar exams. . . . Well, the other night I suddenly thought, 'Jay Pignatelli! Knows Europe like the palm of his hand.'" He began whispering eagerly. "I've got news for you. We'll be putting troops in Europe somewhere within a year. Top secret. I know you speak French. I bet you can speak a little wop."

"Damn little," said Jay.

"Jay, you know perfectly well I've always been on your side. I know it's been slim pickings since you've been on your own. . . .

When you come out of the service with a really brilliant record, you'll be ready to go into a good firm like Potter, Pierce and Perkins ... International law. Think big, man."

"Larry, I guess I ought to have appointed you my business manager years ago," said Jay.

"It isn't so funny," said Larry peevishly. "It's God's truth."

Jay went to a booth and called Lulie. She gave one of her little shrieks. "No no," but right away she was talking quietly and sensibly. "Modesto, you've got to do it. You can really be useful. ... I'll be the most miserable war widow you ever saw. ... Get back in time tomorrow night. We're going over to dinner with Annie and Ugo."

Jay filled out papers all afternoon. Next morning he stood in line two hours for a physical. Though Larry had only been a month in Washington, he'd learned the ropes. Jay had his commission all set except for the final swearing-in in time to catch the one o'clock back to New York. Thirty days to arrange his private affairs. During the five hours he sat reading the Articles of War and the printed manuals he had been handed in the various offices, he went through, in anticipation, all the pains of the separation from Lulie. Back at the apartment, he found Lulie herself briskly making plans to follow him wherever they sent him for training. "This is going to be fun," she said. "We'll see men and cities."

Halfway through a course in military justice at Fort Meade, Jay was transferred to a military government school in Kansas City. Lulie patiently endured a long hot summer there. One hot afternoon in August 1943 the whole Italian section was ordered into the war zone. Lulie and Jay had a last dinner together at the musty old Auerbach Hotel. Lulie cried a little but not much. She was too full of plans. "Modesto," she said, "instead of moping I'm going to make money for us while you're away. I think I've got *Redbook* convinced on a series of short shorts about the homefront from the woman's point of view. I'm planning for us to get rich after the war and maybe adopt a couple of war orphans. ... I don't seem to be able to produce the little varments, but I know I could raise them. ... Is it a deal?"

They shook hands mock-solemnly. Suddenly it was time to leave for the airfield. He kissed her desperately and, leaving her to settle the bill, dashed for a cab.

Getting into the European theatre proved a complicated business. Jay's group of Lieutenants and Captains kept being bounced off planeflights because they didn't have combat status. The Army flew them to Miami. There Naval Transport took over and wafted them by flying boat to Trinidad and Natal. In Natal they had a long wait. Most of the men almost died of boredom there, but Jay amused himself trying to learn Portuguese and writing Lulie long detailed letters about everything that wasn't military that came into his ken. At last there was space on a plane to Casablanca. From Casablanca they were flown to Algiers and then to Messina. In Messina they were stalled for weeks because Italy became a sort of semi-Ally after the armistice was signed with Badoglio. Finally Jay and two Lieutenants were assigned to Catania.

Catania was too much like the slummier sections of Brooklyn to be interesting. The military government office was swamped by Sicilians who'd spent half their lives in the States. Each one of them had some private racket to exploit. Trying to outwit the Sicilians and keeping warm kept Jay busy that winter. He had to admit he wasn't making much headway in either direction. It was a great relief when the military government team was pulled out of Sicily.

After cooling their heels for some weeks in Palermo, they were placed on a homewardbound Army transport that put them ashore at Southampton. A short jeep-ride took them to an American Army camp where military government officers were being briefed under top-security wrappings for service in Germany. Security was so tight that none of them was allowed to leave the special compound in the camp where they messed and slept and attended classes.

They heard rumors of buzzbombs but no more than rumors until a couple of them came into camp one fine afternoon. By a stroke of luck, the military government detachment had been ordered out to the airfield to emplane for Brussels. As it happened, they didn't emplane that day or the next. People kept turning up from the camp to tell them what a close call they'd had. The officers' mess was splintered to matchwood.

Brussels was British. British mess, British officers' clubs, British beer, British weather. They had hardly settled down to the routine of waiting for transportation before von Rundstedt's counterattack threatened all of Belgium. The Battle of the Bulge. The Americans had an uneasy feeling the British were getting ready to pull out.

At a Christmas party at the officers' club, Jay found himself spinning around the room until he was dizzy, breaking up arguments between Americans and Britishers as to whose fault it was that the Germans had broken through. He kept setting people up to drinks and making them vow eternal friendship. Jay never knew how he did it, but he kept the peace. When the steward assembled his chits the next day, it took every cent he had in his pockets to clear the score.

By New Year's the krauts were on the run again. That party was much pleasanter. A nice oldfashioned redfaced Colonel Blimp took it upon himself to set up the American officers, who hadn't had any pay for three months, to all the drinks they could stand. With the slow chilly drizzly sleety coming of spring, the news improved day by day.

It was June and fine weather before Captain Pignatelli found himself third-in-command of military government at Heidelberg on the lovely Neckar River. Heidelberg was almost undamaged. It was like suddenly being plunked down into a Grimm's fairytale among Gothic towers and ancient university buildings.

The military government officials met every morning at a huge doughnutshaped table of some light wood, situated in one of the great halls of the *Schloss* way up on the hill. What they thought at first were stone carvings over the enormous mantel turned out to be faked out of painted plaster, but the antlers and roebuck skulls that lined the walls were genuine enough, and the view through the ogival windows equipped with ersatz stained glass was magnificent; the town, the river, all lights and shadows like a steel engraving.

These meetings were a daily strain. Colonel Markham, a sallow regular Army man who had spent most of his life in the Philippines, appeared the first morning, followed by a Staff Sergeant carrying a sign he'd had lettered to set up over the mantelpiece: Don't Coddle the Germans.

Colonel Markham solved every question by reading out of the general orders. If GHQ hadn't foreseen a problem, it didn't exist. His second-in-command was a Pittsburgh politician and more easygoing. Major McGuire tended to look on the local krauts as potential voters. He suspected some of them might have relatives back home. He was against offending German sensibilities except in one direction. He was collecting all the Meissen and Dresden china and

Bohemian glass he could liberate. It was a big day for him when he'd assembled enough loot to fill a packing case to be shipped home through the PX.

Jay and the four Lieutenants, with the help of noncoms and enlisted men, did all the work. Jones and Harris, the youngest officers, had it easy with public health and public order. Siniatski, a Chicago Pole, who had been superintendent of a meat-packing plant, had food and rationing. He did his best to be fair in spite of his Polish hatred of everything German. People were close to starving. The orders were to see that everybody got eleven hundred calories a day and to prohibit the brewing of beer. Beer was the headache. The krauts would rather drink beer than eat. The farmers, denied beer, started drinking their milk instead of sending it into town. Housing was in the hands of a skinny little guy named Upman, who'd been a nightclerk in a Detroit hotel. He had to deal with a constant stream of exhausted and penniless refugees coming in from the Russian zone.

Jay decided it was the krauts that saved military government from being a complete fiasco. The krauts were so lawabiding that they did their best to carry out every regulation, no matter how silly, the Americans made.

The Colonel saddled Jay with denazification. Denazification was thorny. Every German was supposed to make out a questionnaire known as the fragebogen. There were stiff jail penalties for lying on your fragebogen. If it turned out from your fragebogen that you'd been a member of the Nazi Party, you couldn't exercise any trade or profession. All you could do was pick and shovel work. If you were a plumber, you couldn't employ an assistant or apprentice. If you were a baker, you had to bake your own bread.

The regulations were impossible to enforce. Jay's office was encumbered with informers, turning people in from the meanest of motives. Jay dealt with them through Corporal Schultz, a stocky little towheaded fellow with an honest wooden face from Milwaukee. Schultz spoke German. Jay didn't trust the frowsty White Russian woman with noseglasses whom the Colonel hired as official interpreter.

In fact, he couldn't trust anybody. Sometimes he suspected that even Schultz was getting a rakeoff from shifty characters who were operating on the black market.

It was a relief when the first amnesty regulations came through. Jay had already been trying to stretch a few definitions to get the university operating normally again. Heidelberg had certainly been a center of the old Prussiantype military spirit, but was that the same as Nazism? He claimed not. He used to argue with the Colonel about it over drinks in the evening. Colonel Markham was an admirer of Bismarck. Jay finally got him to agree that driving them crazy with fragebogen was more likely to stir up fresh hatreds than to steer the krauts towards a democratic way of life. "Two wrongs don't make a right" was becoming a watchword among the Americans.

One day in late summer a group of lawyers turned up on a sightseeing tour. They were on their way to join the American section of the International Tribunal getting ready to try the war criminals at Nuremberg. Military government put them up in the *Schloss* and set them up to a big spread of brooktrout and venison, washed down by four different kinds of wine served out of magnificent cut crystal goblets.

Jay sat next to a Boston attorney named T. Townsend Marquand. Right away they discovered they had been in the same year at lawschool, though they couldn't remember whether they had known each other or not. Marquand let on that his nickname was Ted. He had a cold kind of good looks. He appeared years younger than he was. For some reason they hit it off. Jay began to think of him as "the frozen undergraduate." Even when they were friendliest, Jay had a feeling he was being held at arm's length.

They hit it off somehow because neither of them had anybody else to talk to. They swapped war experiences and talked about books and odd predicaments in the courts. By some accident Jay let it out that he had made a study of Spanish criminal law. After Ted had asked him a couple of questions, he exclaimed that he was going to need Jay as a consultant. "No, seriously, if you don't mind losing your place on the repatriation orders, I can get Justice Jackson to ask for your transfer. He always gets what he asks for."

"Good enough," said Jay. His one thought in the world was to get out of denazification. By some miracle the order to report for detached service to the International Tribunal in Nuremberg came through in two weeks.

Nuremberg gave him the creeps, but it was interesting. The

old fairytale city of toymakers and Meistersingers was a total ruin, but the industrial sections down on the plain hadn't taken too much of a beating. An idiotic modern *Schloss* that belonged to the Eberhard Faber pencil people and looked as if it was carved out of soap seemed to have been carefully spared.

Jay had barely time to peek into the Bavarian Palace of Justice. It was in a hubbub of renovation by POW's on stepladders with buckets of cold water paint and battalions of neat German scrubwomen in knitted stockings rammed into big boots who were swabbing up the marble floors. As soon as he reported in, Ted put him to work on the indictment.

Jay knew most of the story already but seeing it all set out on carefully typed pages gave him a feeling of physical revulsion very close to nausea. Robert Jackson's phrase "turned the stomach of the world" couldn't have expressed it better. By the time the trial opened, Jay was so saturated with the material he couldn't bear to listen. He tried to watch the show spread out before him as if it were a stageplay.

The courtroom had been freshly hung with sagegreen curtains. Crimson damask armchairs had been brought in for the judges. Floodlights filled every corner of the room with diffused brilliance. There were English judges in wigs, French judges and German attorneys in all sorts of odd apparel, robotlike Russians in uniform.

The Americans were stagemanaging the show and were doing it well. The earphones worked to perfection. You could tune in on any of the four languages with the click of a switch. A row of American MP's in dazzling white helmet liners and white gauntlets stood at attention behind the prisoners' box. Their pink youthful faces, for all the world like a highschool basketball team being photographed before a game, contrasted weirdly with the creased and crumpled faces trampled by adversity of the "twenty broken men" on trial for their lives.

Jay found the daylong reading of the indictments a special sort of torture. He knew too much already. Wasn't there something innately evil in the repetition of these horrors? When Robert Jackson opened the case for the prosecution, next day, almost everybody breathed easier. Jackson's voice was the voice of reason in a madhouse. His speech opening the case for the prosecution was the highpoint in American prestige.

It wasn't until Jay got onto his cot to try to sleep that night that he began to match the Nazi crimes with the crimes of the Allies: the thousand-plane raid on Dresden when that virtually unarmed city was stuffed with refugees, the partition of Poland, the refusal to help the Finns, the abandonment of the Baltic republics to Stalin's murder squads, the ousting of the East Germans from their homes. "You will say I have robbed you of your sleep." "Indeed you have, Justice Jackson." Jay found himself sitting bolt-upright on the hard cot. *"Nicht schuldig.* No sir, it's not my fault." Nobody had consulted him. Still he couldn't sleep.

This was the first time in his life he'd suffered from insomnia. He wrestled with it so long as he stayed in Nuremberg. It proved harder to get out of the International Tribunal than to get into it in the first place. After the convictions, nobody wanted to stay. Ted Marquand had long since resigned and gone home.

At last Jay decided he needed sleeping pills. Next door to the Medical Corps clinic he noticed a sign fastened with adhesive tape on the inside of a groundglass door. It read Major H. Tybalt—Enter Without Knocking. There was a waiting room and a nurse at a desk. Beyond another open door, Jay caught sight of Dr. Tybalt's red face. He was in uniform. In front of him, on an intricate Louis XV desk liberated out of some poor kraut's drawing room, stood a particularly large stiffvisored khaki cap well garnished with scrambled eggs.

"Major Tybalt, may I come in?"

Tybalt jumped to his feet and greeted Jay effusively. "It can't be you're coming for advice." They both began to laugh. Jay said no, all he needed was sleeping pills, something harmless, please.

"Getting on your nerves, is it?" Tybalt asked eagerly.

"Isn't it getting on yours?"

Tybalt was rubbing his hands. "I've been much too busy. That's why you haven't run into me anywhere. I've hardly gotten out of this office since I arrived. And then I've had to attend all the sessions of the court. I'm under contract with a New York publisher to do a book entitled *A Psychoanalyst Looks at Nuremberg.* This has been the most interesting experience of my life. Seventeen of the prisoners are fascinating studies in abnormal psychology and the employees of the Tribunal are a Kundry's garden of international psychoses."

"What do you hear from Larry?"

"Nothing good. He's back at his office . . . unfortunately my enlisting interrupted Nora's psychoanalysis. An interrupted psychoanalysis can be a very dangerous thing . . . my assistant is completely helpless with her . . . I've suffered from guilt feelings about it. I shouldn't. The war for civilization had the first priority."

"Civilization," sneered Jay, "how much have we saved?"

"Jay, speaking as a friend and not as a physician, you strike me as being under severe hypertension."

"Do you think I'd rate a medical discharge?"

"Could be. . . . I've been sending everybody home I could. No use having them hanging around in Germany until they collapse and take up hospital space. . . . You just tell me what the trouble is. This won't be psychoanalysis. There's no time for that. First let me remind you that you'll be getting the services of one of America's leading psychoanalysts free, gratis, for nothing. . . . Oh, for an hour's free association out of your subconscious."

Jay started to giggle.

"Laughter is a defense mechanism," said Dr. Tybalt severely. "I'm sure you know that."

"I just thought of an old proverb," muttered Jay. " 'Never say to the fountain I shall not drink of your waters.' "

He let himself drop resignedly into the chair across from Dr. Tybalt's at his desk.

Jay's transportation orders home were made out through Paris. All the planes out of Le Bourget were packed solid with the big brass. The Nats man suggested he take the train to Havre and try to get aboard a baby flattop due to sail in a couple of days. The *Trenton* was horribly crowded but he argued his way up the gangplank. Every crack between decks was filled with tiers of bunks. The only difference between officers' country and the enlisted men's quarters was a scattering of chairs. The trouble with the chairs was that there was always somebody in them.

It was a rough crossing. They bucked a northwest wind all the way. Jay was asleep in his bunk most of the crossing. Since leaving Nuremberg, though he didn't take a single one of the sleeping pills Dr. Tybalt prescribed for him, Jay could hardly keep awake. When he did wake, he lay listening to the bull-sessions below.

A dark young man from Michigan kept complaining of the looting of German homes, the laxity of GHQ in plugging leaks in supply lines. Why didn't they crack down on the plundering of military gasoline? At this point a squarebuilt Major who looked like a professional football player would come charging out of his corner: "Lust, liquor and loot are the soldier's pay."

They reached New York in a snowstorm. Slipping and sliding through the slush on the dock, Jay managed, after a scramble, to get his duffle and footlocker into a cab. The stairs at the Stuyvesant Square apartment had a homey smell. No answer to a knock. His heart fell into his boots. Sick? Dead? Gone away? He still had his key. He walked all around the four big rooms. Everything neat and quiet, a pot of chrysanthemums beside a book and her reading glasses on the living-room table. Everywhere an aroma of Lulie, as if she were in the next room. She couldn't be far.

He was asleep in the big chair when she came in. The first thing he saw was her eyes full of green sparkle when she came in. "Modesto!" He jumped up and kissed her all over her face. Her cheeks were cold and rosy from the snowy wind outside. She held him at arms' length and looked him over carefully.

"Do you know how long it's been since we had dinner at the musty old Auerbach?"

"Dinner wasn't musty, I haven't had such a good meal since."

"I bet you didn't keep count. Well, it's two years, three months, thirteen days and ten and a half hours."

They were so full of things to tell each other that for a while they could hardly say a word. Lulie, pleased as a little girl showing a good report card from school, ran to her desk to get her passbook from the savings and loan association.... "Look ... five thousand, four hundred and twentythree dollars. And the Army allowance is untouched in our joint account in the Chase National. Didn't I tell you I'd keep busy and make some money.... But Jay, how did you get back so soon? You wrote it would be months."

"Dr. Tybalt," he said trying not to crack a smile. She let out a shriek. "Tybalt turned out to be a kingpin of the Medical Department of the International Tribunal . . . not such a bad fellow according to his lights. He got me invalided home. 'Nuremberg shock.' He made up a lot of rubbish, but when you're looking for a travel order home you don't ask questions. . . ."

Jay went into the bedroom, took off his uniform and his puttees and his Army boots and got into a blue flannel shirt and a pair of gray slacks.

"Now I really believe I'm out of this man's Army. . . . It's an experience I wouldn't have missed for anything on earth but thank God it's over."

Lulie ran into the kitchen to look at the clock.

"It's four o'clock. Suppose I make us some tea."

"We can have a spot of bourbon with our tea."

She put some buttered bread sprinkled with cinnamon to toast in the gas oven. The smell was unbelievably delicious. Jay followed her around like a poodle while she collected the tea things.

He was saying that he'd done a lot of thinking on the trip back; that is, when he wasn't asleep. The Army was coming back disgusted, at least the most intelligent fellows were. Our Generals did a pretty good job but our statesmen loused it up. We need to put down what we did wrong and what we did right before everybody forgets about it.

"You mean a new magazine on foreign affairs. . . . Oh Modesto, let's do it. We need to have a great big fling after all this absenteeism."

"Do you suppose Annie would finance us?"

"But Modesto, what about the law? You wrote me you were going into international law and make a million dollars."

Jay admitted that he had had a tentative offer from a Boston firm.

"We've got to find a proper editor," insisted Lulie. "Your place is on the Board of Directors. Ugo will be good on foreign affairs."

Jay fetched a long yellow pad from Lulie's desk in the bedroom and started writing.

Mistakes in strategy: 1. Inability to use our power while we had the monopoly of the atomic bomb. This was one time unique in history when a supreme power could be used to a good purpose. 2. Allowing the Russians to capture the three key strongpoints in

Central Europe: Berlin, Prague, Vienna. 3. It was idiotic to give the Soviets three votes to our one in the United Nations.

"These are things that are plain as the nose on your face," he almost shouted at Lulie. "All you have to do is look at a map. . . . Then there was Eisenhower's brutal policy of turning the fugitives from Vlassov's army over to Stalin. Pershing would never have allowed it. Compared with our troops in World War I, there's a lack of moral fiber about our troops in the European theatre. These things come right down from the Commander-in-Chief."

Lulie poured them each another cup of tea. Jay added a little bourbon.

"It was the knowledge of the crimes and follies of the American command," Jay went on in a more matter-of-fact voice, "that robbed me of my sleep, in Justice Jackson's famous phrase."

"But Modesto, the Russians did destroy Hitler's armies."

"With the help of General Winter and American supplies. F. D. R. wasn't himself since he fell under the old murderer's spell at Teheran. Yalta was sheer treason. All Truman could think of at Potsdam was to play 'The Missouri Waltz.' . . . The Russian people mustn't be allowed to forget how hideously they were betrayed by their leadership. Stalin mustn't be allowed to forget that without him this pretty little war might never have started."

Lulie yawned: "I swear I'd forgotten the Hitler-Stalin pact."

"If you've forgotten, think of the ordinary newspaper reader. . . . Don't you remember Stalin's charming little arrangement with Hitler for the partition of Poland?"

"People sure do forget," admitted Lulie.

"That's why we've got to have some kind of periodical that presents the plain facts in simple black letters. . . ."

"Suppose we call up Annie right now." Lulie was catching fire again. "She and Ugo and the Sylvester children are down at Naples. I've got her phone number." She jumped to her feet.

Annie was on the phone. "Come right on down," she said. She had a nice quiet guest cottage waiting for them right on the beach. They both said yes almost with one voice . . . as soon as Jay had completed the little formality of getting out of the service.

When they hung up, they fell into each others' arms. What they needed was a trip, any old trip. . . . It was so long since they had had a trip together.

There were still things to do in the dank end-of-winter cold in New York. Arranging his discharge through an office way downtown proved no problem. There were a few frazzled strands of his old law business he needed to piece together. Their Plymouth roadster, which had been new in 1942, had to be rescued from storage and reconditioned. It was almost the middle of March before they got started.

Crossing New Jersey was grim: trucks, trafficlights, filthy thawing snow in the ditches. At least rationing had been repealed so they didn't need to worry about gas. At the Delaware River, they had a glimpse of late afternoon sunlight. They spent the night in Newcastle and walked around the lovely little old town in a lashing wind, looking with delight at the old fire station and the beautiful brickwork of the houses. Next day they reached Cape Charles in time to eat crab Norfolk for lunch, looking out from the dining saloon of the ferry on a boisterous gray chop between the Virginia Capes. That next night they spent in a tourist home in Wilmington, North Carolina. There were camellias in bloom, daffodils everywhere, mockingbirds were singing. They had reached the spring.

Next morning they drove on south down Route 17. The day was so warm they could drive with the top down. The air was full of the tang of long leaf pines with an occasional briny puff off the Atlantic beaches. They'd never been happier. Their poor deprived carcasses fitted into each other so aptly in the sagging rattly beds of the tourist homes. They felt closer than even in the first days in that little house in Maine they remembered with such happiness.

Charleston was next. White porticos hung with wisteria, azaleas, every kind of flowering tree, pretty little alleys between hedges and brick walls in the gloaming, massive churches, the ancient exchange, business buildings that still had an air of cosmopolitan grandeur of the early eighteen hundreds. After a remarkably good dinner in a restaurant back of a tobacco shop their landlady told them about, they called up Annie to tell her what a good time they were having.

Annie seemed a little miffed that they were taking so long getting down to Florida. Jay promised rashly that in two days they would be knocking at her door. Annie said she'd do her best to hold on to Ugo. He was getting restless because he had articles to write in New York and she wanted him in on the plans for Jay's journal.

Late the next afternoon, they were crossing the flatlands of the Georgia coast. They had left Brunswick behind where Lulie looked longingly at an old hotel with cast-iron balconies where they had stopped pleasantly before. Jay insisted that they must try to push on to Jacksonville. Intermittently, the setting sun spread a red dazzle through the roadside trees. Just at sunset the road took a sudden turn into the west.

"Sure you don't want me to drive?" asked Lulie.

"I'm not a bit sleepy."

Lulie curled up for one of her little catnaps on the seat beside him.

The huge round sun was right at the end of the road. Fiery light poured into Jay's eyes. There was a crash, sudden blackness. Jay never knew exactly what happened. The first thing he was conscious of was of the horn's unending shriek from the crumpled hood. Broken glass. Her skull crushed like an eggshell, Lulie lay dead on the seat beside him.

It was almost dark. Headlights of cars. It wasn't until two state policemen lifted him out of the wreckage that he noticed how much he was bleeding. He could still see. Right ahead in the glare of a headlight was the tailgate of a truck he'd run into. The truck was parked at an angle with its open tailgate sticking out into the road. What did it matter? With Lulie dead nothing in the world mattered. Maybe he would die, too.

Light glinted off the white enameled paint of an ambulance. Men in white jackets were helping him onto a stretcher. He blacked out again.

I I

A Family Tragedy

The breeze drops with the sun. There's a hush. Standing with your legs apart to cast from one of the rock ribs of the island's shore, your feet tread the grooves the ice left in the granite. This time of day the colors run. Greens from emerald to olivebrown seep out from under the clustered spires of sprucewoods into the lake's sheen. The open reaches are still blue from the sky, and rosy buff and white from clouds reflected. As your lure comes twinkling towards you through the dark clear water, the ripples catch a hundred hues.

The air is steeped in redolence of spruce and fir and the mossy loam smells of untrodden woods. There's silence now. Not an outboard, not a plane. In the hush you feel the quiet of ten thousand silent years since the last glacier melted back into the Arctic north and left this immensity of pools and watercourses for the forest to take over. Silence. Except for the lapping of tiny waves and the sudden idiot titter of a loon. It's startling at first. The lake is full of loons.

It was Jim Knox who taught us to feel at home with the loons. Jim came from up north in the Canadian plains, but he'd lived on this lake from a boy. Summers he guided and took out fishing parties. Winters he went in the woods for the lumbering. The lake

223

was his life. His pleasure in it was catching. He had a special feeling for the loons on the lake.

He told us how they'd come back soon after the ice broke up and lay their eggs and raise their brood. Both birds look after the young loonlets. Their enemy is the big pike, walleyes, northerns, that will come up from under and swallow a baby loon or a duckling at one gulp. When the brood is grown, Jim says for the rest of the summer the loons just play. They'll dive and sport and swim in circles; sometimes it's like a kind of tag. Maybe that laugh really is when something strikes them funny. At night the loon makes a different sound. That sound at night we thought was owls was a loon crying. "They'll cry all night, night after night, if they've lost a wee one."

That was why he was such an excellent guide. Jim Knox loved fishing. He remembered every fish he ever caught, how the water looked, what time of day it was, what the weather was like. He knew where the northerns lay in the deeps under the steep rocks and how to steer the skiff round the fringes of the weeds to lure the big bass out to strike without tangling up the tackle. He'd grin all over when he scooped one up with the net. If he didn't find them in one spot, he would find them in another.

He was a good cook. Men who live a lot in the wilds have to know housekeeping. He liked to eat well. He described dishes he had at home. He and his wife both loved wild rice. He was a domestic sort of man in a backwoods way.

Fish are so plentiful in these lakes, nobody thinks of cleaning them or scaling them the way we do at home. Jim would just cut a big fillet off each side with a sharp knife and throw the skeleton away. He liked to fry the fish in lard in a cast-iron skillet. He dipped the fillets in batter and cornflake crumbs and fried them a delicate brown. He laughed about the iron skillet. His wife had never seen an iron skillet before they were married. She came from away, from a place way south of here. Everything had been strange to her in this northwoods country. He guessed she'd get used to it in time.

Some of the best fishing was near a lumber camp where there was a sawmill in the woods. Jim and the man who ran the sawmill had married sisters. Jim often worked for him in the woods in winter. Jim had built himself a cabin there. When we went ashore,

Jim showed us a long trailerlike job, neatly carpentered. He was proud of his cabin. He pointed out how tight it was against the weather.

It was built that way so that you could move it on skids through the snow. All you needed to do was tow it with a pickup truck. Even the mess shack could be moved that way. This fall Jim's brother-in-law was planning to shift the whole camp up into a fresh stand of timber. But Jim said what he thought he'd do with his cabin when the ice was firm was haul it down the lake into town. Twenty miles, what's that? Winter was when transportation was really easy on the lake. Why, you could almost tow it with a snow toboggan.

He showed us his snow toboggan propelled by small caterpillar treads. Hardly burned any more gas than a motorcycle, he said. In winter you could go anywhere on a snow toboggan. Winter on this lake was the big time for commercial fishing with nets under the ice. People who'd never lived in the northwoods couldn't guess how fine it was on the lake in winter.

Jim talked quite a lot about how he was going to move his cabin into town and weatherboard it for more insulation and join it onto his house. His wife said she felt cramped there. He showed even white teeth in a grin. Maybe one of these days they'd need more room for a family.

The last afternoon we had terrific fishing trolling around the rocky point of an island. The rocks were white with the droppings of the gulls.

The lake abounded in gulls and terns, and on one outcropping we'd passed a row of gaunt black cormorants, with their wings stretched out in the sun. "Enough to scare you," Jim said. "Look like something prehistoric, don't they?"

Those northerns rose to the bait at a certain spot on every turn. We'd run out of minnows and were fishing with lures. We hauled in a beautiful smallmouthed bass. We always threw back the pretty little yellow perch. It got so that we had to throw the big northerns back, too, because we already had more than we could eat for supper.

Jim was in high spirits. Every time we passed a small reedy inlet we caught a glimpse of a mallard duck with a flock of ducklings. He kept pointing out how she'd swim out from the shore each time the boat passed to hustle her ducklings back behind the reeds. He was delighted with the way that mallard cared for her ducklings. "Now ain't she the careful mother?"

The last time we saw Jim he went into town before supper in the skiff we used for trolling. We'd beached the houseboat cozily in a cove of the big bay that skirted the Indian reservation, not too far from the railroad bridge. He took along the frozen chickens we never got to eat because we caught so much fish. They'd make supper for him and his wife. He grinned happily when he said it. He was going to bring us some lures and leaders and a bucket of minnows. He'd be back early for a last day's fishing.

In the morning we swam at sunup. Practiced casting but there were no fish in the cove. We couldn't imagine what had become of Jim Knox. We roamed in the rocky woods where we thought we found some trace of the passing of a bear. Still no sign of Jim. At last, when the sun was already high, the skiff came shooting out of the sun's sheen on the lake. Instead of Jim's rosy Scottish face, there was a dark face above the outboard.

He was Fergus, he said quietly as he tied the boat alongside. He said his last name, an Indian name, but he said it so low we couldn't catch it. He'd come instead. When we asked what had happened to Jim, he looked grave but all he would say was "A family tragedy."

Fergus was probably around twenty, but the grave air seemed habitual. He may have had a little white blood, but he looked like a fullblooded Indian, not the sort of man you pestered with questions. That didn't mean he wasn't friendly. He was just not talkative. The few English words he used were wellchosen and carefully pronounced. We guessed he must at least have finished highschool. Something about him made us think he read books.

Fergus was knowledgeable about many things. He confirmed our hunch that some birds we'd been trying to imagine were half-grown loons, were really grebes. He knew the European cormorant.

As soon as Fergus started the houseboat's big outboard, he noticed it was skipping. Happily he began to take it apart. You could see he loved to tinker with motors. When he decided to take the skiff out for some trolling, his heart wasn't in it. He kept getting us tangled in the weeds. Fishing didn't seem to be Fergus's strong-point.

A Family Tragedy

When the time came to give up the houseboat back at the float on the edge of town, the Finn who handled the rentals produced an envelope with the money we'd given Jim Knox to buy the minnows.

"What happened?"

"The poor guy." The Finn was so shaken-up he could hardly talk. "The poor guy," he kept saying. "He comes home last night and finds his house door locked. Both doors locked. He breaks a window and goes in and finds his wife lying on the bed with her wrists slashed. The blood was already dry on the floor and the bedclothes. She did it herself. She'd been dead for three days."

12

The Later Life and Deplorable Opinions of Jay Pignatelli—v

Appointment at an Embassy

Waking in a great ache from the stitches they had put in his head, first thing he asked for Lulie. He had hardly said the name before the knowledge that she was dead poured through him. When a nurse came to look at him, he asked where he was.

"You mustn't talk," said the nurse peevishly. She was a plain-looking woman with scrunched-up hair and long horse teeth, but she did vouchsafe the information that he was in the Chester B. Means Clinic in Waycross, Georgia.

"Please make a phonecall," Jay pleaded, "to Mrs. Anne Sylvester in Naples, Florida. You'll find money in my wallet. Tell her what happened."

The nurse's only answer was to pick up his bare arm, dab it with alcohol and inject something into it. He drifted off into that comatose sleep again. Even in his sleep he felt pain. The pain in his head was trifling, but the lack of Lulie filled the whole world with an agony that seared every green thing.

When he came to again, he played with the thought that it was he who was dead. He could hear her laugh, see the green glint of her eyes, feel the sweet aroma of her hair. Presently she would come and stand by his bier. How comfortable it would be to be dead.

Annie and Ugo turned up next day. They couldn't have been kinder. Lulie's brothers appeared late that afternoon to take the body back to Missouri for burial with the other Harringtons in the family plot. They seemed like wraiths out of nowhere. Jay felt dimly that they blamed him for their sister's death.

Jay lay as if dead. He took no part in anything. The day of the funeral, Annie brought Jay an Episcopal prayerbook so that he could follow the service while it was going on. She sat beside him crying wordlessly. Annie's quiet crying gave him a dim feeling of relief. Perhaps after years some of this pain could be wept away in tears.

Ugo, usually so egotistical, behaved like an angel. Ugo and Annie stayed on and on in a dreary motel. Ugo did allow himself to complain of the food in Georgia, "Grits, what a disgusting!" But he said he was reading the Book of Mormon; that made his stay interesting. He'd read the Koran and he'd always intended to read the Book of Mormon. The motel was run by Mormons and there was a book in each room. Ugo brought one to Jay "for light reading," he said with a wink.

As soon as Jay could be moved, they chartered an ambulance to take him down to Naples. Annie had a quiet airy house with a view out across the beach to the blue gulf. There was a patio with a fountain that let out a little sound of trickling water.

As his physical health improved, bereavement grew more painful. All the smells and sights and sounds he enjoyed so turned into agony, like an exposed nerve in a tooth. There was no Lulie to enjoy them with him. But he couldn't think of her as dead. It was he who wasn't alive. He was a hoax, a jumbie filled with aching death.

Annie had a pleasant young physician, Dr. Ayres, who took X-rays and all the neurological tests his office was equipped for. He religiously sent them to a brain surgeon he knew in Baltimore. The answers confirmed his diagnosis, no brain damage. Procedure: rest, no worries or frustrations.

Jay burst out laughing when Dr. Ayres read him the letter.

"No worries or frustrations, that would make a horse laugh," he wheezed. Laughing made his head ache. Dr. Ayres stood looking at him with amazement. "You are going to make it, Mr. Pignatelli. Anybody who can laugh at his own misery."

It was restful at Annie Sylvester's house. She and Ugo were so selfindulgent with their daiquiris at noon and their cheese soufflés and their hot hors d'oeuvres in the evening and the pasta, pasta at every meal. Once Ella caught on, she was crazy about cooking pasta. They were both overweight already. In Jay's strange state when he never wanted to eat anything himself, he found something cozy about sitting in on their cheerful gluttony.

Annie was still a very pretty woman. She had a young girl's complexion and fine dark eyes and brows even if her figure was somewhat out of shape. A sort of naïve kindness just oozed out of her.

One day she came into Jay's room with an air of having made up her mind about something. She didn't seem to know just how to go about saying what she wanted to say. Then she puckered her fine brows and blurted it out. Ugo's wife and four children, three boys and a girl, sixteen, fourteen, twelve and eight—she counted them off on her fingers—had arrived from Italy. The wife was threatening to bring suit for alienation of affections.

"What does Ugo say?"

Annie groaned. "Ugo's sensitive about the whole thing."

"What does Joe Hilton say?"

"He wants me to settle.... You know Joe Hilton.... Embarrassment for my children and all that.... I don't think the children care.... They rather like having an immoral mother."

"Suppose I call up Joe Hilton."

"No. Dr. Ayres doesn't want you making phonecalls yet.... If I'd known about Signora Salvatore," added Annie pleasantly, "things might have been different.... But you mustn't blame Ugo, he's an old dear."

The Salvatore family wasn't Annie's only source of worry. Her children were reaching the age to misbehave. Amanda was seventeen and quite pretty, but she couldn't seem to get ahead in school. She was crazy about boys. Annie lived in constant terror for fear some young upstart would get her with child and marry her for her money. George and Bill, fifteen and thirteen, were getting mean and contrary. They went to different prepschools, but each of them was on probation. Each headmaster wrote her wishing the family every happiness but reporting that if young Sylvester's deportment didn't improve during the spring term, he would have to ask her to withdraw her son from school.

"Jay," she said one day, "I'm telling you all this because sometimes other people's troubles make you forget your own. . . . People act as if being poor were the only problem . . . too much money has its miseries, too."

When their spring vacation ended, the children went back to their various schools. Jay had hardly seen them. None of them had been home much, but he had felt the strain on Annie. A fresh feeling of calm went through the house. Jay began to be up and about and even took a few cautious swims off the beach. He still had to take long midday naps. Whenever he spoke of going up to New York to attend to his affairs, Annie would beg him to wait a couple more days. She was getting Ed Manchester down. There was the new project to talk over.

When Ed Manchester did appear, it turned out that the new project, instead of being Jay's magazine, was a "committee" Annie was financing and Ed was managing, to find homes for Spanish Republican refugees. They put their heads together about it as soon as Ed arrived. The Party was taking care of its own, but the anti-Communist refugees were in a bad way. The Basques were being more or less absorbed by wellheeled Basque colonies all over the world, but the rest of them were getting no help from anybody. There was a possibility that the present Ecuadorian government would allow some of them to resettle there. Somebody had to go down there to negotiate an agreement.

Ed brought several letters written in green ink out of his inside pocket. They were from a certain Rafael Dominguez who represented the Spanish committee in Quito. . . . "We've got funds, thanks to the dear lady here, and other contributors, to bring over a hundred families, most of them from France. . . . It's a drop in the bucket, but it's something. Now, Jay, you see if I've got the Spanish right. The Ecuadorian government will furnish land, not too far from a road, materials for building a house and digging a well if the settler will guarantee to clear a hectare and cultivate it for two years. After that he can either start taking title to it through a series of payments or turn it back to the government."

"Jay," interrupted Annie while Jay was deep in Dominguez's letters, "we thought of this as a sort of convalescent trip."

"So that's your scheme," said Jay laughing.

"There just isn't anybody else we could send," said Ed.

"And I think it will be fun," added Annie.

"I'd decided to swear off this sort of thing."

"But, Jay, nobody else knows Spanish."

"Just give me a week to tie up loose ends."

"Take as long as you want," said Ed and Annie almost in unison.

"I keep forgetting," said Jay. "There's nobody to tie up loose ends for." That last part he didn't say aloud, but they knew what he meant.

The morning he was to drive to Fort Myers to take the plane, he came down to breakfast to find Annie and Ugo having a regular spat. Their faces were both red.

"No, Annie, I will not have your lawyers pestering Maria. I am her husband. She will do what I say."

"But, Ugo . . ."

"I will tell her she cannot interfere with a beautiful platonic friendship. . . . I will make her write you a letter of thanks for assisting her husband when he was a penniless refugee."

"But, Ugo, wouldn't it be better . . ."

Ugo turned to Jay who was leaning on his chairback waiting to say "good morning" before he sat down. "Annie cannot understand that my boys will be running wild in uptown New York. Maria cannot control them. Ugolina, yes, the girls are the woman's business. I shall have to take the boys in hand."

Ugo stayed behind when Annie drove Jay to the airport. "Annie, you won't forget our publishing plans," Jay said. "Relations with the World Overseas. . . . Think about a title." He kissed her on the cheek.

"You know what Ugo says." She put on her most little girlish smile. " '*Chi va piano va sano.*' "

"How about 'At Home and Abroad'?" Jay cried out suddenly.

The loudspeakers were announcing his plane. "Ask Ugo about that."

After a fidgety series of flights with long waits at Panama and Bogota and Cali, Jay stumbled off the plane at Quito feeling half-dead. His last flight had been grounded for hours at a backwoods airport south of Cali. Oil pump trouble.

A dark broadshouldered man met him. He introduced himself as Rafael Dominguez and grumbled that he'd been at the airport since six that morning. He had a trace of a squint in one eye: at first Jay didn't like his looks. When he switched to Spanish, Jay hazarded a guess that his origins were Andaluz.

The high mountain air was delicious, the sunlight very clear. Houses sparkling like tiny lumps of sugar stood out clear against steep green hillsides at great distances. Dominguez carried Jay's bag for him out to a remarkably dilapidated Ford. "Imagine," said Dominguez in Spanish, "I had to put in new piston rings myself. I am a graduate engineer but no mechanic. . . . I did the work by the book: it functions."

Rafael drove Jay to the plainfaced Hotel Ecuador where he had a room reserved for him. Rafael refused an invitation to lunch. Expected at home, he explained. When he'd gone, Jay felt desperately lonely. The room wasn't too bad. At lunch the meat was roast kid, quite eatable, but he hated eating alone. He tried to strangle the thought: if only Lulie were here, but he couldn't. Her absence was more vivid than anything he'd seen in Quito. After lunch he went back upstairs, threw himself on the hard creaky bed and went unhappily to sleep.

Rafael woke him in the middle of the afternoon. He had on a black suit and a stiff collar. "Visits," he explained. Jay dragged a pinstriped suit out of his bag, put it on in the bathroom where, for some reason unexplained, no water ran. On the way out, Rafael expostulated with a tiny little pallid youth behind the desk. "This night," he said, bringing a big hand down on Jay's shoulder, "there will be water."

He started laughing. "Here," he said, "we blame everything, pumps, faulty motors, political follies, flighty women on the altitude." Jay was beginning to think better of Rafael. With his cajoling manner he was showing signs of getting things done.

234

Their first call was on the Minister of Agriculture. By a miracle, they found him in. He did look sleepy. Jay guessed he'd been drowsing at his desk. Dr. Faustino López was a small bushy-browed man whose round glasses and long pale nose made him look a little like a mosquito. At first he seemed not quite sure of what his visitors were after, but when he caught the words "Spanish immigrants" he became quite brisk. "We need fresh blood," he said. "Other efforts have failed. . . . This must succeed."

He produced a sketch map from the drawer of his desk and pointed out several shaded areas. "You must pick one of these sites." Then suddenly he called out, in a ringing voice extraordinarily loud for such a small man, "Isidro."

Isidro appeared at a trot from some back room. He was a small brighteyed Indian in a striped manta and sandals. Dr. López made the introductions gravely. Isidro knew every road in the Republic. "He will be your guide. As soon as you have picked a site, Isidro will bring the blueprint to me and I shall prepare the decree. Congress has already passed a resolution of approval. You will find much sympathy here for the brave Spanish Republicans."

Dr. López bowed them ceremonially out to the vestibule and bade them good-by on the steps.

"Rafael," said Jay jocosely, "you've done everything. You haven't left me anything to do."

"Time will tell," said Rafael.

The doormen at the other ministries all claimed that their excellencies were out. Jay and Rafael solemnly left their cards with the corners turned up. They were performing this ritual at the office of the Minister of War when Rafael gave a little snort. He had caught sight of the Minister through the window. He strode down the steps with Jay at his heels.

They found the Minister of War lost in contemplation of a small sorrel horse an Indian boy was leading around a corral. He was a tall handsome man with a rosy complexion and prominent brown eyes. When Rafael caught his attention, he turned and shook hands very graciously. Colonel Mayo Casas spoke English like an American. It came out that he had learned English at VMI and at officers' training school afterwards. First thing, he asked Jay what he thought of the horse. Jay, who hardly knew one end of a horse from the other, took a plunge and asked if the little stallion had Arab blood. Colonel Mayo Casas nodded delightedly.

He gestured to the Indian to take the sorrel to the stable and turned smiling to his visitors.

"So far as I am concerned, your resettlement scheme is completely okeh," he said. "We need literate and intelligent immigrants. A hundred families are not enough. We need thousands of industrious Europeans."

Jay began to suggest this might be only a starter. Mayo Casas interrupted politely. "Suppose I take you to see the President of the Republic. He's in his office—I just spoke to him on the phone."

An official Packard was waiting at the Ministry steps. At the palace, Mayo Casas walked right past the doormen and guards. "Señor Presidente," he called.

President Romero Fuentes was a modest-appearing man. He seemed somewhat embarrassed to be caught in his shirtsleeves. He was leaning over a large desk piled with cardboard boxes and tissuepaper wrappings. He seemed to be trying to assemble a set of toy trains. It was the saint's day of his grandson, he explained hastily after the handshaking. He wanted to be sure the parts were all there. You must never disappoint children. He shook his finger reprovingly at Mayo Casas. *"Enfant terrible,"* he said.

He noticed that Jay seemed to understand. After that he insisted on speaking French. Jay found his French harder to understand than his Spanish which was quite limpid. Mayo Casas didn't speak French very well and Rafael didn't speak it at all, so they wallowed in a maze of polite misunderstanding until suddenly the President rang a bell for an attendant and told him to wrap up the toy train *"con mucho cuidado."* A doorman held his jacket for him. As soon as he had wriggled his starched cuffs through the sleeves, he shook hands hastily all around again. *"Mil excusas,"* he said, *"son fiestas de familia",* and was gone.

"Well," said Mayo Casas, "at least he knows you are here. If there is anything I can do to make your stay pleasant, don't fail to call on me." As they walked back to the car, he turned confidentially to Jay.... "I thought you liked the looks of the little stallion."

"I'm really no judge."

"The real Arabians are always rather ugly.... I think I'll buy him. He might be good at stud. I always try to think of the future. When you speak of a hundred Spanish immigrants, I think of a thousand."

Weeks went by. They saw marvelous country, snowpeaks, barren mountains, valleys plunging into forests in a roar of waterfalls. Rafael's Ford broke down on every back road in Ecuador. It seemed like a miracle when they got it running again. Isidro was a great help. He was fast catching on to the ways of machinery, and would unerringly find a yoke of oxen or a mule when they were needed to pull the Fordecito out of a mudhole. Jay and Rafael vied with each other cheering him up with a little *propina* when the car, coughing and spluttering, would reach a smooth piece of road again. Sure enough, each night Rafael managed to deliver Jay to the Hotel Ecuador while there were still waiters in the dining room.

At last Jay and Rafael were able to report that they had found the perfect site. Dr. López cried out that tomorrow he would inspect it himself. His official car would call for Mr. Pignatelli at the hotel at six o'clock sharp.

At six o'clock, Jay and Rafael met on the pavement outside in the cold dawn. They stood shivering in a little thin wind off the snowpeaks.

When they ducked back into the doorway for warmth, Rafael suddenly started talking about himself. His father was a Dutch seaman on a freighter that called regularly at Cartagena. Cartagena was where he was born and went to school. So his name wasn't Dominguez at all. He didn't know what it was. He was dark like his mother, but he suspected he had inherited his father's build. He'd known his father, but he'd never known his name. He had regularly left money for Rafael's education. "Outside I am Andaluz, Moorish maybe, but inside I am a blond Hollander. That has made life difficult."

From then on Jay felt he understood Rafael better. They were developing something very like friendship.

The sun was already shining on a mountain to the west when Isidro appeared all muffled-up from around the corner of the building. *"Ya viene. . . . He's coming,"* he said.

The official Packard had a brilliant polish. The brownfaced chauffeur wore a stiffvisored cap and a military jacket. He bowed them solemnly into their places and started off at a good clip down the macadam road that followed the line of the Guayaquil railroad. Dr. López was in high spirits. He tried to teach Jay the name of every sparkling snowpeak on the distant skyline. At Ríobamba he said he had ordered a lunch "very much of the country."

"To kill the frog," they had glasses of the local cane brandy. The meal turned out to consist of a thick soup made of a dozen different kinds of corn, purple, red, yellow, white, with grains in an astonishing variety of shapes and sizes. After that came a mutton stew garnished with potatoes of different colors and flavors. "And people try to tell us," said Dr. López, "that these two important vegetables didn't originate here in the Ecuadorian highlands. Where else?"

From Ríobamba, it was all downhill. The road deteriorated rapidly. The chauffeur rattled along at a good clip. He seemed very skillful in avoiding the small boulders that became thicker as the road wound down loop after loop into the hot country. Dr. López was fully launched on his theory on the origins of maize. He listed the various ancestors of modern maize, all of them still grown within the confines of the Republic. Isidro joined in the game. Jay was jotting them down in his notebook. The chauffeur, very much interested, kept turning to make suggestions. The car got going too fast. There was a sudden crunch and the passengers were thrown all in a heap. When they piled out on the roadway, black oil was running out of the crankcase.

They still had eight kilometers to go though they could see the rich green of the valley below them stretching out from dark ramparts of forest. A couple of kilometers below, where the road ran through a gully between tall mahogany trees, they were startled when a large bearded man rushed out at them from a log hut. Instead of holding them up, he was inviting them into his hut.

He wore a canvas tunic and black high boots that made him look oddly like a Russian peasant. Right away it came out that he was a Russian peasant. His house looked suddenly like an isba. It was an isba.

Inside they found an incongruously bejeweled lady in a high-necked dress and an elderly man in the uniform of the Czar's army seated at a formally laid-out dinner table. From the crossbeams over

238

their heads hung paper flags and Japanese lanterns. They both spoke perfect English. "Come in, come in. It is our Easter."

When they discovered that they were entertaining the Minister of Agriculture, they couldn't have been more delighted. They brought out vodka, sweet cakes, decorated Easter eggs. They exclaimed that they were Cossacks. After twenty years' wandering they had reached Ecuador through Japan. For five years now they had lived in the forest. It was their home. Viva Ecuador.

After a great many toasts and a great deal of vodka, the officer with the monocle found mules for Jay and Rafael and a small wiry horse for the Minister. After that the afternoon began to look rosy indeed. The valley destined for the Spanish settlement, surrounded by an enormous growth of mahoganies, looked to them all like a segment of paradise. They agreed they would like to live there themselves.

The Russians furnished a man to bring back the animals so that they could ride on the long steep road up to the railway station. They found the chauffeur with his cap askew and his face smeared with grease. *"No se compone, señores, no se compone,"* he said in a tearful tone.

The Minister unfeelingly ordered him to stay there on the side of the road to guard the car.

It was black night when they reached the railroad station at Ríobamba. The only transportation they could get to Quito was a brokendown coach crowded with smelly sleeping Indians attached to a freight train. They reached Quito at dawn.

Jay and Dr. López agreed that they had enjoyed the adventure. Dr. López departed for home declaring that after three days the decree would be signed and countersigned so that Señor Pignatelli could take the plane back to New York.

A week went by. No news from Dr. López. No news from Mayo Casas. Jay and Rafael tried to call at the Ministry of Agriculture. Dr. López was out of town. Mayo Casas was reported to be visiting his father's estates in the south. Jay canceled his reservation and made another.

Rafael was in despair. He had taken the precaution of getting on friendly drinking terms with most of the clerical help in the various offices. They reported to him on the status of the decree.

Four ministers had signed it. Five more were needed, and the President. Romero Fuentes was reported to be assailed by doubts.

One of Rafael's friends whispered in his ear that Colonel Mayo Casas was arriving by train from Cuenca. Jay and Rafael managed to be in the station when he stepped out on the platform. They met like long lost brothers. Mayo Casas offered them a lift in his car. This gave Jay an opportunity to point out that he could not stay in Quito forever. He had his law business to attend to. He also explained several times in English and in Spanish that no funds would be forthcoming to move the prospective settlers or start preliminary clearing until the decree was signed. He absolutely had to leave on the morning plane.

"Meet me at five at my office. We will go together to the Ministers."

"My plane," Jay repeated firmly, "leaves at 7:00 A.M. tomorrow."

Mayo Casas was as good as his word. The Ministers signed meekly. By some misadventure, it turned out that the President of the Republic was not in his office. Nobody, not even Rafael's most carefully suborned secretaries, knew where he was.

"He will certainly come to the party at the Colombian Embassy tonight," said Mayo Casas. "It is to celebrate independence. We will get his signature there."

Jay explained that he hadn't been invited.

"No matter. You will wait in the garden at twelve o'clock sharp. I'll get his signature and bring the decree out to you. I have it in my inside pocket." He tapped the left side of his wellcut jacket. "You will have plenty of time to catch your early plane to New York."

The prospect seemed perfectly absurd, but Mayo Casas was so confident, Jay felt confident, too. That night Jay paid his hotel bill and Rafael in high spirits drove him out to the Colombian Embassy in the knocking shimmying old Ford.

Rafael stayed with the car while Jay tiptoed into the garden. A dog barked. He fell over some low bushes into a formal quadrangle in front of the long French windows of the Embassy drawing room. The windows were open. He could hear the chatter of voices and tinkle of glasses. Even an occasional whiff of Scotch reached him. Shadows passed back and forth.

He stood in the garden for what seemed hours under the unbelievable brilliance of the Ecuadorian stars. Suddenly a tall figure plunged through the French windows. It was Mayo Casas. He was doubled-up with laughter.

"I have it," he whispered. "Here is an embossed copy to take home to your committee. Dominguez can get a copy for the Spanish committee in the morning at Dr. López's office. The President finally signed. You may thank that good Colombian champagne."

Mayo Casas was laughing so he could hardly talk. Jay shook his hand warmly. He didn't have the breath to say thank you. Now there were three dogs barking. He slid back through the bushes to Rafael's car. "I never would have believed it," cried Jay. "It's done."

"Viva Gran Colombia," said Rafael.

The plane north from Lima was supposed to arrive at four in the morning so there was no sense in going to bed. They were shivering from the chill off the snowpeaks. Rafael assured Jay that there was heat at the bar in the airport and that it stayed open all night. When Rafael finally brought his coughing and spluttering Fordecito to a halt at the door of the terminal building, Isidro suddenly stuck his head out of the back seat. He'd been asleep in there all along. He snatched up Jay's suitcase and raincoat. *"Para despedir al señor tan bueno,"* he said hoarsely.

Jay insisted he sit at the table with them. He seemed thoroughly astonished. When Jay presented him with fifteen American dollars as a *propina,* he showed signs of even greater astonishment. "If the gentlemen will permit," he stammered, "Isidro pays the drinks."

The crusty old Spanish waiter looked at Isidro with disgust as if he were about to throw him out by the scruff of the neck, but eventually he deigned to understand his order and brought three *copitas* of brandy. Isidro waved them away. *"Lo mejor,"* he insisted. The waiter brought a bottle of Courvoisier. Isidro did the honors and then a few seconds after tossing off his drink, he turned glassy-eyed and all of a sudden fell fast asleep with his head on the table. Rafael looked at him indulgently. *"Son buena gente,"* he whispered, "but here they treat them like dirt."

Jay insisted that Dominguez go over the famous decree to make sure that everything was in order. He read it aloud in a thundering voice. He swore it was. After that Rafael pushed his chair back and took a drink of wine.

"The first thing our Spanish comrades will do when they arrive will be to hire a few starving ragged Indians to do their work for them. I've seen it happen before. After a couple of crops, they will sell out whatever rights they have in the land and move to Cuenca or Guayaquil to start little bars or grocery stores or garages or repair shops and that will be the end of the agricultural colonies which Mr. Pignatelli described so eloquently to our friends, the Ministers."

"But, Rafael, you've told me a dozen times that what Quito needs most is a good service garage."

"Quite right, but what the Indians need is cheap and nourishing food. Generations of undernourishment have made them stupid and weak.... Look at Isidro, he's a fine boy but he can't drink a small *copita* without falling asleep."

"Suppose we have another," suggested Jay.

"*Cómo no?* I can drink anything."

"Perhaps it's the Nordic blood."

"Blood," declared Rafael dogmatically after he had downed another *copita,* "is the most important thing in the world. If it weren't for your Italian blood, Mr. Pignatelli, I would not be talking so frankly.... I find it not possible to talk frankly to Anglo-Saxon Americans."

"But, Rafael, our committee isn't set up to reform agriculture in Ecuador," said Jay in his most soothing tone. "Our aims are limited. Right now it is to find homes for one hundred Spanish refugee families. You must sympathize with them. You told me you were a refugee yourself."

"In a certain sense," answered Rafael, "but practically speaking, I am an adventurer snatching at anything that will furnish a living for me and my wife and three children."

Jay ordered two more brandies. "With coffee, please," added Rafael to the waiter. "What I am trying to explain is that I hate idealism. Without the follies and treasons of idealists, we wouldn't have lost a million men in the Civil War, the bravest, the best. That I shall never forgive."

Rafael had nothing more to say. He sat drumming with his fingers on the table.

Jay suggested that he'd better go home to bed. The plane would certainly be late. Rafael shook his head. "It is the duty of friendship," he said rather pompously, "to see you off."

Stepping out of stuffy heat of the empty waiting room the chill air made them shiver. They walked back and forth along the edge of the airstrip. "I came down here," said Jay with a slight stammer, "at an unhappy moment in my life, but it has turned out to be great fun. . . . I'm certainly hoping we'll meet again, Rafael." Saying so much embarrassed him.

For an instant he had felt that Rafael and Isidro were the only people he had affection for in the world. Rafael smiled complacently.

The snowpeaks caught fire. Their rosy glow faded to a ghostly white as the bright tropical day burst upon them. With the first hot rays of the sun, they began to hear an irregular bumblebee humming in the distance. *"El avión,"* cried Rafael as if he had conjured it up by some magic out of the depth of the sky.

Lights went on in the waiting room, uniformed ticket agents and baggage men appeared behind the counter, customs agents, immigration inspectors in khaki. Isidro, showing every tooth in his head in a smile, came trotting up with Jay's suitcase. At a word from Rafael, who seemed to know all of them by their first names— *"Amigo del Ministro de Guerra"*—they waved Jay and his baggage smilingly towards the plane that was just coming to a halt in front of the movable gangway.

It was a wrench to say good-by. Jay wrung Rafael's hand, then Isidro's. Rafael threw his arms around him for a final *abrazo*. Isidro had resumed his deadpan Indian look.

Jay climbed the gangway and let himself sink into a seat. As he thought back over the scene in the garden of the Colombian Embassy, he couldn't help a feeling of amused satisfaction. He felt like laughing out loud but already he was falling asleep.

The connecting planes were all late, too, so that Jay missed his connection in Miami.

It was late afternoon of the following day before he reached Idlewild. He took a cab straight to Brooklyn. Ella opened the door. She had a puzzled look on her face.

"There's a Dr. Tybalt here, Mr. Jay, says he's a friend of yours."

The name gave Jay a queasy feeling inside. "Did you have a nice trip, Mr. Jay?"

"Exciting," said Jay.

Walking up the stairs, he could hear Dr. Tybalt's voice "Psychoanalysis in the young..." The door was ajar. Jay paused with his hand on the knob. "... without the impacted repressions that make it hard going with adults."

Jay knocked on the door.

"Who is it? Come in," called Annie sweetly. "Why, Jay! Why so bashful?"

"I've got the document in my pocket," he announced triumphantly. Annie didn't look too much interested. He kissed her on the cheek and then turned to Dr. Tybalt.

Dr. Tybalt looked slightly embarrassed, as if he didn't know what attitude Jay would take. He held out his plump hand. Jay pumped it vigorously. "You got me out of Nuremberg when I was ready to blow my top."

"All in the day's work," said Dr. Tybalt airily.

He got to his feet. "Well, dear lady, thank you for a charming afternoon. If you can convince the young woman to call my office for an appointment, we'll squeeze her in somehow."

Jay walked to the door with him. Suddenly Tybalt looked up at him with real understanding in his eyes. "Jay, I've heard. I'm sorry. These things are without remedy."

Jay sat down. For a moment neither he nor Annie could find anything to say. Annie busied herself pouring him a drink. Annie seemed to have forgotten all about the Spanish refugees. It was on the tip of his tongue to ask about Ugo, but he didn't. He tried to bring up his plan for a foreign affairs journal, but all Annie would talk about was how wonderful Dr. Tybalt was. She was sure his treatment would bring Amanda around. She was wondering if she oughtn't to be psychoanalysed herself. She'd been letting herself get upset lately by all sorts of things. She didn't need to tell him she meant the appearance of Ugo's wife and family.

During the whole long plane ride, Jay had been planning on how he would make Ugo and Annie laugh with the story of how he'd finally gotten the decree out of the Ecuadorian government. Annie did laugh, but she was obviously thinking about something else. In fact, his little tale didn't sound as funny to him as he had expected.

Annie suggested he spend the night, but Jay said he would have a thousand things to do in New York next morning and he had better get along over there. Ella looked really distressed when he asked her to call him a taxi. Halfway across the bridge, he decided he couldn't face going to the apartment. He told the driver to take him to the Hotel Biltmore instead. When he got up to his room, he found he was desperately sleepy.

He ordered a sandwich and a bottle of beer from room service and got ready for bed. By the time the waiter came, he was too sleepy to eat. The last thing he was conscious of was his own inner voice telling him: "You go out and make the money."

It was nine o'clock when he woke up. Overslept. He'd have to hurry. While he was waiting for his breakfast, he called Ted Marquand's office on State Street in Boston. He knew Ted was an early riser. Immediately he had Ted's cold crisp voice on the phone. Jay explained he was just back from Ecuador. Ted started with formally expressed condolences. Jay interrupted the condolences. He had a horror of condolences.

The trip was a circus. His voice was more boisterous than he intended.

Ted seemed relieved to lay off the condolences. He said he hoped Jay was calling about the proposition he had made him. . . . His calling was a lucky coincidence. Right now today he and his partners needed advice about South American affairs.

"All I saw was Ecuador," said Jay in a selfdeprecating tone. "Of course, I did get a little peep at Brazil when I was in the Judge-Advocate Corps."

"Do you suppose you could dine with us tonight at the Back Bay Club?" Ted's tone was guardedly casual, as if he were inviting Jay to meet him someplace right around the corner. "It's quiet there. We can talk without being interrupted."

Jay suggested he might catch the one o'clock.

"Good enough," said Ted. "I'll get my secretary to engage you a room at the Ritz."

The next chore was to polish off the Spanish Refugee Committee. Jay called Ed Manchester between sips of coffee over his breakfast and arranged to meet him at his office right away.

It was a beautiful May day. The walk to Ed Manchester's office seemed all too short. Jay found himself enjoying the razzle-dazzle of the streets, the girls in their spring finery, the glint of the morning sun on chrome and plateglass.

It wasn't that he felt himself again. That self was dead. A new grimly determined self was coming to life.

He told Ed his story of his appointment at the Colombian Embassy and Ed laughed like a fool. He proudly spread the decree on his desk for Jay to translate.

Ed Manchester was in an unusually optimistic mood. He said just to give Annie time to get over her infatuation with Dr. Tybalt. She'd come around. The journal would be as much fun for her as it would be for anybody. Jay wasn't so sure. He wasn't underestimating Dr. Tybalt. Dr. Tybalt was a man who knew a good thing when he found it.

Between Jay's embroidering the tale of his trip to Ecuador and plans for a journal to tell the American people how badly their business, foreign and domestic, was being handled by the government in Washington, the morning slipped away. Jay caught the one o'clock at the Grand Central by a hair.

He ordered a double bourbon with his lunch in the diner.

"Keep busy, that's the secret," he told himself, "and when you are not busy, keep drunk."

After lunch he brought a pad out of his briefcase to sketch out the table of contents of a specimen number of a hypothetical journal, but instead he fell asleep and didn't wake up till the train was streaking into Providence.

The Back Bay Club was certainly quiet. Quiet and dark. Jay's feet sank into spongy dark red carpets. The walls were paneled to the ceiling with dark oak. An elderly steward led him silently through a room full of empty brassbound leather armchairs to Mr. Marquand's table in the dining room.

Ted got to his feet. He still had that frosted Apollo look. His handshake was cold. He introduced his partners in an offhand way.

Jake Merlin was a redfaced sandyhaired man in his fifties with a rambunctiously genial manner.

"Jake is the sailor of the firm," explained Ted.

Shawn O'Brien was the youngest, a dark hawknosed sharpeyed little man with glossy hair black as a crow's feathers. He spoke English with the special clarity of the welleducated Irish.

Ted ordered drinks. "Jay, maybe you would tell us about your trip to Ecuador. You described it as a circus," he said.

Jay launched into his story of the refugee committee, the visits to the Ministers, the President with his toy trains, how the Minister of War—a darn nice fellow—had gotten the notion that Jay was an expert on Arabian horses, the expedition with the Minister of Agriculture, the White Russians celebrating their Easter way down in the bush, the way the official cars kept collapsing on the mountain roads. He kept them laughing all through dinner. When he came to the final scene in the Embassy garden, Jake Merlin, who had a particularly deep booming laugh, roared till he cried.

In his chilly way, Ted Marquand showed signs of satisfaction with Jay's performance. "Didn't I tell you that this is the fellow we need on that telephone case in Rio?"

They adjourned to the room with the overstuffed chairs for coffee, brandy and cigars. Ted began questioning Jay about various points of Spanish civil law. Would the Brazilian law be the same?

"I'd have to look it up—the particular cases—but if I know anything about Brazil, the procedure would be different."

"We took a long shot and engaged a Brazilian lawyer, a little sawed-off fellow named Plácido something," boomed Jake. "We had him up here, but we don't know a damn thing about him."

They broke up early. While they were waiting for the ancient steward to come limping out with their hats, they agreed to meet at the State Street office at eleven the next morning. Ted and O'Brien walked off towards Beacon Hill. Jake had his Chrysler roadster at the curb and gave Jay a lift to the Ritz.

Jay had done a little sailing at Bay Head as a youth. He was able to keep Jake talking about his Gloucester schooner all the way. They parted lifelong friends.

Jay arrived at the office promptly on the dot. Ted, wearing a light gray flannel suit that accentuated his look of youthful coolness, was waiting for him behind a bare highly polished desk. He immediately launched into the Rio telephone case. In a few short sentences, he described the firm's predicament. The client was a Canadian who had inherited a large block of stock in one of the Rio telephone companies. He wanted to dispose of it either to private individuals or to some public body if the rumor turned out true that the telephone companies were going to be expropriated.

Jake Merlin came lumbering in. "Good morning, good morning . . . If it were Boston, we'd know who to fix," he said crossly, "but Rio de Janeiro, my God!"

"Even selling the stock at a loss," said O'Brien from the door, "it would amount to a very tidy sum."

"Somebody has got to go down there to size things up," said Jay.

"That's what we've decided," said Ted.

"We decided you were the man," exclaimed Jake, "on Ted's recommendation, even before Shawn and I laid eyes on you." He slapped his thigh as if he found the situation thoroughly comical.

"Well, if your Senhor Plácido turns out as forehanded as my friend Rafael in Ecuador, we may get somewhere."

"When could you go?"

"Any time," said Jay.

"Have you still got your New York office, Jay?"

"I have a share in one."

"Hold on to it. The firm may need a small base in New York one of these days."

"That is certainly looking into the future," said Shawn O'Brien straddling a chair.

"The question of remuneration," Ted went on in a dogged tone, "has us puzzled. Of course, your expenses would be paid. . . . We've been thinking of something like a conditional junior partnership which could become permanent if everybody was happy."

"A baroque idea," snorted O'Brien. "No such conception exists in law. There has never been a lawyer in the world who could write his own contracts."

"Suppose you think up something better." Ted's voice was cutting.

"This is Friday," burst out Jake, "in case nobody remembers. I have some deskwork to finish, but if we skip lunch and just eat a snack on the road, I could drive us all up to my place in Kennebunkport for the weekend."

Ted said he was tied up, but why didn't the other three go? "I think I know Jay already, but it'll give you a chance to get acquainted with him."

"Are you game?" asked Jake. Jay and Shawn O'Brien nodded emphatically. "I can't promise much social life, but we might get a sail to blow the cobwebs out of our brains."

The Merlins' house in Kennebunkport turned out to be a comfortable old Maine farmhouse with whitepainted paneling over ample fireplaces in every room. Mrs. Merlin was a plumpish apple-cheeked New England lady trimly dressed in outdoorsy tweeds. There was plenty of room in the house because the children were away at school. The Merlins' carelessly hospitable manner made Jay feel at home the moment he stepped in the door.

When they sat down to dinner, another woman appeared. She was introduced as Emily Merlin, the widow of one of Jake's brothers who was killed in the war.

"You must have seen her name," said Mrs. Merlin to Jay in a confidential tone, "she writes under the name of Emily Beaufort in the *New Yorker* magazine. She's quite a swell."

"Exclusively on cooking," Emily Merlin said with a laugh. "Nobody reads them except the copy editor."

As they talked along, Emily's broad South Carolina "a's" contrasted with the flat "a's" of the two Merlins; but she was evidently very much part of the closeknit family group. She was a slender woman with a very graceful figure. Dark eyes and dark lashes lit up a rather sallow oval face. By the time Jake had quit complaining and ejaculating over what a hard time he was having carving a roast of beef, Jay had decided he liked the Merlins very much indeed. None of them had any side. Particularly, he liked Emily.

The night came on foggy. They could hear an intermittent foghorn from some lighthouse far away. "Doesn't look as if it would be a good day for *Petrel* tomorrow," Jake apologized, "but you never can tell. If the wind changes, she'll clear in a minute."

They spent a pleasant evening sitting around the fire over some Scotches. O'Brien talked about Joyce and Yeats and Trinity College. He insisted that Joyce, in spite of his great talent, was a frustrated and frustrating writer. Jake told stories about America

Cup races he had seen or crewed on. He was a great man for a nautical anecdote.

Jay was disappointed next morning when Emily didn't appear for breakfast. The men pitched horseshoes under the dripping trees out behind the house waiting for the fog to lift. At last Jake cried out, "Let's go out anyway. At least we can show Jay the schooner."

Mrs. Merlin said if they would send a boat in, she would send out a picnic lunch. Emily wouldn't be coming because she had an article to write. She wouldn't either: groceries to buy.

As Jay had expected, *Petrel* turned out a fine workable sea boat, converted for comfort but not for luxury. No bright work to keep polished. The only crew was an odd little flatfaced Finn named Matty.

They spent several hours out on the schooner and ate a fine lunch of cold beer and roast beef sandwiches Mrs. Merlin sent out to them. When the wind did come up, it blew the fog in thicker.

The tide was low. Jay breathed happily the iodine smell of seaweed and mudflats and brine. To keep busy, they rowed around the harbor looking for a lobsterman Jake knew. When they got back to the wharf, they had three big hen lobsters in a canvas bag.

They had hardly had time to change their clothes before guests started coming in for cocktails. Emily was the center of all eyes. She had a knack for making acid half-humorous remarks in a semi-mysterious manner that Jay found very intriguing.

Before he left, he had jotted down Emily's New York phone number in his notebook. As they shook hands she said, looking him square in the eye with that impersonal smile she had, that she would be crazy to hear about Brazil. He must come to dinner when he got back.

13

Ike's Flying Conscience

After serving as Secretary of State under Benjamin Harrison, John Watson Foster, Civil War General, diplomat, raconteur, American traveler of the old school who rejoiced in the good will of all the world,

was invited by the Chinese,
to serve as their adviser
in their peacetalks with Japan.

The then grand panjandarum of China, Li Hung Chang, so appreciated Foster's performance that he offered him a spectacular salary and a palace full of servitors if he would stay on as permanent adviser of the imperial government.

Foster begged off by saying he had an engagement at home which he positively could not break:

it was to go fishing with his grandson on Lake Erie.
The grandson was
John Foster Dulles,
then seven years old.

John Foster Dulles came of churchgoing people. His father was pastor of the First Presbyterian Church in Watertown, New York, where Foster, as he was known at home, was born, educated in the public schools, and spent the first fifteen years of his life.

The most familiar word in his father's vocabulary: "right-eousness."

His mother's people were righteous folk, too; missionaries, men of letters, diplomats. His aunt married Robert Lansing who was to be Woodrow Wilson's Secretary of State. Public service was writ large in the heritage.

The summer after Foster graduated from highschool, his mother took him and his sister to Lausanne to learn French, then considered the indispensable language of diplomacy.

At sixteen, planning to study for the ministry, he matriculated at Princeton.

Junior year his grandfather Foster took him along as his secretary to the Second Hague Peace Conference where he represented the Chinese government.

Graduating with honors and a Phi Beta Kappa key, young Dulles won a scholarship to study philosophy at the Sorbonne under Henri Bergson. Though he remained all his life a pious Presbyterian, his plans for the ministry faded. When he came home, he enrolled in the George Washington Law School and lived with his grandparents in their great brick house on Eighteenth Street. The Lansings lived there, too. Especially during the Wilson administration, his grandmother was one of the capital's most sought-after hostesses.

His grandfather got him into the famous New York firm of Sullivan and Cromwell. Something in the family background made him specialize in Latin America. International law became his forte. He married a girl from Auburn, New York, whom he loved passionately all his life, was admitted to a partnership and eventually became head of the firm.

When the first worldwide war broke out, his experience in Central American affairs caused Lansing to recommend him to President Wilson for a delicate mission to line up Panama, Nicaragua and Costa Rica for the defense of the Panama Canal from the Germans. Back home he was commissioned a Captain and attached to the General Staff in Washington. His qualities were generally recognized: soon he found himself assistant to the Chairman of the War Trade Board.

At the Paris Peace Conference he was one of Woodrow Wilson's young men.

Back in the law offices of Sullivan and Cromwell, he used to the full his knowledge of international finance.

He was called in to help straighten out the debts of the Polish government. In that connection he struck up a friendship which proved lifelong with Jean Monnet, a Cognac brandy manufacturer and international banker who was in the same assignment. Jean Monnet was to devote his life to his project—dear, too, to Dulles's heart—the United States of Europe.

Dulles had a hand in the development of the Dawes plan for saving the German economy. When the Great Depression loomed he represented the American bondholders in the bankruptcy of the Swedish match monopoly..

The Wall Street panic barely ruffled his personal finances. He was as well off as he cared to be. His position as one of the prime international lawyers of the day offered endless possibilities for moneymaking.

Money was never his chief interest. Ethics was. Profoundly shocked by the moral collapse of New Era capitalism at home and by the far more threatening collapse of the Versailles order he had helped build in Europe, he felt a personal responsibility. As a Christian, he had to do something.

He was returning in his speeches and exhortations to young men to the Wilsonian ideas which he claimed had never been given a fair trial. He began to give time to church organization. Christians must band together against the possibility of another worldwide war.

In 1940 Dulles accepted the post of Chairman of the Committee for a Just and Durable Peace set up by the Federal Council of Churches. Some way must be found to learn from the failures of the League of Nations.

Politics began to attract him. He had long been friends with Tom Dewey, the perennial Republican candidate for the Presidency. Respect for the nonpartisan foreign policy which had come into being during the war effort caused him to dedicate months of work to the San Francisco and London conferences which set up the United Nations.

He proved so much the best qualified by scholarship and experience that he had become the behind-the-scenes mentor of the American delegations.

He had at first accepted the Yalta declarations at their face value but now with Molotov and Gromyko right across the table from him, the Communist reality hit him between the eyes. Eternal aggression; no compromise there. He began to reflect that if liberal statesmen had carefully read *Mein Kampf,* the second war might have been averted. He added Stalin's *Problems of Leninism* to his grandfather's *Diplomatic Memoirs,* the Federalist Papers and the Bible, which were his bedside reading. His business was to avert a third.

When General Eisenhower was elected President, he appointed John Foster Dulles as his Secretary of State.

At the mere rumor, appeasementminded European politicians began to express their dismay which was faithfully transmitted to the American public by New-Dealish commentators. Anthony Eden was "quite upset." Ike stood firm.

Regaining the initiative which the Communists had held since Franklin D. succumbed to Stalin's blandishments at Teheran, even with a superior Navy and superior nuclear weaponry to fall back on, was a large order.

First Dulles had to prove he was no firebrand. In his initial speech over radio and TV after taking office, he repudiated the notion, attractive to some military men, of preventive war. At the same time, he expressed the hope that the United States, by precept and example, might woo the peoples of the world back from the Communist delusion. His words echoed Woodrow Wilson's. He pledged a diplomacy which would be open, simple and righteous in accord with "what used to be the great American tradition of foreign policy."

By January 30, a scant ten days after Ike's inauguration, Dulles was airborne. The essential paperwork of State Department diplomacy he carried on as he flew.

He touched ground in London, where he exchanged greetings with Winston Churchill, and tried to pacify Anthony Eden. The British Foreign Minister was never one of his favorite people. The antagonism was mutual. His plane took short hops to Paris, Hague, Brussels, Luxembourg, and Rome.

In Bonn he laid the groundwork for the friendship, which occasionally assumed almost the qualities of an *affaire de coeur* with old Chancellor Adenauer. They shared a realistic approach to international politics combined with profound religious convictions.

However cold and brusque he was with people he did not esteem, once his defenses were down Dulles was a simple, friendly man.

With Monnet and Adenauer, he was happy. They talked frankly. The two great Europeans shared Dulles's enthusiasm for the formation of a European Defense Community which they hoped might be an opening wedge for the United States of Europe.

Stalin's death in March 1953 set all the diplomatic dovecotes fluttering. The news reached Washington in the midst of a meeting with French and British representatives at the State Department.

Dulles hoped that the confusion sure to result in Russia from the struggle for power inside the Kremlin would encourage the European nations to unite.

The opposite happened.

The French Parliament had not yet ratified EDC. Winston Churchill, still Prime Minister, was following the traditional British balance of power policy. Only Adenauer, who appeared in Washington in April, seemed to understand that European unity was more urgent than ever.

Malenkov, Stalin's first successor, began to make peaceful noises towards Europe. It soon became evident that the peace he advocated was peace Russian style, and largely a dodge to keep things quiet until the struggle for mastery inside the Communist presidium should be resolved.

For the French politicians particularly, the situation meant a happy resumption of politics as usual.

Dulles had hardly bidden Adenauer good-by before he was off to Paris—airborne again—to buck up a meeting of NATO. There Dulles found only resistance to his policies. Beria's execution in June raised fresh hopes of a liberal turn in the Soviet command. Churchill was calling for a summit conference on the problems of Germany and Austria.

Remembering Potsdam and Yalta, Dulles was suspicious of summit conferences.

Finally, Eisenhower and Dulles consented to a meeting with the French Prime Minister and Winston Churchill in Bermuda.

That meeting had to be postponed on account of Churchill's first stroke. When it took place in December, nothing was accomplished except a few banal declarations.

Dulles tried to replace fear of Russian aggression with fear of American isolation. He was convinced the Europeans could be scared into unity. When he landed home from his last flight to Paris in 1953, he declared that European (meaning French and British) unwillingness to make sacrifices for EDC might cause the United States to follow the advice of the conservative wing of the Republican Party and go it alone. He threatened "an agonizing reappraisal."

In January 1954 he was airborne again. The Russians had exploded their first hydrogen bomb in August 1953. The American atomic authorities were preparing to show their muscle by new devastations of the depopulated atoll of Eniwetok. In a speech before the Council on Foreign Relations in Washington, Dulles had talked of massive retaliation. A barely expressed threat, he reminded his audience, had induced the Chinese to put pressure on the North Koreans to moderate their demands at Panmunjom.

The world press raised a howl. "Agonizing reappraisal" and "massive retaliation" seemed too much like fighting phrases. Russian agents were adroitly using the American nuclear explosions in the Pacific to divide the European nations. Russian bombs, they gently insinuated, were bombs for peace.

Eisenhower was against taking risks. Dulles had to eat his words.

At the conference of the four occupying powers in Berlin, Dulles was confronted by a different Molotov. The leaders in the Kremlin still needed a breathing space while they settled their own private feuds. Full of sweet reasonableness, Molotov was trying to prove that the Soviet Union had mellowed and matured. He particularly wanted to attract President Eisenhower to a summit conference which would affirm the world's acceptance of Russia as one of the world's great civilized powers.

Dulles was still leary of the idea. First, he wanted EDC. After that a Summit might be useful. The time was not ripe.

Molotov, whose whole soul was set on blocking EDC, assiduously cultivated the English and French delegations. His tactic succeeded.

The Allies allowed their disagreements to become public.

The French were in a desperate funk. The war was going against them in Indochina. In spite of Franklin Roosevelt's remonstrances, Indochina had been handed back to them when the Japanese let go their hold in 1945. Though they made offers of autonomy, the French seemed intent on bludgeoning the peoples of that rich peninsula back into their old unhappy colonial status. The Vietnamese rebelled. The Vietminh army was giving the French occupying forces a hard time. Ho Chi Minh, an old Communist functionary backed by the Chinese, was proving himself a leader, vigorous, ruthless, resourceful.

Dulles spent so much time in the air that he could never get around to the reorganization of the State Department which had been one of his priorities.

The spring of 1954 he was continually flying between London and Paris and Washington trying to inspire collective action to save Indochina from the Communists.

Churchill and Eden were pulling their weight for a negotiated settlement. They were making as if they still believed in treaties. Dulles knew only too well treaties were worthless without the leverage of power necessary to enforce them. He found Churchill and Eden uncooperative. They were holding their cards close to their chests until they met the Russians and the Chinese at the conference set for May in Geneva.

The French dillydallied. Their Prime Minister, Laniel, was in such a precarious position politically he didn't dare say yea or nay. The French public already had been conditioned to defeat in Indochina by a brilliantly effective propaganda campaign inspired but not led by the Communists.

When Dulles flew into Paris for a meeting of the Ministerial Council of NATO, where plans were supposed to be laid for common action at the Geneva conference he so dreaded, he found French Foreign Minister Bidault in desperate shape mentally, physically and politically. He whispered to Dulles that only the immediate assignment of American bombers could save the French troops that had let themselves be bottled up at Dienbienphu. The Vietminh forces were tightening the noose with the help of firstrate Russian artillery furnished by the Chinese and positioned on the surrounding hills. This was no news to Dulles who had been briefed on Vietnam by U. S. Army observers. Eden promptly declared that Great Britain had no intention of intervening. All he could promise was to support whatever negotiated settlement might be reached at Geneva.

The day before the conference opened, the French capitulated at Dienbienphu.

Molotov and Chou En-lai held all the trumps.

It was the new Molotov again. With an air of genial frankness and detachment, he invited the various delegations to friendly discussions over luncheons and dinners.

Chou En-lai impressed the journalists as an amateur of roses.

Dulles saw the discussions would drag on fruitlessly and left them in the hands of his assistant, Bedell Smith.

The French government fell. Fast talking Mendès-France breezily promised to end the war in four weeks. A respected Vietnamese named Ngo Dinh Diem, who resided in Paris, was induced to accept the precarious office of Prime Minister of such of Vietnam as was still out of the hands of Ho Chi Minh. At a meeting with Chou En-lai, Mendès-France found the Chinese Communist leader willing to accept a "temporary" division of Vietnam, like Korea, into a Communist North and a non-Communist South. Mendès-France's concessions were hailed as triumphs by the Paris press.

Dulles had withdrawn the American delegation from Geneva. Now, feeling he had to bow to the inevitable, he worked out with Mendès-France a formula describing the minimum terms the United States would accept. The final settlement, signed on Mendès-France's deadline date, July 20, was one of those compromises sure to lead to trouble, but Dulles felt it was better than complete surrender. The Russians and the Chinese still had some respect for American power. Dulles refused to put his name to the settlement but gave it a sort of tacit consent. When the question came up as to who would finance Diem, all parties concerned passed the bill on to Uncle Sam.

Dulles had to spend most of the summer of 1954 flying around the Pacific, trying to undo the harm caused by the French collapse in Indochina. He wanted to avoid any more Korean wars. He wanted the Asian countries to unite in their own defense.

While he was exhorting the Asian delegates at Manila, the

Chinese Communists started shelling the islands of Quemoy and Matsu offshore from the province of Fukien. These islands the Chiang Kai-shek government still held. It looked like the beginning of an invasion of Taiwan. All the nervous Nellies in England and America started howling that the islands must be given up. Dulles was for standing firm: the islands were Chiang Kai-shek's outer defenses. Eisenhower teetered. Chiang Kai-shek's troops held on under a series of Communist attacks.

The presence of the Seventh Fleet in the Formosa Strait was a deterrent to both sides. Dulles coolly went about negotiating a defensive treaty with the Taiwan regime. The Chinese eventually got tired of wasting ammunition on the rocky islets.

The upshot was that Washington pledged itself to protect Taiwan from attack and at the same time agreed not to allow Chiang Kai-shek to invade the mainland.

Meanwhile, Winston Churchill, already old and ailing, was putting all his fading energies into engineering a Summit conference at Geneva. Dulles was against it. His doubts were intensified by the defeat of EDC in the French Chamber of Deputies. This meant the frustration of his and Adenauer's and Monnet's carefully laid plan for the United States of Europe. All that was left of it was the Common Market. Dulles had been so busy in the Pacific, he had lost the initiative in the West.

Anthony Eden jumped into the breach by promulgating the notion that the Brussels treaty of 1948, which was supposed to unite the European nations against the threat of a resurgent Germany, might be turned, by the admission of West Germany, into a charter for the sort of United Europe the British could approve.

An agreement to revise the Brussels Treaty was signed in London on October 31. Eisenhower and Dulles congratulated Eden warmly on his achievement.

During the same month, the stability of Europe was further secured by a concordium between Italy and Yugoslavia, according to which the city of Trieste remained in Italian hands, while most of its hinterland was deeded to Yugoslavia. This meant that the British and American troops that had been occupying the city to hold off a war were free to go home. The Trieste agreement was followed by an accord between Austria and Moscow by which the Russians engaged themselves to remove their troops from Vienna if the other occupying powers removed theirs, and if all parties agreed to neutralizing Austria. Dulles could say Amen with some satisfaction to these developments.

When the much-publicized Summit meeting finally came off, Winston Churchill was too ill to attend. For six days in July 1955, President Eisenhower, Anthony Eden, Premiers Faure of France and Bulganin of the Soviet Union hobnobbed together on the terraces of the superannuated palace of the League of Nations. Along with Bulganin appeared a stocky little man named Nikita Khrushchev who was taking full advantage of his first opportunity to strut on the international stage.

Everybody was very civil. A great deal of beating around the bush. No results.

When Eisenhower tried to bring the meeting to life by declaring the United States would never take part in an aggressive war, Bulganin replied that he believed him; but when Eisenhower put forward his "open skies" plan for disarmament by which national interests would be protected by photoreconnaissance from the air, the Russians began to frown. In essence nothing was settled, but for years "the spirit of Geneva" acted as a narcotic on the European nations.

Dulles felt that the American cause had suffered a defeat.

The Russian propagandists played up the Summit out of all reason. They cut the other dignitaries off a group photograph and left Eisenhower and Bulganin seated smiling side by side. This print they spread assiduously all over the world.

When the follow-up meeting of foreign ministers took place in October, Eisenhower was ill from a heart attack. Dulles tried to promulgate his proposals for the reunification of Germany, for elections in the subjugated states, for European security. The answer from Molotov was an emphatic *Nyet*.

The Soviet Union was entering a new phase of expansion. Engineers were already advising that oil reserves round the Caspian region were getting low. The programs of the imperialist Czars for conquest in the Near East were being tailored to Marxist ideology. The Kremlin leaders were responding to the century-old lure of an open Dardanelles and warm water ports.

The opportunity came when an energetic gentleman named Gamal Abdel Nasser supplanted the fairly moderate Colonel Naguib who had led the army coup which ended the torpid regime of King Farouk in Egypt. Nasser was full of lofty notions about making Egypt a great nation. One of Nasser's first claims was that his technicians could run the Suez Canal as well as the appointees of the European company. After a good deal of huffing and puffing, Anthony Eden induced him to sign one of Eden's intricately worded agreements by which, limited by a long set of terms and conditions, he could establish Egyptian sovereignty over the Canal.

Nasser considered this a victory and it was. Next he wanted an extension of the Aswan Dam which he claimed would double the irrigated acreage of the Nile Valley and make Egypt independent of American grain. He began to dream of leading the whole Arab world.

Various holdovers from British domination of Mesopotamia stood in the way and also the troublesome State of Israel which was particularly powerful in the United States through the respect American politicians had for the Jewish vote.

Russian diplomats were at work. They made offers on the Aswan Dam. Here was a chance to eliminate the British and French from the Near East as the beginning of the elimination of the American and international companies that had prospected the oilwells which had rendered some Arab despots deliriously prosperous.

Nasser's game was to play the interested parties off one against the other. He had to see how much money the Americans would be willing to put up to keep the Russians from taking over the projected dam. Already the Russians were furnishing him arms through the Skoda works in Czechoslovakia.

Dulles was finding Nasser slippery as an eel. Nasser kept blowing hot and cold on the terms. He delayed answering Dulles's final proposition for six months. Feeling that he was being blackmailed, Dulles broke off negotiations.

This was the pretext Nasser had been looking for. Amid Soviet style denunciations of American imperialism, he announced the nationalization of the Suez Canal. The Russians would build him his dam.

Dulles, kept out of Latin America by press of business elsewhere, was being made to feel the Latin American politicians were chafing under his neglect. He flew to Peru to attend a Presidential inauguration. When the news reached the State Department, instead of asking Dulles's advice, Eisenhower assembled a meeting of undersecretaries. He declared that he didn't think the Suez Canal was the right issue for war and sent Robert Murphy flying off to London to see what was happening there.

Murphy found the British cabinet uncommunicative but gathered that the French Foreign Minister, Christian Pineau, was urging joint military action. Nasser was another Hitler. He must be nipped in the bud before he could do further damage.

Eisenhower was up for re-election in November. He could only think of his campaign. He cabled Dulles in Peru to proceed to London. What he wanted was to keep the Near East quiet until after the election.

Eden and Pineau felt this was Munich all over again. The French had for some time been planning a military campaign with the Israelis. Nasser's arms shipments to the Algerian rebels were becoming an intolerable nuisance. Pineau was sure he had French opinion behind him. An avalanche of words poured out of all the ministries for foreign affairs.

Nasser held all the cards. Khrushchev, now in complete control in Moscow, had assured him personally he would have Russian help if he needed it.

Unable to make any headway with the French and British, Dulles flew home to see what could be done with the United Nations. He was frustrated there. The Soviet Union vetoed a resolution calling for free passage for ships of all nations through the Suez Canal.

When the Hungarian revolt broke out, which could at least have been used to put the Russians in the wrong before world opinion, Eisenhower was too busy with his campaign to make any significant statement. Khrushchev felt free to turn his machineguns on the people of Budapest.

Dulles and Eisenhower were appalled by a sudden hiatus in communications with London. They soon learned the reason. The British and French fleets were on the move. Troopships were steaming towards Suez.

The only part of the plan which was carried out with efficiency was the Israeli campaign. Israeli columns tore through the Egyptian troops in the Sinai peninsula. The Israelis proved their army was something to reckon with.

The British and French expeditions had hardly deployed before Pineau and Eden lost their nerve. After some desultory bombing of Egyptian airfields, they called a halt.

Nasser appeared to be unshaken in Cairo.

Anthony Eden was completely broken. Pleading ill health after a few weeks he resigned.

Eisenhower, in Washington, was in a pet because he hadn't been consulted. He decided to bring charges of aggression against the British, French and Israelis before the United Nations. It was Dulles's job to introduce the motion of censure on November 1, 1956. It was the most humiliating moment of his career.

The day after he was taken to Walter Reed Hospital for his first cancer operation.

Eisenhower won re-election handily. Congress proved its confidence by authorizing him to give economic and military aid to any nation requesting it under the threat of international Communism. Under that resolution, Eisenhower got away with a small show of American strength in the Middle East when he sent the Marines into Lebanon to bolster a pro-Western regime in that small republic. It was locking the stable door after the horse had been stolen.

After a month's convalescence, Dulles was back at his desk. Amid the ruins of his favorite projects, he still seemed an iron man. He continued almost mechanically his flights to Europe to encourage some pluck amid the dispirited ranks of the NATO organization.

In Russia, emboldened by the success of the first Sputnik, Khrushchev was emitting threats against the liberty of West Berlin.

In France, De Gaulle was President of the Fifth Republic. By abandoning Algeria to the rebel gangs, he had paid a high price for power.

On his last flight overseas, Dulles had the usual satisfactory conversations with Adenauer. Their talk was gloomy: Europe was proving the prisoner of its past. When the Chancellor drove him to the airport, as always with a single trusted interpreter in his own private car, Dulles confided in him that he hadn't been feeling well. He assured him that all that was needed was a hernia operation.

Back in Washington, Dulles characteristically wrote Adenauer from Walter Reed Hospital that he had not intended to deceive him about his health. He had been wrong.

The next operation was fruitless. Cancer was spreading. Dulles was determined to live. He asked Eisenhower to let Christian Herter take over the office of the Secretary of State for a short time.

Eisenhower refused to accept his resignation and held out the hope that a period of recuperation in the south would bring him around. The hope was illusory.

In April 1959 Dulles, who at last admitted he was dying, sent his brother to the President with his letter of resignation written out in longhand on a yellow legal pad.

"I was brought up," he wrote, "in the belief that this nation of ours was not merely a self-serving society but was founded with a mission to help build a world where liberty and justice would prevail."

He had worked hard to help build such a world. He had failed. In another month he was dead.

PART III

THE GREEN REVOLUTION

I

Walt Whitman: "Song of Myself"

Over the sharp-peaked farmhouse with its scallop'd scum of slender shoots from the gutters,

over the western persimmon, over the longleaved corn, over the delicate blue flax

over the white and brown buckwheat, a hummer and buzzer these with the rest

over the dusky green of the rye as it ripples and shatters in the breeze;

scaling mountains, pulling myself cautiously up, holding on by low scragged limbs,

walking the path worn in the grass and beat through the leaves of the brush

where the quail is whistling between the woods and the wheatlot.

2

The Moonrocket Man

The first rocket expressly designed for the exploration of outer space was the work of a Worcester man, a Professor of Physics at Clark University.

On March 16, 1926, Robert Hutchings Goddard made his first successful test of a rocket fueled by gasoline and oxygen.

He was fortyfour. With New England cussedness he had been plugging away at his plans ever since he was seventeen.

The test took place on a snowcovered field belonging to his Aunt Effie in the adjacent township of Auburn. The contraption only rose fortysix feet before burying its nose in Aunt Effie's cabbage patch, but it performed successfully enough to convince Goddard of the correctness of his principles. Also convinced were his assistant and his smart practicalminded young wife, Esther Kisk, who up to then had thought of her husband as a charming madman.

Charles Abbott who was financing Goddard's experiments through a grant from the Smithsonian was less enthusiastic. He wanted results; after the expenditure of nearly five thousand dollars he felt the rocket should have soared higher.

Goddard was a New Englander from way back, closemouthed as Calvin Coolidge. A lone operator, in spite of his reticence he had somehow acquired the knack of infecting coworkers with his enthusiasms.

He was born in 1882 in an old farmhouse known as Maple

Hill that belonged to his grandmother, Mary Pease Upham Goddard, who was very much the head of the family. Known everywhere as Madame Goddard, she presided with genial tyranny over a household of elderly relatives. Her son Nahum Goddard, Robert's father, started his career working as an accountant for a crusty old codger named Hoyt who manufactured machine knives.

When Nahum showed the temerity to woo and wed his boss's daughter, Fannie Louise, described as a frail and lovely girl, the old man cut her off without a penny. Madame Goddard immediately opened her home and her heart to the young people.

After Robert's birth his father showed his mettle by patenting a mechanical cutter of his own. With an associate he bought out a small Boston firm to produce it. The cutter turned out to be useful to the Danbury hatters for cutting rabbit fur. The firm prospered. Nahum moved the family to a comfortable house in Roxbury.

There Robert had his first schooling, attended Sunday school and sang in the choir of the Episcopal Church. Fannie Louise had always been delicate. Mother and son both suffered from a series of respiratory ailments. Robert's schoolwork was set back.

He made up for it by massive reading, first in popular science works and then in serious grown-up books on physics and mathematics. Robert's bent amused and delighted his father who kept him wellfurnished with books and materials to experiment with. First it was a perpetual-motion machine, then he almost set the house on fire trying to melt graphite down into diamonds. As soon as aluminum became available he tried to build an aluminum balloon. "Failure crowns enterprise," was the entry he made in his diary.

It could have been his motto through life. It was only after an incredible number of failures that he developed his successful inventions.

When Robert was seventeen his mother's ailments were diagnosed as tuberculosis: they called it consumption in those days. The doctors advised Robert's father to move his wife back to Worcester where the air would be purer. Nahum Goddard loved his family beyond everything. With a wrench he sold his share of the business and his comfortable Roxbury home and moved back to his mother's superannuated farmhouse at Maple Hill.

Madame Goddard was delighted. Since the death in infancy of a younger brother Robert was the only grandchild. He would be her boy from now on.

Robert was already filling his notebook with what he called "high altitude research." He was working on the notion of a space vehicle somehow powered by centrifugal force.

Nahum Goddard had taken a job as shop superintendent with a man named Hardy who had bought out grumpy old Hoyt. Free afternoons he devoted to getting his ailing son out of doors. All his life Robert remembered with pleasure verdant spring rambles with his father, who always took along a fishing pole and a camera.

By now he was well enough to do odd jobs for his grandmother. One October day when he was pruning the orchard he fell into a reverie. He was sitting in the crotch of a big old cherry tree that had been his pet dreaming spot for several summers. There he had thought up a grandiose plan for Goddard's Frog Hatchery. The brook that burbled through the orchard would run an electric generator which would pump water into tanks and canals and heat an incubation house. The whole thing would be automatic. He would reap a rich harvest selling froglegs.

This time it was a space vehicle that he dreamed. He could see every detail so vividly it was more of a hallucination than a dream. Every item of the spacecraft's design left such a vivid recollection that for years after he marked down October 19 as Anniversary Day in his diary.

He had been reading H. G. Wells' *The War of the Worlds*. The book set off a string of calculations in his diary as to the actual possibility of interplanetary travel. When he read Jules Verne's *Journey to the Moon and Back,* he worried about the practicality of the giant cannon Jules Verne had dreamed up to propel his projectile. Shouldn't there have been a series of cannons each adding propulsion where the other left off?

At nineteen Robert was well enough to enroll as a sophomore in Worcester South High School. This was in 1901, the year Marconi sent his first electrical impulses across the Atlantic. Morse's telegraph, Alexander Graham Bell's telephone and Edison's incandescent bulb had long been in use. The successful flight over the Potomac of Langley's model "aerodrome" was five years back. T. R.

273

was in the White House about to usher in the great age of Yankee imperialism with the Panama canal. H. G. Wells' fantasies seemed all about to come true.

In spite of his shut-in life, Goddard had this knack with people. He was received as a sort of marvel by his younger classmates in highschool and twice elected class president. An Emersonian essay written for his English class caused a stir among the faculty. The Physics instructor found him the brightest pupil he had ever had. In spite of their disparity in ages they remained lifelong friends.

Robert read all the scientific magazines. In 1902 he submitted an article to *The Popular Science News*. It was called "The Navigation of Space" and suggested that Jules Verne's cannon should have been a multiple-stage affair. Thus he launched what was later recognized as the germ of the many-staged modern rocket. The rejection slip from the editor came unusually promptly.

His graduation was glorious. He was appointed class orator. A tune he made up won the contest for class song and he fell in love, almost at first sight, with a charming Biology major named Miriam who was salutatorian.

His mother had insisted on his taking dancing lessons. How right she was. Miriam was his date for the class dance. Robert bought her a bouquet of roses. The evening passed in a golden whirl.

Students and faculty came away pondering the phrase that capped young Goddard's oration: "The dream of yesterday is the hope of today and the reality of tomorrow."

There followed a long courtship. Miriam went through Smith while Robert went through Worcester Polytechnic. She came out with ideas of her own as to how to conduct her career. After some postgraduate work in Germany she found herself less and less interested in Robert's rockets. Robert as a lover was proving cautious. When in an effort to patch up something permanent she asked him to come to Paris to marry her, Robert answered that the family had to be present at any wedding of his.

For Miriam that was the end. Robert was sorry but he was too busy with his space plans to feel really crushed.

Robert had been taking all the science courses offered at Worcester Polytechnic. Privately he experimented with rocket fuels.

When he tried a mixture of charcoal and potassium nitrate he produced a violent explosion that filled the Physics lab with smoke. The authorities were not amused by this exploit of their star pupil.

As a matter of course he went on to Clark University for graduate study. Clark, recently founded on the model of Johns Hopkins, was a remarkable institution. G. Stanley Hall, who had inaugurated Psychology at Hopkins, was president; A. A. Michelson headed the Physics Department. Freud and Jung, though Goddard doesn't seem to have taken any interest in their vagaries, both lectured there during his first year. Arthur Gordon Webster, who took over Physics when Michelson moved on to Chicago, was one of the most remarkable Physics instructors of his time. His special gift was charging his pupils with enthusiasm for the poetry of science. Practical application interested him very little. He was a most demanding teacher; in all his years at Clark he awarded only twentyseven doctorates. He found Goddard's thesis good, but his oral exam he declared "spectacular."

Goddard stayed on at Clark to study and teach. His reputation was growing. When he accepted a research fellowship at Princeton, his grandmother went with him to keep house. Woodrow Wilson's campaign for the Presidency nearly distracted him from his rocketry. He walked in the torchlight parade the students put on to bid their controversial president farewell.

Easter vacation after Wilson's inauguration Goddard came home very tired. His mother's doctors declared he was suffering from advanced tuberculosis and gave him only a few weeks to live.

They reckoned without the young man's will.

Goddard never took much stock in doctors. Dutifully he went to bed in a room off the upper porch in the fine new frame house his father, who was by now doing quite well in the machine knife factory, had built for his wife on Bishop Street. Then he carefully nursed himself back, if not to health, to the unstable condition which was to furnish him with strength for an immense amount of work during a fairly long life. This time what worried Goddard was that his handwriting had gotten so crabbed he was afraid nobody would be able to read his notes if he did die.

In bed he spent half a day working up patent applications.

Worcester was a community where men were esteemed according to the number of patents they controlled. The rest of the time he lay watching the birds, trying to figure the aerodynamics of the skimming flight of swifts and swallows.

To everybody's amazement his fever abated. He conducted his convalescence as meticulously as he would any other experiment. As soon as he was able he went down to see the patent attorneys his father had picked out for him. One of the partners, a thinlipped Vermonter named Charles T. Hawley, showed interest in his plans. During the rest of his life it was Hawley who reduced his multifarious projects to suitable form for submission to the Patent Office.

His first patent, granted in the summer of 1914, described a rocket motor propelled by a mixture of gasoline and nitrous oxide injected at a very low temperature. A second patent that same year was based on his conception of a multistage rocket.

When the assassinations at Sarajevo set off a general war among the European nations, he made his first suggestion to Naval Ordinance that they think about rockets for anti-aircraft defense. Someone wrote back asking for samples. He had nothing to send. Illness and lack of funds had delayed his production of models.

That fall he was well enough to teach part-time at Clark and to take advantage of their wellequipped laboratories for research. In the course of the following year he proved experimentally that a rocket could fly in a vacuum. He was already on the edge of laying down the basic formulae upon which the science of rocketry would be founded.

Teaching and studying at Clark, Goddard was deep in research on the various fuels which might power his rocket. He applied for funds to the Smithsonian. In January 1917 the news reached him that, upon the advice of Dr. Abbott, an astrophysicist who was assistant secretary, a five-thousand-dollar grant would be forthcoming.

One of his old professors at Worcester Tech turned over an unused laboratory for his private use. He was so intent on secrecy that he covered the windows with heavy blankets and installed a burglar alarm.

Inevitably, as a patriotic citizen, when Woodrow Wilson declared war on the Central Powers he began looking for immediate applications which might be useful to the Army and Navy. His fame had spread. The Signal Corps made him a grant of $20,000 to explore the military possibilities of his rockets in a laboratory furnished by the Mt. Wilson Observatory in California.

The result was a number of rockets to be fired horizontally and a set of plans for the bazooka which the Army kept on the shelf till World War II. In the fall of 1918 he came East, with his very capable assistant Clarence Hickman, to demonstrate his rockets. The tests at Aberdeen Proving Ground were successful. The Army Aircraft Armament Section urged him to proceed at once with the development of a high-velocity rocket to be fired from planes. An appropriation would be forthcoming.

Four days later Germany surrendered. With the end of the war all plans for improving military hardware were forgotten.

Goddard went back to his classes at Clark. When Einstein announced his relativity theory Goddard seemed to have grasped the whole purport at a gulp. He was kept busy lecturing to faculty groups on its probable consequences. Already he was dropping hints that the break-up of the atom might some day furnish a source of power.

Meanwhile, Dr. Webster, the head of the Physics Department, was urging him to publish an article on the progress of his work. In fact, he threatened to make the work public himself if Dr. Goddard didn't.

Goddard was further alarmed by a flurry of newspaper articles which had been set off by some wellintentioned puffs in the *Worcester Gazette*. He was beginning to feel he had to make the true facts known, though all his instincts were against seeking publicity before he had some practical accomplishment to report.

The story was going around that the Goddard rocket could outperform the "Big Bertha" cannon with which the Germans had bombarded Paris towards the end of the war. A dispute over priorities had already begun. The British were citing the Congreve rockets their fleet had used to bombard Copenhagen a hundred years before. The continental press became inflamed to the point of adding that Goddard's rocket could attain a height of seventy miles and was being vigorously developed by the American War Department.

Goddard, who knew only too well how untrue all this was,

.suggested to the Smithsonian that they publish the original paper which he had sent in with his appeal for funds. Dr. Abbott cautiously asked Goddard whether he was willing to let the Smithsonian pay for publication out of his grant. Goddard consented and his paper appeared during the last days of December 1919 under the title of "A Method for Reaching Extreme Altitudes."

For two or three weeks there was no mention in the press of Goddard's report, which has remained to this day a basic classic of the science of rocketry. Then a rash of headlines broke: "Modern Jules Verne Invents Rocket to Reach Moon."

His mother's death distracted him from the noise of the headlines. His grandmother had died at eightythree, three years before. Her mind was sparkling to the end. Since boyhood his grandmother had been the confidante of his secret aspirations. Her innocent enthusiasm for new inventions had buoyed him up in the darkest times of his adolescence. She was buried, he noted, on October 19, the secret "Anniversary Day" of his dream in the cherry tree which he always remembered in his diary. Now in January 1920 his gentle affectionate mother quietly passed away. Their deaths left him with an acute need for female companionship.

Already he had astounded his colleagues in the Mt. Wilson laboratory by his futile efforts to date up certain young waitresses and secretaries. At thirtysix he was a baldheaded youngishlooking bachelor with a trim moustache. He was a very neat dresser. He started looking for a mate with the persistence he showed in his scientific work. He attended weekly dances at Terpsichorean Hall. The names of young women began to appear in his diary along with notations of pressures and experimental velocities.

Eventually he zeroed in on Esther Kisk who worked as a secretary in President Atwood's office. She had been kind about typing papers for him. Nineteen years his junior, she was the daughter of Swedish immigrants. Her father was foreman of a woodworking shop and her mother ran a lunch counter in a manufacturing plant. They were working overtime to put their children through college.

It took Goddard years to convince the Kisks that he was the right man for their daughter, but in the end he had his way. Quickwitted and longsuffering, she turned out to be the perfect wife for him.

Meanwhile the inventor was of two minds about the sensational stories on his "moonrocket" that occupied the Sunday supplements and provided occasional headlines for the daily papers. He didn't want to discourage public interest which might result in more funds for research. At the same time he wanted the journalists to get the story straight. The high-altitude rocket and the calculations it was based on were in the beginning stage. A great deal more experimentation was needed.

The cost of publication of his paper had cut down his grant from the Smithsonian. As there seemed no possibility of getting it renewed, he applied for a similar amount to the trustees of Clark University. They whittled the sum down to a paltry thirtyfive hundred dollars to be spread over two years.

Again he tried to interest the military. After a good deal of futile correspondence, the Navy Bureau of Ordinance offered him a hundred dollars a month, travel expenses, fifteen dollars per diem to work on designated projects at a designated place. The place was an abandoned powder factory at Indian Head on the Potomac River. There, working alone with only occasional help from mechanics from Dahlgren, working on weekends and holidays and summer vacations, he designed a depthcharge rocket for use against submarines and a rocket capable of propelling an armor-penetrating warhead. By 1923 the funds ran out. A careful report pointing out the opportunities for further development was filed away and not uncovered until the Second World War.

At the same time, with one assistant, in a sheet-iron extension he had added for safety's sake to the Physics laboratory at Clark, he continued experimenting with fuels. Smokeless powder would not work. He would try liquid oxygen. He thought of liquid hydrogen but that gas was not yet available in usable form.

Meanwhile, Goddard became rudely aware of the theoretical development of rocketry in Europe. A number of complimentary letters from French students of aerodynamics were followed in May 1922 by a letter from a student of mathematics at Heidelberg which troubled him greatly. The letter, signed Herman Oberth, asked for a copy of his Smithsonian paper. Immediately the suspicion rose in Goddard's mind that the Germans were more interested in the military applicatons of his rockets than in the exploration of interplanetary space. He was convinced that they had knowledge of his plans which, to be sure, were available to anybody at the U.S. Patent Office. When he received Oberth's brilliant paper called "The Rocket into Interplanetary Space," his worst suspicions were confirmed. It is unlikely that at this time he had heard of the pathfinding work which a schoolteacher named Konstantine Tsiolkovski published in a Russian scientific journal in 1903. Goddard could console himself with the fact that none of his European competitors had actually built an experimental rocket.

March 16, 1926, he proved his primacy by successfully firing his liquid-fueled rocket in his Aunt Effie's field in Auburn Township. In spite of his disappointment with the limitations of the flight, Dr. Abbott of the Smithsonian drew on one of the funds at his disposal to the amount of twentyfive hundred dollars which he sent on in driblets of five hundred dollars each for further research. It was July 1929 before Goddard was ready for the final test of a rocket equipped with a parachute that would let the necessary instruments down gently to the ground when the flight terminated.

By this time he had several assistants. His wife Esther operated the motion-picture camera. The rocket rose eighty or ninety feet. Though it didn't rise high enough to trip its parachute, most of the instruments were recovered in fairly good condition.

The rocket landed with a bang. One of Aunt Effie's neighbors was so alarmed by the explosion that she telephoned the police that an airplane had crashed. While Goddard and his crew were still collecting the scattered parts a police siren startled them. A police car and two ambulances drew up in Aunt Effie's barnyard. Eager spectators poured out into the field. Among them were two reporters who began to examine suspiciously the charred rocks under the launching tower. The next morning the national press reported with some glee that another effort to reach the moon had ended in failure. The Moonrocket Man was becoming a figure of fun in the public mind.

The Auburn police took a serious view of the explosion. They ignored Goddard's protestations that he was engaged in a harmless scientific experiment to which his aunt, the owner of the land, had gladly consented. The people of Auburn made it clear that they wanted no more explosions. The Massachusetts Fire Marshal issued an edict that no such tests were to be conducted within the bounds of the state.

Goddard was forced to seek help from the Smithsonian to find another site. The War Department was induced to allow him to use an abandoned artillery range, known as Hell's Pond, within the limits of old Camp Devens. Moving his equipment used up most of his remaining funds.

His situation would have been hopeless if Charles Lindbergh hadn't read of his tribulations in the *New York Times*. Catapulted to fame two years before by his solo flight across the Atlantic, young Lindbergh was conducting himself with innocent modesty in his position of fortune's favorite. He remained full of youthful enthusiasm for every possible development of aviation. What he read of Dr. Goddard's experiments fitted in with his own cogitations on flight beyond the atmosphere. He promptly took off for Worcester.

The same afternoon he appeared in the office at Clark which Goddard had occupied since the unexplained suicide of Dr. Webster a number of years before had promoted him to head of the Physics Department. The two men hit it off immediately. Before he knew what he was doing, Goddard was outlining his complete plans to young Lindbergh in a way he had never done before, even to his closest collaborators. He found Lindbergh's simple honesty irresistible. After they had talked a couple of hours he took the young aviator home to meet Esther. She brought out chocolate cake and coffee to celebrate the occasion.

Lindbergh went to work to find a sponsor for further experiments. His first attempt was with the Du Ponts. Goddard got the notion the Du Pont engineers were pumping him to reveal details of his invention for their own use and clammed up on them.

Lindbergh flew him back from Wilmington to New York in his own plane. It was Goddard's first flight. Lindbergh's aerial gymnastics gave him quite a turn.

A meeting with a group of Washington scientists at the home of the president of the Carnegie Foundation produced nothing more tangible than the offer of another five thousand dollars. It was obvious to Lindbergh that the work had reached a point where financing was needed on a much larger scale, but Goddard, always optimistic, came away encouraged by the feeling that the scientific community was beginning to appreciate its importance. He was further buoyed up by a flock of invitations to lecture.

Meanwhile, there was much noise in Germany about rocket developments. German newspapers joined in the chorus of derision at Goddard's efforts. Though nobody in America knew it, German Army Ordinance was beginning to take great interest in the military possibilities of rocketry. The Treaty of Versailles forbade them from building big guns or airplanes but nothing had been said about rockets. Such notions had never entered the heads of the nearsighted politicians who imposed that treaty.

A German Interplanetary Society was courting publicity. Oberth planned a model rocket to be shot off at the opening of a film called "The Lady in the Moon," but he never managed to complete it in time. It was not till May 1931 that the first liquid-fuel rocket would be flown successfully by the German society. In that same month, G. Edward Penray, a science-fiction writer who had founded the American Rocket Society, reported on the German developments and invited Dr. Goddard to collaborate with his society. Dr. Goddard replied that he had not yet carried his experiments far enough to collaborate with anybody. He would have to carry them on alone.

Meanwhile, Lindbergh was screwing up his courage to ask Daniel Guggenheim to support Goddard's work. He was encouraged by the old man's interest in aviation but hesitated to use his friendship with Harry Guggenheim, who had been a Navy flier, as an opening wedge. At last in a single interview he convinced Daniel Guggenheim that Goddard's work would be a worthwhile project to put twentyfive thousand dollars a year into for four years. After that he could expect results.

As soon as he got home from the Guggenheims' great stone castle at Hempstead, he called up Goddard to tell him he thought he had a firm offer of support. All that remained was for the Guggenheim lawyers to write up a contract. Not quite convinced that the arrangement was final, to celebrate Goddard merely took his wife out to a Chinese restaurant. They did order the biggest meal on the menu.

Daniel Guggenheim was good as his word. President Atwood of Clark gave Goddard leave of absence from the university and loaned him the equipment he had collected in his laboratory.

The Moonrocket Man

On the advice of the chief of the U. S. Weather Bureau, Goddard picked the town of Roswell, in New Mexico, for his tests. He was assured that there was plenty of space there. He had no trouble in inducing his crew: Harry Sachs, Esther's brother Albert, Larry and Charles Mansur, to come along. He and Esther drove west in a freshly purchased secondhand Packard.

Roswell was then a town of eleven thousand people. The local boosters were eager to put it on the map as a resort for tuberculosis sufferers. Instead of obstruction Goddard found eager cooperation. The Secretary of the Chamber of Commerce helped him rent an abandoned ranch house three miles out of town on a deadend dirt road for quarters; and a local rancher allowed him to use part of his range for the test site, free on the understanding that his crew would close all closed gates after they went through them and leave all open gates open. The range was known as Eden Valley. Esther was amused by the contrast with Hell's Pond.

As soon as the equipment arrived they set up the launching tower in Eden Valley. The first static test was a failure. For some years now the rocket had been known to Goddard's crew as "Our Nell." A professor at Clark launched the nickname commenting on the uproar at Auburn "They ain't done right by our Nell."

After several more failures, on December 30, 1930, Nell soared from the tower to a height of two thousand feet, reaching a velocity of five hundred miles an hour.

Very much encouraged, Goddard attacked the problems of guidance and of coolants for the motor with fresh vigor. On the whole the climate agreed with him. He paid little attention to respiratory trouble that occasionally put him to bed for a few days.

Daniel Guggenheim's death at the end of the first year did not affect the operation of the fund. Goddard merely had to convince the trustees from time to time that the work was progressing. All seemed to be going smoothly when the Great Depression started to erode the Guggenheim fortune. The family lawyers reluctantly explained to Goddard that work would have to be suspended.

The fall of 1932 Goddard was back teaching at Clark. In his spare time he worked out a method of gyroscopic steering and a new centrifugal fuel pump which he patented with the help of his friend

Atwood. A doctor who examined his lungs told him urgently to get back to New Mexico. There he would have a better chance of survival than on the eastern seaboard. Lindbergh again came to the rescue but this time all he could manage was a grant of twentyfive hundred dollars from the Guggenheim Foundation. It wasn't until 1934 that the trustees, needled by Adolf Hitler's and Mussolini's warlike gestures in Europe, restored the full amount of their support.

In September 1934 the Goddards stopped off at the Chicago Exhibition on their way west. A Buck Rogers exhibit amused them mightily. Dr. Huer, the professor who fixed everything in the comic strip, was obviously a cartoon of Dr. Goddard himself.

The new series of tests at Eden Valley, though failures were as frequent as ever, showed advances in stability and power. An enlarged Nell flew fortyeight hundred feet before wobbling off course. Another flew seventyfive hundred feet. In September 1934 the professor and his crew felt they could hazard a public exhibition. Two rockets they had prepared for a visit from Harry Guggenheim and Lindbergh came to grief on the launching pad. It was an embarrassing occasion.

By this time it was obvious to everybody but Robert Goddard that the problems of rocketry would only be solved by putting many minds to work in a cooperative enterprise. All Lindbergh could accomplish, after much tactful argument, was to induce him to prepare a new report for publication by the Smithsonian. Goddard began as a loner and a loner he would remain.

Meanwhile, in 1930 the German Army Board of Ordinance under strict security set up a rocket program under the brilliant General Karl Becker who later committed suicide when he found he couldn't see eye to eye with the Fuehrer. According to Dr. Dornberger who headed the group, they failed to get details of Goddard's later inventions but worked out their problems by trial and error. Adolf Hitler was no help because he had dreamed that it would be dangerous to try to use rockets to attack Great Britain. His only part in the program was to name their first operational rocket "Vengeance Weapon #2." The success of their program first at Kunersdorf near Berlin and then at Peenemünde on the Baltic Sea put them years ahead in spite of Hitler's dreams.

By 1940 Goddard had completed his final version of his enlarged rocket without being able to report a completely successful test flight. In May of that year at the request of Harry Guggenheim, he came to Washington for a final appeal to the Armed Services. The U. S. was already threatened with engulfment in the European war. Since his pact with Stalin for the partition of Poland, Hitler's armies had toppled nearly every government in Western Europe.

With Guggenheim as his sponsor, Goddard had no difficulty in obtaining interviews with top officials of the Army and Navy. Goddard presented a detailed program. They listened to him but their doubts remained. The result was the usual frustration.

Back at Roswell, Goddard, aroused for once to the point of beating his own drum, filled the mails with protests and programs. His old associate Dr. Hickman, now heading one of the Bell Telephone Company's research departments, put his case bluntly to the various Chiefs of Ordinance. Another old colleague from Clark, Dr. Thompson, appointed to head up research at Dahlgren Proving Ground, introduced him to the Chief of Naval Ordinance.

Two months before Pearl Harbor, under the influence of younger officers who had become Goddard's fervent disciples, Naval Ordinance offered him a contract. He immediately went to work at Roswell on the adaptation of rocket propulsion to a takeoff of airplanes. In June 1942 the Navy decided to move Dr. Goddard's work to Annapolis. His lungs had not been behaving too well even in the high dry air of New Mexico, but he accepted the change without a murmur. Annapolis would be nearer the center of things.

The first test of his takeoff rocket, in the Severn River, proved as usual part success and part failure, but within two years his jets were operational. By 1943 his old projects were being taken off the shelf. It was a development of his bazooka that stopped the German tanks in Tunisia.

The Goddards were now established in a large cottage at Tydings on the Bay. While he gave most of his time to the projects entrusted to him by the Navy and Air Force, privately he was organizing his notes on space travel into a hasty writeup which he labeled "The Ultimate in Jet Propulsion." He sent to his friend Hawley in Worcester detailed projects labeled "cases in storage" out of which Hawley was able to devise successful applications for a hundred and thirtyone more patents after his death.

Though he seems to have been conscious that time was running out for him, he paid no attention to his wife's suggestions that he transfer his work—the terms of his contract left him free to do so—to Roswell, where a rebuilt workshop and a restored Mescalero Ranch were waiting for them. His voice was getting so husky he sometimes had to use the Morse code to communicate with his assistants. He suspected that he might be getting the same cancer of the throat that had carried off his father. When he was assured by a throat specialist at Johns Hopkins that cancer rarely appeared in connection with tuberculosis, he dismissed any further worry about his health.

The war situation furnished worries enough. In January 1944, Naval Intelligence reports confirmed his hunch about developments in Germany. He didn't have to wait for the appearance of the V2 to announce that the Germans had a ten-year lead in military rocketry. His diary in the following months reported for the first time spells of discouragement. His work at Annapolis was leading merely to the production of minor gadgets. Navy scuttlebutt had it that his contract would not be renewed when it expired.

The Goddards heard the news of the successful Allied landing on the French coast at breakfast June, 1944. This heartening news was followed almost immediately by reports of the buzzbomb, the German unpiloted plane that was seeking out targets in England. Soon after came news of the much more dangerous V2. The Goddard patent which covered most items of the V2 had been published in a German aviation journal five years before. It seems to have been news of the V2 that caused a sudden change in his attitude towards solitary work. He accepted an invitation of the American Rocket Society to lecture and consented to serve on its Board of Directors. It was too late.

In March 1945, the Allied armies crossed the Rhine and captured a V2 plant in full production. Goddard inspected a model shipped to Annapolis and reported to Harry Guggenheim on the similarities to his own plans which had been shelved due to the lack of interest of the big brass.

May 1, 1945, in revising a new edition of "A Method for Reaching Extreme Altitudes," Goddard wrote ironically "the subject of projection from the earth, and especially a mention of the moon must still be avoided in dignified scientific and engineering circles, even though projection over long distances on the earth's surface no longer calls for quite so high an elevation of the eyebrows."

As the summer of 1945 progressed, his health became desperate. He was operated on for a growth in his throat that had been described as benign. It was found to be malignant. His vocal cords were removed at the University Hospital. He lived long enough to read of the first atomic bombs. August 10, when his nurse arrived for the morning shift, she found him dead. The day the Japanese surrendered in Tokyo Bay he was buried in the Goddard's family plot in Worcester.

3

1948

Nov 1   Truman confident of ground swell
First trainees called in new draft reach Fort Dix
New York campers expelled by CIO as slaves to REDS
Goal of Chinese Communists the same as Reds
Berlin Airlift Working Despite Weather
Mukden is bombed by Nanking planes as Reds capture it
Airlift Backfires on the Russians
Truman Leads Dewey in Late Returns

Nov 4   Truman Wins with 304 Electoral Votes
   Race called Miracle of Electioneering

Mr. Thomas declared in an analysis of
   Tuesday's election that the liberal and
   labor elements of this country can be
   expected to capture the Democratic Party

4

Corn and the Common Man

The Common Man was the hinge of Henry Wallace's political preaching, but he himself
was the most uncommon of politicians,
researcher into the genetics of the cornplant,
statistician,
agricultural missionary with some of the selfrighteousness of the Presbyterian elder, a hint of the swami;
there had been nobody quite like him in American politics since Thomas Jefferson rode out from Monticello.

Franklin Roosevelt brought him to Washington in 1933 to give an Iowa touch to his Department of Agriculture.

The Wallaces were already one of farming's first families. Henry's father was Secretary of Agriculture under Harding and Coolidge; and his grandfather's good friend and close associate "Tama Jim" Wilson served in the office right through the administrations of McKinley and Teddy Roosevelt and Taft.

In Iowa the Wallaces were a dynasty: editors of farm journals, teachers in agricultural colleges, missionaries of improved farming methods.

The first Iowa Wallace left the family farm in Pennsylvania in the 1860s to follow the railroad out to the black soil belt.

A Presbyterian minister, he had served as a chaplain during

the Civil War. He gave up the ministry claiming the confinement ruined his health, but he never stopped preaching. He promoted choice breeds of cattle and speculated in corn acreage. He fished and he hunted. Evenings he wrote editorials for the farm journals.

Farmers read his lay sermons at family prayers.

He was affectionately known as Uncle Henry the whole state over.

His son, the second Henry, known as Harry to the family, taught agriculture at Ames and edited a farm journal of his own. He not only wrote about farming—none of the Wallaces ever stopped writing for a minute—but he was a dirt farmer himself. When he married he took on one of the family farms, five miles out of Orient, as tenant. There the third Henry—H. A. to his friends—was born, the oldest of six, in 1888.

Money was scarce in those years. Harry Wallace did most of the field and barn work himself; as they grew up his boys were expected to do likewise. H. A. was raised to the morning chores, to milk, and plow and read the Bible like any other Iowa farmboy. To that he added botany. From a tender age, he had a hobby for classifying grasses.

One of his father's contemporaries at Ames was a lanky Negro man named George Washington Carver. Born of slave parents, Carver had worked his way through all the courses in botany and agronomy offered by the middlewestern colleges. The tall Negro and the touslehaired white boy had a passion in common: grasses. Together they tramped over field and hill seeking out strange grasses. All his life Henry Wallace was grateful to Carver for teaching him the minutiae of the fertilization of grasses.

With the advent of McKinley's full dinner pail, good times dawned for Iowa. H. A.'s father moved his journal *The Farm and Dairy* to Des Moines. *Wallace's Farmer*, Uncle Henry's paper, was already going great guns. "Good farming, clear thinking, right living" was its motto.

People still lived the old country life in the burgeoning state capital. H. A. attended public school, pumped water up into a tank in the attic for the bathroom, fed the fowls, milked the family cow. He was a shy awkward untidy sort of boy; his cowlick kept falling over his eyes; all his life he never could quite keep his shirttails tucked in. He never learned any smalltalk. Under his silence he hid a welter of enthusiasms. He had a passion for grasses. Corn was a grass. Corn was king of the grasses.

Corn was the focus of the Iowa economy as much as it had been the focus of the life of the farming Indians who developed, through centuries of selecting the seed they liked best, the incredible range of the corn plants' shapes and varieties.

In those days every farmer strove to produce the smooth enormous ears that won blue ribbons at the county fairs. But how did they yield? Young H. A. had heard sceptics say that the seed corn from prizewinning ears yielded no better than seed corn from the sorriest nubbins.

His father encouraged him to make a test. In the spring of 1904 he plowed up ten acres and carefully handsowed it with seed from thirteen ears, some prizewinners and some rejects. It was a good growing season. He worked his corn all summer with one horse and a planet junior cultivator. When harvest came he discovered that the seeds of the prizewinning ears weren't the best yielders at all.

Yield depended on something else than looks.

What was wrong?

How to select for the largest crop?

From then on H. A. was hooked on the genetics of corn.

In college he read reports of the work of two professors in the East. Stimulated by Mendel's laws of heredity, which had remained lost in the drawer until a German professor rediscovered them in 1900, Dr. Shull was crossing inbred strains of sweet corn on his small experimental plot on Long Island. Meanwhile, on a farm that had once belonged to Eli Whitney near New Haven, a middlewesterner named E. M. East was laboriously recommencing a series of experiments which he had never been allowed to finish at the government station in Illinois.

Both men produced hybrid corns; the problem was what good were they? East and Shull agreed that the key to improvement lay in crossing inbred strains which, though weak in themselves, carried in their chromosomes the traits which might combine to form a productive and vigorous hybrid.

H. A. was intrigued, but he liked his work to be thorough. He had to prove these theories. He started in his backyard in Des Moines laboriously fertilizing each ear by hand to obtain a cross.

Then he hit on detasseling.

Let the wind do it.

He knew that corn, or "maize" as the scientists called it, was a manmade plant. Careful men in prehistoric times, selecting the best seed from season to season, had developed the four great families of corn he knew. The plant had a gift for mutations. But no known variety could subsist by itself. Men had to shell the grains off the cob and plant them and tend them.

Where had it been developed? Mexico, the Andes, China?

Mysteries unsolved.

No botanist had found the ancestor of modern maize but that did not mean it might not exist in some faraway mountain valley. Nothing was certain.

H. A. felt, as few men, the awe of the unknown. He was as steeped in cornworship as the farmer-shamans of the planting tribes.

A passion to do good was bred in the bones of the Wallaces.

Scotch-Irish to the core. H. A. caught fire at the thought that hybridizing might bring the first radical improvement in a food grain since the days of prehistoric man.

When he graduated with honors in Animal Husbandry, he decided, instead of working for a college professorship as his friends had expected, to devote his life to the growing of corn. Like his father and grandfather before him, he would pay his way during the early years by writing editorials for the family press. First he had to see a little of the world. Already he had mountainclimbed in the Rockies on fishing trips with his grandfather.

He invested in a student tour of Europe. On the way to the steamer, he spent four days in Washington with his grandfather's friend, the veteran Secretary of Agriculture. The Wallaces and Wilsons fell easily into the role of the rural elite. James Wilson's bureau chiefs were impressed by the shy young man's knowledge of every recent development in the breeding of corn.

In Europe, H. A. was more interested in learning how the farmers grew corn than in seeing the sights. For many years his chief interest in Europe was in the crisis in agriculture provoked by Napoleon's wars.

Back in Des Moines he threw himself ever deeper into the slow careful work of hybridizing. A record had to be kept of each plant. The removal of the male tassel to keep the ears from being self-fertilized in the female rows was a timeconsuming operation. Every detail had to be noted with consummate care.

The accepted theory was that inbreeding was disastrous, yet East and Shull had developed their most desirable varieties by crossing inbred strains. The more he experimented, he told a friend, the more he found himself driven into the arms of East's and Shull's theories. These theories were turning nineteenth-century genetics topsy-turvy.

People called H. A. a visionary. Visionary was right, but he wasn't the only one. DeKalb in Indiana and Funk in Illinois had eager groups of young visionaries working to make East's and Shull's theories come true.

H. A. was absorbed in his work. His friends were amused when they found that his courtship of a young lady named Ilo Brown consisted in reading her a book about Chinese farming. Abstracted. Absentminded to a degree. After the wedding the story was told that he jumped into the car first and closed the door on his bride. He had no time for anything but corn.

In 1924, by crossing an inbred race of "Leaming," sent him by East in Connecticut, with a waxy type of Chinese corn known as "Bloody Butcher," he produced his first practical hybrid. He named it "Copper Cross."

He had enough of the foundation stock to plant an acre the next year. A friend who worked for the Iowa Seed Company contracted to market the product. H. A. wrote the come-on in the catalogue: "A foretaste of what is coming in the cornbreeding world. Ten years from now hundreds of crosses of this sort will be on the market."

Copper Cross earned a gold medal. East wrote him kiddingly that Leaming ought to get half the credit and H. A. mailed him the medal.

A dollar a pound.

The farmers grumbled at the price. Those Wallaces were a visionary lot. The idea of having to buy seed each year instead of saving your own! But the funnylooking yellow corn caught on. It became a problem where to find the acreage to grow more hybrid seed. His wife traded her family farm for land nearer Des Moines. H. A. through personal talks and editorials in *Wallace's Farmer* was reaching the young farmers. He ransacked the agricultural schools for adventurous souls willing to take on the extra labor and risk of growing the new hybrids. In 1926, with a couple of friends and some funds his wife had inherited, he founded the Pioneer Hi-Bred Seed Corn Company of Des Moines.

The beginnings weren't easy. Hybrids had to be produced that had strong stalks, resistance against drought, insects, blight. No matter how deep he went into the mathematics of genes and chromosomes, hybridizing remained a hit-or-miss business. Copper Cross wasn't good enough. Other strains turned out faulty: H. A. had the knack of attracting fellow visionaries. He stimulated the enthusiasm they needed to surmount frustrations and failures. Within ten years all the researchers at Pioneer were convinced that his prophecy was coming true. After twenty it was abundantly fulfilled.

Pioneer wasn't alone. Every year the competition spread. Funk in Illinois and the DeKalb Company in Indiana were producing hybrids immune to lodging and disease. Hybrid seed corn was never the invention of any one man or any one company. The basic strains the hybridizers used had been developed over a hundred years by corn growers who took up where the Indian planters had left off.

Somehow during those deep Depression years, when journalists and intellectuals were wringing their hands over the failures of American society, the hybrid corn workers were bringing about one of the first radical and revolutionary steps forward in farming since the aboriginal planters selected out the first fecund strains of corn and wheat and of all the food crops the farmer grows today. In 1933, only one percent of Iowa cropland was planted with hybrid seed. Nine years later the percentage was nearer ninetyeight. Mechanization, weedkillers, improved fertilizers all played their part, but hybrids, tailored to the climate and the land, were the basis of the increase in yield. In the 1920s, forty bushels was considered a good crop; in the 1960s, many a cornbelt farmer would be unhappy if he missed the two hundred mark.

It was a wrench to leave the experimental plots of Des Moines for a Washington office, but H. A. was as much a preacher as he was a research scientist. The Department of Agriculture was a family tradition. He was stepping into his father's shoes. In the Hundred Days he was in his element.

Republicanism had been the family creed. H. A. had left that long since for the New Deal. Now he began to equate Republicanism with original sin.

He was the most active Secretary of Agriculture the nation ever had and probably one of the best. A frugal man who never smoked or drank, his intoxicants were experiment and innovation. In agriculture he was on firm ground. Rural electrification. The ever-normal granary. The war on erosion.

Nineteen thirtyfour and 1935 were the years of the dust storms. Searing drought in the Middlewest, ferocious winds. On March 25, 1935, while the Senate Committee on Public Lands was in session at the Capitol, the Washington sky was darkened with dust from the Great Plains. The rich farmlands of Kansas were blowing away in the wind.

Drought and depression, scourges out of the Old Testament. H. A. was a great reader of the minor prophets. Micah and Amos he felt to be farmer prophets. With the assurance of the Hebrew prophets, Henry Wallace denounced the ungodly who didn't agree with him.

The Wallaces were outdoor people. To get out of doors Henry played tennis, and well. He took long drives at high speed on lonely roads. He threw the boomerang.

The boomerang delighted him. Why when you threw it right would it land at your feet? He amused himself figuring the aerodynamics of this strange toy.

Practical men scoffed, sometimes with good reason, at the New Deal visionaries. Earthy old George Peek, Roosevelt's first Agricultural Adjustment Administrator, resigned in a huff, declaring that presenting facts to the New Dealers was a sheer waste of time. "The administration," he wrote, "was a curious collection of Socialists and Internationalists, men who have never earned their livings in industry, commerce, finance or farming and who have no comprehension of how such livings are earned."

He had this to say of Henry Wallace: "He had tended rather to specialize in the study of corn"—neither did Peek have much idea of how corn was studied—"and was a dreamy, honestminded and rather likable fellow. He had a mystical religious side to him. Never having been in the rough and tumble of life—for he simply went on the family paper as a matter of course—he was apt to view clashes of economic forces as struggles between good and bad men, and not as between groups, all of whom believed that right was with them. Since Henry was with the good men he never quite got the whole of any picture."

Just the man to give the messianic touch to Franklin Roosevelt's third campaign for the Presidency. As Vice-President, Wallace began to interest himself in Latin American agriculture. For some years now he had been studying Spanish. Sent to Mexico to represent Franklin Roosevelt at the inauguration of Avila Camacho, he was fascinated by the corn he saw.

He shared the Indians' reverence for the sacred grain, but he was horrified by their poor yields.

In Mexico City he delivered himself of a modest speech in Spanish which pleased the Mexicans, astonished that a gringo politician would take the trouble to learn their language.

Wherever he went he asked about corn.

As soon as he reached home, he induced the Rockefeller Foundation to undertake a program to improve the culture of Mexico's three basic food crops. The result was, in twenty years, a tripling of Mexico's production of corn and a fivefold increase in wheat. The research in new strains of wheat at Ciudad Obregon was the starting point for the runaway improvement in tropical wheats that bids fair to revolutionize the agriculture of the hungry countries.

After four years as Vice-President and the production of a flood of cloudy speeches somewhat too Socialist for the public taste, Franklin Roosevelt decided that H. A.'s head was in the clouds. He let the organization Democrats fight it out with Sidney Hilman's New York radicals.

Dr. Win-the-War was beginning to take the place of Dr. New Deal.

At the 1940 convention the administration forces ditched Henry Wallace for Harry S. Truman. H. A. proved his loyalty to F. D. R. by attacking Wendell Willkie, the Republican candidate, as Hitler's favorite. He was rewarded by being made Secretary of Commerce.

He was developing a colossal blind spot where the Communists were concerned. As a geneticist, he knew that innovations didn't always work, but as a political economist he closed his eyes to the failures of social engineering at home and abroad. When Roosevelt died at the beginning of his fourth term, President Truman dropped H. A. from his cabinet for making a speech against American imperialism that would have made a good editorial in *Pravda*.

On a trip to Siberia while he was Vice-President, Wallace saw only the technological potential and never the human degradation of Stalin's regime. At home he could only see capitalism's faults and never the fantastic material advance it was bringing about for the very common man whose cause he espoused.

He was revolted by Winston Churchill's speech at Fulton, Missouri, where the deposed British war chief pointed out that concessions at Yalta and Potsdam had only made the Russians more greedy for conquest.

He grumbled about the Marshall Plan and flatly opposed Truman's aid to Turkey and Greece. He quarreled with Bernard Baruch's proposals for a treaty that would mitigate the danger of an atomic arms race and proposed to turn over the atomic formulae outright to the Russians. Every word he said was applauded in *Pravda*.

As editor of the *New Republic* he became the chief guru of the Russophile liberals. A gaggle of oneworldites, Socialists, Communists and misinformed idealists organized the "Progressive Citizens of America" to boost him for the Presidency.

A Presidential aspirant lives in a narcotic haze. "No danger on the left" became Henry Wallace's slogan.

Everything Henry Wallace said was applauded worldwide by the Communist press.

He made a bid for the Negro vote. As a friend and lifelong admirer of George Washington Carver, he could not abide segregation. Wherever he spoke, even in the South, he insisted that Negroes be seated in the audience.

Whether what he said made sense or not, he was derided as a crackpot by the large circulation newspapers. Letters were printed that showed him seeking advice from a clairvoyant. He was accused of weird dealings with a certain Roerich, an enigmatic Russian, ethnologist and mystic, half scientist, half charlatan, who flourished in an endowed museum on the upper West Side in New York. His more levelheaded supporters were sometimes surprised at the company they found themselves keeping.

In 1947, the May Day marchers in New York carried—Soviet-style—a sixty-foot portrait of Henry Wallace at the head of their column. An improvised Progressive Party, aimed to exploit the popularity of the La Follette name in the Cornbelt, nominated him for the Presidency. The Soviet press cheered him on. He was for full employment, production for use, and close ties with the Soviet Union: the century of the Common Man.

That truly common man, Harry Truman, took him on, along with the Republican candidate and a small States Rights Party in the South, and beat them all when the ballots were counted.

Defeat was a release in a way.

Settled back on his new farm, which he named Farvue, at New Salem, New York, away from the clamor and contention, Henry Wallace could interest himself in his line of hybrid chickens, which was proving a commercial success in the hands of his son in Des Moines. He started a new branch of research in the hybridizing of strawberries. He frequented flower shows with examples of his hybrid gladiolus.

He lived as a quiet country gentleman, served on juries, attended the Episcopal Church and began admitting to his friends that he had allowed the Commies to pull the wool over his eyes just a bit during his Presidential campaign. When he allowed himself to be quoted in support of President Truman on the Korean War, it caused a break with his Progressive Party. From that day on the Communist-inspired press never had a good word to say for Henry Wallace.

Freed from the delusions of politics, he became again the rational researcher. He lived just long enough to learn the final solution of the mystery of the corn plant's origin.

As early as 1948 and 1950, archaeologists excavating the anciently inhabited Bat Cave in New Mexico found tiny ears of a pristine podcorn in deposits which were carbon-dated to somewhere around 3600 B.C. This was figured to be close to the uncultivated ancestor.

Paul Mangelsdorf of the Bussey Institution at Harvard set to work to cross podcorn with popcorn and backcrossed his hybrids till he produced a podcorn which could conceivably disperse its own seed.

This artificial throwback gave the archaeologists a hint of what to look for in their search for a wild maize.

Developed forms of maize were already turning up in four-thousand-year-old human deposits in caves in Northern Mexico. Meanwhile, a strange fossil pollen isolated from drillcores taken from the old lakebed seventy meters down under Mexico City was suspected by botanists to be the pollen of a primitive maize that flourished there during the last interglacial period. Presumably this antedated the appearance of man in the Valley of Mexico.

The story of the beginnings of maize in America is the story of the beginnings of farming.

The key discoveries were made in a series of caves in the Tehuacan Valley. Beginning in strata from the first human occupancy five thousand or so years ago, enough wellpreserved cobs have been dug up to trace the development from the early wild prototype of the four families of maize now grown in Mexico. The latest tiny ears of wild maize were found in strata carbon-dated at around 250 A.D.

Not a trace of wild maize has been discovered growing today in that valley or anywhere else in Mexico. Its close relatives, tripsicum and teosinte, range from Mexico to Bolivia. They interbreed with maize but that is all. Where did the wild maize go?

In a paper published in 1964, Paul Mangelsdorf, Richard MacNeish and Walton Gallinat, prime researchers into corn history, launched an ingenious theory. On the one hand, the early farmers pre-empted all the land suited to the plant's growth for their cultivated varieties, and on the other, since corn hybridizes readily and its pollen is carried immense distances by the wind, the very improvement of the cultivated varieties tended to produce hybrids unsuited to propagate themselves in the wild.

Henry Wallace died at seventyseven. His life spanned not only the discoveries that cleared up the origins of corn but the development of hybrids that increased its range and increased fivefold the food value of a crop on a given piece of land.

The increase in farm productivity was the work of many hands and many minds. No one man had more to do with it than Henry Wallace.

5

Iowa Takes the Lead

Will Henning was born into one of the founding families of the little farming town of Poplar Falls, Iowa. His father, Josiah Henning, as owner and manager of Henning's Emporium, had been a leading citizen as long as anybody could remember. Henning's Emporium, carefully stocked, well lighted and spotlessly clean, was famous all over the state. A silent, cogitative man, who had found time to do considerable reading, and to think about what he read, Josiah Henning was great friends with "Uncle Henry" Wallace and "Tama Jim" Wilson. He hated social events and smalltalk but enjoyed talking philosophy with a few cronies. He owned a couple of farms on the outskirts of town. He didn't care too much about general farming but he was an enthusiast for fine breeds of cattle. He had a small herd of English shorthorns that were his pride and joy. A beautiful Percheron stallion he kept at stud improved the breed of workhorses for miles around.

Horses and mules were an important part of the life of Poplar Falls. The town supported three blacksmiths. Farmers in the back country still plowed with oxen. The Missouri mule was proving more suitable to work with the farm machinery fast being developed by the great number of concerns that followed on the heels of the McCormick Company. The buying and selling and swapping of horses and mules were the main business of the farmers who crowded the streets and livery stables Saturday afternoons.

Josiah Henning didn't live on either of his farms. He was a small-town man. He raised his family in a yellow frame house with wide porches ornamented with scrollsaw work on Center Street opposite Lancaster's Livery Stable. The Henning house was at easy walking distance from the store.

Will was the youngest of the three boys. He had an indulgent older sister. Will remembered his brother, Merrill, the oldest boy, with affection all his life, though he was a rather dour fellow, because he taught him to swim. Merrill hated school. He was irked by the chores the boys had to do around the house. He was only happy when he was fussing with machinery. When Dad bought their first Model T, Merrill must have taken it to pieces and put it together a dozen times. Merrill became the family chauffeur. Mr. Henning had been in the habit of having his pair of sleek matching bays hitched up to the surrey and driving out to visit the farms at eight o'clock every Saturday morning. It was the only time he could go because Saturday afternoons he had to be in his office back of the store to greet old friends from distant farms and to watch over the line of credit his clerks were giving out. He kept the oldtime Presbyterian Sunday. He never would learn to drive a car, and Mama, who was as skillful with the reins as he was, called cars devil machines and refused to touch the wheel. Driving the Ford touring car over the bumpy graveled pikes and the rutted farm tracks that served for roads in those days, Merrill was in his element.

Joe, two years older than Will, was the bookworm of the family. Joe was tall and dignified and always at the head of his class in school. He parted his sandy hair in the middle.

Though they were so different, he and Will were very close. Will was always after Joe for help with his lessons. When they were in college, he used to declare that without Joe he would have failed every course. It wasn't that Will didn't like to learn. He was curious as all get-out and crazy for information, but he just couldn't keep his mind on homework and reading. He liked to have people tell him things.

When they were in gradeschool, Will was a rolypoly little fellow with untidy brown hair and bright pink cheeks. He was a great one for talking people around. From the time he was six, he never stopped asking questions. He'd question Mr. Lancaster and the stable boys about how much corn and oats the horses ought to eat. He would rush into the kitchen, where he wasn't supposed to go, to ask Lizzie, the Irish cook, how much baking powder she put in the hotcakes. Until his father ran him out, he would hang around the store pestering the clerks with questions about where the goods came from. He would spend hours listening to Jake Stepanovich, the elderly Slovak warehouseman, tell about how they used to farm in the old country. Jake had a way of slowly stroking his grizzled walrus moustache as he talked that Will found particularly impressive. He secretly planned to wear a walrus moustache when he grew up.

Meals at the Hennings' were solemn affairs. Dad would preface them with a long Presbyterian grace. Sister Sarah and brother Merrill would sit like undertaker's mutes. Joe would wriggle and squirm, but he kept his mouth shut. Even Mama who liked to chatter and laugh was subdued. Only Will could get away with piping up to ask his father one of his irrepressible questions. People found it hard to get mad at Will.

Will's first flyer in business was a paper route he operated with two other small boys. Every morning he'd meet the train that came in from Des Moines at seven fifteen and start staggering around town with big bundles of the *Des Moines Register*. He'd keep the other two kids on their toes. The papers had to be distributed, rain or shine, snowstorm or blizzard, no matter what. Sometimes the paper route made him late at school. He produced such plausible explanations that Miss Inglestadt, the principal, found it hard to punish him. At that he spent many an afternoon writing out maxims from his copy book in what never did approximate a Spencerian hand.

"The quick red fox jumped over the lazy hound," he would write out fifty times with cramped fingers. He'd wonder if he was the lazy hound or the quick red fox. He favored the fox. His high spirits bubbled up so inside him that the teacher once caught him whistling as he labored over his copying. Whistling in the classroom was the unforgivable sin.

When they finally turned him loose, he'd be off like a shot for Dad's farm across the bridge. He loved everything that happened on the farm. Winters there was bobsledding on the hilly pasture and skating on the river, and Saturday afternoon sleighrides out to farms belonging to friends of Dad's. Bunches of shouting, squealing, singing kids would be packed under buffalo rugs on one of the big drays on runners they used for hauling firewood. There would be hot bricks to keep their feet warm. The big horses would snort out steam and they would go skimming over the snowy hills. Years later when Will was driving his car fast over hardtop roads, he would sometimes remember that feeling of speed. Eighty miles an hour in a Chrysler Imperial couldn't touch it.

Summers he spent on the farm. The tenant, Ray Venner, had a big family of kids, four boys and three girls. They came all ages and shapes so that there was always somebody to play with. When Will went out there, Ray and Mrs. Venner just treated him like any other of their kids. Everybody helped with the chores. They learned how to milk, and fed the hogs and cleaned out the chickenhouse. They didn't have haybalers yet. After it had been winnowed, the boys would follow along pitchforking the hay into the wagon. The hay smelt better than anything in the world.

Haying seemed to attract thunderstorms. Great purple and yellow and white cauliflower clouds would start making up in the western sky. The boys would pitch and pitch until they were ready to drop. The horses would stamp their feet and whinny nervously at the sight of the lightning. Finally the great creaking wagon would start ponderously in the direction of the barn. As the first curtains of rain moved towards them across the green green hills, the boys would run for it. It was a race. The last one in's a rotten egg.

For reasons Will could never fathom, everybody's parents frowned on their swimming in the Poplar River. After haying or pulling cornfodder on a hot July day, a man couldn't live without a swim. Merrill had taught his brothers the rudiments of swimming in the pool at the YMCA in Des Moines, when they went over on the train to spend a weekend with him after he left home to take a job in a repairshop there. This was before he moved east to Detroit to go to work at Ford's. Merrill and Dad didn't get along. He wouldn't come back after he left home, not even to see Mama. After that they never did see him, not even at Dad's funeral.

The Venner boys and Will would sneak out in pairs when they were supposed to be straightening out the harness room in the barn or doing some other light aftersupper job and creep down along a hedgerow to an old hickory that overhung a deep pool. There was a bend in the river so people couldn't see you from the bridge. They'd leave their clothes in the hickory roots and slide down a steep bank into the cool brown water. Will never did get caught at it though Ray Venner caught his two younger boys there one Sunday afternoon and gave them a hiding they never forgot.

When World War I came on, Joe was a freshman at Ames. Will and Joe put their heads together the weekend after President Wilson declared war. They both admired Bob La Follette, but they agreed that Make the World Safe for Democracy was a slogan that carried them away. And hell, neither of them had ever been any further out of Iowa than Chicago. Joe went to Des Moines and enlisted and was sent to an officers' training camp in Indiana. He got stuck in the Quartermaster Corps and wasn't shipped overseas till after the armistice.

Will tried the Navy, but he never got beyond the Great Lakes Training Station. He made a great hit with the girls when he turned up at the highschool prom in his sailor suit in the spring of 1918. By midyears in 1919, he was out and applying for admission to the freshman class at Ames. Dad died in the flu epidemic and Mama was pretty well strapped while the estate was being settled and before she found a proper manager to run the store, so Will and Joe were on their own. The State College authorities were pretty helpful to boys whose schooling had been interrupted by military service. Joe came back in the late spring and they both stayed on in summer school to catch up. Will worked on the experimental farm and helped himself out selling books, encyclopedias mostly. He had a persuasive way with him. Joe, who turned out a brilliant student, had nailed down a scholarship while he was still a freshman. He came back from overseas very much bucked-up by having spent four weeks at Cambridge, England, while waiting to be shipped home. He said the economics courses were fine, but they just didn't have any idea about agriculture.

It was when Will was a junior and Joe a senior that the brothers first got to be real friends with H. A. Dad knew his redheaded father Harry Wallace quite well. They'd met the Wallaces at home several times when Dad was alive, but H. A. was so much older that he didn't notice them much. Now Harry Wallace was Secretary of Agriculture under President Harding and *Wallace's Farmer* was the leading farm paper in the country and the Wallace family was very much in the public eye.

The boys caught fire when they got word that H. A. was going to speak in the auditorium, about improving corn production. They had already read his articles about how they were hybridizing corn at the Connecticut and Harvard experiment stations. There was a good deal of controversy at Iowa State about H. A.'s theories. Corn in Iowa was a topic that hit everybody where he lived. The agricultural school had been holding up show corn for years as the type the farmers should work for, and many of the professors were sore at this young upstart who claimed it was no good. The students would argue the proposition on their way to class.

The auditorium was nearly full the night H. A. spoke. There were even girls who had driven over from Grinnell and the Teachers' College. H. A. certainly didn't have the platform manner. He mumbled his words and talked up at the ceiling, but what he said really made Will's heart beat faster. He had already read it in one of H. A.'s editorials in *Wallace's Farmer,* but it sounded better when he said it in his brooding, kind of offhand tone: "We are on the edge of a real revolution in farming. It may take ten years, and it may take twenty years; but all our preconceived notions about yield and productivity are going to be knocked into a cocked hat."

Will swore to himself he'd be in on it. The muffled fervor in H. A.'s voice excited him tremendously. He and Joe had been wondering whether they ought to advise Mama to sell Dad's farms. Right away Will decided No. The rise in farm values was just beginning.

Will had other reasons for being excited that evening. Among the girls was one with dark eyes and brows and a lovely creamy complexion and just the nicest kindest manner you ever saw. When Will and Joe crowded up to ask questions after the lecture there she was in the front row looking up at H. A. out of big brown eyes full of adoration.

H. A. wasn't paying any attention to the girls but seemed genuinely pleased to see Will and Joe. "I was looking around for a friendly face," he muttered. "There are people here," he let out his dry laugh, "who'd like to put a knife in my ribs."

Straggling after H. A. towards the entrance, Will managed to get into conversation with the darkeyed girl. Her name was Antonia

Hayek. The girls called her Tony. Right away Will made up his mind he liked Antonia. Her people were Bohemians. They lived in Des Moines. Right away he asked her if she'd let him take her to the commencement dance that was only three weeks off. She batted her eyes and looked bashful. "I'm the world's worst dancer," Will added cheerfully. That seemed to please her. "Maybe I can teach you," she whispered. Right then something clicked between them.

Will turned his attention to what H. A. was saying. He was telling Joe about a new test he was advocating of the prizewinning ears at the next state fair. He'd plant two or three rows of the prizewinning ears and two or three rows of kernels off any old nubbins and wager they would yield just as much.

H. A. had a way of going suddenly silent when he finished talking about something that interested him. The three of them stood constrainedly waiting in the gloaming for the car that was to pick him up. Junebugs buzzed around their heads. None of them could think of anything to say. It was a relief when the car came.

The girls had disappeared. Joe stalked off to the library. There was nothing for Will to do but go back to his room to pore over a thick volume on economics in preparation for next week's test. "Tony Hayek," "Antonia Hayek," he kept whispering to himself. Prettiest name he'd ever heard. The pages in the economics book went blank.

Will didn't do too much studying at Ames but he did everything else. He had a finger in every campus activity. For a while after they came back from the service he and Joe became regular Christers. They campaigned for the prohibition amendment. They threw themselves into YMCA work to bring light to the poor and shiftless across the railroad tracks. When a shirtsleeve evangelist named Ed Smithers appeared on campus, Will drank in his every word. He began to think he might have a calling for the ministry. He was going steady with Antonia Hayek by that time. When he began to sound her out as to whether she'd be willing to share the perils and privations of a missionary's life, she almost laughed herself sick. "I might," she said, "but, Will, I know you wouldn't."

From the moment Will and Antonia set eyes on each other, there wasn't much question as to who they were going to marry. The parents all wanted them to wait for a while after graduation from college. Antonia had been planning to teach and had a job waiting for her next fall. Will said he wasn't going to let her slip through his fingers like that. Now was the time.

He talked the parents around. The pair were married in July and set up housekeeping in a new little bungalow-type house on a new street a little outside the fashionable residential section in Des Moines. Will had gotten himself a job with Vickers and Wise selling real estate. He used his first commission to make a downpayment on the house.

Credit was plentiful. Everybody talked New Era. The Iowa farmers had sold all their products at boom prices during the war. They'd weathered the after-war Depression better than industry had. The value of farmland was soaring. Farmers' supply towns like Des Moines were full of business. Everybody was buying everything he could lay his hands on on the slimmest possible margins. Will told Antonia he was planning to make a pile of money and then they would decide what they really wanted to do with their lives.

That was the year H. A. launched Copper Cross. As Will cruised around the country showing farmland to prospective customers in his secondhand Essex, he never failed to stop off at H. A.'s experimental farm. He followed every detail of planting and detasseling until he could deliver a better lecture on the process of hybridizing and the future of hybrid seed corn than H. A. could. Particularly, Will kept track of the farmers who had bought H. A.'s seed at a dollar a pound. Most of them boasted about the crop: the best yield they'd ever had.

Babies started coming. The year their first little girl was born, Mama took sick. She hadn't been herself since Dad passed away. They took her over to the hospital in Des Moines: cancer. Mercifully, she died in three weeks.

The day of the funeral Will and Joe, who had come back from Leland Stanford where he was studying for his master's, received curious identical letters from Merrill. Merrill renounced his inheritance. They were to share it with their sister Sarah. He wrote that he had no use for private property. He had joined the Communist Party that had established the rule of justice and equality in the Soviet Union and would soon spread it throughout the world. Meanwhile, he was quite able to earn his keep. He wished them well and hoped they wouldn't be too disappointed when they learned how empty the rewards of capitalism were.

Will was rocked back. Joe, who was developing a leaning towards Socialism which was only held in check by his enthusiasm for the cooperative movement, said, "But it's all too drastic. . . . Remember when you were mad for Ed Smithers and thought you had a calling for the ministry?" Will winced and grinned. "I guess it's a preacher streak that runs in the family." He gave Joe a slap on the back. They put on their funereal faces and went out to rejoin the family gathered around the coffin in the living room.

Will's and Antonia's second boy was born in 1929. Three months later the stockmarket crash brought down the whole structure of New Era finance. Banks failed. Customers defaulted on their payments. Foreclosures didn't help because suddenly there were no buyers. Vickers and Wise filed a petition in bankruptcy. One fine autumn evening Will came home to supper and announced to Antonia that he was cleaned out.

"Let's have a good supper," she said with a schoolgirl excitement in her voice, "and then we'll decide." Susan and Little Will were already putting themselves to bed. When Antonia had gotten the baby to sleep, she cooked up a marvelous supper of steak and onions and scalloped potatoes. Afterwards while they nibbled on some leftover chocolate cake with their last cup of coffee, Will cried out, "What the heck! Let's move back to Poplar Falls and be peasants." One of Dad's farms was free and clear. They'd have their share of the profits of the store if there were any. They'd go back and be peasants. "My people were peasants for three hundred years." Antonia's eyes filled with tears. "They're not sorry tears, Will," she blubbered. "They're happy tears."

Before leaving town Will went around to see H. A. He had a notion he might grow a little hybrid seed corn. H. A. was in the dumps. Three years before he'd founded Pioneer of Des Moines with a couple of friends and a slice of his wife's money, but they were having heavy sledding. They could sell every bit of seed corn they produced, but they weren't producing enough to keep up with the expense of researching new strains. H. A. had collected a first-rate bunch of young fellows to help in the research. If he was going to hold them together, they had to be paid. Will said he had a hunch he could expand the market if he set up a company in Poplar Falls. "But what with. . . . I haven't got a warm dime."

That afternoon he went around to see Ed Jenks in the hospital. Will and Ed had gone through school together. Ed's father owned the only grist mill in Poplar Falls. Ed was an ambitious young fellow and mad about farming. He was convinced that mechanization was the answer. He was probably the first man in Iowa to try out a mechanical cornpicker. It was an early model. It worked all right when it didn't get jammed. Trying to clear the damn thing of a wad of stalks he'd gotten his arm caught. The bone was crushed. Will found him propped up in a hospital bed with his arm in a Balkan frame. Besides being in great pain, Ed was horribly depressed. He saw no prospect of getting back the use of his arm. How was he going to farm with a withered arm? He was the unhappiest guy you ever saw.

Will started to talk up hybrid seed corn. He had a hard time getting Ed to listen, but by the time he'd worked on Ed for an hour, he had at least talked himself out of his own depression. When he went back next day, he found Ed more cheerful. Ed's wife Hazel said Will had done him more good than the doctors. After a couple more sessions, Ed became really absorbed. It would be a partnership. Ed would furnish the initial capital and part of the land. Will would throw in his father's farm, superintend next summer's crop and sell the seed. By the time Will was ready to move the family back to Poplar Falls, the firm of Henning and Jenks had taken shape.

Corn that winter sold at ten cents a bushel. What they couldn't feed to the cattle and hogs farmers burned in the stove. Ray Venner after being the Hennings' tenant for so many years had moved his family out to California the summer before. He said if they were going to starve they might as well starve where it was warm. Will still had a little cash. He took Ray's dairy cows and a few steers and some pigs off his hands. Antonia was planning to raise chickens in the spring. The Venners left a woodshed full of wood and a cupboard full of canned goods and preserves they couldn't take with them. The house was tight. Will and Antonia had good stoves and an inside pump in the pantry. They'd eat and keep warm.

Will's first problem was to sell a few hundred bushels of seed corn left over from last summer's crop. How could you get farmers to pay a dollar a bushel for seed when they couldn't sell the corn in their bins for a dime?

Will thought up a scheme. He'd furnish the hybrid seed corn free if the farmers would pay him half their gain in yield. He sketched out a simple contract.

Will was never a man to hide his light under a bushel. He talked up his plan to a group of men he felt pretty cozy with, gathered for a cup of coffee at the Ideal Café one November afternoon. Charley Dirk said he ought to have his head examined. Robert Evans, who was cashier of the bank, muttered sourly that Will was one of the few men who still had a little credit left in this town; he hoped this wouldn't be the end of it. But Fred and Viv Stover, a couple of active fellows trying to make a living for their young families on rented land, cried out that they thought it was great; there was no way they could lose. Sure they'd go in on it.

It was a snowy winter. Will had trouble keeping the old Essex on the road. He'd have been in a mess if Fritz Lancaster, who ran the Poplar Falls Garage, hadn't let him hang up his repair bills. It was Fritz's father who had run the livery stable when Will was a boy. Will did part pay him with some loads of firewood off the farm. Sometimes he felt he was spending more time putting in fresh links in his chains and digging himself out of snowbanks than selling his customers.

The way Will put it was that he was peddling his corn out of the back of the car like a huckster. "Call that selling?" said Charley Dirk when Will cornered him in his barnyard where he was shoveling corn into the feeders for some woollylooking Hereford steers. "Will, I think the world of you and Antonia, but even if I didn't have more seed corn than I needed, I wouldn't buy it on those conditions. . . . I'd feel I was contributing to the delinquency of a minor."

Some of the other farmers who weren't special friends of Will's were even more suspicious. Must be something wrong with a deal where you get something for nothing. They studied the contract form, which Antonia had so painfully typed out after she'd put the kids to bed in the evening, with bent brows to find the catch in it.

At Christmastime Joe came east to help. With him he brought

Hellen Waring, his new bride. Hellen turned out just the nicest girl you ever saw. Her folks must have been pretty welloff because they had given her a new Chevrolet for a wedding present. The car made a sensation in town. No one in Poplar Falls had sported a new car since the stockmarket crash. Hellen was as smart as she was nice. She was taking her M.A. in Botany while Joe worked for his in Economics. She helped Antonia with the housework while Joe cruised around with Will selling seed corn. When Joe and his bride were ready to go back to the coast, they had to leave their fine car with Will. A blizzard had blocked up the roads. They went home on the train but every last grain of the '29 crop had been sold and even a few orders chalked up for 1930.

That spring was the leanest time Will and Antonia ever went through. They just didn't have any cash. They couldn't have kept clothes on the children without their credit at Henning's Emporium. At the Ideal Café the boys kept razzing Will about his giveaway program. Ed Jenks was home, but he still carried his arm in a sling.

Ed was down in the dumps again. A talk he had with an agronomist from Ames shook him all up. At the famous corn experimental station at Purdue, they had decided to give up working with hybrids. Interesting scientifically but no commercial future, was the word. All Ed could talk about was the expense of planting different seeds in different rows. Suppose you didn't get it detasseled right? The crop would be a dead loss. He'd stick by the agreement, he told Will, in a shaky voice, but Will would have to match any funds he put in. Ed was convinced they were going to lose their shirts.

Will and Antonia had one of their quick conferences over a cup of coffee after the children had been put to bed. Nothing to it but to put a mortgage on the farm. At that it was like pulling teeth to get two thousand dollars out of the Poplar Falls Bank.

When spring came and the business of plowing and harrowing the land, Will felt better. He didn't have time to worry. He could only get enough foundation stock from Des Moines to plant ten acres, but no ten acres in the State of Iowa ever got so much manicuring. When the male rows of the foundation stock came up looking wizened and weak, the boys at the café didn't have the heart to kid Will any more. They treated him like someone who had just suffered a bereavement.

Detasseling was a chore. They had to reach up and pull down each tassel of the female rows. Immediately Will began to plan a movable staging that would fit between the rows, but there was no time for anything like that this year. Ed and Viv Stover pitched in to help after they'd gotten their own corn laid away. Antonia put on an oldfashioned poke bonnet and worked like a Trojan in the field, but it was hard for her to reach up far enough to pull out the tasseling stalks. It was the captain of the highschool basketball team who turned out to be the prize detasseler. Phil Meyers was a lanky awkwardlooking lad with a big Adam's apple, but he sure could pull out those tasseling stalks. Will got him to work free with a promise of a share in the profits.

When the hybrid ears ripened, they looked a good size; but the grains were puny. Will's farmer friends turned them incredulously between their thick fingers when he laid out a handful of shelled corn on the oilcloth counter of the Ideal Café. Most of them shook their heads. Mule corn they called it. "Ain't nobody goin' to buy corn that won't breed true. A man ud be a fool to buy fresh seed every year."

"You wait and see," was all Will could say. It was a long wait, through another rough winter and a dry spring. Will never would have made it if it hadn't been for Antonia. They had four children now. She claimed she didn't know how she did it, but Antonia managed somehow to keep them fed and clothed. Their cows gave plenty of milk.When the hens stopped laying they didn't eat eggs. There was always oatmeal. Antonia never seemed to tire of thinking up new ways to cook beans. The babies were healthy. Will and Antonia were as healthy as they had ever been in their lives.

That spring Will had fifty acres planted in hybrid corn besides another fifty in foundation stock to hybridize for seed. It was a dry summer. Everywhere curled leaves and pallid stalks. Only the hybrid corn fought the drought. Even the earworm didn't raise such Cain as it did with the open-pollinated corn. Drought resistance and insect resistance were bred in. This was what convinced the farmers. The boys at the Ideal Café laid off razzing Will about his mule corn. They were all lining up to buy hybrid seed for next season.

It was 1937 before Henning and Jenks chalked up their first sale of fifty thousand bushels. As Will sat in his little office at the end of the warehouse down by the railroad tracks checking over the salesmen's figures, he swelled up with satisfaction until he was nearly ready to burst. "The happiest day of your life," he told himself; "No, the day you married Antonia was happier. You lucky bastard. All in eight years."

Eight years before even Henry Wallace, the most sanguine of men, had been skeptical. They had been bargaining—they were good friends, but H. A. drove a hard bargain when he wanted to—over the terms on which Henning and Jenks would sell the seed for which H. A.'s Pioneer Company would furnish the foundation stock. H. A. wanted a twentyfive percent royalty on all sales. Will claimed the royalty should go down as sales increased. "At five thousand bushels, twenty percent. At ten thousand, eighteen percent; at fifty thousand..." H. A. cut him off: "I love your optimism, Will," he said, "but there will never be fifty thousand bushels planted in your lifetime or mine."

Will burst out of his warm little office at the end of the warehouse by the railroad tracks into the raw April drizzle and walked fast up Main Street to have a cup of coffee with the boys. Nobody there but Charley Dirk, who had come into town to ship some old broodsows he was getting rid of. Disappointing. Charley Dirk was one of those guys who made a point of never being surprised at anything. Buz Lewis the counterman, now, was a good listener, but Will wanted somebody he could really get a rise out of. Will sat there stirring the sugar into his coffee and getting redder and redder in the face as he bottled up his good news. At last Robert Evans, who had slipped over from the bank, turned up on the seat beside him. Robert—nobody called him Bob—was Will's first cousin and they got along fine. Robert was rangy and sandy-haired, with a cool statistical mind and a sarcastic way of talking. "What are you looking so pleased about, Will?" he asked right away.

"Guess what Henning and Jenks sales were for the season."

"Thirty thousand bushels," drawled Charley Dirk from the end of the counter.

"Did better than that the year before," said Will, his high spirits bubbling up all over.

"I happen to know," said Robert in that omniscient tone he liked to put on, "that you sold 50,523 bushels. Ed came in the bank and told me this morning."

Buz in his deferential way said, well wasn't this a good time to have a cup of coffee on the house. He gave the oilcloth counter an extra polish with his cloth.

"Robert," Will said, "do you remember my telling you what H. A. said eight years ago when I told him we'd be selling fifty thousand bushels within a decade?"

"Not within my lifetime or yours," answered Robert. "Will, you are only thirtynine years old. Many a bushel to sell yet."

"We haven't half gotten started," said Will. He drank the hot coffee down as fast as he could. "I'll certainly razz H. A. about it next time I see him even if he is Vice-President of the United States."

He slipped off his stool. "Thanks, Buz. So long fellers."

As he left he heard Charley Dirk let out a hoot: "Will's got the gall to do it."

Will hurried down the street to where he had left his car parked. He couldn't wait to tell Antonia. He jumped in and drove across the Poplar River and up the hill to the farm. Antonia was in the kitchen. When she heard the news she threw her arms around him and hugged him. She was getting ready to roll out some piecrust and her hands were covered with flour.

They stood there looking at each other and laughing while Will brushed the flour off his jacket. Her eyes filled with tears. "Will, some of it has been a tough row to hoe, not all of it." She gave him a big blubbering kiss.

It had been a tough row to hoe but the turning point had come two years ago when Henning and Jenks had found themselves definitely in the black. The farmers had already begun to renege on Will's deal by which he furnished them free seed in return for half of the increased yield. They decided that Will was making too much money out of it. As the demand increased, Will contracted with Fred and Viv Stover to grow seed corn for him. He paid off the mortgage on the family farm and while prices were still depressed got hold of several hundred more acres of good land: Wisconsin drift. Some of it had black soil eighteen feet deep. At that he didn't have enough acreage to meet the demand. By 1937 he had all the best farms in the neighborhood growing seed corn for him under contract.

He didn't have time to do any farmwork himself any more. All day he drove from farm to farm in his Chevrolet stationwagon keeping tabs on his farmhands, checking his machinery, seeing that broken parts were renewed. Detasseling time everybody worked from dawn to dark. He was developing a knack for getting their best out of people. He directed his operations like a General marshaling troops in the field.

Increased production meant increased investment. He and Ed had to raise money to build storage barns, to install dryers and conveyor belts. They bought an elaborate machine for shelling corn. Right away they found they needed another. Every time Will went out to raise money, Ed Jenks yelled like a stuck pig, now they'd go broke for sure. Will couldn't do anything with the three old men who ran the Poplar Falls Bank. They hadn't yet recovered from their fright at the bank failures in '33, but in Des Moines and Omaha he found bankers that took a cheerier view. Will could show them half the cornfields in Iowa planted with hybrid seed. Give him the right statistics and Will could talk money out of a stone.

What made Will feel really good was that Antonia didn't have to work so hard. The oldest girl was starting school. When a fifth started to come along, Will got in a hired girl to do the heavy chores. He added two rooms to the house to make more room for the kids as they grew.

Phil Meyers, his boss detasseler, developed into a firstrate manager of the shelling, drying and storage plant. Charley Dirk's eldest son Steve grew up to be foreman of the farming operation. Steve saw that the hogs got fed, and the steers Will fed on clover, hay and nubbins and discard from the plant. Will hadn't yet cut loose from the ageold theory that you had to rotate crops: corn, small grain and clover, then soybeans maybe before you could plant corn again. With Phil and Steve in charge, Will was free to spend a couple of months on the road each year selling the next year's crop.

The war in Europe gave all middlewestern farming a boost. Wartime is the farmers' bonanza. After Pearl Harbor there was a limitless demand for every conceivable product. Corn was at a premium. Soybeans were in short supply. Steers cost money to feed, but there was an increasing demand for beef. Hog prices rose. It was a far cry from the days when Henry Wallace almost tearfully presided over the slaughter of the little pigs because there was no market for them. In 1940, a bare ten years after Will Henning made his agreement with H. A. to market his Pioneer corn, Will and his salesmen sold a hundred and twentyfive thousand bushels.

A hundred and twentyfive thousand bushels of shelled corn meant mountains of cobs, Himalayas of corncobs. Will used them for bedding in his feed lots. He gave them to anybody who would haul them away. Finally he had to hire trucks to dispose of them. Sheer loss. Will would wake up in the night dreaming of strangling under piles of corncobs. He didn't like to waste money any more than Ed Jenks did. He wracked his brains trying to think of what to do with them.

All at once he decided to feed them to his steers. The first hint had come from Joe at Leland Stanford. He had seen an article in a scientific journal about feeding cattle in Finland. Some farm-research man had tried to treat woodshavings in vats to remove the lignose. The residue was then impregnated with the proper bacteria to break down the cellulose for cattle food. Urea and molasses were used in the process. Just an experiment with no commercial possibilities. While Will was reading Joe's letter, it dawned on him that corncobs were mostly cellulose. Every cow and steer had vats full of bacteria inside their multiple stomachs. Let the cattle do the work. That fall he started feeding cattle on ground corncobs mixed with urea and molasses. It worked. They didn't gain quite as fast as cattle fed on corn, but they gained.

He wired Joe to come on to Poplar Falls. With Joe he worked out different ratios of molasses and urea to experiment with. One penful of steers was fed one; another penful, another. At the Ideal Café the boys had a field day. Imagine feeding cattle on corncobs. What kind of crazy ideas would Will Henning get next? Though his son Steve had begun to educate him, Charley Dirk laughed till he thought he'd split. Maybe the steers would eat corncobs, but how about the meat?

Joe went back to Palo Alto to write up the results. He called it a breakthrough. He was beginning to worry about how the world's population was going to be fed.

World War II and the years after it was a period of breakthroughs in agriculture. As fighting slackened in the European theatre, war machinery plants turned to building tractors, diskplows, cornpickers. The uniform ears the hybrid strain produced made the mechanical cornpicker feasible. Nitrogen plants built for the emergency turned over from explosives to the production of nitrogen fertilizers.

Weedkillers began to appear—chemicals you could spray on to kill cornweeds in the cornfield without damage to the crop. Liquid nitrogen displaced the oldtime guano in bags. Production soared though the planted acreage decreased. In 1924 the average yield nationwide of corn was twentyone bushels to the acre. Thirty years later it was sixty.

Will Henning became a great lecturer. "You see," he'd say to a visitor as he drove him over the rolling green Iowa country where the cornstalks filed past the car mile after mile, rank on rank, waving their darkgreen leaves that shimmered with blue from the sky where they curved into the light. "A lot of things meshed in together, improved machinery, plentiful fertilizer, growing demand, but at the center of it all was the hybrid plant, the ability to encourage good characteristics and discourage others. Now these hybridizers can tailor a variety for short summers or long summers, for resistance to drought and insects and fungus. Without hybrids that produced evenly shaped ears the cornpicker would have been impractical. With the old open-pollinated varieties all this fertilization would have been wasted. They just didn't have it in them to produce a hundred bushel corn. And it's just a beginning. Our farmers used to be happy with forty. Now some of them are just a teeny bit miserable if they can't beat a hundred. . . . That's what we mean when we talk about the revolution on the farm."

Twenty years after Henning and Jenks got their start, the firm was grossing a million dollars annually. Will Henning didn't care too much about money; what he cared for was growth and production and sales and the endless detail of the business that kept him busy from dawn to dark. Antonia was radiant. The children were thriving. Every year topped the last. Will Henning was a happy man.

6

The True Believers—ii

Ginny's baby was born in time to save Paul Edwards from the draft in World War II. Paul had landed a Washington job he was crazy about. If the baby had been a girl, they were planning to name it Peace. Since it turned out a boy, they named him George Morris after Ginny's father. George Morris, Senior, with loans from a government agency, had managed to buy his business back in time to take advantage of the war boom in cereal prices. He and Mrs. Morris drove to Washington for the baby's christening on special gasoline coupons issued him by the Department of Agriculture as a consultant to a Committee on milling and processing.

It had taken a good deal of correspondence before Paul and Ginny would consent to have the baby christened at all, but Dr. Edwards discovered that the Most Reverend Philander Ruskin, Rector Emeritus of the Washington Cathedral, was an old friend from seminary days. The prospect of a christening in the cathedral was too much for Ginny. She gave in.

The grandparents met the day before, an early spring afternoon, at the cozy little apartment Paul and Ginny had found for themselves at the edge of Georgetown on Q Street. The Morrises, in spite of their setbacks during the Depression years, now had a brisk and prosperous air. Dr. Edwards looked shabbier and more oldfashioned than ever. There was still that accursed reek of stale pipe tobacco. Paul couldn't help feeling embarrassed at the sight of him; and his poor mother was wearing a shapeless flowered dress that made her look as big as a house.

Dr. Edwards hardly let them catch their breath before he started to tell them about the abecedaries recently discovered at Ugarit . . . "now known as Byblos," he added for the benefit of the Morrises.

He was interrupted by the arrival of Philander Ruskin. The Rector Emeritus was a tall stately man in neat ecclesiastical togs. As befitted a High Churchman, a faint whiff of incense came with him.

The old friends shook hands vigorously.

"Saint," said Dr. Ruskin, obviously using a seminary nickname, "it's a pleasure to meet your family." He had a benevolently booming voice.

"Wonderful of you to come, Phil. I was just trying to bring the children up to date on the discoveries in Syria and Lebanon. Paul seems to occupy a position of some influence in the administration. I keep hoping that some fact I can uncover might influence him and Ginny to recognize the prime importance of the alphabet in the teaching of reading."

"This is indeed a coincidence," said Dr. Ruskin beaming all around. "The purpose of my visit is twofold. One is to renew old affections. The other is to beg you to publish a résumé of the work that is being done. Your article in *Canaan* was much too short."

Dr. Edwards' eyes glowed as if someone had snapped on a light behind them: "Well actually, Phil," he said, "what seems to be the missing link between the proto-Canaanite texts and alphabetic writing seems to have turned up in a hoard of inscribed arrowheads excavated at Bethlehem. The signs on the arrowheads, which probably had magical significance, were something between pictographs and phonemes."

"We can now rest assured," he continued in his lecturer's tone, pronouncing his words in that meticulous manner that so annoyed Paul, "that the alphabet had its origin in an acrophonically derived pictographic script in the Syria-Palestine region, if not actually in Ugarit. The influence of Egyptian hieroglyphics was there but it was almost certainly indirect."

Guy Rogers Stephenson had slipped in through the still-open

front door while Dr. Edwards was delivering himself of this pronouncement. Dr. Stephenson was Paul's immediate boss at the Department. Even Paul, who knew he prided himself on his unconventionality, was surprised to see him wearing a track suit with YMCA insignia on the back. "Got to keep my weight down," he explained panting.

He certainly didn't look overweight. He was a skinny dark hairy man in his late thirties. His black eyes under black brows jutting out from a narrow skull thickly matted with short black hair gave him a red Indian look.

"Excuse this outfit," he said laughing, as he shook hands all around. "I was taking a little run around Georgetown before supper. . . . Just wanted to say howdoyoudo to the baby and to have a few words with Paul."

The baby let out a yell when he saw Dr. Stephenson advancing towards him. His mother, flanked by the two grandmothers, whisked him into the other room. "I don't seem to have very good luck making friends and influencing people," Dr. Stephenson said ruefully. "But what were you saying, Sir," he turned to Dr. Edwards, "I'm afraid I interrupted."

Dr. Edwards showed his yellow teeth in a quiet little smile. "I like to tease the young people about the alphabet. If they knew more about it, they would treat it with more respect. The fashionable schoolteachers are all for giving it up. I hope it's a passing fad. It's not too early to start worrying about how I'm going to teach my grandson to read."

Paul felt nettled, but he tried to laugh the subject off. "Dad's a volunteer archaeologist," he said.

"I wish I had time to go into this, Dr. Edwards. When were you saying the alphabet originated? I suppose you mean the Phoenician?"

"A chronology is gradually unfolding," put in Dr. Ruskin in his booming tone, "as fresh discoveries are made. The Phoenician was one of the scripts that grew out of the parent stem. The order of signs in the alphabet used in Ugarit seems to have been established as early as the fourteenth century B.C. Alp the oxhead, bait the house, gaml the throwing-stick became six centuries later the alpha beta gamma of the Greeks. But why am I taking up your time? Dr. Edwards is the real expert."

"Fascinating," said Dr. Stephenson, "but I have to keep running. . . . Good night all."

He motioned to Paul with his head. When Paul came back into the room, he burst out enthusiastically, "Well, everybody says Guy Stephenson is one of the most remarkable men in Washington . . . and I certainly think so. He started as a farmboy on the family farm in West Kansas. Harvard, Bussey Institute, London School of Economics. The chief authority in this country on agricultural economics. F. D. R. brought him to Washington in the days of his first Brain Trust. He can tell you the whereabouts of every surplus commodity stored in the United States."

"I hope you invited him to the christening," cried Paul's mother.

"He actually said he'd come."

"I think he wants to hear more about the alphabet." Paul's mother made a little mocking face behind her husband's back.

At the christening the grandmothers took over so that Paul and Ginny felt like outsiders. After the service, Dr. Ruskin asked the whole party into his private study for a glass of sherry. Dr. Ruskin and Dr. Edwards never stopped talking about the inscriptions at Byblos. Dr. Stephenson listened intently. Paul discovered to his surprise that his boss looked at him with fresh respect on account of his father's erudition. He didn't exactly like that.

All in all it was a relief when the grandparents went home.

Dr. Stephenson ran his office like a track coach. Everybody on the double, so it was a rare evening when Paul didn't have to work. The Edwardses had found a nice highschool girl to come occasionally as a sitter. They would snatch at the opportunity to walk the few shady blocks to Grover Wilson's house. Dotty was such a darling. Drunk or sober, Grover was a good host. The garden made the place seem in the deep country. It was more like home than their apartment.

Grover made everything fun with his jocular manner. There was always plenty to eat and drink. Though Paul and Ginny stuck to their old plan of never touching hard liquor, they got a sort of reflected glow from what the others were drinking. The company was always good; you never could tell who you would find there, anybody from a Supreme Court Justice to a group of highschool seniors. Grover called them all by their first names whether he knew them or not.

Grover was a great man for causes, and Dotty, bless her heart, always believed in what Grover believed. Grover never stopped to explain why some particular cause was right. He took it for granted that if he was for it, it must be right.

During Paul's first months in Washington, Grover's cause was a second front in Europe. We were letting our Russian Allies bear the full brunt of the war against Hitler. He was suspicious of the British. Churchill, that old reactionary, was secretly working to let the Germans and Russians polish each other off. If any public man wasn't in favor of a second front, right now, immediately, Grover wrote him off as a Fascist. He saw Washington full of unconscious Fascists, particularly among the military, who were interfering with the flow of arms and equipment to the great Socialist state. Grover was a plausible fellow. He advanced his opinions in such a cheerful friendly way that they rubbed off on people.

Dr. Stephenson—at the Wilsons' he was always known as Steff—was one of Grover's few intimates who kidded him about his phobias. Since his wife had left him, Steff had taken to eating Dotty's cozy dinners a couple of times a week. They distracted him from the lonesomeness of being what he called a reluctant bachelor.

"Grover," he would cry out occasionally, "these generalizations don't help. Give me chapter and verse and I might be able to do something about it." Grover would reply soothingly that he'd get up a whole dossier by the next time they met, but Grover never quite got around to it.

Seeing each other so much outside of hours produced a special relationship between Dr. Stephenson and Paul that didn't go down well with some of the other people in the office. Paul timidly started calling him Steff when they were alone together. Steff was finding Paul a useful fellow to send on confidential missions. Paul still had a touch of the eager highschool student about him that people found disarming. He was physically attractive. There was an innocent look about his crewcut that made women want to stroke his blond hair.

He had a good memory, and a naïve way of sizing people up that Steff found revealing. He became dedicated as a poodle dog to Steff's ideas and interests.

After the success of the Normandy landings, Grover's obsession became the Pacific war. To save American lives, every concession must be made to get Russia into the war against Japan. For once he agreed with the Army that only an amphibious landing would bring about a Japanese surrender. His old friend Ezra Goodbody, just back and burned a deep brown by the Pacific sun after three years as a war correspondent, said this theory was all nonsense. The Japanese were licked already and had been for months. All that was needed was a strict blockade.

Grover was horrified. Though he stopped short of implying that Ezra was a Japanese spy, he declared him to be grossly deluded.

The bombs on Hiroshima and Nagasaki broke Grover all up. The only way to save the world's peace was to share atomic formulae with the Russians. When it turned out that the Soviets, through their busy espionage, had been helping themselves to these formulae all along, Grover said it served us right for not coming clean with our Allies.

The end of the war and Harry Truman's accession to the Presidency caused anxious moments at the War Emergency Board, but Steff managed to reorganize his little group as a liaison agency between the Department of Agriculture and UNRRA. Paul, as Steff's righthand man, found himself scooting around the world on missions to Italy and Turkey and Greece. More foreign travel than he had ever imagined. He found the postwar world excruciatingly confusing. Steff kept his mind on statistics; crops, reports, shipping, movements of populations, lists of available nutrients. For reassurance as to what was white and what was black, Paul had to rely on the discussions at Grover Wilson's house.

In those days Grover was on the wagon though he poured drinks for his friends as liberally as ever. Having attended the San Francisco sessions he claimed to be writing a book called the *World's Last Chance* in favor of the United Nations. Washington he saw dominated by a sinister band of America Firsters, isolationists, Ku-Kluxers and military adventurers, among whom he occasionally placed Harry Truman. These were opposed by Men of Good Will, clear thinkers who gave first priority to that accommodation with the Soviet Union without which the peace would degenerate into a war of attrition. He was a little out of sorts with Steff's plans to feed the world off surplus American crops. Wouldn't that mean the survival of disguised Nazis and Fascists, and hysterical anti-Communists ready to upset the orderly transition from capitalism to Socialism?

Grover would never have admitted, even to himself, that he was in favor of allowing anybody to starve, but he couldn't help letting it be inferred that he felt the fewer Germans there were, the better. He was all for the Morgenthau plan to reduce Germany to an agricultural state.

When they got home to their new little house out in Bethesda that still smelt of fresh plaster one night after one of these conversations, Ginny suddenly cried out, "It's all too cruel. . . . We ought to do what we can to repair the war damage. . . . We caused a lot of it ourselves."

Paul looked at her sharply. He wasn't accustomed to having her come out with opinions of her own like that. In the glare of the overhead light in the hall, she looked haggard. Her hair was straggly. Her figure wasn't as tight as it used to be. They had three children now, George and Guy and Eleanor. Being cooped up with them without a car, cooking and cleaning all day because she couldn't get a maid, was telling on her. He'd been so busy with his special missions around Europe he hadn't been paying enough attention to Ginny. Dim silhouettes of treacherously lovely women he would rather forget passed before his eyes: Berlin, Vienna, the Polish girls.

A wave of tenderness for Ginny welled up in him. He hugged her to him. For a second he felt the old feeling of being completely at home in her arms. "Ginny," he whispered, "underneath we are just like we were . . . remember in the highschool play."

"I was beginning to think that was water over the dam," she answered in the little plaintive singsong voice that had always touched him so.

"Ridiculous," he said out loud. "The first thing we've got to do, Ginny, is get us a car so you won't be isolated out here."

They walked back into the children's room to send the sitter home and see how the little things were sleeping.

In the spring of 1948, Ginny and Paul decided they ought to come out for Henry Wallace. Here was a man who spoke their language. They ought to back him. Steff talked Paul out of it.

He invited him to play handball one hot April afternoon and waited till they were both good and sweaty. Then when they paused for breath, he said, "Paul, as you know, I have the greatest admiration for H. A. We worked closely together under Franklin D. What I like to think of as the agricultural-biological side of his brain is terrific, but now he's being taken for a ride.... You'll see. Besides, anybody working for the government has to be a bit cautious about coming out for Presidential candidates. It never hurts to keep your mouth shut. If a man's not careful, he'll cut his own throat. That would not only be silly but unethical."

He got the ball flying and they played a couple of volleys.

Steff picked up the spent ball and bounced it in his hand. "The little gentleman in the White House is scrappy and vindictive."

"Maybe he won't even be nominated," said Paul.

"Don't you be too sure."

They played on in silence. Steff never mentioned the subject again.

Grover, who was telling everybody he was planning to campaign for H. A., pursed his face up when Paul told him that if he contributed to anybody's campaign it would be to Harry Truman's.

"The meal ticket!" bellowed Grover. Then suddenly he slapped himself on the forehead. "A wife and three children.... Me, I've got an independent income ... it's not large, but it's there. I have no right to criticize anyone."

He started walking back and forth in the library on his short legs. "Maybe you think I misplace my righteous indignation, when I'm madder at the Un-American Activities Committee than I am at the Russians for taking over Poland and Czechoslovakia and Hungary. Maybe it's illogical but that's how I feel. I can do something about injustice at home: the witch hunts, the hysterics over Red spies. Abroad, I'm helpless."

"Well," said Paul, "we've got the Marshall Plan. That is something I can really go for."

"I'd like it better if it was under the United Nations."

"Speaking of the United Nations, Grover, how's your book coming?" The minute he spoke, Paul knew he shouldn't have asked that question. Grover looked as if the wind had been knocked out of

328

him. The next time Paul went by the Wilsons', no Grover. Off on one of his benders. Hadn't been seen for three days.

Paul was making fifteen thousand a year. That summer he and Ginny were able to take the children to Rehobeth Beach for two weeks. It was a pleasure to see how they throve in the sun and the sand. Ginny turned brown as a nut. Paul told her she looked just like his schoolgirl sweetheart.

"Who was that?"

"Don't you remember? *Romeo and Juliet.*"

She nodded and batted her lashes at him. He kissed her.

"Daddy's acting just like a movie star," said George, who was seven and wise beyond his years.

It was as if he'd fallen in love with Ginny all over again. He was mad about the children. That part of his life was fine, but privately he was unhappy all through the vacation. Too much time to think. His conscience bothered him. Here was Henry Wallace, who believed in the things Paul believed in, making the fight of his life for the Presidency, and he wasn't lifting a finger to help him. Paul felt better after he'd gone to the post office and mailed a twentyfive dollar money order to the Progressive Party's Campaign Committee. He didn't send a check because he was afraid they might list his name as a contributor.

When he went back to Washington, he joined Americans for Social Action. He attended a meeting and came away thinking that at last he had found a group of likeminded people. As soon as he got home, he made Ginny write out a check and send in her application for membership.

Grover Wilson nearly laughed himself sick when Paul told him about Americans for Social Action. "Paul, these are the sterilized radicals with all the naughty Communists left out. . . . They won't accomplish a goddamn thing."

When Truman fooled the wiseacres and got himself re-elected by a comfortable margin, Steff didn't even say "I told you so." He was too busy. The winter that followed was a nervous one for Washington officeholders. Harry Truman came back cocky after his successful campaign, ready to reward friends and punish foes. The Marshall Plan was going great guns in Europe in spite of Russia's refusal to cooperate. Truman's administration dreamed up the

329

Point 4 Program, a sequel to give the rest of the world a taste of American prodigality. Technological assistance was Steff's meat and it didn't take him very long to get his agency reorganized under Point 4. Paul got a raise in salary out of it, to seventeen thousand five hundred. That meant the Edwardses could start buying a little wisteria-covered brick house in Georgetown and that Ginny could have a proper full-time maid. Life with Ginny became fun again even if she did go fill out her absentee ballot for Henry Wallace. For voting purposes, they still listed Dr. Edwards' house in Shelbyville as their residence.

Paul was in South America a great deal that winter. Though it was a little off his beat, he was helping set up the Menhaden fishing industry and fishmeal factories in Peru.

The collapse of Kuomintang China and the Berlin blockade following so soon after Communist takeovers in Czechoslovakia and Hungary had Grover somehow boxed in. Some evenings he could even be heard glumly denouncing Communist aggression. He took it as a personal affront that the Reds went to such extremes after he'd done everything he could to give them a break.

Just before Christmas, Paul came home from a fact-finding mission to Venezuela to find Grover Wilson in high spirits. He was on the wagon again and tremendously worked-up over a new monster of iniquity he had discovered in Congress. The junior Senator from Wisconsin was letting it be known that something had to be done about spies and subversives in government. He was about to lead an attack on the Democratic administration. "Twenty years of treason."

Paul felt miffed because he wanted to tell about Point 4 successes in Latin America, and how Nelson Rockefeller had entertained him at his ranch and what a fine fellow he was, but nobody would listen to anything except Joe McCarthy. It was the first time Paul heard the name.

It wasn't the last. The next time he spent an evening at the Wilsons' house, later that same winter, Alger Hiss had been convicted and sentenced to the Federal Penitentiary, a day of mourning for all good men; and McCarthy had just delivered his outrageous speech in Wheeling, West Virginia, claiming to know the names of eightyfour "cardcarrying" Communists still on the State Department payroll.

When McCarthy tangled with Millard Tydings in a long drawn-out debate over who was responsible for the loss of China to the Communists, Grover clipped out every word that was said. His living room was filled with stacks of old newspapers. In the 1952 campaign, he followed McCarthy to Maryland to hear the "intemperate speeches" which helped defeat Tydings for re-election to the Senate. He blamed McCarthy for the faked photograph of the respectable Maryland Senator in friendly conversation with Earl Browder, which he claimed was the final straw that elected in his place a gentleman whom Grover always spoke of as "an obscure Republican named Butler." This time he really was going to write a series of articles on the reasons for the Democratic debacle.

A not so obscure Republican named Eisenhower won the Presidency that fall. Grover worked like a demon, but he couldn't get his articles ready for publication before the topic became old hat. Amid the excitements of the Eisenhower inauguration, he fell off the wagon and wasn't seen again by his friends for some months. He reappeared looking pink and healthy after a long rest in the country in time to rejoice over the bad reception given McCarthy's attack on George Catlett Marshall. "He's digging his own grave, just see if he isn't."

The TV series where McCarthy was seen in a disgraceful shouting match with the Army brass was one of Grover's finest hours. The Wilsons turned the televised hearing into a protracted party. Dotty furnished pitchers of cold beer and really excellent sandwiches. People came from all over Washington to watch the hearings at the Wilsons'. Grover somehow gave the impression he was putting the show on himself.

It was at one of these sessions at the Wilsons' that Paul met Steff's new wife. Originally Cecelia Adler from Baltimore, she had been married a couple of times before. She wore her black hair short, showed prominent teeth when she laughed and wore a lot of clanky Mexican jewelry. "I never met Dr. Peress," she said, "but I did take a course under Professor Lattimore.... He's a very nice man but anybody who would enlist him for a secret agent would be mad."

Paul was never quite so intimate with Steff after his second marriage. Steff had become wrapped-up in the experimental work that was producing new strains of wheat which he hoped would feed an overpopulated world. While he was away encouraging the agronomists at Ciudad Obregon and in the Philippines, the routine work of the office fell on Paul.

It was a surprise to find a telegram from Grover in the incoming mail one morning. URGENT CALL MY HOUSE IMMEDIATELY. His secretary put in the call. Dotty answered. "Grover has somebody here you have absolutely got to meet. Can't talk about it on the phone."

Paul made some readjustments on his calendar, made sure his secretary had Grover Wilson's number and took a cab to Georgetown. Grover met him at the garden gate. His curly red hair seemed to be standing up all over his head. He was seething with excitement.

"This may be the bomb we need to blow McCarthy sky high," he whispered. "Now you tell me whether the guy is on the level."

Paul followed him through the broad French windows of the living room. "Jeff Lovejoy, meet Paul Edwards."

Jeff Lovejoy was a tall gangling young man with a long neck and a small head of sandy hair. He had a nervous way of throwing his arms and legs around that made Paul think of a baby giraffe. He was smoking a cigarette as if his life depended on it.

"Now, Jeff, you tell Paul what you've been telling me," said Grover soothingly.

Jeff talked in bunches. Occasionally he stuttered a little. He said he'd been given an honorable discharge from the Air Force after serving many years at bases in the Middle East. The Communist subversion at some of those places was just terrible so he'd come to Washington last fall to report this situation to somebody who would do something about it. Patriotic duty. Of course, he got the old runaround. He'd gone to see some Army officers who wouldn't pay attention to him. The publicity in the newspapers gave him the idea that McCarthy's Committee was the place to go. He'd seen a Mr. Malone, and Mr. Malone had told him he looked like the kind of man who might be useful for secret work. "From that minute I swear to God I couldn't call my soul my own."

"What happened?"

"They took me down in the basement of the Senate and

threatened me with a Luger. They have a whole cache of arms down there, rifles, machineguns. Then they made me spy on people."

"What people?"

"All kinds of people. Every day they gave me a different list."

"Are you still working for them?" asked Paul.

Jeff gave a gulp: "Patriotic duty. It's that Committee that ought to be exposed. That's why I decided to stay on to collect evidence."

"Are you on their payroll?"

Jeff snatched for another cigarette, lit it and inhaled deeply. "The secret payroll," he gasped. He had large protruding gray eyes. He rolled them eloquently.

"Let's check," said Grover. He went up to the bedroom phone and called Ezra Goodbody at the *Globe*. He asked Ezra to call the McCarthy Committee and to ask them if a man named Jeff Lovejoy was on their payroll. Just as Dotty was serving up lunch, Ezra, curious to find out what was going on, arrived in person with the answer. There was no such name on the regular payroll.

"That clinches it," said Grover. "Jeff must be telling the truth. He's on the secret payroll."

At lunch Jeff ate a great deal. In fact, he ate as if he hadn't eaten for several days. He rambled on between mouthfuls. He said he had the run of the files. He could sneak out documents, minutes of secret meetings, vouchers, affidavits. He didn't stop smoking once all the time he was eating. "They give me the run of the place."

Over his third cup of coffee, he told Grover confidentially he needed more money for photostats. He'd spent all his earnings on photostats. He was behind on his rent. He had alimony to pay if he was to stay out of jail. He had to have a thousand dollars.

Paul looked at his watch. He said an important appointment was coming up and started back to the office in a hurry.

When he reached home for supper, Paul called Grover. "I advanced the money," said Grover. "He'll pay me back when Ezra arranges for a series of articles for the *Globe*." Paul could almost hear him rubbing his hands. "This really is going to fix the junior Senator."

Paul ate his supper all in a glow from Grover's enthusiasm. "I think we've really got the goods on him now," he told Ginny.

Paul next heard of Jeff Lovejoy through Steff. Steff's wife's brother, Simon Adler, was a brilliant young lawyer who had just been elected Chairman of the Americans for Social Progress. He had told her in great secrecy that Lovejoy had come to him for funds to hire an assistant to help in the tremendous task of going through the McCarthy files. They had already turned up all kinds of evidence of wrongdoing. They were on the trail of a conflict-of-interest situation. The Senator had been paid ten thousand dollars by a firm that wanted to furnish prefabricated houses to the Federal Housing Administration. Cecelia told the story to her husband.

Steff sniffed disdainfully. "There's something phony about this story somewhere. That's what I told Simon. What's the use of giving people advice? Simon wouldn't tell me how much he paid the guy."

Before Simon Adler left for a summer trip to Europe, he and Paul and Ezra Goodbody had a conference with Jeff at Grover's house. Jeff arrived in a cab with a large carton full of photostats and mimeographed sheets. There were copies of letters to and from a lawyer about how the Senator's wife was seeking a divorce on account of his immoral behavior. There were a lot of vouchers for petty cash that none of them could make head or tail of. Jeff turned his popeyes pleadingly towards Simon. "This is just the bulk evidence," he said. "That's why I need an assistant, to organize it and refine it."

Then he started on a long tale about how a friend of his who was a respectable college professor had been browbeaten into testifying by the Senator's threat to release the story that he had an illegitimate Negro son.

"The man is not only a blackmailer but he's a racist," shouted Grover.

"Somebody has got to publish this stuff while the Army hearing is still going on. It will make a lot of those Senators who are still a little favorable to McCarthy change their minds. It might mean expulsion from the Senate," said Paul.

"If somebody will get the material into understandable shape, I'll see that we work up a series of articles and publish them," said Ezra. "It's time we put an end to this witch hunt. How about you, Paul?"

Paul explained that he had a new mission coming up: Point 4.

Simon was leaving town. Ezra was too busy. Grover was the only one left. He promised faithfully he would go over the material and send the choicest items to Ezra Goodbody to work up.

Three weeks later, when Paul came back to town, he couldn't reach the Wilsons at their house. It turned out they had gone to their place in Rhode Island. He called Ezra at the *Globe* and Ezra gave him the lowdown. Ezra had put an experienced reporter on the story. The reporter had discovered that all of Jeff Lovejoy's material was fake. He'd never had any connection with the McCarthy Committee. Instead of hiring an assistant, Jeff had cashed the checks himself made out to him by Americans for Social Progress. Now he'd gone to the FBI claiming that it was Simon Adler who had induced a Communist stoolpigeon named Wiener to reverse his testimony in another case quite separate from the McCarthy investigations. For some reason Lovejoy had it in for Simon Adler.

"This can't be true," said Paul. "Could your reporter have been reached by some agent of the Senator's?"

"Paul," said Ezra quietly, "my reporter knows his business. . . . Excuse me, this is my busy time." He hung up.

Paul and Grover held an indignation meeting over the phone that afternoon. They refused to be convinced until a Federal Marshal served subpoenas on them to appear before the Grand Jury that was preparing Wiener's indictment for perjury.

The scene in the Grand Jury Room was fantastic. Boardly, the Assistant Federal Attorney, was making it his business to discredit Lovejoy. Somewhat against his will, he caused Simon to admit he had been paying Lovejoy with funds that belonged to Americans for Social Progress to produce evidence to discredit Senator McCarthy.

When Grover took the stand, he agreed, in his hearty way, that he'd had the wool pulled over his eyes and declared, to the great amusement of the assembly, that he'd acted like a perfect ass.

Paul took the attitude that he'd been out of town while most of this was going on and had never given the matter careful consideration.

Boardly, an agile prosecutor, gave Lovejoy a hard time. First he let him declare under oath that the material he had furnished Grover Wilson was genuine and then he produced an affidavit of the *Globe* reporter declaring that it was a fake.

"Now, Mr. Lovejoy, you tell us which is the true story."

Lovejoy was standing. His tall skinny figure began to wobble. He broke into sobs. "I needed the money.... I got a wife who persecutes me for alimony.... I wrote every damn word of those papers myself.... I sat up nights working on them.... I didn't have any assistant, I did all the work myself."

Boardly gently led him through his story again to make sure every point was covered. Then he dismissed the witness and suggested that the Grand Jury prepare an indictment for perjury against Jeff Lovejoy. Jeff turned and shouted back at the jurymen. "It's them ought to be indicted.... They knew my story was a lie. They didn't care how much money they spent to smear the Senator."

Simon and Grover and Paul really had their tails between their legs when they turned up at the Wilsons' house for lunch. Dotty bustled among them in a pretty pink and white hostess gown, making sure they were properly fed. "What is the matter? You three look as if you'd lost your last friend on earth!"

It was quite a while before they told her.

"Well, I'll be goldarned," was all Dotty said.

"Dotty," said Grover, "I know better than anybody when I make a fool of myself so don't rub it in." She got up and walked around the table and kissed him.

PART IV

THE IMAGE

I

Vacancy

Weary of the motor's purr, speed buzzing in the ears, the traffic's challenge, the slither on asphalt of rubber, the landscape's green flicker unrolling along roadsides, the slide past of billboards, the trees pirouetting, the glimpses of revolving rivers, lakes, hills, never quite thoroughly pictured because your eye's on the highway;

by the time the sun—August is the touring month, the family month—the dogday sun sultry in decline, that glares so hot off brightwork and sheening paint, is three-quarters down the sky,

the vacationers are ready to turn in

to the nearest motel: stationwagons packed with camping equipment and little children's heads, convertibles, twodoors, fourdoors, Volkswagen buses, hunched trailers in a dozen shapes (Man like the Snail can drag his house with him wherever he goes), pickups mounted with bunks and a gas stove, the old gypsy wagon motorized and enameled a delicate blue. There's a pet dog in every other car; even horses ride; a Chrysler with a brace of Scotties on the back seat and a horse pullman in tow turns in right now.

Community housing. The motel's a latterday pueblo, a pueblo for transients, built instead of adobe, of stuccoed cinderblock and glass. The traveling public—Dad and Mom and Aunt Susie and the kids—pack themselves into identical cubicles, only these are draped and airconditioned and furnished with wall-to-wall carpets and tiled baths. The men rush for the icecube machines—there's a bottle of bourbon in the traveling bag. The children raid the cold-drink dispensers. Already in sportshirts and madras shorts, the barelegged tourists as they line up for the cafeteria show an assortment of knock knees and bandy legs, seats so tight they'll surely split. Why do the broadest-bottomed women sport the startlingest designs? Purple and green petunias. The baboon effect: Miss Mandril 1963! Bobbypins and serried curlers have reached the distinction of a formal hairdo, like the shockheads of oldtime Hottentots. The teenage children, whose legs are more often brown and shapely, favor tornoff jeans. A lot go barefoot. Only the old people still dress like citizens.

Other families smelling of sunburn oil and insect repellent straggle towards the swimming pool. A swim, even in chlorinated water asquirm with kids, delightfully strips away fatigue.

We are all hung with cameras. Maybe it's not quite too late for Kodachrome or to use up the last few feet of movie reel on sister in a red bathing suit poised on the springboard to dive, or junior standing on his head: "Now everybody watch this."

NO VACANCY

Every cubicle is full.

Poocho is fed and bedded in the car.

The kids have been treated for sunburn and poison ivy, Band-Aids applied where needed, and tucked away. Their sleep's a little restless in anticipation of tomorrow.

Thoughtfully, Dad and Mom put fresh rolls in their cameras. A wonderful day but the pleasure's too soon gone.

The way the children looked lined up against the balustrade in front of the great curl of water that hangs glass green over Niagara's thunderous fall before it is lost in the mist of the gorge, the twins up topside on the blockhouse of the old reconstructed fort, the whole gang grinning as they bite into Mom's sandwiches at the roadside table, or the littlest peering quaintly down into the clear spring behind the picnic ground. The hours go fast. None of us will ever be quite this way again.

Images of the fleeting world.

The sunny moment's fled, the pictures of a wonderful day have faded from the retina, the loved voice no longer sounds in the ear. Who can recapture the fragrance of swamp magnolia? Tomorrow's here before we had a chance to taste today, and death waits to rub it all out at the end of the road.

The snapshot stays. Click. The camera will peel a casual thin scrim of immortality off the fading scene. That's why we spend so much on film.

And that's why

Mr. George Eastman who slung all these cameras round everybody's neck and used to live in a big old stone house among marvelous flowergardens in the handsomest broad elmshaded street of Rochester, New York,

made such an incredible amount of money.

Image Maker: the Kodak Man

George Eastman was born in 1854 in Waterbury, in one of those white frame houses, with a flavor of the classical revival about the trim, that give such elegance to the towns and villages of upstate New York.

His people were not welloff but they were proud of their first settler stock. The father, George Washington Eastman, taught the lost art of penmanship. There were two girls but George was the only boy.

The year the Civil War broke out, when George was six, the family moved to Rochester. Mr. Eastman hoped to make a better living by setting up one of the first commercial colleges. Besides the fine Spencerian pen, he taught his students double-entry bookkeeping, the writing of business letters and the rudiments of office management. Mrs. Eastman took in boarders to help out.

Young George had to go to work as an officeboy at fourteen. Whatever he could earn was sorely needed to make ends meet. He worked for an insurance firm.

He was a conscientious lad. When at twenty he secured a position as bookkeeper with the Rochester Savings Bank, the family and friends thought his career was made—but George had a hobby.

He was an amateur photographer.

He improvised a dark room.

He developed his own plates.

His equipment didn't satisfy him. He had a hunch he could make better. He read the British Journal of Photography from cover to cover, tried out every formula, snatched at every hint that would help him develop a more sensitive emulsion. He coated his own plates. It took too long by hand.

By the time he was twentyfive he had worked out a mechanical process for coating dry plates. He put through a patent and managed to interest a local promoter named Henry Alvah Strong—who was then running a plant for the manufacture of wagoner's whips—in the factory production of photographic plates on a large scale. They founded the firm of Strong and Eastman, Incorporated, capitalization one hundred thousand dollars.

George Eastman resigned from the bank. From that day on he hardly left his factory. He directed every move. He watched every process with an anxious eye. His equipment never satisfied him. Everything had to be improved. He experimented early and late. Trial and error. Many a night he slept in a hammock slung in a corner of his workshop.

Glass plates were awkward to handle and easily broken. If only he could spread his emulsion on some flexible substance.

In 1884 he patented a paperbacked film you could roll. The business was already thriving so he could afford to hire a professional chemist. He and Strong reorganized the company with three times the original capitalization. There was no question now whose company it was. The new name was Eastman Dry Plate and Film. Colonel Strong stayed on as president.

Eastman never forgot that he was an amateur photographer. He wanted a product cheap and practical enough for everybody to use. He drove himself tirelessly.

He hired more chemists. He drove them as hard as he drove himself.

"The technical men," he wrote in an instruction manual, "must make a record to hold their jobs. If they do not, they are no better than uneducated men: in fact not as good, because an educated man who is not efficient is a spoiled man."

Eastman was not the only man in America who was working on the problem of producing a light and flexible negative. Another amateur photographer, who was rector at the House of Prayer in Newark, New Jersey, was experimenting with a gelatin roll to take the place of glass slides so that he could show Biblical scenes in his Sunday school. The Reverend Goodwin wrote Eastman for advice.

344

When Eastman learned that Goodwin had applied for a patent for "a photographic pellicle," he told one of his chemists to lose no time in patenting his own transparent film.

In 1888 he marketed the first Kodak, a fixed-focus box camera that took round pictures two and a half inches in diameter on a paperback roll of a hundred exposures. When you had exposed them all you mailed the box back to the factory for recharging. They developed the negatives and printed the pictures. "You press the button and we do the rest" was the salesman's slogan.

Already Eastman had established his four principles: mass production, low unit cost, copious advertising, and international distribution, that were to make Kodak the word for camera the whole world round.

He called it a Kodak because that was what it sounded like when you clicked the shutter.

George Eastman's whole being was in his factories. Even after his company had several plants, he personally supervised them all. He remained a wifeless, childless man. He had no time for any life of his own. The Kodak caught on so fast that when the company went through one of its periodic reorganizations in 1889 it was capitalized at a million dollars. Three years later it was five million. By now the Kodak was a folding camera equipped with a roll of transparent film you could load in daylight. It was Eastman's film that Edison used in his early experiments with the kinetoscope that foreshadowed motion pictures.

By the turn of the century the Eastman Kodak Company was capitalized at thirtyfive million dollars and had plants in Rochester, and Kingsport, Tennessee, in Harrow, England, and Vincennes, France; in Germany and Hungary and Australia, and agencies and subsidiaries in every city in the world. When, after a quarter of a century of unremitting work George Eastman found himself one of the richest men in America, he'd been too busy to know exactly how it had happened.

When in 1913 Hannibal Goodwin's heirs won a judgment against him of five million dollars for infringement of patent, it was a drop in the bucket.

All the paternal feelings he might have lavished on a family and children were spent on his company and on his home city of

Rochester. He early introduced profitsharing for executives, accident insurance, wage dividends, and pensions for his employees. He started a building-and-loan association and made it easy for the men who worked for him to buy stock in the company. Childless, he had a pathetic concern for children and young people. He endowed the Rochester university with thirtyfive million dollars for a medical department and a music school and a women's college and a theatre. He gave twenty million to M.I.T. He financed a dental clinic in Rochester where school children could have their teeth attended to free, and tonsil and adenoid operations, and where harelips and cleft palates could be remedied. When he saw what bad teeth the English children had he started a dental dispensary in London.

Now he could give his hobbies and crotchets full rein. Everything done in his name had his personal attention. He raised prize dairy cattle and choice cotton on a farm in North Carolina. He enjoyed flowers, so he built fabulous greenhouses around his home. He liked music, so he invited his friends to hear the world's greatest performers at his Sunday evening musicals. He had a taste for painting, so he made his own private collection of old masters. He assembled a unique museum of photography. He financed movements for calendar reform and for the use of motion pictures in teaching.

His Eastman Kodak Company was the largest producer of photographic material in the world. Already known as one of the world's great philanthropists, George Eastman remained a lonely unapproachable man. Publicity he dreaded. Whenever possible, he made his donations anonymous. He never talked to reporters. The master of mass photography hardly ever let his own photograph be taken. In the great age of public millionaires he was the least known of them all.

When war broke out in Europe he was concerned about the children left homeless orphans. He spent weeks at a time at a sort of home orphanage he set up in the South of France he called le Chateau des Enfants.

When he was seventyone he retired as president of the company but as Chairman of the Board continued on the lookout for what he called "interesting new developments."

Even so, time sometimes hung heavy. He had no family. He'd

reached the age when a man's best friends are dying all around. He'd treasured his friends.

At seventytwo he got up a party to hunt big game in Africa, "with gun and camera." They joined the Martin Johnsons, who were the famous wild-animal photographers of the time, and spent four months driving in trucks and touring cars around the great plains shooting lions and buffalo, rhinoceroses and cheetah, impala and gazelle. He was still a pretty good shot.

Cooking was another of George Eastman's hobbies. In camp he set up a private little kitchen of his own where he could turn out mince pies and ostrichegg omelets for his party.

As the trip neared its end, he wrote home to his secretary: "We have traveled four thousand miles with motor car, camel and porter safaris without serious mishap or even discomfort. . . . Whether anybody is justified in killing a lot of wild animals (mostly harmless) just for the pleasure of taking home so-called 'trophies' to show his friends and bragging (inferentially at least) of his prowess as a hunter, is of course a matter that is open to the opinions of the onlookers, but from whatever viewpoint it is looked at, from that of the sportsman or that of the sentimentalist, the fact remains that the adventure is now over, and this adventurer with his mind filled with memories of many new things he has seen and experienced, now at the end, as always, is turning his face eagerly homeward, to a place where there is an abundance of pure water, where the great majority of the inhabitants are not hopelessly and unspeakably filthy, where the mosquitoes are not allowed to spread disease, where the roads are smooth and the streets clean, where the four seasons follow each other in glorious sequence, where there is music, art and science, and boundless scope and unlimited opportunity for the development of all that is admirable in man, and above all where he hopes to enjoy the priceless privilege of a few more years of contact with the friends whom he has gathered about him during the course of a long, interesting and eventful life."

Six years later, at his home in Rochester, when at the age of seventyeight he decided he had lived long enough, he wrote a note in his firm regular hand before he killed himself: "To my friends: my work is done. Why wait?"

House of Fame

Headlines are another sort of death. It was hard not to be reminded of the mortician's train of funeral cars as the somber limousines crawled past the portal of the fiftystory hostelry so discreetly discharging—black tie and girls in glory—the invited guests who in some past incarnation had been the subjects of cover stories in this weekly magazine of national—nay, international—circulation.

"I saw your picture in the paper."

Impeccably gladhanded, the guests throng room after salmontinted room where waiters, who left their own faces behind in the pantry, deftly circulate cocktail trays. The aroma of luxury. Every alcoholic exhalation: gin, vermouth and zest of lemon, warmsweet of bourbon, smoky reek of Scotch, all buoyed on rafts of toasted cheese, caviar canapés, fat gooseliver, anchovies, olives . . .

Camera men abound. The camera men neither eat nor drink. Tirelessly they snap famous faces, twisting in and out between eminent waistcoats, squirming with dervish whirls under brassiered bosoms, converge on politicians whose eyes roll come hither at the nearest lens.

The photographers are mad for angles. They crouch behind their cocked cameras, shoot up, shoot down, back off on all fours. They teeter on stepladders, they balance on mantels, they crawl up the walls.

The public image is the photograph.

A dozen cameras pin down each frontpage phiz. Lens stare into lens. Say cheese. Flashlight blanks out flashlight, making eyes blink behind the glare on glasses, picking out a swollen ear, shiny pores on a nose, creases on a woman's neck, or the peevish wrinkle at the corner of a mouth smiling the public smile.

In the flicker and flare, face stares into face. There's a phrase that freezes unspoken on every tongue: "By God I thought you were dead."

Can it be that the Arabs are right, and the dour pueblodwellers of our own Southwest, when they say the camera takes away something that can never be recovered, skims some private value off the soul?

The tactful greeters, the girls sorting indexcards at flower-scented tables, have managed, through their intricate engineering of mass hospitality, to find chairs for this multitude, placecards. Now we are grouped at tables in the grand ballroom that rises tier upon gilded tier into a dim empyrean.

Posycolored ladies and their whitefronted escorts throng every box. The dance floor is all tables. White spotlights cut satin swaths through the smokeblue air, trays glitter as nimbly the waiters pass brook trout in aspic, some marvel of soup, rare roast beef veiled in sauce, pour just the right wine. . . . Nebuchadnezzar never feasted so the day he spelled his doom off the Babylonian wall.

We must listen too. Public address. These tidings are all glad. Keep it light. Informal. Let's not get stuffy. Penguin figures talk and teeter behind the distant mike, extolling, explaining, wise-cracking why and how

each of these poor humans:

bundles of nerves, hearts resolutely pumping blood, anguished tubs of guts, congeries of interacting braincells, suffering nocturnal despair, rejoicing in inexplicable morning aspirations,

became,

out of all the infinite possibilities of humankind

Material for a Cover Story.

Palms sting from clapping. On a screen above the stage the enormous simulacrum shines while a tiny black and white figure

collared by an inquisitive spot

pops up to bumble and bow behind his table.

That simp on the screen can't be me. Where? When? A case of mistaken identity. No never. Least of all in a photograph redrawn and tinted by the art department. Some inkling of a former self now long since scrapped? It is today's self that lives. The dead selves linger on as photographs.

"Wouldn't it be funny," I ask my neighbors, "if it turned out that we were really all dead, and this Hall of Fame was an ingenious Hell?"

Nobody seems the least amused by the suggestion.

The Greeks might have thought so. For the Greeks, the spirits of the dead were simulacra, very like a photograph, bereft of blood and brain and nerve. Those ghosts, that Odysseus, at another famous banquet in the royal hall of the rich Phaeacians, told Alcinous about—

who crowded so fearfully about him when he cut the ram's throat on Ocean's shore, that he had to draw his sword to cow them,

were mere images of men, antique celebrities crowding out of Erebus to drink of the live blood. Achilles hissed he'd rather be a slave, a poor man's slave on earth, than King of all the celebrated dead. When Odysseus' own mother's ghost rose up before the pool of blood he tried to take her in his arms, but like smoke she drifted through his fingers; the image has no life.

The party lasted till long after midnight. Then we all went home to search out our pictures in the morning paper.

2

Walt Whitman: Democratic Vistas

I am now once again in New York City and Brooklyn.
... The splendor, picturesqueness, the oceanic amplitude and rush
of these great cities, the unsurpassed situation, rivers and bays,
sparkling sea-tides, costly and lofty new buildings, façades of marble
and iron, of original grandeur and elegance of design, with the
masses of gay color, the preponderance of white and blue, the
flags flying, the endless ships, the tumultuous streets, Broadway, the
heavy low musical roar, hardly ever intermitted even at night. ..."

"The average man of a land at last only is important. He, in
these States, remains the immortal owner and boss, deriving good
uses, somehow, out of any sort of servant in office, even the basest;
... a nation like ours, in a sort of geological formation state, trying
continually new experiments, choosing new delegations, not served
by the best men only, but sometimes more by those that provoke
it—by the combats they arouse. Thus national rage, fury, discussion
etc. better than content. Thus also the warning signals, invaluable
for after times."

"When I pass to and fro, different latitudes, different seasons,
beholding the crowds of the great cities, New York, Boston, Philadelphia, Cincinnati, Chicago, St. Louis, San Francisco, New Orleans, Baltimore—when I mix with these interminable swarms of
alert, turbulent, goodnatured, independent citizens, mechanics,
clerks, young persons—at the idea of this mass of men, so fresh and

free, so loving and so proud, a singular awe falls over me. I feel with dejection and amazement that among our geniuses and talented writers or speakers, few or none have yet really spoken to this people, created a single imagemaking work for them or absorbed the central spirit and the idiosyncrasies which are theirs and which thus in highest ranges so far remains entirely uncelebrated, unexpressed."

"Democracy in silence biding its time, ponders its ideals."

"How long it takes to make this American world see that it is, in itself, the final authority and reliance."

"Thus we presume to write, criticize, upon things that exist not and travel by maps yet unmade."

"I see over my own continent the Pacific Railroad surmounting every barrier

I see continual trains of cars winding along the Platte carrying freight and passengers,

I hear the locomotives rushing and roaring and the shrill steam-whistle,

I hear the echoes reverberate through the grandest scenery in the world,

I cross the Laramie plains, I note the rocks in grotesque shapes, the buttes,

I see the plentiful larkspur and wild onions, the barren, colorless sage-deserts,

I see in glimpses afar or towering immediately above me the great mountains, I see the Wind River and the Wahsatch Mountains

I see the Monument Mountain and the Eagle's Nest, I pass the Promontory, I ascend the Nevadas,

I scan the noble Elk Mountain and wind round its base,

I see the Humboldt range, I thread the valley and cross the river,

I see the clear waters of Lake Tahoe, I see forests of majestic pines . . .

Bridging the three or four thousand miles of land travel

Tying the Eastern to the Western sea,

The road between Europe and Asia."

3

Wild Life in the Hills

After the long straight swoop across the pancake-flat prairies, hour after hour of harvested lands streaked with yellow wheatstubble to the horizon, it's exciting to see hills ahead, dark hills under clouds against the West. For the dwellers in the flatlands the hills are a tourist attraction. But on what a scale. The advertisers have gone mad. There's a sign on every fence post. Billboards zigzag along the highway: *Marvels Ahead*.

Genuine Prairie Dog City
Dog Town Ranch Store
They are Alive
Show children wild prairie dogs

Reptile Gardens
free ice   free water
Born Lucky See Free Zoo

THINK TALL
Chuck Wagon Quartette

See the Thunder Mine
LOST INJUN MAKE RESERVATION
SIOUX MOTEL

Now the plains heaving up into slopes. Railroad lines converge. Water tanks glint above the distant checkerboard of towns. Grain elevators ride the hills the way cathedrals do in Spain.

THE GATEWAY TO THE BLACK HILLS
In Rapid City the traffic is bumper to bumper. It's a shock after days of empty country under the spacious prairie sky.

DIZZYLAND
Where Weight Turns Upside Down
Instructive Educational Exciting
Alligators   Crocodiles   Iguanas   Giant Lizards
Miss this show and you'll be sorry the Rest of Your Life
THE GRAVITY SPOT
Wild Animal Cubs
Snakes

Inside the National Park every parking lot is packed. Tents rub elbows with tents under the great black pines in every allotted campsite. Lakes are black with boats. The green upland meadows are dotted with hikers. The Black Hills seem as crowded as Central Park on a fine Sunday.

The narrow road through the hills to Mount Rushmore turns out unbelievably winding. Can all these loops be necessary? The cars advance by inches bumper to bumper past marvelous outlooks through pineforests poised above the cloudshadows that travel across the rusty plain. At last they come into view, the poor spooks, the enormous faces carved at such expense out of the cliff upthrust into the sky. The parking places are all full. Every viewpoint is dense with craning heads, brandished cameras, fieldglasses, pointing hands, tots held up so that they can see above the crowd. But it's not sculpture. Somehow the rockhewn faces look flat like old photographs badly reproduced on newsprint. George Washington hasn't enough chin. He looks more like Susan B. Anthony. Teddy Roosevelt has lost his glasses. Poor Jefferson has the air of a female impersonator. Abe Lincoln at least has a profile. Sidewhiskers give his face some shape. The effect is depressing. They don't look big at all way up there on that enormous cliff, under the vast sky and a threatening thunderstorm. "They'll stand out more at night" whispers someone hopefully. "The spotlights set them off."

Won't do us any good. By night we'll be a hundred miles to the west, out in the empty drylands of Wyoming.

The National Park Service must be proud of that road. It's a whimsical road. The touring cars are squeezed along it by the press of traffic like toothpaste out of a tube. It winds up and down the steep mountainside, makes figure eights and switchbacks and actually ties itself in knots. At the sharp curves, underloops pass beneath bridges stoutly built of the great unpeeled trunks of the black pines of these mountains. There are tunnels through the cliff.

The last tunnel is most ingeniously contrived so that we get a final look at the effigies of The Four Great Americans framed in rock. They flicker in the distant sunlight as unsubstantial as faces painted on balloons. Coming out of the tunnel there is a curve. The four faces slip out of sight behind a magnificent great stand of black pine.

We breast a final hill and wind down into sunlight again in a less-crowded valley where every blade of grass glistens from the shower. The lodge we just passed was where Calvin Coolidge used to come to his vacations from the Presidency. There's a lake and crowds of campers beside a hundred parked trailers.

The traffic is held up again. What can be wrong? The people on the oncoming lane have a look of blank wonder on their faces. Incredulous wonder. It can't be an accident. They look pleased. Our lane's completely stalled.

We climb out of the car. "Goats," says someone in the car ahead. "Goats nothing," says a young man in a sedan with a Connecticut license, "they are bighorn sheep. . . . There is nothing else they could be."

His wife reaches out a Triscuit to a tall slender darkhoofed creature. The long dark muzzle munches. The eyes are dark, liquid as brooks.

There is this ewe and a lamb and up on the hillside a big old ram with spiraled-back horns.

"But they are so tame. . . . They haven't any right to be so tame. . . . They are the shyest animal that lives."

The ewe pokes her head into another car and backs off munching. The lamb seems shyer. Somebody hopefully produces a pretzel. The ram stands on the steep flank of the cutting a few feet above the two lanes of cars. His hoofs are firmly planted in the shale. Every camera whips out of its case. The mountain sheep hold still while shutters click all about them.

"Ovis canadiensis," insists the young man from Connecticut. His voice is shaking with excitement.

People begin to think of the mileage before them, the stalled cars behind. Cameras are shoved back into cases. Motorists climb into their cars. Everybody drives very carefully as the two lanes of traffic start moving again.

"Tame bighorn sheep . . . Don't that beat anything?"

The ewe and the lamb hold their ground, pushing their muzzles towards the passing cars for another cracker, while the ram looks on from his post above the road, for all the world like an old gypsy who's sent his women off to beg.

4

The True Believers—iii

Paul Edwards came out of the McCarthy business with his reputation for liberalism somewhat enhanced. He and Grover Wilson were favorably mentioned in a volume flaying the Senator alive which was widely read. Instead of joining in the "whitewash tactics" of the Eisenhower administration, so this man told the tale, at considerable risk to themselves, they had helped uncover some of McCarthy's more scabrous doings. The author's sense of moral outrage glowed so hot that he quite forgot the anticlimax that topped off the Lovejoy revelations.

In 1960 Paul came out enthusiastically for Kennedy. The time had come, he felt, to break away from the nonpartisan tradition of the public service. He had developed into a passable afterdinner speaker. In his middle forties he hadn't quite lost his cowlick or the disarming look of being a strayed highschool senior. Enough of Shelbyville had stuck to him to make him a rather efficient fundraiser with cornbelt audiences. He began to cultivate a Middlewestern twang. None of this went unnoticed by the very competent professionals who directed the Kennedy campaign.

After John Kennedy's somewhat marginal victory, the dyed-in the-wool liberals left over from the New Deal and the Fair Deal felt that the New Frontier should offer them a step up on the bureaucratic pyramid. A good many of them were disappointed. The U. S.

Department of Agriculture already employed a hundred thousand persons.

Top positions tended to go to men who had been useful in the campaign. The Secretaryship went to a California lawyer named Eli Goodman who had administered agriculture for that state under the Honorable Pat Brown. So far as anybody knew, Mr. Goodman's contact with agriculture was limited to the possession of a large ranch stocked with highpriced cattle, whose chief purpose in life was to establish a loss for income-tax purposes.

Guy Stephenson, whose whole career was bound up with the production of new grades of wheat, found himself heading the Office of Stabilization and Conservation. By some miracle Paul was appointed Assistant Secretary in charge of Latin American programs. In the days when he worked for Steff he had had some experience with counseling plantation owners south of the Rio Grande.

The raise was a godsend to the Edwards family. Though Paul maintained his air of innocent indifference at the cocktail parties tendered him by friends and by people who wanted to seem friends, at home he and Ginny rejoiced mightily over the near doubling of his salary.

The education of the children was a drain on their resources. Though Paul's father objected vigorously in a chain of carefully connected letters from Shelbyville, they had all gone to private schools. All their little friends in Georgetown went to private schools. They seemed outraged when they were threatened with a public school stuffed with Negroes. George Morris, the eldest, was about to graduate from Harvard and wanted to work for a master's degree in literature. He thought of it mostly as a way of keeping out of the draft and who could blame him. The younger boy, Guy Stephenson, was graduating from Protestant High in Alexandria. He had largely been kept in school, in spite of a number of teenage scandals, by the benign influence of Dr. Ruskin. The youngest, Eleanor, was doing quite well at St. Matthew's in Baltimore, but board and tuition there kept increasing every year. Paul and Ginny had only kept up with the cost by putting an expensive second mortgage on their Georgetown house. Fortunately, the house and land had gone up in value even faster than the cost of the childrens' schooling.

Inauguration that winter was almost a national festival. Kennedy's popularity had grown daily since election. Every hotel in town overflowed with an effervescence of deserving Democrats.

A few days before inauguration there arrived by special messenger at the Edwards' house a heavily embossed invitation to a dinner honoring John Kennedy's contribution to agriculture. The host was Buddy Lee Engle of Plainview, Texas. Paul immediately called up the Department to find out who the gentleman was. He was told he was a rich Texas cotton-grower, a contributor to the Democratic campaign. Nobody seemed to have anything against him. The dinner would bridge a gap between watching the parade and the opening of the inaugural balls they had promised to attend, so they decided to go.

Paul and Ginny had hardly got seated in one of the upstairs banquet rooms at the Mayflower Hotel when they began to wish they hadn't come. The room buzzed with young reporters for Buddy Lee Engle's own newspaper in Plainview. They were putting down the name and opinions of every guest.

Buddy Lee was on his feet at the end of the table greeting his guests into a battery of mikes. He was a tall broadshouldered pale man with wide glowing eyes. He wore a pinstriped business suit which contrasted with the tails and white ties of most of his guests. Paul immediately thought: "Why he talks like a streetcorner evangelist."

He was apologizing. Buddy Lee was apologizing for not serving liquor. His religious convictions. He said he hoped the good thick steaks, off his own Santa Gertrudis cattle, would make up for it. Good rare beef was as much stimulant as any man needed.

Then he started to toss around the word vision. Vision was God's stamp of approval on man. It was through the intensity of his vision that John Fitzgerald Kennedy had been elected to the highest office in the land. Vision had motivated the empire he, Buddy Lee, had built for himself in Texas and the greater empire he hoped to build overseas. It was the man of vision who went furthest out on the limb to pick the fruit. Vision was God's way of choosing those who would succeed in this world. He thanked God for his vision and for the vision of John Fitzgerald Kennedy. By this time his speech had become so confused it was hard to tell whether it was Buddy Lee or John Kennedy who had been elected President.

Paul and Ginny ate a little of the thick and tender but thoroughly cold steak and made their excuses. Inauguration day was a day of comings and goings. They had to honor a previous engagement.

"Paul, did it occur to you the man may be crazy?" asked Ginny when they found themselves alone in the elevator.

"But his personality pervaded the whole room," said Paul.

"I'll say it did," jeered Ginny. "It's like the smell of a pulp mill. You can't get it out of your nose."

"Crazy like a fox," said Paul thoughtfully. "An almost illiterate combine operator from East Texas—he's collected a fortune of twelve million dollars."

In the lobby they met friends. With them they looked in on another dinner. Paul clean forgot about Buddy Lee and his vision.

Merely getting a grip on the routine work of his office, combined with time-consuming and fruitless Departmental conferences kept Paul from thinking of anything but matters on his desk for several weeks.

Then one day he had a telephone call from Simon Adler suggesting they eat lunch together.

Paul was surprised when he found himself being ushered into a White House car. He knew Simon was well entrenched with the administration but he didn't know how well. "I hope you won't mind if I take you out to my place for lunch," said Simon. "As you know, Washington is the one city in the world where a man can't have a quiet lunchtime talk with a friend without being overheard. . . . I suppose you've heard of Buddy Lee Engle."

"We were one of the couples he invited to dinner inauguration night," said Paul laughing. "Ginny says he's madhatter mad. I must admit he's an oddball."

"You just wait," said Simon.

They went up in the gleaming aluminum elevator in one of the new apartment houses in the west end of G Street. There was no one in the apartment. A table was set for two in front of a bright window that afforded a magnificent view of Arlington and the river and the Key Bridge and the oldworld pile of Georgetown.

Simon went into the kitchen and came back with a cold chicken, a bowl of salad and a bottle of white wine in a cooler.

"My, this is pleasant. Simon, you and Olive sure do live well."

Simon grinned. "The best is none too good," he said. "I never found a lack of baked meats at the Edwards' house either. If you just took an occasional glass of wine."

"Not after the number of promising men I've seen ruin themselves in this town by too much drinking. In that I agree with Buddy Lee."

"Is he a dry too?"

"Teetotaler. Won't serve it to his guests."

"I have news for you," said Simon, his eyes popping. "It turns out that he's one of the most gigantic swindlers on record."

"Something told me I shouldn't have accepted that dinner invitation."

"Sitting a few minutes at a man's table on inauguration day isn't compromising, though the way the *Plain View Gazette* wrote it up one would have thought the President himself was giving it. . . . The trouble is, Paul, that some people high up in the Department, including some Kennedy appointees, have been taking handouts from Buddy Lee. He's no lavish spender in that line but he's been broke often enough himself to know when a check for a thousand dollars, or even a suit of clothes or a pair of shoes will be very much appreciated."

"Simon, what is his racket?" asked Paul who was chewing with appetite on a chicken leg and a crisp roll.

"Racket number one. He trades in cotton allotment transfers, mostly forged or obtained by illegal means." Simon lifted one finger.

"Racket number two. He trades in government contracts for the storage of grain. He's borrowed money from every loaning agency in the Southeast. For collateral he puts up government contracts, many of which may be fraudulent."

Simon lifted two fingers. This was his courtroom manner.

"Racket number three." Simon lifted three fingers. "He's shaken down that huge Industrial Solvents Corporation of New York by presenting them with mortgages on tanks of anhydrous ammonia—we used to call it nitrogen. The tanks are phantom. The ammonia must be real but I imagine most of it had been sold to local farmers."

Simon poured himself a second glass of wine. He cleared his

throat. "I must admit this amuses me. These businessmen are always saying the government is so inefficient and here they've been taken for a ride themselves, a million-dollar ride. This is the deal the FBI will probably jump him on. It turns out to be a Federal offense to transport fraudulent mortgages across state lines."

Simon paused to savor his wine. "The minute this story breaks, Paul, every reactionary John Bircher in the country is going to start howling corruption. Agriculture will be the Department involved. The newspapers— It's going to be God's gift to the Republican Party."

"Thank God it's not in my bailiwick."

"How much influence do you have with Stephenson?"

"He's your brother-in-law."

"Paul, you know perfectly well if Cecelia or I suggest anything he'll do the opposite. He's in the Office of Stabilization and Conservation and I suspect that's where the lightning is going to strike. How he ever got there is a mystery to me. Steff is a serenely honest man and a genius but his lifework, like he's always said, is in directing research. And now we have a man who believes in nothing but the truth, the whole truth, so help him God; in a spot where we need tact and a certain amount of evasion. You know, an operator."

They got to their feet and started walking distractedly about the room.

"It's going to be a riproaring scandal," said Paul. "I suppose you'll have plenty of people to handle the White House end."

Simon came right back in almost an accusing tone. "Your business, Paul, is to see the Department keeps its skirts clean. What about Goodman?"

"He hasn't practiced corporation law for nothing."

Simon was staring out the window. "John Kennedy is so popular right now nothing can touch him," he said at last in a relaxed tone.

He locked up the apartment and they went back to the elevator. "Better not speak of anything sensitive in the car," he whispered in Paul's ear. "We don't know who the driver might be working for."

Back at the Department, where Paul half expected to see tornado shelters being built, everything was quiet.

Weeks went by; yellow forsythia bloom started to appear in the Georgetown gardens. The young managed to assemble at home for a spring weekend. They had time for a picnic at Great Falls before taking Eleanor back to St. Matthew's.

Then one morning a headline stood out as Paul gathered up the *Washington Post* from his doorstep: "Texas millionaire arrested by FBI. Charged with transport of fraudulent mortgages."

By the end of April the story was building up daily: "Top DA officials possibly involved in defalcations." "Farmers sue Buddy Lee." "Buddy Lee empire collapses under revelations of Texas District Attorney."

Eli Goodman had called a conference in his office for that same morning. Several men arrived with a haggard look as if they hadn't slept too well. Eli Goodman's oval face showed some peevish wrinkles around the mouth. After a sullen silence he blurted out, "Well, gentlemen, this isn't a very happy way to initiate our spring season. . . . I shall accept with regret the resignation of anyone who feels that that's where his duty lies, but the fewer resignations we have the better. . . . I want to warn everyone against talking to newsmen. . . . If you possibly can, pass the buck to me. I shall give a formal press conference whenever there is a new development. What they want is headlines. We'll try to give them headlines favorable to us. . . . Thank you very much."

When Paul got back to his office he found a note from the Secretary: "Mr. Edwards—this is to authorize you to take over the Office of Stabilization and Conservation from Mr. Stephenson. Explain to him that this is entirely in his own interest. We have been busy for a long time getting him back to his real work at Ciudad Obregon."

"Steff must know something," thought Paul, "or they wouldn't be in such a hurry to get him out of town."

Steff was perfectly pleasant but he said he would be damned if he would get out of his office until something was done about the material he had collected in his safe. He'd been doing research himself during the last six months. He had complete documentation on seven cases of favoritism to various projects, all unsound from the point of view of the Department, which had been initiated by Buddy Lee. In each case he had found a penciled notation along with the authorization: *endorsed by Senator Straub.*

Paul heard him out. Then he said very gently: "Steff, you know there is nobody in Washington I have more respect for than you, but Secretary Goodman has ordered me to take over your office. If I don't do it someone else will. He suggests you take a tour of duty with the Rockefeller outfit at Ciudad Obregon."

"Ciudad Obregon be damned. What we have to do is clean up this mess. This is the biggest government scandal since Teapot Dome."

"It could be if we let it grow to that point. Secretary Goodman has spent the last week going over the records. He claims the government hasn't so far lost a thin dime . . . not a thin dime."

Steff gave a snort. "You'll have to prove that to me."

Paul stared blankly in his face. He was trying to think of an argument. "Steff, you just keep your shirt on and promise not to do or say anything hasty. Won't you do that just for me? If the newsmen get to you in the corridor tell them you can't make any statement until a full report is placed on your desk."

Paul tossed back his cowlick suddenly. His blue eyes shone. For a moment he looked all of fifteen.

"I know what let's do. Let's sleep on it. You come over to our house for breakfast in the morning. I'll bring the Secretary's figures. We'll compare them with yours back at your office. I think you'll find that the parties who really fell for the swindle were Industrial Solvents and the loan companies. They kept making him advances on his phony collateral."

"They wouldn't have done that if he hadn't been able to toss around some big names. What's this Texas Senator getting out of it? Why should the V.P. take such an interest?"

"After all his years in Texas politics and his years in Washington, Steff, think of the thousands of people who could claim to be buddy-buddy with the Vice-President. Think these things over tonight. Then, too, you have to decide whether you are a Goldwater man and a John Bircher or a Democrat. . . . Ginny and I will expect you for bacon and eggs at seven thirty. I can't quite promise popovers but I might be able to convince Ginny she ought to make them."

In the outer office Paul saw a familiar face. "Why Hattie McGuire, where have you been all these months?"

"To tell the truth, Mr. Edwards, I had a long sick spell."

"I hope you haven't come back to work too soon. Lots of people do." Paul's voice dripped with sympathy.

"The doctor says I'm right up to scratch."

Paul left her his most lingering blueeyed smile.

Next morning Steff arrived at the Edwards' house promptly at seven thirty. He and Paul sat drinking orange juice and coffee, and looking over the CPA figures that had been furnished to Goodman. Ginny occasionally came trotting out to say the popovers were unconscionably slow this morning. By the time she brought out the bacon and eggs and popovers it was eight thirty.

Steff began to get restless: "I suppose you know," he said as he pushed his plate back, "a representative of the bureau who was down here looking over Buddy Lee's cotton leases came to an untimely end. The coroner found it suicide. The coroner must have been an operative of Buddy Lee's. If the suicide story is true the man must have first poisoned himself by exhaust fumes, then shot himself four times with a bolt action rifle and then run himself over with his truck. It sounds like murder. Don't you think the Department should investigate the murder of one of its agents?"

"That was George Warren," said Paul. "It is somewhat of a mystery. I understood he had reported favorably on the leases."

"That question is, as the lawyers say, moot," said Steff gruffly as he got to his feet.

Steff, who was particularly fond of Ginny, thanked her warmly for a marvelous breakfast. When they walked out to the garage Paul discovered he had left his key upstairs in his other trousers. It took him a long time to find it. It was nine o'clock in the full jam of morning traffic before they started for the Department.

Paul parked his car in its usual place in the basement. They found an odd sort of bustle outside of Steff's office. Several Security Guards stood in the hall assuming belligerent attitudes. A maintenance man was working on the lock.

"Who's been tampering with my door?" asked Steff angrily. "Nobody is supposed to have a key but me and Miss McGuire."

Sounds of squeaking and whimpering came from Miss McGuire's desk within.

"Orders from the top floor, Mr. Stephenson," said one man

politely. "Perhaps you could get Miss McGuire to give us the combination to your safe. She seems quite upset. We have orders to open it."

Steff immediately called the Secretary's office. The telephone girl knew nothing. Secretary Goodman was on his way to a cabinet meeting and couldn't be reached.

At the same time Paul called Emergency Services on the other phone. A doctor was needed right away to care for a secretary who was going into hysterics.

Paul felt his face getting red. "Somebody jumped the gun on us," he muttered sheepishly.

"You lying doublefaced son of a bitch," said Steff, leaving long pauses between the words, "and all these years I thought you were a friend of mine."

He was hauling off with his left when two Security Guards stepped deftly between them.

"When you cool down a little you'll realize I still am. I'm keeping you out of a muddle you might have found deeply embarrassing. . . . If you want to see my authorization here it is." He flattened out Goodman's note on the desk under Steff's nose.

Steff strode over to the safe, manipulated the lock and threw it open with a bang. "My resignation will be on the Secretary's desk before I leave the building."

Hattie McGuire sat sobbing at her desk in the office entrance. Steff patted her on the shoulder. "Hattie, don't take this too hard," he said. "I'll make sure you don't get penalized for my evil intentions."

A man in a white coat had appeared. A nurse tagged after him with a wheelchair. He asked Hattie McGuire if she minded if he gave her an injection of a tranquilizer.

"I'll only take it if you say it's all right, Dr. Stephenson."

"I don't see why not. You lay up for a couple of hours and you'll be fine and dandy."

Steff had been ramming a few books and other personal possessions into an old Gladstone bag Paul remembered from a trip to Mexico way back.

Hattie McGuire was trundled off by the nurse, in the wheelchair.

366

Before Steff left, Paul tried to shake hands. Steff's dark eyes narrowed to slits. His long ruddled face behind the sharp beak looked more Indian than ever. "I'd as soon shake hands with a rattlesnake," he said, giving his words a snakelike hiss as he said them.

Paul went home with a throbbing headache that night.

"It turned out very painful," he told Ginny. "The end of twenty years of friendship. What can you do if people will act so emotionally?"

"Anyway, we gave him a good farewell breakfast," said Ginny cheerfully. "Look what we got."

She trotted to the living-room mantel with her girlish scamper and came back with a large embossed envelope bearing the Presidential seal. "It's an invitation to the next White House dinner."

Paul had the usual difficulty trying to find enough matching studs. Ginny got all out of breath tying his white tie. At first the car wouldn't start. All dressed up, they sat staring at each other in helpless despair. Paul kept turning the key this way and that. Suddenly the starter turned.

Ginny was studying the invitation. They were supposed to enter by the east entrance in the back of the White House.

It was a balmy May night. Moonlight. As they paused in the line of cars they got a whiff of magnolia, mingled with just a tang of buttery French cooking from some kitchen.

Ginny's eyes were sparkling. She put her hand on Paul's sleeve. "This is the most wonderful thing that ever happened to us. Paul, does it make you think of anything?"

"Of course," said Paul in his offhand way. . . . "Highschool graduation."

"You still remember *Romeo and Juliet* and the dance afterwards?" whispered Ginny.

Paul had no time to answer. He was driving up in front of a brilliantly lit entrance. An operative in a natty business suit was ready to take over the car.

Paul slipped the check into his breast pocket. As he hadn't anything to leave in the cloakroom he waited for Ginny while she left her mink stole on the ladies' side. It was a handsome room.

People were pointing out to each other the imported wallpaper Mrs. Kennedy had had the walls papered with; people were guessing how much it cost. Since most of the guests were walking slowly up a broad shallow stairway, Paul and Ginny followed.

Paul was getting worried because he hadn't seen anybody he knew yet. He had a panicky thought that maybe it was the wrong night. He brought the invitation out of his pocket to study it. Someone must have been looking over his shoulder because as soon as he reached the top of the stairs into the East Room, an usher suddenly bawled out "Assistant Secretary of Agriculture, Mr. Paul Edwards and Mrs. Edwards."

Paul half-expected a lot of people to come running up to say "How do you do?" Nobody did. Then he saw Simon Adler. Simon with his beaked face of a scavenger bird and his sideburns and his pale skin looked particularly well in evening dress. Over Simon's shoulder Paul caught sight of Olive's brown face with its usual discontented look. She was taller than Simon.

Paul and Ginny made their way towards them through a sprinkling of Secret Service men in white jackets. "Well," said Simon to Ginny, "how do you like it?"

Ginny whispered hoarsely that it was like a dream.... "I keep thinking I'm going to wake up."

"Ginny, you are wonderful," said Simon. "Can you beat it," echoed Olive in her deep voice, "she's still the naïve little girl from Shelbyville, Ohio, who came to town twentyfive years ago."

"I'll tell you one thing," said Simon. "For my sins I've occasionally attended these functions under three administrations and they are a whole lot more palatable now. The Kennedys have the knack. They don't get along too well together but as entertainers they make a team. Jackie understands French food. They both know about wines. Somebody told me this was the largest seated dinner ever given in the White House and see how smooth everything runs. This sort of thing needs management and management begins at the top."

A waiter came along with a trayload of champagne. Simon scooped up a couple of glasses. "I suppose you won't indulge," he said mockingly to Paul. "Olive, it's up to us to live it up for four."

After a while Simon added, giving Ginny an exaggerated

ogling look. "Ginn, let's agree to consider it part of your rustic charm."

When a tray of soft drinks came by, Paul eagerly snatched off a couple of Cokes. The crowd, the lights, the excitement made him thirsty.

The guests were cuing up in alphabetical lines. Wellknown faces began to show up, off front pages, out of sports and theatre columns and TV news spots.

"Imagine getting all this gang seated and fed," whispered Ginny. Paul had her firmly by the arm and was leading her into the E column.

Ginny gave a little gasp when the Marine Color Guard resplendent with flags and gold fringes appeared suddenly against the wall. A double door opened behind them.

"Ladies and gentlemen: the President of the United States and Mrs. Kennedy," announced the usher's voice, and there they were, looking exactly as Ginny had expected them to look—Jacqueline dark and sleek and wide-eyed and John with that lovable crinkly hair.

Putting aside their empty glasses on whatever trays and tables they could reach, people pressed forward. It all happened surprisingly quickly. They were shaking hands. The President seemed to know all about Paul. His face puckered up in a grin. "I certainly hope you've got that fellow out of your hair over at the Department," he was saying. "Wasn't that something?"

Ginny found herself having a tiny chat with Jacqueline about St. Matthew's. Jackie said it was a lovely school. A friend had told her they were all mad about Eleanor Edwards. Charm, intelligence. She gave Ginny a deep brown smile. "She must take after her mother." Ginny came away almost swooning.

The Marine Band was playing. Ginny wanted to dance. She hummed a few bars, but nobody was dancing yet. Paul left her to find his table in the State Dining Room. An obsequious usher indicated her place at Table 8 in the Blue Room.

She found herself sitting next to John Ingoldsby of State. It was a relief to find somebody she knew. Who should be across the table of all people but Steff? He was so busy talking Spanish to what looked like a Mexican diplomat that he paid no attention to her.

John Ingoldsby could talk about only one thing. He had a son at Harvard and he knew the Edwardses had a son at Harvard. "Graduating this year," said Ginny brightly.

"What's your son's name?" asked Ingoldsby.

"George Morris."

"My son Richard is a straight A-boy but I'm tremendously worried about him."

"Ours don't come that bright but they do all right. We've always let them have their own ideas and work things out their own way," said Ginny stoutly keeping up her end. "Is it the long hair and whiskers that worry you? It's silly but I don't see any real harm in it."

"Ever heard of LSD?"

"What exactly is it?"

"I'm no chemist but I know it is very easy to make by anybody who has the most rudimentary chemical training. Richard is a chemistry major. The kids in his group are experimenting with LSD. It is a very dangerous drug and none of the doctors I've consulted seems to know much about its long-term or short-term effects. At that age you think you know all the answers but you don't."

John Ingoldsby was so upset he piled his salad in the middle of his meat plate. He was drinking wildly every different kind of wine the waiters poured out. When the brandy came he put it away in one great swallow.

Ginny, who had always thought of him as one of the most severe of the striped-pants contingent, was appalled by his show of emotion. She was so busy trying to console him she couldn't find a word to say to an agreeable little grisly man who looked like a foreign professor on her right.

Some of John Ingoldsby's agitation came off on her. It was a relief to get away from him and to join Paul who was waiting in the last row of little gilt chairs in the East Room. A lectern was set up facing them. A well-known actor was fiddling about, waiting to read something. Neither Paul nor Ginny could remember his name, though they both recognized his face. The piece turned out to be an unfinished short story about Caribbean adventures in World War II by Ernest Hemingway, a writer they both admired. Ginny kept thinking about what Ingoldsby had said. She got so nervous she couldn't follow the plot. At last the actor stopped reading. Ginny tugged at Paul's sleeve. "Would it be rude if we slipped out?"

"Not quite yet. I've seen a number of people I'd like to say good evening to."

They cruised around the room. The Marine Band played. A few couples were desultorily dancing in odd corners. The Kennedys and most of the headline faces had disappeared. At last Paul consented to let Ginny fetch her wrap and meet him at the car port.

"You mustn't let Ingoldsby upset you. His boy is probably too bright for his own good."

"But anything about drugs gives me the creeps."

They slept badly that night. After Paul had left for the office a special-delivery letter appeared addressed to both of them from Dr. Edwards.

From the first line she felt the voice of doom. Her hands grew cold.

"Dear children," Dr. Edwards wrote, "George has just written me—as from one researcher to another. He's become very much interested in LSD, he says, in a scientific way. After all, that is a much better approach than that of some boys and girls I've heard about, but his letter worries me. I don't suppose we can do anything to interfere with his graduation but I'd like to see him do his postgraduate work in England or on the continent. There is something unhealthy about our attitude towards these things in America. Studying hallucinatory drugs might make sense if he were majoring in Psychology or Pharmacology, but it seems to me that Coleridge and De Quincey have polished off the subject so far as English literature goes. I suggest that one of you fly right out to Boston to see George. I'd go myself but Ruth absolutely draws the line. She says I'm much too old to go rattling about the country and that what I'd say couldn't have any influence with the young man anyway."

Ginny called Paul and by noon she was on the shuttle to Boston.

George met her at the airport. What she could see of his face through his whiskers looked pale. He kept twitching his fingers. They looked pathetically thin and tobaccostained. He smoked one cigarette after another.

They sat down in the lounge to talk. "I guess I shouldn't have written my grandfather, Mom, but I thought it was the easiest way of tipping you off without throwing you into a fright. I can take care of myself. I'm just doing my thing. The one I'm worried about is Guy.... Eleanor and I are husky types—we can take things, but Guy isn't too stable. You must know that. You and Dad should have been worrying about Guy years ago. He may need psychiatric treatment. The lack of interest of parents in their children in this day and age is a national scandal."

"George, tell me exactly what you mean."

"Guy is not only smoking pot but he's hooked on it. He's one of a group of lively young highschool students who are buying and selling it.... Those kids just think they can do anything. One of these days he's going to get caught and that won't look good in the son of a man high up in the government service. I'm not criticizing Guy. I'm criticizing you and Dad for not catching on."

Ginny burst out crying. "But George, what could we have done?"

"Dad could have turned him over and paddled his rump good and hard. That kind of medicine applied years ago might have brought him around."

Ginny was sobbing. She went to the ladies' room to wash her face.

When she came back George was walking nervously up and down in front of the bench, occasionally glancing at his watch.

"Mom, I've got a very important date. At my time of life dates are more important than parents, something else you and Dad have to learn.... There's a plane at five. I suggest you take it back to Washington and get hold of Guy as soon as you can. You and Dad might get a little sense into his head before it's too late.... Mom, I haven't intended to be cruel or unkind, but as soon as I knew you were coming I decided that the time had come to give you the works straight from the shoulder."

"But George," she whispered in a little childish voice, "there are so many things I wanted to talk to you about."

He grabbed her two hands in a sudden burst of affection. "Mom, there's nothing you or Dad can tell me that will help me right now. Call it the generation gap if you want to."

He was gone.

Ginny walked back up the ramp on the plane. She let herself drop into a seat. "This," she told herself, "has been the most terrible day in my life." She asked the hostess for an aspirin and a glass of water and buckled her seatbelt and leaned back with her eyes closed.

When she tried to remember what she had been so anxious to tell George about, all she could think of was the White House dinner.

5

The Later Life and Deplorable Opinions of
Jay Pignatelli—vi

The Long Arm

August is a lovely month in Rio. Jay flew down for another eight days on the same Telephone Company business which had afforded him several pleasant trips in the past. Every member of the firm had called up the Canadian client in Montreal to explain that Goulart's expropriation decree had made the situation hopeless, but the client, a stubborn Scot by the name of McGregor, replied that in Brazil nothing was ever quite hopeless. He was willing to throw good money after bad for one more try. So in his capacity of Latin American expert for the firm, Jay found himself again on the nonstop Varig flight to Rio.

Plácido Gonçales met him at Galeão, as he always did. He was unusually silent during the long lunch which, according to established custom, he set Jay up to in the quiet splendor of the restaurant at the Museum of Modern Art. This was one of the most expensive places in town but it had the advantage of being on the direct road between the airport and Jay's hotel. As always the food was extraordinary, small broiled red snappers washed down with Portuguese *vinho verde,* green beans, filet mignon with sauce Béarnaise. A good Beaune. Plácido never spared the horses.

Just as the waiter was bringing in the pineapple au kirsch for dessert, Plácido almost jumped out of his chair, like a fish lunging at a lure.

It always amused Jay that the excitable little man, chain-smoker, drinker of an incredible number of *cafezinhos,* each of which made him more jumpy than the last, should be named Plácido.

"I have an idea. The famous governor of the state of Guanabara is not only a friend of mine but a relative. Actually, he is the most intelligent man in Brazil. He went up to Washington last spring with what seemed to me an excellent formula for compensating the foreign stockholders, but your State Department, as always rewarding its enemies and punishing its friends, would have none of it. They stupidly acquiesced in Goulart's plan a few weeks later.... I know we can see the governor up at Petropolis on Sunday."

"But Plácido, our client is a Canadian."

Plácido hurriedly poured Jay an extra brandy.

"Do we have to wait till Sunday?" Jay asked impatiently. "This is only Wednesday."

"Wait. I shall call him."

Plácido trotted off into the corner of the restaurant.

He came back breathless. "I spoke to his son ... Sunday afternoon. In the week he is too busy. Up at Petropolis. I shall drive you. He is vitally interested. We must see him before we meet the bureaucrats. Now I shall take you to the hotel. Always the Gloria?"

Jay nodded yawning. He felt woozy after sitting up all night on the plane and the rich lunch and the extra brandies.

"First you must sleep and then you must imagine a new formula."

"Damn well better be new," said Jay.

Plácido, after signing the bill with a flourish and leaving a wad of *cruzeiros* for the waiters, handed Jay into his white VW and plunged into the stream of traffic. The hotel was virtually in sight but it took three-quarters of an hour of dodging trucks and buses, weaving in and out among taxicabs in intricate eddies of traffic, before they reached the comparative calm of the ramp in front of the Gloria.

"Meester Pignatelli, thank you very much."

"*Senhor Plácido, muit'obrigado* . . . Saturday morning at ten," added Jay, looking Plácido firmly in the eye, "we confer at your office."

"*Hora inglesa.*"

"And Sunday Petropolis?"

They shook hands on it again.

What a place to do business, thought Jay going up in the elevator. If people aren't in Petropolis they are in São Paulo. . . . "But how damn pleasant," he said aloud as he pulled up the blind that closed off the balcony of his shuttered room. The azure sky and the bay and the Sugarloaf and the sailing yachts and the steamers poured into the room in the flutter of picture postcards on the briny South Atlantic wind. Under him through the shimmering palms was the clear aquamarine of the pool. It was the pool that saved his life whenever he came to Rio. Nobody in it now. In Rio they thought of August as midwinter.

He was asleep before he hit the bed.

It was about five when he woke up. Now for a swim. It was the same as last time. To reach the pool from his room he had to go down a long corridor to a greasy-smelling freight elevator. From the lower level he worked his way through an old ballroom that was being replastered by a swarm of little brown workmen. They civilly wished him good afternoon as he passed them.

The water was just right, not too cold. The lusty vegetation springing from every corner of the court made it summer enough for him. It was eminently restful to lie on his back in the clear cool water making gentle frogmotions with his legs while he looked up through the shining leaves into the paling blue of the late afternoon sky.

No way of escaping the traffic. Its hissing and roaring rose from the broad jampacked avenues between the hotel and the bayshore, but its stridence was strained through the palms and the balustrade and a group of English twittering over their afternoon tea under the striped umbrellas on the terrace. The phone was ringing when Jay got back to his room. It was an American voice. At first he didn't recognize it. It was a professor of English who was a friend of Emily's in New York.

"Jay, this is Paul Bates."

"I'm kicking myself I didn't insist on Emily's coming down. . . . You know, she's so scared of hot weather."

"Ruth and I are wondering if you couldn't have dinner with us. We're in Copacabana. I'm winding up my teaching job so we are leaving at the end of the week."

"Fine," said Jay. He would come out as soon as he could corral a cab.

Paul added that their little place was hard to find. They would meet Jay in the Copacabana bar. "And Jay," a hesitant note, almost a stammer came in Paul's voice. "Would you mind eating dinner with Danny DeLong?"

"Who?"

"You know, the embezzler."

"Not the fugitive there has been so much about in the papers? Why not?" Jay burst out laughing. "I'm always dining with thieves in my business."

"Of course, he says it was all an administrative error." Paul was laughing at his end of the line.

"That's what they all say. . . . Don't worry if I'm a little late. You know the taxi problem. Love to Ruth."

Jay dressed as fast as he could. Wait till I write Emily, he was muttering to himself. She'll be furious. She loves to meet notorious characters. Under the glass awning the doorman was desperately blowing his whistle. Several groups with a dressed-for-dinner look were already waiting. "Just no cabs tonight," muttered the doorman when Jay approached him with a piece of change. "Don't know where they have gone."

A slight drizzle had come on but he had his raincoat. He decided to start walking. The buses were all bulging with passengers. Beyond the slow line of buses and cars, and the trucks and pickups smoking and blatting, and the decrepit jalopies of every American and European make, a last slanting saffron glare out of the west picked up windows across the bay and sails and the superstructure of steamers gilded the purple pinnacles that thrust up out of every backwater. Pinpricks of light already crowned the crest of the Sugarloaf. In spite of the smell of scorched rubber and burning oil from the pandemonium of traffic, there was a lift about the evening that brought back a thousand city twilights, the

Champs Élysées, the Castellana, the East River Drive. This was the moment cities lived for.

Jay walked and walked. Copacabana was turning out further than he remembered. At length he tried to cross the stream of traffic to the broad sidewalk by the bay side. He found himself pushing his way through a crowd on a traffic island. Everybody was looking at something on the pavement. Men were taking their hats off. Jay was stopped by the smooth black-covered heads of two women kneeling right in front of him on the pavement. Beyond, in a clear space under the streetlight, was something stretched out. A man neither old nor young. The face was wizened, the color of green tobacco. The eyes were closed. The torn shirt was caked with blood. Bare toes protruded from a broken shoe. Someone had put two candles at his head and one at his feet. The women fingered their rosaries as they prayed. A small policeman with a yellow frogface was writing in his notebook by the light of the streetlamp overhead.

Jay gave up trying to cross through the traffic and backed off into a narrow sidestreet where streetcars advanced slowly with clanging bells. Clusters of youths in blue jeans hung on front and back. He walked and walked. He felt shaken by the grim little scene. The thought of sudden death brought the old pain back the way a wound sometimes tingles under the scar tissue. Just before the tunnel he found himself, as if by a miracle, stepping into an empty cab. In a flash he was through the bright-tiled tunnel and stepping out in front of the Hotel Copacabana Palace.

Paul and Ruth Bates were waiting for him at the bar. They both looked up at him at the same time. It struck Jay that this was one of the moments when husband and wife look alike. There was the same pleased smile on both their faces. "We thought it might amuse you, Jay. For several days we have been eating in the same restaurant. We had seen this rather strikinglooking young man," explained Ruth. "Then he sat down at the next table and began to talk."

"He talks to everybody," said Paul.

"I'm an old hand with embezzlers," said Jay with a broad sweep of his arm.

Paul had paid the bill. "You mustn't forget," said Ruth as she got to her feet, "he claims he isn't one."

Paul and Ruth Bates were so full of Danny DeLong Jay didn't get a chance to tell his little tale about the man, laid out on the traffic island. The drizzle had stopped. High above the tall buildings and the trafficlights there hovered a great full moon. They had to thread their way in single file along the main avenue of Copacabana. An extraordinary assortment of people in all the shapes and colors of the world's races jammed the pavement. Every conceivable costume. Couples of all colors and breeds, cheek to cheek, thigh to thigh. It brought back the Paris boulevards years ago, except for the fantastically vivid green of the leaves in splotches of light overhead and the growling of the warm South Atlantic surf at the end of each cross street.

Manfredo's turned out to be a barn of a place flooded by bright white light. There was the familiar Italian smell of Parmesan and tomato paste and garlic and oil. Through openings in the latticed walls, broad banana leaves, garish in the glare, swayed in the seabreeze.

The restaurant hadn't filled up yet. Jay recognized Danny DeLong from his pictures. He was sitting alone at an empty table. He did look young. He had dark hair and vivid blue eyes with lashes so dark they looked as if he used mascara. He balanced on the balls of his feet like a boxer when he rose to shake hands. He seemed smaller standing up than he did sitting down.

Danny DeLong started talking right away. Jay had hardly settled in his chair before he was shoving newspaper clippings under his nose: "Youthful Financier Takes It on the Lam. Boy Wonder Bolts to Brazil."

Before Jay had time to read down the column, Danny was pounding his ear. "They got the story right as far as it goes. What they didn't get was that I was working for the stockholders all the time. This whole acquisition program was for their benefit and the benefit of the companies and the customers. In the days when I could do no wrong the Acme directors gave me permission to buy up to half a million shares of Wallboard. What the building industry has needed for years is coordinated distribution, and that is what I was going to give them. . . . I still think I could have gotten away with it if the SEC hadn't stuck its ugly nose in just at the wrong moment. If Malachi and Joseph had kept their word I would have lost a lot of money personally but the companies would not have suffered. When the market picks up they will be as solvent as they ever were, including my little Delphic Corporation."

Danny suddenly turned his attention to the steak and fried potatoes that had been getting cold on his plate and ate them up greedily.

"When you've been the blueeyed boy all your life it's a shock," he said with his mouth full. "It's a damn funny feeling to have your friends walk out on you. Of course now I realize that it would not have made sense for Dad to ruin himself. It would have taken a Rockefeller to put out the kind of money needed to bail me out. Dad's been shelling out plenty for legal advice as it is. Now what I want to do is dream up some way of making three million dollars and paying back every man woman and child who was damaged by my stupidity. Did it once. Why shouldn't I do it again? Actually I had very different ideas when I got on that plane. I had a gun with me. I was planning to go to the best hotel and blow my brains out.

"Sounds like the last act, don't it? . . . Well, it didn't work out that way. I bet you can't guess why. . . . Table tennis . . . Ping-Pong. . . . That's been one of my funny little hobbies ever since I was a kid. Well, after I'd been here three or four days writhing around in agony at the Copacabana Palace, I read in the paper about this table-tennis tournament, open to all comers, down at the Club Flumense. That's one of the great soccer clubs. I hadn't played for a year since I last gave the kids a workout. I didn't know what the hell to do with myself so I went down and signed up. I took an interpreter down, but I didn't need to because the boys spoke pretty good English. Well, I told the secretary the whole story. I didn't want to go in there under false pretenses. Damned if he didn't laugh and say well I hadn't broken any Brazilian law and what happened in New York wasn't any of his business. Would you believe it, those guys treated me like a long-lost brother. When they found I really could push the little balls around they couldn't make enough of me. They didn't even get mad when I won the cup."

"Bravo," said Ruth Bates, making gentle applauding motions with her hands.

"Seems silly, but that set me up. It wasn't winning the cup. It was the attitude of those nice Brazilians. Made me feel I wasn't such an outcast. That and a letter"—his face crinkled all up with smiles— "a letter from my girl. She's sticking. She said she would but now she has put it in writing. Excuse me . . . I've got to go. I see my man waiting for me at the door." He got to his feet and shook hands all around in a disarmingly boyish way. He grinned. "I got some little deals on . . . finance consultant to some Brazilian companies."

He said good-by to Paul and Ruth, thanked them for the good dinner and then turned his blue eyes on Jay. "Mr. Pignatelli, if you have a moment's spare time I need an American attorney to do a very small job. . . . I'm writing a book. . . . With all this publicity a book might sell. I haven't got time but I've hired an Englishman to write it for me. As told to . . ."

"What's it about?"

"About me, of course. Who else would I write a book about? But libel. Libel is beginning to worry me. No use to go to all this expense and find I can't publish the book. Some red-hot libel suits when I get home, with all my other troubles, would sink me for fair."

Jay was in a quandary. The insistent blue eyes were burning into him. "I could come tomorrow," he heard his own voice before he knew what he was saying.

Danny snatched a visiting card out of his pocket: Avenida Copacabana 84 terceiro andar.

"I can't promise to make any recommendations."

"No matter. Make it 3:00 P.M."

Danny was off down the street in the company of a stocky darkbrown man.

"Well," said Paul, "isn't he a ball of fire?"

"He makes me feel kind of motherly," said Ruth.

"Let us know what happens," said Paul. "We may have gotten you into something."

"Nothing I can't get out of," Jay said firmly. "The fellow may have a story to tell."

A cab had just discharged a passenger at the corner. Jay hopped in before the driver could close the door. *"Feliz viagem* and thanks."

"We'll bring Emily up to date." There seemed to be just a touch of malice in Ruth's parting shout.

When Jay rang, the Englishman opened the door of the apartment. Jay extended his hand. "Mr. Pignatelli?" he asked. Jay nodded. "I'm Armistead Grimes." Jay looked at him narrowly but he couldn't make out much about him: a personable young man.

It was a large bare apartment, must be costing plenty. At a typewriter by the window sat a toothy blonde girl with straggly hair. "This is Miss Irma, our secretary." She wrung Jay's hand.

Nobody seemed to know what to say next. Grimes stood first on one foot, then on the other, like an actor who has forgotten his lines.

"Danny was called out for a moment," he said, as if suddenly remembering his cue. "Maybe you would like to read over an early chapter."

Jay allowed himself to be settled in an easy chair by the window with a pile of typed sheets in his lap.

It was five o'clock before Danny came in the door.

"Well?"

Jay stacked the sheets and laid them neatly on the chair as he rose to his feet. "But I couldn't make any pronouncement about libel without looking up some points. That would have to be in my office back home. How about your divorced wife?"

"She's not divorced yet; that's the trouble," said Danny.

Grimes came ambling in from another room. "And I'm only a sportswriter," he broke in. "Didn't Danny tell you? He found me at the Ping-Pong tournament."

"Gentlemen, I wonder if the time hasn't come to have a drink," said Danny. "Irma, suppose you do the honors. . . . That a girl." Danny tapped her lightly on the behind as she passed him.

He looked insistently up into Jay's face. Jay was getting a strange feeling he had seen him somewhere before. "May I call you Jay? The real reason I asked you around is that I thought, since you know the country better than I do, you might advise me about some of these deals I'm being tempted by. This is a country where you could make a lot of money fast if you knew how to do it."

"You can lose a lot too," said Jay, "fast as winking."

"How busy are you going to be in Rio?" asked Danny.

"After Saturday I'll be tied up for the next week."

"I have a proposition to make. Would you be my guest in a social way? Tomorrow I want to drive down to Angra dos Reis—

that means anchorage of the kings. . . . It is another great bay down the line here. There's a man who owns what is said to be an incredible tract of virgin mahogany. I've got a driver named Socrates—he knows the way. Maybe you would come just for the fun of it? It ought to be an interesting drive if you like scenery. Just you and me and Armistead."

"Well, that's very nice of you."

Danny grinned. "It's a deal. I've got one more suggestion but I shan't make that until you've had a drink."

For some time Jay had been hearing tinkling sounds in the hall. Irma appeared with a tray laden with bottles and glasses.

"It's the ice," said Irma. "I had to send Socrates for some ice. . . . Now," she giggled, "we've got enough for a champagne wedding."

"Not tonight," said Danny. He poured himself a very small drink of Scotch and Jay a very large drink and let the other two pour their own.

"Skoal," said Danny, lifting his glass towards Irma. Jay found the Scotch excellent. "I got this through Bad Jack Skinner. . . . You've read about him. He's a real confidence man. He just thinks I'm an amateur. He says not to worry about the label. This is imported by the barrel. So far he's been right. There are four or five other fugitives. They came trooping around trying to blackmail me as soon as they heard I was at the Copacabana. They found I didn't scare easy. Now Skinner claims he has a proposition. I'd like you to come along. To see what you think of it. . . . I'll have my gun."

"Danny," said Armistead Grimes with a nervous titter, "if you don't mind too much I'll stay here. I'm still taking bitters for that little touch of travelers' disease."

"I guess I'm elected," said Jay.

"Well, Armistead, suppose you go out and buy a lot of cold meat and stuff for dinner and a bottle of Portuguese wine, not the sweet kind. Casal Garcia."

"Shall do. Well, ta-ta."

"For some reason," said Danny as they went down crowded into the pocketsized elevator, "I expect the English to be brave. . . . False notion number four thousand and fortytwo."

"This'll amuse you. Up on Corcovado. There's a little shelter up there. Skinner says it's the only place in Rio where there is any privacy. Socrates knows where it is. It's where we've been going to pick up the Scotch."

"It's the one place in Rio where they've been holding people up regularly," said Jay dryly.

"I'll be darned. . . . Maybe he's in cahoots with the holdup men. If he is they won't bother us."

A small cheerful little black man with very white teeth came out from behind a black towncar parked in the tiled lower story.

"Senhor Daniel, boa noite!"

"Socrates, this is my friend Jay. You know where to go," Danny tapped Socrates on the chest. "See that ribbon? It's his football club, Botofogo, eh? . . . I'm for the Ping-Pong!" Socrates grinned even harder.

The dusk was thickening fast. It turned out a long drive, first through twilight streets where strings of lights were coming on round the shores of the lagoon and then up a series of breakneck curves into the mountain beyond.

Danny talked and talked. He'd been all around Europe and the Riviera but he'd never found a place that bugged him the way this place did. This trip up the hill was probably a damn fool wild goose chase but it would be fun. A way of learning about the country and they would go back to that little flop with a good appetite for supper and he would sleep like a top. For months he hadn't slept without Nembutal. This was how a man got his courage back.

As the road swept up from hairpin curve to hairpin curve, the houses dropped away. Few cars. The only lights were pinpoints far below. Suddenly the road was blanketed by driving mist. Socrates turned his lights down and climbed slowly. Fifteen minutes went by. He slowed up alongside a dim little edifice. "Is this the place?" "Yes sir," said Socrates, who knew only a little English.

Jay noticed that Danny pulled his gun out of his back pocket and slipped it in the pocket of his jacket. Socrates turned the car neatly around and left the motor running.

"Who's that?" came a hoarse voice from behind the shelter. Dim lights came on in another car.

A man wearing a hunting cap and a turtleneck sweater emerged from behind the car. "Danny, of course."

"Who's the other guy?"

"Friend of mine; just came for the ride."

It was completely dark now. The lights of the cars lit up a stone picnic table. The air between was a confusion of swirling mist.

Bad Jack Skinner sat down at the table. "Let's go ahead with our business." Bad Jack didn't look so bad as all that. He was a rather handsome young man with an amused twinkle in his eye. "My friend says this is the best place in all Brazil to get held up."

Bad Jack showed crooked teeth in a grin. He laid a Colt automatic on the table before him. "They won't bother me," he said. "I suppose this guy's all right or you wouldn't have brought him."

"He sure is," said Danny.

"Well, here's the deal. . . . If I could get hold of ten thousand dollars U. S. currency I could buy into a huge consignment of machineguns, ammo, etc., that one of those revolutionary groups is smuggling into the hills. It is right here in Copacabana somewhere. But the guy in charge won't let it be moved until he gets his deposit."

"How do you know he wouldn't just keep the deposit?"

"He'd be scared to. The buyers are tough hombres. They've got *cruzeiros* to burn, crazy mad all of them."

"How much do you figure to make on it?"

"Whoever puts up that dough stands to make fifty thousand next morning."

"Dollars?"

"Dollars, but it might be in Brazilian currency."

"Suppose somebody did put up the dough, what kind of security would he have?"

"We could leave a couple of cases at your apartment till the deal was completed."

"Cases of what?"

"Machineguns. Why not?"

Danny burst out laughing. "Thank you very much." He and Jay got to their feet at the same moment. "Next time, Jack, let's deal in Scotch."

Bad Jack Skinner put away his Colt. "You bigshots just don't have what it takes."

"Now Jack, you just think it over from my point of view. Now if you find some Brazilian with a nice tract of timber he wants to sell cheap . . ."

"Title," whispered Jay. "That's the problem down here."

"With a clear title . . . we still might do business in American dollars. Meanwhile, I wish you all the luck in the world."

Socrates had the car in gear. The motor roared. He went plunging down the dark winding road. *"Calma,* Socrates, *calma."* Jay leaned over the front seat to whisper in his ear. "We don't want them to think we are scared of them."

When Jay arrived next morning Danny came down in the elevator to meet him. Socrates was busy polishing the car. He seemed in high spirits.

"The gentlemen certainly gave me a fright. Like in a movie." Socrates laughed heartily. "Today it will be perfectly safe. Beautiful scenery, a good dinner, perhaps a boatride." He was rubbing his hands with his rag.

Danny told him to get some breakfast. They would be leaving in fifteen minutes. Socrates nodded and smiled. He understood words like "breakfast."

"I'm afraid we haven't much to offer," said Danny as they crowded into the tiny elevator. "Armistead makes the world's worst coffee."

Jay said he'd had his at the hotel.

"What did you think of Bad Jack? Isn't he a card? The worst one is Loring Bronson. He's been indicted on sixtyseven counts in the States and here he is successfully smuggling in Cadillacs, importing semen of blooded cattle. That may be legitimate. We'll know when the calves are born. And he's organizing charter flights for businessmen who want to buy land. He looks like a Baptist elder, dresses carefully. He'll work hard all day cooking up these phony deals and raise hell like a nineteen-year-old all night. The man must be fortyfive or fifty. You ought to see him dance the samba. He tried to hook me first thing on his Cadillac deal. He's got a local lawyer named Spandini who's as crooked as he is. Bronson's a kind of magician among embezzlers. He not only takes their money but he makes companies disappear without leaving a trace. He transported a small insurance company he'd bought across the Canadian border, looted its assets. When policyholders began complaining to the New York District Attorney's office it took them three months to find the address." All this time Danny had been fumbling with the latchkey.

"I can't get the damn key to work."

He started banging on the door.

Jay took the key. By the time he had the key turning, Armistead, looking very tousled in his pajamas, was pulling the door open.

"Armistead, we're leaving in ten minutes," said Danny severely.

"Ready in a jiffy." As he trotted off, Armistead indicated a nicely set breakfast table in a sunny window. Orange juice, toast, fried eggs and bacon, coffee, everything. "We've got service," said Danny laughing. "You'd better have some. We don't know when we'll get another meal.... What I've been meaning to say," he explained as he settled himself at the table, "is that a man trying to rehabilitate himself doesn't want to be caught playing around with those jokers."

He took a last swallow of coffee, wiped his mouth and got to his feet.

"Let's go."

The morning traffic wasn't too heavy. Socrates managed to get them out on the São Paulo road through a bypass in fairly short order. The day was brilliant with piled-up cumulus clouds shaping up over the bare hills. "Did you ever think," said Danny, "that clouds could look like women's hairdos?"

The fourlane was unfinished with long detours but there weren't too many trucks that morning. Where the road wound over a very considerable hill Socrates suggested they stop for a snack. Rather proudly he showed off a spotless little restaurant with a terrace shaded by traveler's palms overhanging a pool of water. They sat at wicker tables eating small meat pies, drinking cold beer and looking out over an enormous valley striped and checkered with the different greens of sugar cane in various stages of growth which extended over rolling hills past processions of palms and vivid green banana groves into the blue distance. "Who was saying we weren't going to get anything to eat?" cried out Danny. "I don't see why this isn't the life."

After leaving the São Paulo fourlane, the road to Angra wandered off into a beautiful wooded farming region. There were clumps of palms and eucalyptus on every hill, occasionally little lakes between. Socrates claimed to have been there before but he had to stop at various farmhouses to ask the way. No signs on the road. Armistead was asleep. Even Danny had stopped talking. Jay spent his time carefully assembling Portuguese remarks to make to Socrates.

At last they found themselves climbing a steep recently graded red clay slope. Socrates showed all his teeth when he turned back to his passengers and raised a hand with the thumb and forefinger pressed together in a gesture of satisfaction. "Wish he'd keep his hands on the wheel and look where he's going," muttered Danny pettishly. "He knows," said Jay. "We are already climbing the coastal range."

As the car surmounted one smooth rise and then another Danny started talking again: "There's no question in my mind that I intend to stage a comeback. If that guy Bronson can collect eleven or twelve million dollars—that's what he's supposed to be worth— by crooked finagling, with my knowledge of Wall Street and of the building-supply business I ought to be able to make a million dollars a year without any funny shortcuts.... That would sound big to anybody not in the know ... but I've seen it done."

The road wound up a stony mountainside. Palisades of steep rimrock rose high overhead, veiled at the top by dazzling white cloudcover.

Danny wasn't looking. "There's nothing like a drive in the country. It's all coming clear now. I'm sure you understand, Jay, without me telling you, that my problem is whether to try to do it here in Brazil—that's why I wanted you to come along to hear Bad Jack's proposition last night—or to go back and try to bull it through at home. The trouble is there that the DeLongs are kind of upstarts. A lot of people would like to see us go under and stay under. My Dad was in trouble with the law before I was born."

The pass through the summit proved to be a series of gulches deep in dripping rainforest. Now the roadway was made of small square stone blocks. Everything took on a faraway longago look.

"Pedro Segundo," said Jay.

Socrates nodded his head vigorously. Danny wasn't the least bit interested.

"Then there's the problem of my image," he was saying. "You aren't exactly conscious of what you're doing, but you spend your whole life building up an image and something like this happens and crash, it's gone."

The cold air had waked up Armistead. "I keep telling Danny I'm only a sportswriter."

"Damn it, that's the business of sportswriters. Baseball stars, football stars, tennis champions, they are just images. I used to be the boy wonder. Little me underneath, I was just the same as I am now. Well, what have we got here?"

Socrates had put his foot down hard on the brake. They stopped with a thud at the entrance of a narrow tunnel cut through the live rock. The rock faces glistened with moisture. The tunnel was choked with mist that poured in from the other end. From the tunnel came a tremendous clattering and banging. Then a dim light. A dilapidated truck emerged, then another. Both were loaded with great drippy bulks shrouded in seaweed. A choking smell came from them.

"Socrates says it's whalemeat. No place to try it out at Angra so they truck it to the nearest Japanese post down the coast."

The car plunged into the tunnel.

The other end was plugged with mist as solid as cotton wool. Beyond they came out on a valley dark as night under the overcast. A roaring torrent plunged under a great stone bridge. "Pedro Segundo," said Danny kiddingly to Jay, "didn't allow cars much room to pass."

"He was thinking of muletrains."

Another tunnel. At the other end a light drizzle was falling but the air was clearer. They turned down a long escarpment. There were orchids in the trees that overhung the road, pink and white flowers in the ditches. As they wound down the mountainside the clouds lifted. Through long pearly tatters, strips of blue sky appeared; then sunlight over forested hills and a huge bay, islands and the ocean beyond.

"Jay, which of these trees is mahogany? It's silly not to know what it looks like."

"Socrates says they are all mahogany. There are a hundred different kinds."

"Isn't that Brazil for you?"

They were driving through sunlight now, along a reedy bay with occasional beaches, then up a rocky hill again.

"This is going to be one of those tough decisions," went on Danny. "I won't know whether to toss a coin or split a deck of cards. . . . Jesus Christ," he cried out suddenly.

Socrates had slammed on the brakes but hard. The car slithered in the loose gravel. Right in front of them they could see paved streets, sunny tiled roofs, arcades, stone towers, a dome in the deep valley beneath them. The tower was right under the car. They were looking down into the valley through a jagged hole in the road. *"Perigo!"* cried Danny much too late.

Socrates burst out laughing and pointed to a crumbly slope to the right where cars had been passing.

"Just a washout," murmured Jay.

"Looked like the end of the world."

"And he said this drive would be safe," muttered Armistead.

Five minutes later Socrates, broadly grinning, was driving up in front of the local hotel. He made eating motions with his fingers. "Very good," he said, pronouncing his English well. As soon as they stepped into the restaurant they knew what he meant. The place smelt of hot butter and herbs and fresh fish frying. A young man in a striped smock was slipping a large tray of freshly boiled rosy shrimps under the glass counter the waiters served from.

The proprietor turned out to be a very considerate mein host. He was proud of his fare. While he ordered them a meal of turtle soup, mayonnaise of shrimps and turtle steak he sent a boy down to the waterfront to arrange for a little launch for the afternoon. He knew Senhor Afonso who owned the timber and sent a smaller boy chasing after him.

After lunch they found Senhor Afonso waiting on the stone wharf beside a narrow black motorboat. He was a square redfaced man with a slight cast in his eye. Under his arm he carried an enormous black briefcase. Everybody shook hands. "The boatman knows where to go," he said in English. After that he spoke Portuguese to Jay. "Mr. Pignatelli, I hope you won't consider me indiscreet if I say I know why you are here . . . the beezness of McGregor." His eyes searched Jay's face with every word. "If you allow me to be so indiscreet I shall ask our friend to allow me to accompany you to Rio tonight."

"You know Plácido?"

"Everybody knows Plácido, a delightful man."

"Danny, our friend wants to go back to Rio with us. You won't mind?"

"I was going to suggest it. That way we'll get a chance to talk."

Socrates arrived running. He explained breathless that he had been putting the car in a safe place.

Senhor Afonso stepped heavily into the boat. "Let's go." He began reaching into his briefcase and came out with a penciled map which he spread out on Danny's knees. He pointed out the features with a stubby forefinger. "Beach . . . fifteen kilometers without anything and behind virgin timber, a thousand hectares."

The bay was terrific. Great reaches of smooth water with a peacock sheen, fishingboats with slack sails, piny islands, islands of purple rock, islands punctuated with cypresses. Saffroncolored villas lurking among the palms. One island harbored a chapel and a cemetery Socrates said was a great pilgrimage spot on the saint's day. Everybody came in boats.

"Do you remember that picture 'The Island of the Dead'?" said Danny. "It used to hang in our upstairs hall. Isn't that just it?"

He spied a long stretch of beach. Senhor Afonso nodded and smiled. "That's it."

"My lord, look at that beach and this is all within striking distance of Rio. Let's take a look at it."

"It is very far," the boatman shouted over his put-put.

"I've got to see it."

Senhor Afonso in his soft authoritative voice explained to the boatman they would come right back afterwards.

"If I do go back to the States," whispered Danny for Jay's ear alone, "I sure would like to have you on my legal team."

"Suppose I consult my partners. I'll be calling them tomorrow about something else."

"Maybe I ought to stay here and develop these magnificent properties."

"But you don't own 'em yet, Danny," said Jay and Armistead almost in unison. Danny laughed at that.

"Do you know something?" whispered Danny suddenly, keeping his voice under the racket of the put-put. "You and I have met before." For some reason his face had turned very red. "I was afraid you wouldn't like my mentioning it. I was a little twerp scared to death trying to get away from those triggerhappy Spaniards. . . . I recognized you the first moment I saw you at the restaurant. I never forget a face. . . ." Jay stared at him blankly. "Don't you remember a redheaded guy named Don Carp? He took me along to your hotel and we slept on the floor in your bedroom."

"Well, I'll be damned," said Jay. He began to laugh. "I'd only expected one of you and I had to explain to the Catalans that you were both my private secretaries. . . . Of course they never believed a word of it but they let me take you along. They were really nice people. When Franco took over he shot all the members of the generalitat he could lay his hands on."

"All I remember is that you were the bigshot that saved my life," said Danny sentimentally. "Maybe one of these days I can pay you back."

The eastern sky over the mountains was breaking into thousands of pink clouds crisp as spilled popcorn. A head wind came up. The return trip took a long time. Senhor Afonso, after excitedly pointing out the great trees back of the beach, took to studying documents in his briefcase.

"Jay, what do you think about when you look at all that scenery?" Danny asked all at once.

Jay cleared his throat. "Music maybe; it certainly affects me like music."

"I look at the pretty clouds and the pretty mountains and I make plans to make mountains of money and I love it."

The new offices of Marquand, Merlin and O'Brien were on the twentieth floor of a sparkling white skyscraper near the Civic Center. As soon as Jay appeared in the door Ted Marquand whispered to his secretary over the intercom that he was in conference and was not to be disturbed.

"Jay, it is a relief to see you face to face. I couldn't make out a word of what you were saying in that last phonecall from Rio."

"The gist of it is, Ted, that a certain Senhor Afonso de Fonseca e Hoffsteiner—that isn't his full name but that will do—is willing to buy out McGregor's holdings in the Rio telephones at twentyfive cents on the dollar payable in Canadian dollars in Montreal. I imagine the sum will be transferred from one of those famous Swiss bank accounts."

"I'd rather have it paid in American dollars in Boston," said Ted screwing up his usually placid brows. "We would be more sure of our fee. . . . Did Plácido dream this gentleman up?"

"Senhor Afonso appeared on the scene out of nowhere. . . . It's a long and extremely funny story . . . at least it seems funny to me."

"Let's get Jake in. Shawn is in court."

Jake pumped Jay's arm with one of his heavy handshakes.

"Jay, did you bring home the bacon?"

"Exactly one-quarter of it but Ted won't believe it isn't going to be paid in confederate money."

"Go ahead. I haven't got too much free time," said Ted.

"The story is somewhat complicated. I'd hardly gotten to my favorite Hotel Gloria after a sumptuous lunch with Plácido when some old friends called up. They are more friends of Emily's than mine." Ted and Jake smiled when Jay mentioned Emily's name. They were both soft on her. "Paul and Ruth Bates asked me to dinner with them in Copacabana. You know how I hate to dine alone so I went hightailing out. Copacabana is the Miami Beach of Rio with a strong infusion of Greenwich Village. Well, it turns out that they were dining with a man they got to talking to in a restaurant, none other than Danny DeLong, one of the American embezzlers now hiding out in Brazil. Would I mind meeting him?"

"The Boy Wonder of Wall Street," cried out Jake letting out a guffaw.

"None other."

"High society," said Ted in an acid tone.

"Anyway, he's one of the greatest talkers in the world. I'd hardly sat down before he started pounding my ear. Didn't leave out a detail. He blamed the whole business on Malachi and Joseph. According to his story, they'd promised to back him and then let him down the drain for the express purpose of buying up his companies cheap. One thing I've noticed about confidence men, they are often extremely gullible."

"What about Afonso?" asked Ted impatiently. It was obvious that Ted felt the morning hours ticking away.

"I'm coming to that. But first enter the long arm of coincidence. Danny DeLong when he was about nineteen and working as an officeboy for his father ran off to Spain to join the Loyalist army. He was afraid he'd knocked up a girl and would have to marry her, that's the story he tells."

"So this isn't the first time he's taken it on the lam," broke in Jake.

"It may be a habit," said Jay laughing. "The Communists were shooting everybody they imagined might be a Trotskyite. So Danny gets the wind up and slips away from the International Brigade, along with another American radical who was in real danger . . . deviationist. That's another long story. . . . Anyway, I helped them across the border to France. I'd forgotten all about it but Danny insists he never forgets a face. . . . Well, he tells me he owes me eternal gratitude for saving his life and asks me to read a manuscript of his, free gratis by the way, for libel. He has a phony Englishman writing his autobiography for him. Thinks he can recoup his fortunes that way. . . . I tell you, he's a card. Then he invites me to go down the coast with him to inspect a tract of timber he's thinking of buying. The owner of the timber, the most magnificent stand of mahogany you ever saw, was this Senhor Afonso. Driving back with us to Rio he proved to be familiar with all the ramifications of the McGregor claim, surprisingly familiar. I met him at Plácido's office next day and he made us this proposition."

Ted was tapping with his fingers on the desk.

"Is the fellow on the level? What does Plácido think?"

Jay laughed. He could feel that Ted was relaxing a little. "On the level isn't the right phrase. He's a crooked politician of the old school. Also he's a violent political opponent of the present governor of Guanabara."

"That's the reformer who is supposed to have caused the dictator Vargas to commit suicide," said Jake. "You see, I read my *New York Times.*"

"If Ted will give me an extra minute," said Jay teasingly, "I have to explain that there is no political connection between the State of Rio de Janeiro and the city of Rio. The capital of the state is Niteroi, a kind of Brooklyn across the bay. The state of Guanabara was created to take the place of the Federal District when it was moved to Brasilia. The governor of Guanabara outranks the mayor of Rio."

"Do I need to remember all that?" asked Ted pettishly.

"You had better remember some of it, Ted, because it explains what's behind this deal. . . . Well, Plácido told me Afonso Fonseca's life history while he was navigating his little Volks up the breakneck curves of the road up to Petropolis that Sunday morning. Senhor Afonso, as everybody calls him, is the grandson of one of the great *fazendeiros* of the state of Rio in the old days of the sugar plantations. Used to be the richest state in Brazil but now its glory has departed. . . . Plácido knows everybody. Seems to be on good terms with everybody. He first knew him in law school. He didn't have two *cruzeiros* to rub together until he got into politics in Niteroi and began to make money fast. He got in with a political gang that terrorized and plundered the state of Rio for years and now he's a big wheel in President Goulart's entourage. He can raise as much money as he wants to. Plácido says he probably has several millions stashed away. Not *cruzeiros* but dollars. He hates the present governor of Guanabara with a deadly hatred on account of being flayed on TV, and the reason he's in earnest about this proposition is he wants to drop a monkey wrench into the present governor's plans to reorganize the Rio telephone service."

"Then why can't we get more than twentyfive cents out of him?" asked Ted.

"We worked on him for two days. We fed him drinks and one of those magnificent lunches Plácido knows so well how to order but he wouldn't budge from his original offer. He's a very plausible man and far from stupid. He knows he has to make his profit when he turns over his block of shares to the Federal Administration. There may be others who expect their cut too. He has to think of the daily inflation of the *cruzeiro*. He put his offer in writing with a time limit. Here it is."

Jay produced an imposing sheaf of documents with a dangling red seal out of his briefcase.

Ted scrutinized them carefully.

"Well, the next thing is for me to call McGregor. It's too late now. He goes to his lunch at twelve sharp."

"Suppose we eat too?" suggested Jake. "Well, Jay, it looks to me like mission accomplished. . . . Congratulations."

It was Jake who corraled the cab. He was light on his feet for such a large man. On their way to the club Jake asked many questions about the reforming governor of Guanabara. Jay told about the delightful afternoon he and Plácido had spent with him up at Petropolis. A very brilliant personality.

"His interest in the telephone business is to get decent service for the people of Rio. You can't imagine how bad it is. . . . He couldn't care less about compensation for the foreign investors. . . . He certainly won't be too pleased when he finds we've sold Mc-Gregor's stock to his arch enemy . . . but we've got Plácido to talk sweet to him. Nobody ever gets mad at Plácido."

While they waited for the waiter to bring the bill of fare, Ted said offhandedly, "By the way, Jay, did you know that your friend Danny told the newspapermen yesterday he was coming home to face the music?"

"From the way he was talking I thought he might."

"Let me ask an impertinent question, Jay. Did you make any commitment to give him legal assistance if he did come?"

Jay felt his face getting red. "Only in the most conditional way," he stammered.

All Ted answered was "Humph."

PART V

OF FORTUNE AND MISFORTUNE

"Then will man indeed confront Nature, and confront time and space, both with science, and con amore, *and take his right place, prepared for life, master of fortune and misfortune."*

—Walt Whitman, from *Democratic Vistas*

I

Ten Days in the Ice Age

The wind swings into the north and the sky clears. By the time the ferry leaves the Juneau dock the sun is breaking through. After rounding Douglas Island, Admiralty Island where there are said to be more brown bears to the square mile than anywhere lies to the southwest. The Lynn Canal stretches ahead into the bright north. The ruffled water is a dense jade green. To the right of us Shelter Island, which we couldn't see for the mist of the day before, stands out bright, bristling with darkgreen pointed spruces. On the mainland beyond, a few small white houses, dotted along the road into Juneau, shine like cubes of sugar. Above them the gray mass of Mendenhall Glacier streaked with icegreen rises to the broad white shoulders of its snowfields. An S-shaped streak shows up dark down the middle where the torrent runs off from the melting ice.

The ferry plows into the scalloped jade water. I keep remembering a steel engraving that made an impression on me when I was a child: "Whalers Under the Arctic Circle." The waves were indicated by the same crisp peaceful scallops. Now, to the left, the Chilkat Range stretches as far as you can see, peak after jagged peak with snowfields and glaciers draped between. Snow bright, ice gray, rock charcoal-dark. To the right rise the Kakuhau Mountains. As the channel narrows into the north, snowmountains rise higher and whiter on either side. There is an unearthly brilliance about the day. Sky of a robinsegg blue. Jade water. Clouds suffused with rosy amber. Snowcones glisten. Foaming waterfalls catch the sun. Peaks parade past like circus performers in their glittering finery.

Marine life, the man said. Yes indeed. Porpoises roll near the ship. Blackfish surface. Whales spout in the distance. Some creature shows a great shining fluke as it sounds right off the bow.

We are entering the ice age. Here glaciers still carve out the valleys. With your own eyes you can detect the piling of moraines. The streams that gush, gray with rock flour, from under the ice, wind and wander over plains of broken stones. Some day they may dig themselves beds and become rivers. Now they are mere torrents that flood the land in the spring thaw. Water pours from sievelike cliffs. The grinding weight of the ice and the rush of thawed water towards the sea is fashioning these gorges. Escarpments stand up raw and new. Between snowfields, seamed and splintered by frost and storm, the rock ridges strain towards the sky. It is a land in the agony of creation.

Standing on the ferry's firm deck that shakes ever so slightly from the throb of the diesels and the competent lunge of propellers through the calm seawater, you feel a bellyknotting excitement in the unfolding of peaks and snowfields. Terror perhaps. The hackles tingle. Life has little part in this landscape. Stunted spruces cling to the lower buttresses; a few alders and dwarf willows grow in the sheltered hollows. There is moss and lichen on the slopes, enough Arctic herbage here and there to support a few mountain sheep, berries and wild pea vines enough to feed an occasional bear. No trails. No sign of human habitation. Through the centuries Athabascan hunting parties have camped on these shores; or in more recent years an occasional prospector, searching the rock with hammer and chisel for gold-bearing ore, has labored up these frosted valleys. Captain Cook noted the vast terror of these mountains. They are out of human scale. A man is struck with the sort of awe Ezekiel the priest felt when, standing among the captives by the river of Chebar, he saw fiery wheels in the whirlwind that came out of the north.

In Juneau the air is damp. The wind has gone into the south. The warm moisture-laden breeze off the Japanese current will condense when it hits the great snowfields behind the hills. Already melting snow pours off in cascades through every runnel in the shaley slopes behind the town. Eighty inches a year is a moderate estimate of the rainfall there.

In a last burst of sunlight we catch a glimpse of the unearthly blue fissures in the face of the Mendenhall Glacier fifteen miles out of town. A small iceberg in the gray lake beneath glows blue as a Bunsen burner. Then the rain closes in.

In the bars in Juneau the talk's all of fishing, investments in trolls and nets and fishingboats, shares of the catch. Fishing's been pretty good this year. Big money.

The Alaskans are optimistic people. They delight in the rugged country, the rugged climate. They are proud of everything. The biggest state. More than twice the size of Texas. The biggest bears. A fisherman tells of a youngster who stumbled on a grizzly in a wooded valley near the glacier. Before his brother could come up behind him to scare the bear off, the bear had chewed out his eyes. While we were in Juneau three school boys drowned in the Mendenhall River that pours gray, and heavy with glacial flour, out from under the lurid face of the glacier. One of them, trying to do monkey tricks on a log, slipped and fell in. Two others tried to save him. The water's so cold a man can only live three or four minutes in it. All three were swept away and drowned.

"There is no juvenile delinquency in Alaska," says the young man eating a sandwich beside me at the lunch counter at Percy's. Percy's is a combination newsstand, sodafountain, notions store and snack bar that is the social center of downtown Juneau. It is a teenage hangout too. There are boys and girls in blue jeans and leather jackets, and Scandinavian sweaters and sandals and sideburns. Indian young people wear the same clothes and talk the same lingo as their paleface contemporaries.

This young man has just moved up from L. A. The lack of juvenile delinquency is one reason why he's come, this young man goes on after giving an approving glance round the room; that and the excellence of the school system. His son is just reaching school age.

He's a toughtalking young man with a scar on his nose, obviously the product of city streets. He was raised in East Los

Angeles where juvenile delinquents crowd every streetcorner, he confides as he munches his hamburger. Nothing else for them to do. No jobs, no sports except for the rich, no outdoor life.

Life was rough in Alaska. The kids had their hands full and they loved it.... The young man expands.... He's just settled down in Juneau. He's in shoes. He has a job managing a store at more money than he's ever made in his life. Do I know that laborers here make six dollars an hour? Of course, living is high, house rent out of sight. His wife and his boy and his three-month-old daughter will be joining him soon. She came from Northern Michigan so she wouldn't mind the climate. She'd catch on right away. He loved it himself. Alaska was the only state in the union where you could bring kids up decent. When they came he'd get himself a trailer and live up at Glacier Village. They had thirty inches less rainfall a year there than in downtown Juneau.... He gives me a canny look. "If there should be another earthquake, a trailer's the safest place to be."

2

Eager Beaver—iii

Danny DeLong Speaking

Well, I've made my decision. Hope it's the right one. Better be. One reason is Dad says he can't spare any more cash for living expenses or there won't be anything left to pay the lawyers with. He sounded so old and tired on the long-distance phone that I felt like crying. Part of it was the bad connection but it broke me all up. He hasn't been himself since they kicked him out as Chairman of the Board at Northern Millwork. Made me feel I'd better go home if I wanted to see him again in the land of the living.

The other thing was Kathleen's letter. She's heard through that old bitch Fanny Sherwood that Delphine is suing for a divorce. Desertion. She's moved her residence to Connecticut. Can't get rid of me fast enough now that I'm in real trouble. Maybe just scuttle-butt but it certainly wouldn't make me mad. Kathleen said please come home and make sure the divorce goes through. Actually my coming home might work the other way. She's talked to the lawyers Dad hired and she's sure they can get me off. I'd been begging her to come down here just for a visit. I'd find the money for a plane ticket somehow. But she said no, it would be just too painful to run around with me until we could get married. That girl sure does have principles. She believes in her religion all right, but suppose she got tired of waiting or some other guy came along?

To tell the truth, I'm not too sure I could have raised the money for the ticket. I'd expected to pick up a little extra change acting as a financial consultant here, but my clients don't come through with any cash. To tell the truth, it's not so easy as I thought to make a living in Brazil. A foreigner has to deal through the local nationals and they take a lion's share of the spoils, if there are any. The only one of the exiles, as we laughingly call ourselves, that made a go of it was Loring Bronson. He's a genius in his particular line. I couldn't pass for a Baptist elder if I went to Max Factor himself. Believe it or not the evangelist gag goes big in Brazil. Bronson gets away with the same old mahula with the Brazilians he got away with on gullible Americans.

What did I do the moment I made my big decision but call in the reporters. They had the wires humming in no time. The District Attorney can't claim I didn't give him ample notice. The only thing left open is the date.

Pignatelli thinks all this publicity has done me more harm than good. That's the last thing he told me before he left. He's one of those lawyers likes to settle things on q.t.

But hell, I've been working on my image so long I can't stop now. The Associated Press man sure seemed to eat the story up. Armistead Grimes is all for publicity. He thinks there's a million dollars in my life history. He can't wait to peddle the story around the New York publishers. He hasn't done any work on it since I had to let Irma go. Now I'm keeping my own diary. He thinks the autobiography ought to stop when I make my great decision.

I'm going to miss Rio and table tennis with the nice Brazilians at the Club Flumense and swimming at Copacabana and all that, but New York is where the action is.

My God I'm going to have to play my cards carefully when I get home. First thing will be to get the lawyers started on my defense and keeping away from Delphine on account of the divorce. I can't seem too anxious or else Delphine will start holding out for bigtime alimony. But I would like to see the kids, poor little devils. They are only adopted but I think I can raise them better than Delphine can and Kathleen would be just dandy with them. Another reason I got to go back to New York.

I've been wondering if Pignatelli wouldn't be the guy to represent me in the divorce at least. He'll appeal to Delphine. You know, the continental background and everything. He's supposed to be a good lawyer, but how can he be if he doesn't go after the money? The good lawyers I've known couldn't get rich fast enough.

I've always been told good lawyers had no visual sense, but this guy's crazy about scenery and old architecture ... and causes. He claims he's sworn off causes but they crop up all over. He honestly believes that if a few good men got together and spread the proper information, they could get rid of crookedness and demagoguery in public office and put the poor old United States back on the rails.

The guy's so scrupulous it makes you want to throw up. He absolutely refused to give me advice as to whether I ought to go back or not. When I asked him whether he would join my team of lawyers if I could get a retainer for him out of the old man, he said absolutely not. He would decide after he talked to his Boston partners. He wants to check on my lawyers and read the indictments etcetera.

I happen to know that the guy is horribly at loose ends since his wife was killed in an automobile accident. My only chance is to get him to take me up as a cause. A lawyer with scruples in the year of Our Lord 1962. Can you beat it? A lawyer with scruples is so rare in a New York court he might pull a lot of weight; who knows? I gave him a copy of the indictments to read on the plane when he took off.

Pignatelli's trip down here seems to have been pretty successful. Wrapped up a deal for a client who's unloading Rio telephone stock. He should be grateful to me for pulling Senhor Afonso out of the underbrush.

Now that's a guy scares me out of a year's growth. Power Incorporated, like the head of the Mafia or something. Seems to be the political boss of the state of Rio de Janeiro, buddy-buddy with the President of the Republic and all that.

It turned out he understands English perfectly well but he insists on Portuguese when he's talking business. He's got a sense of humor too. The deals he suggested to me on that timber gave me gray hairs just thinking of them. They would have put me in his power for life. I suspect that's the secret of his political oomph. He's got everybody in the state owing him money.

Getting aboard the plane was something. I had trouble keeping my voice steady when I called up Varig to make a reservation. They always leave in the middle of the night. Well, my plane was two hours late from São Paulo. I got jumpier and jumpier sitting there with Grimes in that old barn of an airport. Grimes seemed to be struck dumb. I never know what that guy's thinking. I'd just about reached the screaming jeebies when who should turn up but the Ping-Pong team from Flumense . . . and Socrates . . . he'd gotten tired of sitting in the car and came in to cheer me up. He understands more than he lets on with his big white smile in his black face. I sure hated saying good-by to Socrates. I'd gotten fond of the little guy.

The Flumense boys ordered up champagne at the bar and Socrates had a glass and they all gave me a send-off. When the loudspeakers finally announced the New York plane I was feeling no pain.

I went right to sleep and didn't wake up till I smelt coffee with hot milk. I'd bought a first-class ticket for Grimes, just so that he could take down a few deathless words while we flew, but here we were off the Carolina coast and I hadn't told him a thing. The steward came around apologizing in various languages because the plane would be late at Idlewild. Couldn't be too late for my taste. I was praying the damn plane would crash coming in for a landing.

Going down the gangplank was like diving into cold water. When I hit it wasn't as bad as I'd expected. An Assistant District Attorney and a Federal Marshal were waiting for me all right but they didn't put handcuffs on me or anything like that. Actually, they looked sort of perfunctorily sympathetic, like undertaker's helpers at a funeral. I couldn't imagine what they had on their minds until one of them cleared his throat and told me Dad had died of a stroke the day before. That rocked me back. I asked them anxiously how Mom was. They said she was fine. "She's waiting for you with your lawyers in the Terminal building."

There she was all in black crepe but looking in the pink. She hugged me and cried and blubbered that it was God's mercy I'd gotten home in time for the funeral. Then she introduced me to the lawyers Dad had retained. Joe Schlessinger, who'd been my standby on corporation procedure, said he couldn't take the case. It was years, he told Dad, since he'd defended a criminal case; he felt that was a job for younger men. He recommended Wise and Gattling. He told Dad they'd kept every client they ever had out of jail.

Fred Wise was a sharplooking little guy with wavy black hair and sideburns and gimlet eyes. Lloyd Gattling was a big dreamy-faced bozo. He had a funny smothered laugh way down in his belly and looked a little like Wendell Willkie. I sure looked 'em over carefully but there was nothing I could do but reserve decision till I saw how they acted.

After I'd gotten through Customs and everything the Sheriff and Marshal drove me downtown. They sat on each side of me in the back seat with their jaws clamped tight while some sort of plainclothesman who looked like an unreformed convict drove us in. Mom followed with the lawyers in a chauffeur-driven Lincoln she must have hired from the local undertaker. I felt I was going to my own funeral instead of Dad's.

Armistead said ta-ta, he'd catch a cab. The last thing he did was borrow ten bucks. That was the last time I laid eyes on the son of a bitch. After he'd stuck to me like a leech all those months in Rio. He did call up a couple of times to say what ill success he was having trying to sell my story to a publisher. Bad cess to him. I'd seen his face fall when he noticed how few reporters came out to meet the returning hero. Only the regular Idlewild gang, no feature writers or TV crews. Only three photographers. He's a cold bastard. I could see him writing me off his books then and there. Last thing I heard he'd gotten himself a job on *Sports Illustrated*.

Proceedings in the two courthouses took all day. The lawyers had their bondsmen waiting. I formally turned myself over to the State of New York and the Federal District. That's not the proper way of putting it: I listened to so much legal gobbledygook that day I couldn't remember half of it. By closing time at four we were ready to start out to Montclair in Mom's lugubrious Lincoln. It took a special deal to let me go to Montclair, which was out of the jurisdiction of the court. Everybody said my lawyers had done a remarkable job of bailing me out so promptly. Most people would have spent a couple of days in the cooler. I began to think they might be all right and arranged to meet them next morning at their office downtown.

Montclair hadn't changed so much as you would expect. I felt the way I'd felt being taken home by the seat of my pants after getting into some teenage scrape like that Spanish fiasco. Only poor old Dad wouldn't be waiting there to scold me.

Someone was waiting though. Right in the front hall. You wouldn't believe it but I'd been so busy with the legal flimflam I'd forgotten Kathleen. First thing when Mom unlocked the door of the old Tudor house I felt in my nose that tiny little scent Kathleen used that brought out the flavor of her red hair. She looked so pretty all in black I couldn't help hugging and kissing her right in front of Mom.

Mom didn't seem to care. Then suddenly it came over me that Mom and Kathleen were getting along fine. Mom never had felt Delphine was the right wife for me: woman's instinct I guess. As we went around the house I could see Kathleen helping her out and deferring to her in little things just like a favorite daughter. That was going to make life a lot easier for me. Suddenly it all seemed worthwhile. What the hell, suppose I did go to jail. There'd be Kathleen to look forward to when I got out.

I began to feel pretty good and Mom seemed as chipper as a sparrow. She wasn't going to miss Dad that much. He'd been more trouble than pleasure during the last few years. Under a whole lot of nonsense women are damn practical creatures.

Mom said we had to go over to the undertaker's to "view the body." That broke me all up. She was bound we'd give him a bang-up funeral if it killed us. If it hadn't been for Kathleen I never would have made it. The silverplated coffin, the flowers, the painted-up waxy face on the satin pillow. The undertaker, Mr. Gorman, with his mouth full of mashed potatoes. None of it seemed to have anything to do with Dad. He sure looked more Jewish dead than he had alive.

I tried to beg off from the funeral that was at eleven o'clock next morning on account of my appointment with the lawyers, but Mom wouldn't hear of it. Kathleen backed her up.

The funeral was horrible. I had to say the right thing to all the old reprobates Dad used to play gim rummy with and the ladies from the Montclair Garden Club and the Book Club and the Croquet Club and the Library Association and the League of Women Voters and the Wilderness Society and the Associated Bird-watchers and I don't know what the hell else. It wasn't Dad, it was Mom who had been active in all of them. Looked like poor Dad hadn't had a friend left in the world.

There was only one reporter, a longhaired lanky young punk who'd been a Latin and English major and graduated at the head of his class at the Montclair High School. He had a little hunchback photographer limping along after him. It may have been that highschool kid's first real assignment. He was knocking himself out trying to get in the irony of it all. Capitalist greed gets its own reward. "Indeed ironical" was his favorite phrase. He whispered to me he was covering for the *New York Times* as well as the local sheet. He cottoned up to me but he sure didn't give me any breaks. Young people are so treacherous. He inferred much more than he said. It was indeed ironical that when Dad and I had been so prominent in the financial world a few months ago, not a single prominent figure from Wall Street or banking or even the building-materials business turned up at the funeral.

He must have thought he'd hit the bigtime with "indeed ironical" because he used it several times. The piece was just like a prize essay in a highschool paper. He tried to end with a Latin quote: *Sic transit gloria mundi,* but the rewrite man must have made him translate it because it didn't come out that way in the *Garden State News.* The reason I know is because the conceited little squirt sent me a carbon of his typed-out article. He thought it was Holy Writ.

In the *New York Times* they hashed it all up and mixed it in with Dad's obit out of their morgue. Their editorial writer got in a dig at me for bringing my father's gray hairs down in sorrow to the grave. He didn't say it in so many words, but you could see that was what he meant.

Dad's funeral turned out mighty poor public relations. All the wrong people. . . . The whole business broke me up so I was on the ropes. I went up to my room when I got home. It was the same little old room with faded curtains I'd had when I was a college boy: group photographs of tennis teams and football teams and swimming teams on the wall, and college pennants and the Dartmouth

College seal and cups I'd won in different events. The same old bed where I dreamed up so many boyish hopes. I lay down on that old bed and just gave way to the shakes.

I'd have sure died if Kathleen hadn't brought me up a stiff Scotch. Now that's the kind of girl a man wants for a wife.

I wasn't in any shape to see my lawyers so I called them up to say I'd be in next day. My story was I had to stay with the old lady who was inconsolable from her husband's death.

Next morning I woke up perfectly fit and ate a good breakfast with Mom. She seemed bright as a button. Kathleen had gone home. I went in with the rest of the commuters on the seven-forty train: the unsinkable Danny DeLong.

Wise and Gattling had their offices in a kind of old building on William Street. The elevators were oldfashioned, and their receptionist was a dowdylooking old hag. That all put me off until Lloyd Gattling told me this had been his father's office and he'd been keeping it for sentimental reasons.

Right away the two of them started working on me like I was on the witness stand. First they asked me to give them my idea of a defense. I said I was planning to tell the court I was sincerely sorry the gamble I'd taken had turned out badly, but it was an honest gamble. My intention was to work for the good of the stockholders.

"All those shares you had in your own name, were they for the good of the stockholders?" asked Fred Wise staring me down with those sharp eyes. I tried to laugh him off with the proposition that what's good for General Motors was good for the country.

"The stockholders would have come out all right if those Paris bankers hadn't doublecrossed me. There was no intent to steal. If it was larceny it was unintentional." Is there such a thing as technical larceny, like manslaughter instead of murder?

What I wanted to do now was to work up some sort of deal with the District Attorney's office so that I could use whatever funds Dad left me to build another fortune. I told the newspapermen in Rio I was going to see to it everybody who lost money by my mistakes got reimbursed and that was my intention if I spent the rest of my life doing it.

"How much did your father leave?" Fred Wise put his question in such a sharp tone I figured he wanted to be goddamn sure where his fees were coming from.

I said I hadn't the slightest idea. Dad's will had been prepared by a local attorney in Montclair and we'd get the family together to read it as soon as Mom felt a little calmer.

"Any brothers and sisters?" asked Lloyd.

"There's my brother Dave and one sister."

"Nephews and nieces?"

"A few."

"If we are going to be your attorneys," rumbled Lloyd, "we'll need a copy of your father's will."

Fred nodded. "Coming back to your defense," he said in his most sarcastic tone, "repentance and restitution are all right if you are going to plead guilty and throw yourself on the mercy of the court."

"I intend to cooperate with the court in every way. That's what I told the newspapermen."

"That's only if you plead guilty," said Fred Wise impatiently. "We have got to decide right here and now whether you are going to plead guilty or innocent."

"First, Danny, you've got to get the picture," put in Lloyd. "We have two DAs to deal with. George McKenna, the State of New York man, is a public official at the end of his career. He likes to get along with everybody. If the accused is a decent-seeming sort of person he keeps his prosecutors, a bunch of youngsters fresh out of the ivy league lawschools, more or less on the leash."

"But the Federal District Attorney," interrupted Fred Wise, "is a hellroaring Democrat, Kennedy appointee, who likes to eat malefactors of great wealth for breakfast."

"But I'm not a malefactor," I broke in. "There was never any larceny—at least only in a technical sense. I never intended to commit the crime for which I have been indicted. The newspapers have been giving everybody the idea that I ran away to Rio with a suitcase stuffed with other people's stock certificates. That's just not so. All I did was put the stock up as collateral—. You know very well that people do that every day and get away with it."

"But Danny," said Floyd soothingly, "the reason we are all here today is that you didn't get away with it."

"Now you've changed your plea to not guilty," snapped Wise. "Which one is it going to be?"

And so it went on until I jumped to my feet in a pet and

shouted, "The way you fellows talk I can't tell whether you're working for the defense or the prosecution."

Then to get myself in hand I told them the latest funny story that's going around Brazil. The Brazilians are great storytellers. This one is about the friend of the jaguar—that's the South American wildcat. Two countrymen are whacking their way through a dense jungle with machetes. "What would you do," one asked the other, "if we suddenly came on a jaguar?" "I'd cut his head off with my machete." "Well, suppose you missed him," asked the other. "I'd pull out my gun and shoot him in the eye." "Suppose your gun wasn't loaded." "Then I guess I'd climb a tree." "Suppose he climbed after you."

The second countryman stopped in his tracks and started making passes with his machete. "Whose friend are you anyway?" he asked angrily. "My friend or the friend of the jaguar?"

It didn't strike Fred Wise funny at all, but Lloyd Gattling's big frame started rumbling all over with that dry internal laughter. "The friend of the jaguar," he sputtered.

"The Brazilians," I explained, "thought it was the funniest joke ever."

At least I'd cut the grease of what seemed to be developing into a shouting match. That old scoundrel, Senhor Afonso, told me the story in Rio the last time we wrangled over the price of that tract of mahogany. Just telling the story made me homesick for Rio.

"We are going to do our damnedest for you," Lloyd was saying. "Don't forget that."

"But you've got to make up your mind," snarled Fred. "Guilty or not guilty."

Finally I said suppose we all slept on it, and started for home. Down in the entrance lobby I spied a phone booth. I went in and called Jay Pignatelli. His voice sounded friendly, another thing that reminded me of Rio. He wasn't any Brazilian but he was kind of like one in a way. He said he was tied up for lunch, but would I come in this afternoon about three? It would be only partly a business call, I said. Jay said come along, he wanted to hear how I was making out.

Then I called Kathleen to ask her if she'd take a cab down to Sweet's for lunch. It would be a way of keeping me from jumping off Brooklyn Bridge. It was the first time in my life I'd been in the downtown district without being in a desperate hurry with a dozen engagements. I kind of enjoyed rambling along the oldtimey streets. The lunchtime crowds filled every sidewalk. I half-expected people would recognize me from my picture in the papers but nobody did.

I had to wait in line for a table. I'd just sat down at one end and the waiter was busy putting on a fresh tablecloth when there standing behind the opposite chair was Kathleen. As the weather was cool she had on a darkgreen tailored suit with a little fur trimming that matched her hair. Suddenly I was in heaven. I didn't know what we ate, I didn't know what we talked about. All I knew was we were together.

All too soon it was two thirty. She had to go uptown to her job on *Holiday* Magazine and I rambled off towards Beaver Street. I felt like a lost soul but now I kind of liked the sensation. I'd always been an insider and here I was looking at the Financial District from the outside.

Over the entrance the sign read Marquand, Merlin and O'Brien, but inside on a groundglass door was the name Jay Pignatelli.

The receptionist was blonde and nicelooking though certainly middleaged. She gave me a cozy smile and said, "Mr. Pignatelli is expecting you, Mr. DeLong." To tell the truth, I was so accustomed to having receptionists fall all over me that it still gave me a shock to be treated just like anybody else. Jay opened his door and let me in. He still had that tall stringbean look he had in Rio. I noticed how prominent his Adam's apple was.

I blurted right out I wanted his advice—should I plead guilty or not guilty? He stared at me but not in that mean way Fred Wise had this morning. There was a sort of twinkle in his eye.

"Danny," he said, "you know perfectly well I can't give you that sort of advice. You've engaged a highly respected firm of attorneys and I'm afraid you'll have to leave it up to them. I know it's a difficult decision because you are a sort of borderline case between guilt and innocence. You are just going to have to thrash that out with Wise and Gattling."

Well, if he couldn't do that, I asked him right out if he could represent me in a civil suit.

"What's that?"

"My previous wife Delphine is divorcing me." That sounded silly; I began falling all over myself explaining. "Of course, we are technically still married but I feel we ought to have been divorced years ago. Desertion. She resides now in the State of Connecticut."

"What is your position, Danny?"

I said I wanted it to go through as fast as possible. As I had told him that night in Rio, I wanted to marry somebody else. I told him I'd just had lunch with her—she seemed like an angel from heaven. All I wanted from Delphine was to be a little moderate in her demands for alimony on account of my embarrassed situation and to let me see the children as often as possible. She used to kinda like me, after all.

He asked why couldn't Wise and Gattling handle all my legal business?

"They are too highpowered, Jay. I want this divorce handled quietly and tactfully. You are just the man to do it."

"What's the name of her lawyer?"

"Harry P. Moore in Hartford, Connecticut."

Jay reached for the phone.

He always seemed so impractical in Rio. Now sitting there at his own desk in his own office he was right on the ball. After all, I told myself, all the time he acted so carefree in Rio he was wrapping up this big deal on the telephone stock.

Mr. Moore was on the phone. He said Delphine started this suit a year ago soon after she bought that little house in Farmington. I thought she'd moved out there just to be bitchy but actually she wanted to have a countersuit in case I got my decree in Nevada. That was all to the good. It meant I wouldn't have to wait so long to marry Kathleen.

"Well, Danny," said Jay, "Mr. Moore sounds like a most reasonable man. Mrs. DeLong ought to get her decree in three months. Then it will be up to the Hartford County Court to determine questions of alimony and custody of children. If I can't appear for you personally I'll find some qualified person who can."

I told him he'd taken a great load off my mind. He said he wished the rest of it was going to be so easy. Then he asked me to come along with him to call on who he said was a very attractive lady who he knew wanted to meet me. A friend of that Mr. and

Mrs. Bates we'd had dinner with that night in Rio. I called Mom to tell her I wouldn't come in till the seven fourteen and we took a cab up to this lady's apartment on West 13th Street between Fifth and Sixth in one of those old Victorian houses.

The lady's name was Emily Merlin. She was a widow and just about as tall and skinny as Jay. I'd have bet my bottom dollar they were shacked up but I couldn't be exactly sure. She had that way I've noticed before in South Carolina dames of looking just a little past the top of your head.

The apartment was beautiful, all furnished in old mahogany. No reproductions. Must have been heirlooms. I'd gotten an eye for colonial furniture when Delphine and I were furnishing our apartment in Waldorf Towers. The silver service on the bureau must have been worth five thousand dollars if not more. With the drapes and some of those family portraits that are just getting fashionable on the walls I figured the one room I saw couldn't be matched for less than twentyfive thousand dollars, if not more. Some of those portraits might turn out to be worth a mint. I wanted to whisper to Jay when she went out in the kitchen for ice for drinks that he'd landed in clover, but I dassn't because I knew it would make him mad and I needed every friend I had in the world.

Mrs. Merlin was nice and friendly but she sure had a sharp tongue. I was thanking my stars Kathleen wasn't too damn witty. She said she couldn't imagine why in the world I'd come back from Rio. Kathleen is full of cheerful banter but she doesn't say those cutting things about other people New York intellectuals set such store by. I slipped off after one drink to catch that train to Montclair.

I went on spending money on my defense with no hope of return. Weeks went by. It was Mom's money at that, because my inheritance from Dad wouldn't be available until the estate was settled. Damn lucky Dad had settled what amounted to pretty near a million dollars on Mom before this scandal broke. He knew he had high blood pressure. I love to spend money but I like to make investments where there's some hope of return. It costs money to make money; speculate, gamble if you want to call it that, but it just made me sweat blood seeing all that money go down the drain to Wise and Gattling when I wasn't even sure it was going to do me any good.

The one thing that went through smoothly was Delphine's divorce. Jay wouldn't take any retainer, just said he'd send me a bill when the arrangements for alimony and custody of the children were settled. It turned out that Delphine didn't want André and Jeanette anyway. I'd always suspected she didn't like them much. I guess she just thought of them as windowdressing. I'm naturally generous. I took on their entire upkeep and education and allowed Delphine more alimony than I could afford. Anything to be shed of her.

Kathleen and I were married quietly in a little chapel on 86th Street. I'd been undergoing instruction in the True Faith just in case I had to turn Catholic if we couldn't find a priest who would marry us on account of my divorce. Kathleen found this Father Doheny who said Delphine and I hadn't been properly married anyway; we had just been living in sin and that didn't matter. I had to sign a paper that any children would be brought up Catholics. There was nobody present except a sweet old aunt of Kathleen's who lived in Brooklyn and Mom. Anne and Dave just hadn't been associating with me since I turned out to be a prospective jailbird. Last time I saw them was when they turned up with the inlaws at the reading of Dad's will. Dad had appointed me and Mom executors; that made them real mad.

One thing that set Kathleen and me up was a long cable from Kathleen's folks in Ireland. They must be broadminded people because they invited us to fly over and celebrate the wedding in proper Irish style after I had solved "my little difficulties." That made Kathleen so happy she almost cried. "The old dears," she said, "I knew they would stick by me."

It looked like we had a smooth and happy life ahead of us if it weren't for those indictments. Remaining in the jurisdiction of the court was sheer hell. No way of even taking a summer trip to Maine to take the children out of the heat. All Wise and Gattling seemed to know how to do was obtain postponements.

Kathleen got along wonderfully with the adopted kids. I knew she would. We had them in firstrate dayschools and that proved damned expensive. No way of turning over any money because everything I had in the bank was impounded until after the trial. I did manage to make a couple of quick killings on investments in Mom's name and Mom lent Kathleen a few thousand to try her luck on the market. She did all right too. It made me feel good because naturally I picked out the stocks. Maybe my luck was coming back along with the bull market.

The kids were delighted when Kathleen told them they might soon have a little brother or sister. I was worried for fear having a child might spoil her looks. Since she'd been living happily with me she'd turned into a raving beauty. There is nothing improves a woman's looks like being loved. But not a bit of it. After little Kevin was born her figure was prettier than ever. I would have been happier than I ever was in my life if it hadn't been for this cloud about going to jail hanging over me. It looked to me as if every time the trial was postponed the DAs got more vindictive. I'd come away from sessions with Fred Wise and Lloyd Gattling feeling like a whipped dog. At last one day I went into the office to find them smiling and pleased. "Danny," they both said together, "it looks as if we might have you fixed up."

Their proposition was that if I'd plead guilty and furnish the SEC with a report on all the transactions connected with my defalcations so that they could suggest legislation that would make something of the sort impossible in the future, the DA would see to it that the Federal judge commuted my sentence.

The first thing I asked was what about the state court. They said the state court would do what the Federal court did. Well, that was the beginning of my undoing.

I pleaded guilty and waived a jury trial in Federal court and then the judge doublecrossed me or maybe it was the DA or it might have been Wise and Gattling. The Federal court sentenced me to two years in the Federal Penitentiary for grand larceny.

The lawyers appealed. That meant more bail, transcripts, more expense, more delay.

I'd been calling Pignatelli desperately to get his advice, as a friend at least, but his secretary said he was down in South America on legal business. I didn't know where to turn.

Then the damnedest thing happened. Dave called up one Monday morning. He'd turned into a moderately successful corporation lawyer and after divorcing his first wife had married a distant relative of the Loeb family who was hellishly wellheeled. That was why he put so much effort into keeping his reputation separate from mine. If he could have changed his name this late in the game he sure would have done it. Well, Dave's voice was almost cordial.

He said he and his wife had been weekending with some socially prominent people at Bridgehampton and at a cocktail party had run into a guy named George Denikin who had taken him aside and said that he knew Dave didn't like the idea of having his kid brother Daniel shut up in the poky and that Denikin had a notion that by contacting the right people he might be able to do something. The man might turn out a phony but it would be worthwhile getting in touch with him anyway, he was pleasant to talk to. He gave me Denikin's phone number and then he hung up.

When I called Denikin he immediately invited me out to lunch at the Roman Forum. He turned out to be a large rolypoly man with a pink face and fuzzy blond curls all over his head. The Circassian type. He was laughing all the time from the moment he pumped my hand with his big fat fist. He led me in to his table as if I was a grand duke. Then he started ordering up vodka and beluga caviar and followed that up with lobster *à l'americaine* and *boeuf stroganoff* with appropriate wines. It was a long time since I'd had a meal like that.

He seemed to have a ferocious appetite. Talking with his mouth full he told me what he claimed was his life history. He was a White Russian, a relative of the late lamented general's. After the general's death he'd escaped through the Red lines to the nomads of the Gobi Desert. There he'd passed himself off as an incarnation of Buddha and lived for years in high style. When things began to get hot for him there he'd ridden off into China on his favorite mare and served as a doctor—a horse doctor—with Mao Tse Tung's route army. From Shanghai he'd sailed in a Chinese junk across the Pacific and, after spending some time as the queen's paramour on a Polynesian island, drifted to Brazil. In Brazil he helped build Brasilia as a common laborer and saved up enough to come to this country where he'd done pretty well selling some diamonds and emeralds he'd picked up in the Mato Grosso. Now what would you say my profession was? He burst into a guffaw: "Adventurer, of course; ask about me at the Explorers' Club." The way he told it, it certainly was funny. He had me in stitches all through lunch.

When I eat a meal with a stranger in one of those plush restaurants I always watch the waiters' faces. They know as much about their customers as a credit bureau. This time the head waiter kept fluttering around the table. They all seemed to know him. Denikin was obviously a customer who paid his bills and left good tips. Financial rating must be pretty high.

Denikin didn't get around to his business until we were drinking our coffee and cognac. He said he had a friend who was a specialist in getting people out of jail. He had an important contact with a highly placed gentleman in Congress. In fact, he was the highest-placed gentleman in the House of Representatives. He said this gentleman was an elderly man and thoroughly convinced that Denikin's friend, whom for the purposes of this conversation he would call Lerner, could do no wrong.

"I myself needed his services," Denikin burst out laughing again, "once in connection with some gems that the Customs officers found in an old shoe. Can you believe it? Of course it was the purest accident. They threatened confiscation, jail, all sorts of unpleasant things. A phonecall from Mr. Lerner quieted them immediately. His charge was five thousand dollars, which I thought was very reasonable."

So much for the lunch. Denikin—now I realize it was so that I shouldn't have time for second thoughts—insisted on going right to the downtown office where he said Mr. Lerner was cleaning up some paperwork before leaving for Washington. Denikin kept saying we were lucky to catch him in the city. He spent most of his time in Washington.

It was a niftylooking office all right, at the top of one of the new buildings on Broad Street. We were ushered into a conference room with a view of the harbor and the Statue of Liberty and all. Lerner was seated at the far end of the long conference table writing on a yellow pad. He was a quiet little dark man in a pinstriped suit. He seemed to know all about the case. He talked in cutoff sentences. He said it was obvious that my lawyers didn't know the right people. He said the first thing to do was to get a postponement of sentencing in the state court. He could attend to that right today. He looked at his wristwatch. No, it would have to be tomorrow. Then he would see about getting the sentence nullified in the Federal court. He would need about fifteen thousand dollars for—he gave a dry cough—expenses.

I didn't say anything for a while. Was the guy on the level or was it just a swindle? Denikin had helped himself to a cigar out of a brass box at the other end of the conference table. I could hear his shoes creak as he roamed heavily about the room. He seemed very much interested in the shipping in the harbor. Lerner was tapping with his fingers on the desk.

"Well," he said, "I can't sit here all day. If you want to take up my proposition bring fifteen thousand dollars in bills to this office tomorrow morning at eleven thirty sharp." I noticed Denikin had stopped in his tracks at the mention of fifteen thousand dollars. I could hear his heavy breathing somewhere behind my chair. "Naturally," went on Lerner, "if the slightest breach of confidence occurs between now and then the proposition is withdrawn."

In the lobby I found a phone. Both Wise and Gattling were out of their offices. By some miracle Jay Pignatelli was back. Just in from Rio. I pled with him to let me come around to talk for a moment. "Sure," he said, "if you promise only to stay ten minutes. . . . I'm as busy as a onearmed paperhanger."

In five minutes I was sitting in the chair in front of his desk. He listened carefully while I told my story. When I came to the part about George Denikin, he burst out laughing. "He got out of Brazil the hard way in a smugglers' boat from Amapá, with the police after him for smuggling precious stones. Plácido Gonçales told me all about him. He's a notorious international crook."

"Well, that part of his story was true," I said. "That was just about what he told me."

Jay got to his feet. "Danny," he said, "forget it. Drop the whole business. You'll just be throwing good money after bad. You'll be lucky if they don't blackmail you."

I hurried out. I didn't want to overstay my ten minutes. From the lobby I called Mom and said I'd be over for supper. Then I called Kathleen to see if she could join us, but she said she couldn't get a sitter for the kids at that short notice, so I said I'd tell her what we decided when I got home. She whispered something about the jurisdiction of the court, but I said, "Who'll be the wiser?"

Mom was all for paying the fifteen thousand. She said they could have fixed my poor father's case only his brothers were dead set against it. She always felt they should have done it. "Jail leaves a stigma," she said with a shake of her head.

After supper she drove me to the station. We'd agreed that I'd meet her at ten next morning at the downtown branch of the Chemical Trust Company where she had an account. I decided not to tell Kathleen what I was doing until later. I let myself in the apartment with the latchkey. Kathleen was asleep. The baby was asleep in his crib. Jeanette and André were asleep in their rooms. Fast asleep they all looked pretty as pictures. I tiptoed around in a kind of happy trance at all the sweet responsibilities I had taken on.

I did tell Fred Wise. I got to his office so early I met him going up in the elevator. As soon as he'd closed the office door I told him the story.

He pressed his lips together tight while he listened.

"I think I know who those fellows are," he said. "It's a sort of ring of influence peddlers. They do have contacts with highly placed personages in Washington. They've managed to quash indictments for several members of the Mafia and when you work for the Mafia you've got to deliver, or else." He made the gesture with the flat of his hand of cutting his throat. "I don't know what to tell you. . . . If you want to spend that much money, it's up to you." He cleared his throat. "I know you feel we ought to have done more for you, but don't forget, we did get you a light sentence and we may be able to reduce it to probation on appeal. . . . Don't let them sell you on any of those crooked lawyers who work for the Mafiosi. They don't dare doublecross them but anyone else they'll take to the cleaners." He pounded with his fist on the corner of the desk. "Once and for all I want you to understand that if we'd realized what an uphill fight this was going to be we never would have taken the case. We are proud of our record of never letting the client go to jail."

That got me mad. "You can't say you haven't been paid. I've paid every bill as soon as you sent it."

"That's not what I was talking about," said Fred Wise pushing his little hawkface up into mine. "Get wise to yourself, Danny DeLong. You were the whitehaired boy for so long you don't know what's happened. Didn't you read that article in the *Wall Street Journal*: 'Financial Playboy Gets His Comeuppance'?"

He settled down behind his desk and started bawling me out like a judge laying down a sentence. "The financial community wants you to go to jail. They are sick and tired of brash intruders giving them a bad name with their monkey tricks. That feeling is reflected in the courts."

To say that we parted on poor terms is an understatement. He left me no choice but to see what those highbinders could do. God knows I ought to have had better sense.

Mom surprised me that morning. She'd been surprising me ever since Dad died. So much guts and initiative. I'd always thought I had taken after my old man, but maybe it was Mom I got my drive from.

When Mom took the fifteen thousand-dollar bills from the cashier at the Chemical Bank she buttoned them into her handbag.

"Daniel," she said, "I'm going with you. It'll be much better if the money comes from me . . . in case somebody wanted to come up with a charge of bribery or something; and besides, I want to see what this man looks like."

We were sitting in the lobby of that office on Broad Street at eleven thirty sharp. I hadn't noticed before it was called the Universal Airspace Company. Now what the hell did that mean? Lerner came out to the reception desk to meet us. I could see he was set back when he saw Mom. He didn't offer to shake hands. Mom piped up right away, right in front of the receptionist, "Since I'm putting up the funds, Mr. Lerner, I wanted to see who I was dealing with."

"Mrs. DeLong," said Lerner as soon as he'd closed the door of the small groundglass box he ushered us into, "you are dealing with a man who knows how to get things done." He poked out his thin wrist all furry with dark hair and looked at his watch. "By one o'clock I'll be on the shuttle to Washington. By three or four somebody in great authority will be phoning Judge Hoskins that there is nothing in your son's history to prove he hasn't always been an honest respectable person. He made his plea of guilty only upon the court's promise of a suspended sentence. That should bring results."

It didn't. It was as if I'd fallen into a sort of sausage machine to grind out convicts. The courts, state and Federal, ground relentlessly on and on. The appeal failed. A date was set for me to give myself up to be sent to Sing Sing to start serving my New York State sentence. I lost hope entirely.

When Denikin turned up in Montclair and sweettalked poor Mom out of an additional twentyfive thousand to obtain a writ of error, I didn't even try to stop her from giving it to him. His story was that Lerner had found a judge who was an old pal of my Dad's and who would certainly give me a break. This was a Judge Epstein. He would have been friendly all right but when we looked him up he'd been dead five years. The writ of error came up before a different judge. Denied.

Worried about the amount of breaking and entering going on, I arranged for Kathleen to sublet the apartment and move the family out to Mom's house in Montclair. The crime wave.

Who are you to complain about the crime wave? You're a criminal yourself. As if these years of misery with courts and lawyers hadn't atoned for any little wrongdoing in using the company stocks as collateral. Then falling like a sucker for a couple of common swindlers. I was so disgusted with myself I was ready to puke. I had only myself to blame. Poor sweet old Mom, I was to blame for letting her waste her good money on a pair of swindlers.

If I was disgusted with my own idiocy, I was at my lawyers' too. I'd hardly speak to them when they took me down to the DA's office to give myself up. I felt like a poor damn fool.

Repentence, restitution, hell.

I never felt less like a criminal than when I was handcuffed to a deputy sheriff who smelt of a combination of garlic and rank pipetobacco and taken up to the Grand Central Station to be loaded on a grubby day coach guarded by deputies with sawed-off shotguns with a lot of other poor devils, each handcuffed to a deputy, on the way to prison at Sing Sing.

3

The Coming of the Assassins

If ever a man had an illstarred childhood it was Lee Harvey Oswald.

His father had been dead two months when he was born. His mother, a selfcentered woman who alternately bossed and neglected her children, had already put away in an orphan asylum Lee's older brother Robert and a halfbrother by a previous marriage which had ended in divorce. Her story was she had to work so hard for a living she couldn't take care of them. Lee followed into the orphanage as soon as he could toddle.

Mrs. Oswald had a high opinion of herself. For a while she tried to sell insurance. Her deceased husband had been connected with an insurance company. Then she worked in oddtime jobs in department stores. Occasionally she gave her occupation as practical nurse.

When Lee was about to turn five she moved the family from New Orleans to Fort Worth where for a while she claimed to have represented the Literary Guild. Along the line she'd met a gentleman named Ekdahl, a New Englander described as an engineer.

When they were married—it was Marguerite Oswald's third try—Ekdahl seems to have done his best by the children. He placed the older boys in a military boarding school and saw to it that little Lee was entered in first grade.

In a matter of weeks the newlyweds found they couldn't get

along. Marguerite carried off Lee to Covington, Louisiana, and re-entered him in first grade there. Almost immediately she attempted a reconciliation and moved Lee back to first grade in Fort Worth.

The reconciliation ended in Ekdahl suing her for divorce. According to neighbors, Lee, who was badly in need of a father, had become deeply attached to him.

For some years Lee continued his schooling in Fort Worth. There he formed another attachment, for a pet dog named Blackie. He had to leave Blackie behind when his mother decided to take off for New York, where her eldest son John Pic was stationed in the Coast Guard. She and Lee moved in with Pic and his wife.

Lee was nearing his thirteenth birthday. So far, though his schoolwork had deteriorated from good beginnings, he had been rather meek and affable and had given his teachers no trouble. Now he began to show signs of an uncontrollable temper.

During an argument with Mrs. Pic he drew his pocket knife on her and threatened to use it. Immediately she insisted the Oswalds pack up and leave.

Up to that moment Lee had idolized John Pic. They were never friends again.

His mother took an apartment in the Bronx and entered Lee in a junior highschool. Mrs. Oswald, described at the time as being fashionably dressed, would take Lee to school and then spend the day downtown selling stockings. Long ago she had taught Lee to get his own meals. She seemed to prefer not to have him play with other children. He was a loner in a hostile world.

Right away his schoolmates started teasing him about his Texas drawl and Western dungarees.

Lee decided there would be no more school for him. He would hang around the building until his mother had left and then sneak back to the apartment to read magazines and watch TV. The truant officers caught up with him looking at the animals in the Bronx Zoo.

Admonitions availed nothing. He was taken into Childrens' Court as an incorrigible. The judge sent him to Youth House for observation and diagnosis. The chief psychiatrist there found him in desperate need of treatment. Efforts to discuss his case with his mother were met with a blank stare. A volunteer organization, Big Brothers, tried to help. Mrs. Oswald said it was all nonsense and refused to cooperate. When the lease ran out on their apartment in January the Oswalds took off for New Orleans without leaving a forwarding address.

Back in ninth grade in New Orleans Lee's deportment improved. He'd discovered public libraries. According to his own account, this was when he started reading up on Socialism. He was becoming convinced that it was the iniquity of American capitalism that was making his life miserable. From the age of fifteen he claimed to have been a dedicated Marxist.

When he turned sixteen he forged a letter to the school authorities, supposed to be written by his mother, to the effect that she was taking him out of school because they were moving to San Diego.

His brother Robert had enlisted in the Marine Corps and sent Lee the manual. Lee knew it by heart when he went around to the recruiting station to try to enlist. His mother didn't mind making a false statement about his age. She wanted to get rid of him, but he failed to convince the recruiting officer he really was seventeen.

He spent a year waiting, doing odd jobs for pocket money. With the first money he made on his own he bought himself a parrakeet. He named the bird Blackie.

He had made no friends in highschool. Among boys and girls he ran into in his various jobs, his overbearing manner quickly choked off any approach to intimacy.

Finally he reached his seventeenth birthday. The Marine Corps accepted him. In spite of his bad spelling and reading difficulties he passed the general classification test with such a high score he was sent to the radio and radar division. He trained at Camp Pendleton in advanced electronics.

He caught on quickly. He was promoted to Private First Class and passed the examination for Corporal. His promotions never stuck because he couldn't conceal his resentment at having to take orders from men he fancied were his intellectual inferiors. He had an inflated idea of his own capabilities which he found it hard to keep to himself. While stationed in Tustin, California, he started to study Russian. He was bound that he'd make his mates understand he was a very superior fellow.

The adolescent swelled head took the usual forms. Insolence. Dirt. He was the sloppiest man in the company, never took a shower. He would get into a fight at the drop of a hat. He was usually beaten but he was game. He seemed to want to be picked on. He had a way of coming into the barracks without speaking to anybody with a superior smile on his face that drove the other men mad.

His unit was sent to Okinawa and then to Atsugi Air Base in Japan. Atsugi was a very special air base. It was the point of departure for some of the U2 overflights across the Soviet Union.

His mates never saw him when he went on leave. He was supposed to be shacked up with a Japanese girl. Later he claimed it was the poverty of the Japanese that first called his attention to the wickedness of American imperialism.

Francis Gary Powers suggests in his autobiography that Oswald—whom he never met—might already have been transmitting information to the Russians on the U2 planes. Certainly by the time Powers was shot down on May 1, 1960, the Russians seemed to know a good deal about the overflights. It would be a way of accounting for that superior smile.

At Atsugi, Oswald distinguished himself by two courtmartials. The first was for possession of an unauthorized pistol which went off and shot him in the leg and the other for abusive language to a Sergeant.

Back in California he made no effort to hide his political attitudes. When he played chess he chose the red pieces. He ostentatiously read Russian newspapers and magazines. In his unit he was kiddingly known as Comrade or Oswaldovitch.

Three months before his enlistment expired he induced the Marine Corps to issue him an honorable discharge on the plea that he was needed at home to take care of his mother who had been hurt in an accident.

Whatever else he did in the Marines he managed to save up some money. The day before his release he had secured a U. S. passport good for travel in the Soviet Union. Paying no attention to his mother he bought himself a ticket on a freighter out of New Orleans to Europe.

By early October 1959 he was in Moscow. The question arises: how did he secure a Russian visa so quickly?

He arrived in a state of morbid excitement. He was told by whatever authority he consulted he could only stay two weeks. He went back to his hotel and slashed his left wrist. He celebrated the event by an entry in what he labeled his "Historic Diary." "... I am shocked! My dreams! I have waited 2 years to be accepted. My fondest dreams are shattered because of a petty official.... I decide to end it. Soak wrist in cold water to numb pain. Then slash my left wrist. Then plunge wrist into bathtub of warm water ... somewhere a violin plays as I watch my life swirl away."

Before his life had time to swirl completely he was discovered and carted off to a hospital. Two days after being released from the hospital he hurried to the U. S. Embassy to renounce his American citizenship.

He talked so big that he got to see one of the higherups. Interviewed by a Mr. Snyder, Second Secretary and ranking consular official, he told him that he wanted his American citizenship revoked. His application for Russian citizenship was pending. He wanted to live in the Soviet Union forever.

He hinted that his service in the Marine Corps had given him an opportunity to gather information which might be useful to the Russians.

Leaving Mr. Snyder thoroughly baffled, he returned to the Hotel Metropole "elated at this showdown. I'm sure the Russians will accept me after this sign of my faith in them."

From the hotel he followed the conversation with Mr. Snyder up with what he seems to have considered a formal written renunciation of American citizenship. An American newspaperwoman who interviewed him still got the impression that, in spite of all the bluster, he wanted to leave a tiny crack open at the Embassy in case he ever wanted to go home. He was delighted by the attentions of the press. He had just turned twenty and already he was hitting the headlines.

To his brother Robert, in answer to an affectionate letter telling him that even if he renounced his family his family was not renouncing him, he wrote savagely: "Ask me and I will tell you I fight for *communism.*... Look for yourself at history, look at a world map. America is a dying country. I do not wish to be a part of it nor do I ever again want to be used as a tool of its military aggressions. In the event of war I would kill any American who put on a uniform in defense of the American government, any American."

One of the men in his Marine Corps unit who had had somewhat friendly relations with him, broken off as always in a fit of rage, said of him later: "He looked upon the eyes of future people as some sort of tribunal and he wanted to be on the winning side so that ten thousand years from now people would look in the history books and say 'Well this man was ahead of his time.' . . . That was why he chose the peculiar method of defecting he did. It got him in the newspapers. It did broadcast his name out."

It's too bad that the Russian record of his defection is unavailable. It would clear up a great deal. He had at the tip of his tongue a good deal of information useful to the enemy.

According to the report of a retired Marine Lieutenant, who had taken a certain interest in Oswald while he was under his command, Oswald's defection caused a stir in the Marine Corps bases in California. "It compromised all our secret radio frequencies, call signs and identification codes. He knew the location of every unit on the West Coast and the radar capability of every installation. We had to spend several thousand manhours changing everything and verifying the destruction of codes. Oswald was a very unpopular man that month."

It is not surprising that the Marine Corps withdrew his honorable discharge.

The Russians treated him quite well, perhaps in return for a report on call signs and identification codes. He was awarded a subsidy of eight hundred rubles a month and placed in a radio factory in Minsk at eighty rubles a month. This, combined with a specially good apartment, put him on the economic level of the manager of the plant where he worked. The Russians did draw the line at admitting him to the university.

The unfavorable discharge gave him a new grievance. He began to write letters, half wheedling, half abusive, to public officials in the States demanding that it be rescinded. One of them was to John B. Connally. Oswald didn't know Connally had resigned as Secretary of the Navy to run with Vice-President Johnson's blessing for Governor of Texas.

At the same time he was making entries in his Historic Diary critical of life in the U.S.S.R. He complained of the lack of bowling alleys and nightclubs and of forced attendance at political information meetings. When the whole shop went out to the potato fields on Sunday to help bring in the crop, he flatly refused to go.

Even before he met Marina Prusakova, whom he married after a six-week courtship, he was pleading with the Embassy in Moscow to find some way of sending him home. Marina was younger than Lee, but already a licensed pharmacist. She was well connected. Her uncle was a Colonel in the MVD. Lee, who had decided that Russian Communism was as bad as American capitalism, was now in a fever to return to hated America. He bombarded the Embassy with letters. He wrote Senator Tower of Texas that he was being held in the Soviet Union against his will.

Time dragged on. Marina was brought to bed of a daughter. May 24, 1962, the State Department authorized the Embassy in Moscow to amend Oswald's old passport to include wife and child. How an exit visa was procured for them from the Russians remains a mystery. Maybe Marina's uncle helped.

The State Department furnished $435.71 for their tickets to America. The Oswalds arrived in New York on a small Dutch steamer on June 13, 1962.

They were met by representatives of the Travelers' Aid. Oswald was beginning to make a scene because he had no funds to continue to Texas when two hundred dollars arrived, telegraphed him by his brother Robert. He lived a month with Robert's family in Fort Worth. His mother came around and tried to be helpful in buying things for the baby.

In spite of the fact that Lee wouldn't let her learn English, they all liked Marina. The better Marina got along with the family the sourer it made Lee. When his mother tried to buy her some clothes he blew up. In October 1962 he moved his wife and daughter to Dallas without leaving an address. He never wanted to see his mother again.

In Fort Worth he had worked for a sheetmetal company. Though his work was satisfactory, he told Marina he had been fired as an excuse for moving to Dallas. In Dallas he took a set of capability tests at the Texas Employment Commission. He made such a good impression that they recommended him for a highly technical job preparing photographs for a commercial advertising firm.

Oswald was twentythree years old. He had learned to dress neatly and to put up a plausible front to the world. Marina declared later that he changed completely after their arrival in America. Their marriage was becoming more and more painful. There were days when she wouldn't speak to him. At one point she took the little girl and moved out altogether for two weeks. He often urged her to go back to the Soviet Union.

In spite of his disillusionment with life in Minsk, he still considered himself a Communist. Hatred of his own country was the mainspring of his life.

Denunciations of American imperialism and of President Kennedy poured out daily from Fidel Castro's radio in Havana. Oswald decided that Castro's Cuba was the home of "pure communism." He began to talk to Marina about hijacking a plane to take them to Havana. She would have none of any such crazy notion.

His delusions were taking practical shape. In March he ordered a Mannlicher-Carcano rifle from a Chicago mail-order house. It was to be delivered to a post office box he had rented under the alias of A. H. Hidell. A little later he sent for a Smith and Wesson .38 caliber revolver from a firm in Los Angeles. The distorted mental processes of his adolescence were hardening into adult determination: he must kill some important American.

The first victim he chose was a retired Army Major General.

General Edwin A. Walker was a plainspoken man who had resigned from the Army to defend the American cause. His speeches before rightwing organizations were arousing animosity among liberals and Communist sympathizers.

Meanwhile, Oswald exulted in the possession of deadly weapons. He had two photographs taken, with rifle and revolver. In one he held a copy of *The Daily Worker,* in another a copy of *The Militant.* He told Marina to keep one of the photographs for his daughter June.

He planned his attack on General Walker with great care, writing down every detail in a notebook. He took photographs of the Walker house, collected bus schedules to and from the suburban street where Walker lived, and photographed the bushes along the railroad track where he intended to hide his rifle after the shooting.

Before he left their apartment on Neely Street he carefully wrote out a note in Russian to Marina telling her what to do in case he did not come back. He included the key to his post office box, explained that the rent, water and gas had been paid and that his next paycheck would probably furnish enough cash to keep her and the baby for a month. He noted the position of the county jail in case he should be taken there and told her she must immediately let the Russian Embassy know what had happened and send them all the newspaper clippings that dealt with the affair.

General Walker was sitting under a lamp at a table in his living room, slaving over his income-tax papers when a bullet came through the window behind him missing his head by about an inch. He immediately snatched up a revolver and started searching the backyard. He found nobody.

Oswald came home very late, pale and shaking, saying he was sorry he'd missed him. Marina made a scene; if he ever tried anything like that again she would use his note against him. She had already hidden it. She did insist he burn his notebook. In spite of her he kept the snapshots of the Walker house and of the location where he had buried his rifle.

Though no one connected him with the attempt on General Walker's life, the managers of the advertising firm decided they had had enough of Oswald. Work inaccurate. Couldn't get along with the other employees. Insisted on flaunting Communist newspapers in their faces.

He decided to move to New Orleans and took Marina, already big with a second child, and little June to Ruth Paine's house in Irving. Ruth Paine was a warmhearted Quaker Marina had met at a Russian conversation class arranged by the small but lively émigré Russian group in Dallas and Fort Worth. Marina's friendship with these people disturbed Lee considerably. He didn't get along with Ruth's husband Michael either, but he couldn't at that moment quarrel with Ruth's kindness to his wife and child.

The only work he could get in New Orleans was as oiler and greaser in a coffee processing plant. He was so ashamed of this menial job that when the Paines drove his wife and child over to join him at an apartment he had rented on Magazine Street, he let on that he was working as a commercial photographer.

In New Orleans his actions became more and more bizarre. Though no such organization existed in the city, he represented himself as chairman of the local branch of a Communist front known as the Fair Play for Cuba Committee. The president's name he listed as A. H. Hidell, which was the alias Oswald used when he rented the post office box in Dallas.

He engaged in correspondence with the real Fair Play for Cuba Committee in New York and sent membership cards in his phantom organization to such Communist dignitaries as Gus Hall. How he managed to pay for these posters and leaflets out of his wages as an oiler remains an unanswered question.

So great was his selfconfidence that he allowed himself to fall into a trap when a man named Bill Stuckey invited him to appear on a TV program called "Latin American Listening Post."

At first, Stuckey had been quite taken with Oswald. Oswald talked abundantly into a tape recording for him. He seemed "a nice bright boy and extremely believable."

A little investigation brought out the facts. Helped by a director of the Information Council of the Americas who appeared on the same program, Stuckey confronted Oswald with his defection to the Soviet Union and completely destroyed his credibility in the New Orleans region.

Oswald told a different story to his Communist correspondents in New York. He wrote them that as a result of the broadcast he had been flooded with invitations to debate and that his office—which didn't exist—was crowded with people coming to join his Committee.

Actually, he was on his beam-ends. When the Paine family stopped off at Magazine Street on September 20 on their way home from a trip east, they decided they'd better put Marina, who was expecting a baby in October, and little June and as many of the Oswald goods and chattels as they could carry, into their station-wagon and take her home with them to Irving. Lee told them he was off to look for a job. Since the TV broadcast he had no hope of one in New Orleans. Maybe he'd go as far as Philadelphia.

On September 25, leaving the place filthy according to his landlady, and owing her two weeks' rent, he departed for Mexico City. He lived so frugally informants of the Warren Commission figured the whole trip could hardly have cost him more than eighty-five dollars. He went straight through on the Mexican bus from Nuevo Laredo and put up at a cheap hotel called the Hotel del Comercio. The night clerk remembered that he left early next morning and came back late every night while he was there. Except for his visits to the Cuban and Russian Embassies, the Mexican police were able to report very little about his activities.

At the Cuban Embassy he seems to have talked to a friendly Mexican employee named Señora Duran. He showed her his documents, said he had a Russian wife, had lived in the Soviet Union, was a member of the Communist Party and the New Orleans director of the Fair Play for Cuba Committee. He hoped to be admitted to Cuba as "a friend of the Cuban Revolution." Señora Duran helped him fill out an application for a visa and suggested he come back that afternoon.

At the Russian Embassy his story was that he wanted to take his wife and child back to the Soviet Union. The official he interviewed there was almost certainly a member of some secret-police organization. There's a chance that he already knew about Oswald. If there was ever a plan to use Oswald as an agent in the United States he had been rated so unstable the plan had been given up. The official told Oswald he'd have to wait until the Embassy could communicate with Moscow. Back at the Cuban bureau Señora Duran told him this would take four months at least and that the Cubans couldn't do anything about transit until the Russian visa was granted.

Oswald was getting so jumpy that to pacify him she let him talk to the Cuban consul on the phone. Oswald immediately lost his temper and so did the consul, who shouted into the phone that people like Oswald were doing the Cuban revolution more harm than good and he didn't care if he never got a visa.

Oswald left the Cuban consulate thoroughly discomfited. Nothing to do but make a stab at seeing the sights and catch a bus home. He bought some postcards of bullfights and made his reservation. October 3 he checked in for the night at the Dallas YMCA.

Before getting in touch with Marina he went around to the Employment Commission for recommendations for jobs. His rating was high in their records. At the first place they sent him, a printing shop, the manager was on the point of hiring him when he called his last employers in Dallas, the commercial art people.

They said they couldn't give him a recommendation so there he was back on the sidewalk again. Finally through a neighbor of the Paines he got work at the Texas Book Depository.

The baby, another little girl, was born in October. Mother and children got along well in Mrs. Paine's hospitable house. Lee lived in Dallas and enjoyed weekends with the family in Irving. Life moved smoothly. Through the early weeks of November he attended to his duties at the Depository and drove to Irving every weekend with a neighbor named Frazier. At this point he seems to have been fonder of Marina than she was of him. At the Paine's house he was tender with the children and helpful with household chores such as hanging out the baby's diapers. No amount of argument could induce Marina to join him in Dallas.

When Marina asked him not to come to Irving the weekend of November 16 and 17 because there would be a birthday party for one of the Paine children, and Michael Paine, whom Oswald disliked, was going to be there, he was very much put out.

He was at loose ends the whole weekend.

Sunday afternoon, Ruth Paine and Marina tried to call him but couldn't reach him because he had rented his room under the somewhat transparent alias of H. O. Lee. Next day, he called Irving and tried to explain to Marina that he had to use an alias on account of constant persecution by the FBI. Marina cried out it was time to put an end to all these comedies and hung up on him.

Marina was right. The persecution was imaginary. No FBI man had been near Oswald since an interview, which according to one report Oswald insisted on himself, in New Orleans during the period when his broadcast had earned him a transient notoriety. An agent visited Marina twice in early November but the interviews had been reassuring. She begged him not to come back because her husband was so upset when he heard of them.

It may have been during his lonesome weekend that Oswald decided to kill President Kennedy. He had already had a telescopic sight attached to his rifle. He had been seen practicing marksmanship at various local rifle ranges.

As part of his preparations he took brown paper and gummed tape from the shipping department at the Depository to construct an oddshaped package in which he planned to transport his takendown rifle. He was working out every detail with as much care as he had planned the attack on General Walker.

The newspapers were furnishing him with ample information

on the course of the President's motorcade on Friday, November 22. On the way to the underpass that led to the Trade Mart where the President would be tendered an official luncheon, the President's car was almost certain to take the westbound street that passed right under the windows of the Depository.

Sometime Thursday Oswald asked Frazier to let him ride to Irving with him that evening. Oswald had called the Paine house several times on Monday but Marina had refused to speak to him. When he turned up in Irving Thursday afternoon Mrs. Paine was sure he had come home to make it up with Marina.

Marina played hard to get. Oswald tried to convince her she should come to live with him in Dallas. Marina said she did not want to talk about that until after the Christmas holidays. There was an argument about a washing machine Marina wanted him to buy her and they separated.

Since his return from New Orleans Oswald had kept his rifle in an old green blanket in the Paine's garage. While the women were putting the children to bed he had plenty of time to take the rifle down and stow the parts in the brown paper parcel he had so carefully contrived.

That night he went to bed before Marina did. When she joined him she didn't speak, though she thought he might be awake. When she woke up he had already left. She found his wedding ring in a glass in the bathroom and his wallet with a hundred and seventy dollars in it on the bureau.

When he met Frazier he explained that the brown paper package he was carrying in an odd way under his armpit contained curtain rods. When Frazier parked the car in the usual parking lot, Oswald with his package pressed under his armpit walked faster than usual to the Depository. Frazier reported that usually they strolled along together watching the freightcars being shunted through a marshaling yard behind the building. Oswald brought no lunch with him that day.

Oswald's duties as orderfiller took him to the Shipping Department on the first floor and to the sixth floor which was used as a warehouse. Towards lunchtime that morning there was no one else in the southeast corner of the sixth floor. By a curious accident packing cases had been moved away from the wall to leave room for repairs on the floor so that they formed a barricade that cut off the view of the corner window. It was easy for Oswald to set up his rifle on its stand and to draw up a small packing case to sit on.

This time he was bound nothing would go wrong. He was ready when the motorcade appeared a little before noon. John Kennedy, for whom this was an important politicking trip to garner votes for the coming election and who wanted to lose no opportunity to "press flesh" with the Texans, had insisted on lowering the bulletproof glass protection on his open limousine. The car moved at about eleven miles an hour.

For an experienced rifleman it was an easy shot. Oswald was cool and exultant. The first shot went through the President's neck and severely wounded Governor Connally who sat in the front seat. The second shot hit the President in the head and caused his death. The third shot went astray.

Having committed the deed which he believed would make him famous in the history books, Oswald walked away from the window. He left his rifle in place and walked calmly down the stairway five flights to the lunchroom. There he was confronted by a police officer looking for suspects, who asked Roy Truly the building superintendent if this man worked in the building. Truly said yes. Oswald appeared so calm the police officer paid him no further attention.

Oswald left the building, walked seven blocks east and boarded a bus. He found the bus too slow. He could hear police sirens in all directions. He got off at a stop and flagged a taxi. The taxi, discovered later to be driven by a man named Click, left him at his rooming house. Mr. Click heard the police sirens and was wondering what the hell was going on, but when Oswald left the cab after handing him a dollar, the traffic was piling up so behind the cab he didn't have time to exchange a word with him.

The housekeeper noticed that Oswald seemed in a hurry. He was in his room only a minute and was still fastening his zipper jacket as he ran down the stairs.

Oswald's description had been broadcast over the police radios. On 10th Street, Officer Tippits, who had been listening to the description, stopped his car to investigate a man he saw walking along the sidewalk. When he stepped out of his car to question him Oswald shot him dead with his pistol.

Oswald was on the run. He shed his jacket and with his gun in his pocket ran eight blocks to the Texas Theatre. He ran into the theatre without buying a ticket and sat down.

Police cars converged on the theatre; about twenty policemen took up positions around the auditorium. When the manager turned up the lights Lee Harvey Oswald was found sitting alone near the right center aisle. An officer told him to stand up. He raised his hands over his head. When the cops converged on him he reached for his gun. He hit one cop between the eyes with his free fist. After a scuffle he was overpowered.

At the police station he became perfectly calm. He denied having owned a rifle. He denied shooting Officer Tippits. He told the police that the only charge they could hold him on was resisting arrest. When he was asked what lawyer he wanted to defend him he named John Abt, the lawyer in New York who had defended Rudolf Abel, the Soviet spy. Abt had worked closely for years with the CPUSA.

Before Abt could be notified, Oswald was dead.

The moment the news of President Kennedy's assassination was flashed around the world, reporters and TV crews poured into Dallas. The corridors and elevators of City Hall where the Police Department had its offices and jails filled up with frenzied yelling pushing crowds. Reporters and TV crews encumbered the corridor outside the police offices to such a point that the District Attorney had to fight his way in and out and the interrogation of witnesses was very much hampered. Instructions had been issued to give the news media every facility and the results were disastrous. When the Chief of Police tried to produce Oswald for a press conference, such pandemonium ensued that he had to be hurried back to the elevator and up to his cell.

It was decided to remove him to the custody of the Sheriff at the County Jail. An armored truck would take him from the basement of the police office in City Hall. TV crews had been notified and had set up their equipment facing the door from which Oswald was to appear. As soon as he was seen, reporters and TV crews went mad. People crowded in from all sides. No real effort had been made to screen the spectators.

A bumbling tub of guts with a disreputable history, known in Dallas where he operated a nightclub and striptease joint as Jack

Ruby, elbowed his way past a police officer, shoved a pistol in Oswald's stomach and shot him. Oswald died in Parkland Hospital two hours later.

The television networks had the satisfaction of being able to exhibit a film which clearly showed the assassination of the assassin.

4

The Execution of Malcolm Little

Though he apologized for it, Malcolm Little occasionally liked to compare himself to Saint Paul, smitten down on the road to Damascus. Only Malcolm had two conversions. The first was in Norfolk prison, when he decided that the Islam of the Honorable Elijah Muhammad was the creed for the Negro and changed his name to Malcolm X, and the second was in Jeddah, when he discovered that the real Islam meant brotherhood, the brotherhood of all believers without regard to race or color. He changed his name again to El Hajj Malik el-Shabbaz. When he got home he tried to undo the harm he felt he had done.

That was why they killed him.

His father,
    a freelance preacher who agitated for Marcus Garvey's
Back to Africa Movement,
    went that way before him.

A few years before Earl Little was killed, nightriders burned his house in Lansing, Michigan. The fire and the fright and the pistol shots were young Malcolm's earliest memory. Earl Little determinedly built himself another house farther out of town, spaded up a fresh garden and raised chickens. When he was killed his widow was left with eight children to raise and feed.

She was a cranky sort of woman from Grenada in the West Indies. She could have passed for white. Her father was white, probably a Scot, because Malcolm inherited red hair.

Malcolm Little wanted his story told before he died. He poured it out to his friend Max Haley. At first he didn't trust Max Haley because Haley knew too many white people; but how could he get the story published without knowing some white people?

Malcolm was the seventh child, his father's favorite because he was so light. His mother preferred the darker children: Malcolm was the one she whipped. She was full of strange hatreds and abstentions, wouldn't eat pork or rabbit, always quarreling with her husband. They had a quarrel about cooking a rabbit Earl shot the day he was killed.

Head bashed in and thrown under the wheels of a trolley car. The Littles had trouble collecting his insurance; the people paid up on one small policy but they wouldn't pay the larger one, claimed his death might have been suicide. Welfare workers crowded into the house. Malcolm's mother tried to drive them out, said she was quite capable of taking care of her family. They said she was crazy to refuse free food. They told the children she was crazy.

June 27, 1937, was a great day. Joe Louis knocked out J. S. Braddock and became heavyweight champion of the world. All the young Littles began to dream of the ring. Malcolm was only thirteen but he was tall and gangling. His brother Philbert was making a name for himself as a highschool pugilist. Malcolm lied about his age, signed up for a match with a white boy and was ignominiously beaten.

The Littles were always hungry. Sometimes they were so hungry they were dizzy. Malcolm started stealing regularly, mostly things to eat from the stores downtown. In school, though his marks were good, he was written off as uncontrollable, wouldn't take off his hat, put a thumbtack in the teacher's chair, expelled.

The truant officer took him to a detention home. There is something twisted about his story here. Malcolm told Haley contemptuously that the white couple who ran the home treated him like a mascot; but as soon as they found that he was intelligent and cooperative they seem to have treated him kindly and sensibly. Instead of sending him to reform school they placed him in the local public school. There were only two Negro families in town,

444

nd they were much respected. Malcolm did well. He was popular with his classmates, elected president of the seventh grade. Everybody praised him but praise from white people went down the wrong way. Bitter news from home. The welfare workers had placed his mother in a mental hospital.

The children tried to go to see her there now and then; often he didn't know who they were. The happiest visit was when Ella, Malcolm's father's daughter by an earlier marriage, came over from Boston. Ella was a big black confident woman who had made her way in the world. She had saved her money and married a successful doctor and invested in Roxbury real estate. She helped other Littles come up from Georgia. When they all went over to the hospital, she made a great fuss over her pale stepmother. Malcolm came away feeling it really meant something to be a Little.

Malcolm was unhappy in the eighth grade. He'd had one of those talks with his English teacher about what he'd be when he grew up. Malcolm said he would like to be a lawyer. He didn't know much about what it meant to be a lawyer but he knew lawyers didn't wash dishes like he had to do for a living. The teacher looked at him strangely and said we all had to be realistic. A lawyer wasn't a realistic goal for him. How about carpenter work? From that moment Malcolm hated the school, the white friends who had been nice to him, Masons and everybody in it.

Ella came to the rescue by getting herself appointed his guardian and taking him to live with her in Roxbury, but instead of going to school and fitting himself for a career, Malcolm started to hang around poolrooms in downtown Boston. He struck up a friendship with a cat named Shorty who hailed from Lansing too. Shorty dekinked his hair for him. Shorty taught him how to shine shoes and a lot else besides. Before long he was buying himself a zootsuit on credit, peddling reefers to the boys in the band, slipping men phonenumbers in the washroom, pimping in a small way. He found he could dance. He was mad for the lindy hop. His friends were prostitutes, pushers, burglars, holdup men. Everybody had his hustle.

When things got hot for him in Boston, Malcolm wangled a job as fourth cook on a dining car. The first glimpse of Harlem seemed heaven: the Savoy Ballroom, the Apollo Theatre, dignified Negro racketeers drinking whiskey in quiet bars. Whiskey and more

whiskey, marijuana, half the time high on cocaine. Like his brother
he was terribly precocious. By the time he was sixteen he was
Harlem character, kept by a white woman who had picked him u
in Boston. He signed his autographs "Detroit Red."

Money, money, all the time he had to have more money fo
cocaine. With good old Shorty and his white girl and her sister h
organized a gang for burglaries. The girls rented a Harvard Squar
apartment for a hideout. His white girl had married a returne
service man but she couldn't keep away from Red. To prove wh
was boss he played Russian roulette for the gang's benefit. Clic
click click with a pistol pointed at his head. Years later he admitte
to Haley he had palmed the only bullet.

At first, things went well, but each time he pulled a job it too
more of the drug to notch him up to it. Everybody was edgy. Th
white girl's husband was looking for Malcolm with a gun. Then on
day when he was trying to get a stolen watch repaired, a detectiv
walked in the jewelry store. Malcolm had a gun but for som
reason—later he claimed it was Allah's direct intervention—h
decided not to use it and handed it to the detective. Being arreste
saved his life because the white girl's husband was at that momen
looking for him in their apartment to kill him. Twice Allah save
his life that way.

Malcolm and Shorty were held on ten thousand dollars bai
each. The police questioned Malcolm but they didn't beat hin
That detective was grateful that he hadn't tried any gunplay. H
and Shorty were convicted and sentenced to eight to ten years o
several counts, sentences to run concurrently. Poor Shorty didn'
know what concurrently meant and nearly fainted when he adde
up all those years.

The girls got off with less. Afterwards Malcolm was bitte
about that. Nobody seemed to worry about the burglary. The rea
crime was tampering with white girls.

He wasn't quite twentyone and hadn't yet started to shave.

Charlestown jail was cold, obsolete, stinking. Malcolm said i
dated from Napoleon's time and had been modeled on the Bastille
He wouldn't conform to anything, shrieked filthy names at th
psychologist and the chaplain, dropped his tray in the dining hall
refused to answer to his number. When his religious brother wrot
him from Detroit that his Holiness Church was praying for Mal

colm, Malcolm wrote back a lot of foul language he later regretted. Even when Ella came he couldn't find a decent word to say to her.

With the money she gave him he bought nutmeg—powdered nutmeg mixed with water was considered in Charlestown the cheapest way of getting just a little bit high. You could buy nutmeg from convicts who worked in the kitchen. From the guards you could buy Nembutal, Benzedrine and reefers for higher-class highs.

He spent a lot of time in solitary. He liked it better in solitary. Fellow convicts called him Satan.

Gradually he quieted down. They put him to work in the shops where they made automobile license plates. There he met a burglar named Bimbi. Bimbi was a lightcomplexioned freckled Negro about the same color as Malcolm. Bimbi was getting along in years. Everybody respected Bimbi. He'd read a lot and had considered opinions on all sorts of subjects: he was the first man Malcolm had ever met who was respected for his learning. He was the prison library's best customer. When he noticed that Malcolm had brains he told him in his dour way that he ought to take advantage of the prison correspondence courses.

Malcolm started a correspondence course in English. His sister Hilda had suggested it too, said she couldn't read a word on the picture postcard he sent her when he was on the road hustling reefers.

After about a year he could write a decent letter. He interested himself in grammar. He took a course in Latin so that he might learn where the words came from.

Ella never gave him up. She worked with the authorities to get Malcolm transferred to the Norfolk Prison Colony, an experimental jail. Norfolk had a magnificent library. The prisoners were to be rehabilitated by education.

Meanwhile, his brothers and sisters in Chicago had joined the Nation of Islam. His brother Reginald wrote him to stop smoking cigarettes and to refuse pork. "I'll show how to get out of jail." What kind of a hype was this? Malcolm determined to try.

Finally, Reginald came to visit him and after beating around the bush for a while suddenly asked: "Malcolm, how many degrees are there in a circle?"

"Three hundred and sixty," said Malcolm.

"If there was a man who knew everything he would have three hundred and sixty degrees of knowledge," Reginald went on, "he would be God. God is a man and his name is Allah. . . . The white man is the devil, especially Masons, but the devil has only thirty-three degrees of knowledge. . . . He's used that to brainwash the blacks. . . . You don't even know who you are. The white man has hidden it from you that you are of a race of people of ancient civilizations and riches in gold and kings. You don't even know your true family name "

Reginald explained that the message had come to them through The Messenger of Allah, the Honorable Elijah Muhammad, who was black as they were, born on a Georgia farm. He had suffered in jail for refusing to register for the draft. He had moved his family to Detroit where he had met a Mr. Wallace D. Ford whom he claimed was God in person. Mr. Wallace D. Ford had delivered Allah's message to the black people of America who were the Lost-Found Nation of Islam here in this wilderness of North America. Then he suddenly vanished without a trace.

Malcolm's sister Hilda came to see him. She told him the white race had been created six thousand years ago on the island of Patmos through the wickedness of a scientist named Mr. Yaccub. His sister told him to write the Honorable Elijah Muhammad for further instruction. He did and got back a tract and a five-dollar bill.

He wrote President Truman and the Governor of Massachusetts and the Mayor of Boston that the white man was responsible for the black man's condition. He began to pray to the east. Praying was the hardest of all; the only way he'd ever been on his knees was picking a lock to rob somebody's house.

He found he couldn't express himself properly in these letters. All he knew was Harlem slang. First thing, he got an English dictionary out of the library and started to copy it down letter by letter into a set of notebooks. He found the dictionary was a miniature encyclopedia. He always remembered the first word, aardvark. There was a picture of the little animal. He'd never known that such a creature existed.

Gradually he learned enough words to understand the books he was trying to read. Lights out at 10:00 P.M. was a plague. He'd sit on the floor and go on reading in the glow from the corridor lights. He read Will Durant and H. G. Wells and Toynbee and all the books about Negroes he could find. The accounts of Negro slavery drove him wild. He read the philosophers. When he liked what they said he decided they must have been black. Spinoza was black. The original Hebrews were black, Moses and St. Paul and even Jesus.

It was at Norfolk that he learned public speaking in the weekly debates. His last year of prison he was sent back to Charlestown. Was it for preaching that the white man was the devil? Or refusing to take some injection?

Already his younger brother Reginald had been suspended from Islam by the Honorable Elijah Muhammad for immoral relations with the secretary of the New York Temple. Malcolm was horrified. He wrote the Messenger begging him to help his brother. Whenever Reginald came to see him he noticed signs of Allah's punishment. He had given up dressing neatly. He had delusions. Finally the police had to pick up Reginald and place him in an institution.

In 1953 Malcolm's parole came up. Shorty's did too. Shorty had studied music in prison. Somebody told Malcolm that he wrote a piece called "The Bastille Concerto." Hilda turned up with some money and begged him to go to Detroit to learn Islam from the ministers in the temple there. Ella wanted him to go to Detroit to make a fresh start but said she wasn't going to become any Muslim.

He stayed at his brother Wilfred's home. Wilfred managed a furniture store for some Jews and gave Malcolm a job as a salesman. Malcolm was delighted with the quiet neatness and discipline of a Black Muslim home.

On Labor Day, Wilfred drove him over in the caravan of cars that took the Muslims from Temple #1 in Detroit to Temple #2 in Chicago. From the moment the small brown man appeared from the back of the hall surrounded by the sturdy Fruit of Islam guards in dark suits, white shirts and bow ties, Malcolm became the Messenger's slave.

For thirteen years he went around the country with no possessions but a suitcase, a wristwatch and a pair of glasses, making converts and organizing new temples for Elijah Muhammad. From four hundred the number of the faithful rose to forty thousand. Everywhere he preached Muslim morality. No fornication, no pork, no cigarettes, drugs or liquor. Women must be respected. There must be no quarreling or fighting. The first task of the new temples was curing the junkies who wanted to get the monkey off their backs. No one could cure junkies like a man who had just been cured himself.

In 1957 Malcolm married a Muslim girl named Betty who was taking a nursing course in a New York hospital. The following year who should he see stand up as a convert when he was proselytizing a new temple in Boston, but his sister Ella.

The Black Muslims became news. Malcolm fast caught the knack of dealing with the media. He became a television figure, was invited to speak in colleges; always he spoke in the name of the Honorable Elijah Muhammad. Books came out. Malcolm found himself a VIP.

Nineteen sixtyone was the peak year. Their newspaper, *Muhammad Speaks,* came out with drawings of a project to build a twenty-million-dollar Islamic Center in Chicago. The Nation was in funds. The Honorable Elijah Muhammad took the opportunity to travel in Islamic countries. The word on the wire was that he was making the pilgrimage to Mecca. While the Messenger was away Malcolm X was the spokesman. He was importuned by offers from radio and television. According to the *New York Times* only Barry Goldwater exceeded him in popularity before college audiences.

Elijah Muhammad came home ill. Asthma. He kept being taken with violent fits of coughing. The doctors said he must move to Arizona. The Nation built a big house with a swimming pool for him and his family in Phoenix.

A coolness grew up between Elijah Muhammad's supporters in Phoenix and Malcolm in New York. The way Malcolm put it was that he believed more in Elijah Muhammad than Elijah Muhammad did in himself. He had been shocked to discover that several of the Messenger's secretaries had been put away pregnant. Two were bringing paternity suits against him. Malcolm had been to see them: he had no doubt that their stories were true. He was shocked to the marrow. He was convinced that the newspapers would get hold of the story. How to explain it to the poor faithful black Muslims?

He consulted one of Elijah Muhammad's sons. They settled on

"Fulfillment of Prophecy." Moses had sinned. David had sinned. Lot and Noah had disgraced themselves, but their accomplishments had been greater than their crimes. As the story got back to Phoenix Malcolm was trying to publicize the Messenger's guilt.

President Kennedy's assassination brought the rift to a head. The Honorable Elijah Muhammad sent messages to all his ministers that they should make no comment on the event. He canceled a lecture he intended to give in the Manhattan Center in New York. When he discovered he couldn't get the money refunded he'd advanced for the hall, he phoned Malcolm to speak in his stead.

Malcolm already had a speech ready: God's judgment on White America. The first question he was asked afterwards was what did he think of Kennedy's assassination. "Chickens coming home to roost" was his answer.

Immediately the headlines echoed it. No commentator missed it. Next day Malcolm flew out to Phoenix for his monthly meeting with the Messenger. Mr. Muhammad immediately told him that it had been a very bad statement. President Kennedy was immensely beloved. It would make trouble for Muslims. He added that Malcolm must be silenced for ninety days.

Back in New York Malcolm began to discover that the silencing might well be forever. "When I discovered who wanted me dead I'm telling you it nearly sent me to Bellevue."

At that moment Cassius Clay invited Malcolm to bring his family to Miami where he was training to fight Sonny Liston. Malcolm had known Cassius and his brother for about a year. The Clay boys were among the very few people he invited out to his home. His wife and children loved them. Since Muslims were not supposed to interest themselves in sport, Cassius and his friends belonged to a whole different world. Of course, the reporters publicized the fact that Malcolm was in Cassius' training camp and in Phoenix his presence was taken as just one more play for personal publicity.

Nobody expected Cassius to win. Malcolm pepped him up by telling him his was the fight between the Cross and the Crescent. Cassius was already a Muslim and Malcolm thought it was his preaching that had done the work. Cassius won the fight by careful planning. He out-thought Liston every round. It made Malcolm very happy when Cassius told the reporters afterwards that he believed in the religion of Islam; there was no God but Allah and Muhammad was his apostle.

It became obvious when Malcolm reached New York that the breach with Elijah Muhammad was final. He began planning a new organization of all black people. First he wanted to learn more of the rites and beliefs of the real Muslims in Arabia. How to raise money for the trip? Sister Ella of course. Ella had been saving up to make the pilgrimage herself but right away she said it was more important for Malcolm to go.

Before he could get a visa to Saudi Arabia he had to have the approval of Dr. Shawarbi of the Federation of Islamic Organizations. Dr. Shawarbi said he had been following Malcolm's statements in the press. He had his letter of approval all ready when Malcolm went to see him. He gave Malcolm a book by Dr. Rahman Azzam which he had just received in the mail. In Arabia too they had been following Malcolm's career. That's what came of having developed what Malcolm called "an international image."

From the minute he climbed on the Lufthansa plane everything was delightful. His two seatmates were Muslims. Certainly a sign from Allah. They had a layover in Frankfurt. Roaming around the town they were delighted by the cordiality of people in the stores. People were cordial whether you bought anything or not.

They took the United Arab Airlines plane to Cairo. There they saw their first pilgrims, a mixture of people from all sorts of different countries. No colorline there, only friendliness and cordiality. The friends he met in Cairo were excited because he was an American Muslim. The fact that he was a Negro didn't interest them.

He had been advised to leave his baggage and cameras in Cairo and just to take a small suitcase along. The pilgrims wore sandals and two loose white garments of what looked like toweling held together by a moneybelt and a bag with a strap for the passport and documents. There were thousands at the airport all dressed alike. You couldn't tell rich from poor, governor from governed; this was the brotherhood of Islam. They all called out "Labbyaka . . . Here I come Oh Lord."

Planes were taking off every few minutes. A special seat was found for Malcolm because they didn't want to disappoint an

American Muslim. He said he hoped they hadn't bumped somebody off for his sake. Packed together in the jet he found brown people, blueeyed blondes with yellow hair, yellow people, red people, all honoring the same God Allah and all honoring each other.

When the plane was airborne the captain came back to introduce himself. He was an Egyptian, darker than Malcolm. The captain invited Malcolm into the cockpit. The Arab copilot was even darker. Never in his life had Malcolm imagined a black man piloting a plane.

They arrived at Jeddah in the middle of the night. The airport was immensely crowded. The Customs men were thrown off by Malcolm's American passport. The letter from Dr. Shawarbi didn't seem to help. Malcolm would have to appear before the Muslim court. His little group of Englishspeaking Egyptians, who were planning to take care of him, would have to go on without him. They seemed heartbroken.

Malcolm was led up into a huge dormitory above the airport. Since tomorrow was Friday he would have to wait there till Saturday. There were so many different kinds of people in that dormitory, Malcolm told Haley, it was like pages out of the *National Geographic*. His guide found him a corner and tried to teach him the proper postures of prayer.

When dawn came, Malcolm tried to communicate with the people squatting on the rugs around him. One Egyptian seemed to speak a little English. Malcolm tried to get it across that he was a friend of Muhammad Ali Clay. People thought he was Clay. Great excitement. Everybody knew how Clay had beaten Sonny Liston and they announced that it was with the help of Allah.

At that point his guide turned up and led him down to a long trough with rows of faucets in the courtyard of the adjacent mosque. The guide tried to show him how to perform the ablutions. It all seemed very complicated but somehow he got through the morning prayer. The guide led him back up to the dormitory again. A Persian came up and invited him to have tea with himself and his wife on their carpet. Malcolm decided it would be presumptuous to accept. Muslims don't like strangers eating with their wives. The Persian brought him tea and cookies anyway.

His guide had said he would be back in three hours but he never did come back. Malcolm made various exploring expeditions down to the courtyard. People were friendly but he couldn't quite get himself to accept invitations to eat from groups round about who ate with their hands out of a common pot. In one of his explorations he found a little restaurant. He bought a roast chicken and squatted down and ate it with his hands the way the Muslims did.

Finally, after evening prayer, he suddenly remembered that he had a telephone number in his letter from Dr. Shawarbi. The son of the man who had sent him the book lived there in Jeddah. He'd seen some officials at a table with a telephone. He dashed down the stairs again and asked them to call the number.

That number proved the open sesame. Soon a handsome six-foot white man was shaking Malcolm's hand. He was white but Malcolm had no feeling of his being white. He had a very polished manner. It was Dr. Rahman Azzam. Why hadn't he called before, he asked Malcolm. In a short time he had arranged everything at the airport, retrieved Malcolm's suitcase and passport and was driving him through the streets of Jeddah. Malcolm was amazed to feel no physical difference between them as human beings.

Dr. Azzam was a Swisstrained engineer. City planning. The Saudi Arabian government had borrowed him from the United Nations to superintend the reconstruction of the Holy Cities. His sister was married to Prince Faisal's son. Malcolm was horn-swoggled.

It was early in the morning when he reached Dr. Azzam's home. His father, the man who had sent him the book, and several relatives were there. They had gotten up early to meet Malcolm. Before Malcolm knew what was happening they had driven him over to the Jeddah Palace Hotel. They put him up in Dr. Rahman Azzam's own suite.

Malcolm was so moved he prayed on the rug in the living room. What could they possibly gain by doing him a kindness like that?

It was that morning, Malcolm told Haley, that he began to reappraise the "white man." As he had been using the words they meant complexion, but it was attitudes towards others that counted.

Dinner that night with the Azzam family was one of the great experiences of his life. They were one of the most prominent families in the Arab world and they treated him, school dropout, Harlem hustler, jailbird, racist, like a brother.

Next morning he appeared in court. After a few questions the judge recognized him as a true Muslim and gave him two books, one in Arabic and one in English. He was taken back to lunch at the hotel. He was napping when the phone rang. It was one of Prince Faisal's heads of protocol. A car would call to take him to Mecca after dinner. The man said to eat heartily because the Hajj ritual required plenty of strength.

The car whizzed along a well-lighted modern turnpike. His guide or *mutawafe* was a short darkskinned Arab named Mohammad but he spoke no English. The car waited for them near the Great Mosque.

They walked three times around the Black Stone getting as near it as they could in the immense crowd. They drank from the well Zem Zem, they climbed the mountain Arafat and threw seven stones at the devil.

When, after he had finished the ceremonial stages of his pilgrimage, some Englishspeaking Arabs asked him what had impressed him most, he answered, "Brotherhood, the Brotherhood of Islam."

That night he wrote a number of letters, to his wife Betty, to Elijah Muhammad's son Wallace, to the ministers of the new orthodox Harlem mosque and to Dr. Shawarbi. He tried to explain his change of heart. The Nation of Islam must merge with the real Islam. It wasn't so much the white man as American racism that was bringing the United States to destruction. He signed the letters El Hajj Malik el-Shabbaz.

Prince Faisal invited him to an audience. The gist of what the Prince said was that the American Negroes had the wrong Islam. With the number of books about the real Islam that had appeared in every European language he could not understand how such false impressions could get about. Malcolm said he was making it his business to correct these false impressions. "That is good," said Faisal and the interview was over.

Malcolm left Mecca with the feeling that this was the first time he had stood before his Creator as a complete human being.

Back home he found bickering and backbiting everywhere.

Even his warmest supporters in the New York mosque were uncertain. The Nation of Islam had brought suit to take back the house on Long Island his family had been allowed to occupy. Malcolm managed to delay giving up the house but when he was getting ready to move somebody set off a bomb in it and burned half of it down. The round of interviews, meetings to create the Organization of Afro-American Unity, press conferences, lectures took every moment of his time. As organization advanced, the death threats became more frequent. His wife had had another baby, a fourth little girl. His organization was bringing in few dues. He was terribly short of cash. "They won't let me turn the corner," he told Haley. "I'm caught in a trap."

On February 21, 1965, he was booked to speak in the Audubon Ballroom on 166th Street. The meeting started late. The Reverend Galimaison and other Harlem notables were supposed to come and never arrived. An assistant spoke first. Friends waiting in the corridor heard Malcolm advancing towards the front of the stage.

They heard his friendly voice. *"Assalaikum,* brothers and sisters." Suddenly there was a scuffle. A man's voice was raised: "Take your hand out of my pocket!" "Don't get excited," said Malcolm. "Let's cool it, brothers."

At that moment three men in the front row rose to their feet and started shooting at him simultaneously, like a firing squad. There were other shots as the gunmen backed away to the doors.

With the first shots Sister Betty had thrown her body over the children in the seats beside her. By the time she reached the stage Malcolm was dead.

5

The Later Life and Deplorable Opinions of Jay Pignatelli—vii

The Common Sense Group

Jay struggled up the steps of the subway into the rasping heat of 13th Street. The rays of the afternoon sun swung about his head like a baseball bat.

It was stifling in the corridor, but when Emily opened the door to her apartment a tiny breath of cool air drifted out. He kissed her carefully so as not to get her mucked up with his sweat.

"Emily, you look worried."

"Why wouldn't I look worried? Somebody broke in last night and carried off about half of the family plate."

"Wonderful," was the first thing Jay said. "Maybe that will convince you that it is time you stopped living alone. Our society has reached a state of degradation when it is no longer practical for a woman or anybody else to live alone."

"Would you really want to marry an old hag like me?"

"Emily Beaufort, you're young enough, and you know it, to be my daughter, but before we start to argue if you don't mind I'll go back to your bathroom and take a shower."

"Meanwhile, I'll make us a gin and tonic."

"A most wholesome proposition."

"Emily," said Jay when he came back refreshed by a long cold shower and a clean shirt he found in the bureau, "let's go into our problems . . . seriatim. First, what did you do about the burglary?"

"I called the police and the insurance. A couple of young detectives came down and an elderly man from Travelers'. They talk like you do. They said it was idiotic for a woman to try to live alone with a batch of valuable antiques. They said I was lucky they hadn't cut my throat. . . ."

"Did you put down their names?"

"Yes." Emily handed over a piece of paper.

"I'll check with them in the morning."

"Emily, did you do anything more?"

She looked in his face with a cute little apologetic smile. "I called the bank about a small vault. They won't have that ready till tomorrow."

"The burglars will certainly be back to complete their haul," said Jay.

"Since the plate was photographed for the insurance, the detectives thought there might be a bare possibility of recovering it."

"Emily, the main thing to recover is you. As you may suspect, I've had a marriage license ready for weeks in my desk drawer, but it's a little late for today. I'll put you up at the Plaza for the night."

"Isn't that extravagant?"

"I fully intend to be extravagant I've even decided to back *Common Sense*. This is the first time in my life I've been really flush."

"How much did you promise to put in?"

"Plenty. . . . I told the whole group to come on down to have a drink here before going out to dinner."

Emily made a face. "Jay, bring me up to date."

"Well, you know Ed Manchester. He's a tall meticulous man with a moustache. It used to be a very small moustache but now he says—Ed always reminds me a little of Dean Acheson—he has to let it grow to keep up with his sons. Si Simonds has grown pretty hairy since he's been teaching Economics at Harvard. He is bringing Edwin Gotfried and his brother Joe. Then there will be a couple of closecropped types from the Thomas Jefferson School of Economics at Charlottesville. One of them is James Francis Delaney."

"It might be interesting," said Emily suddenly off on another tack, "to look up the natural history of beards and see how they correlate with long hair. Women change their hairdos but men go in for much more archaic variations."

"When I was in lawschool"—Jay was thinking back—"elderly professors wore small carefully trimmed beards. Their barbers would have disciplined them if they hadn't."

"Now nobody tries to discipline anybody."

"You wait," said Jay, "here comes the new discipline."

Emily's eyes followed his glance out of the tall window. Two cabs had driven up; a tall man and two short men were piling out of one, and another trio out of the other.

While Jay busied himself getting them drinks, the Common Sense Group delved with gusto into the subject of Long Hair.

"This is the sort of anthropological sociological approach we ought to take up," said Manchester in his somewhat pedagogical manner. "Why did people wear long hair in the forties and fifties, beards now and then and gradually settle down to moustaches and clean shaves that predominated in World War I? Then everybody seemed happy with their Gillettes until the first rumbles of protest over World War II began. The young people began to sprout whiskers but whiskers on an unprecedented scale."

"Let's face it," cried Si Simonds laughing, "the human race has never been studied carefully and consistently. Not even our most superficial aspects."

"Si, you know students better than we do," said Jay wiping his glass on a paper towel. "Would any of them be interested in this sort of study?"

"Barring a few exceptions, most of these poor kids are too ignorant to be interested in anything except their own navels. That goes for the teaching staff first. How did we ever manage to saddle the country with such a race of incompetents?"

"I hope none of this," said Emily, "is going to keep us from eating a very good supper over at Marco's. Jay, do you think you ought to call them up? We'll be eight."

Jay strode back to the telephone. "Pronto spaghetti," he

shouted back, "and let's hope the burglars won't scoop up the rest of the Beaufort plate while we are dining."

"You could send me over my supper on a tray. I'll stand sentinel," said James Francis Delaney, puffing his chest out.

"No, we can't risk losing an editor at this stage of the proceedings."

Marco's was dark and cool and full of the familiar smells of cheese and garlic and tomato sauce and scallopini and chianti.

"I'm certainly glad I was brought up to enjoy Italian food," said Emily sniffing the heavy-laden air.

"Does that go for Chinese food, too?"

"The mainstay of life in New York," she said laughing.

Jay sat at one end of the table and Emily at the other. Waiters bustled about with spaghetti *al burro* and spaghetti *al olio*. In between the heaped plates appeared various forms of antipasto, slices of cheese, prosciutto with pickled mushrooms, a real holocaust.

"Isn't it wonderful?" crooned Emily. "Marco puts on the best imitation of a Roman orgy."

"The real problem in this country," said Delaney abruptly, picking up his classroom manner, "isn't race. It is the degradation of the human element that comes from the coddling welfare psychology. Biologically we have been encouraging the most incompetent strains since 1933 when Franklin D. and Harry Hopkins started encouraging the lame and the halt and the blind. There's always been welfare but it then reached a scale where it became a way of life."

"Should we have let them starve?" asked Emily.

"Biologically it would have been better. . . . But actually they wouldn't have starved."

"What can we do about it at this late date?"

"That's what we are all huddled up about, dear lady. In these thirty years in spite of the prejudice against honest eugenics a certain amount of research has been done. What we'll have to do is explore the whole subject."

"You'll be lynched by the welfare workers. The subject is a sacred cow."

"Barbecue the sacred cows."

"That," said Jay, "is our business in a nutshell."

They had reached the café espresso stage. Jay serenely paid the bill and excused himself by explaining that he had to find Emily a flop for the night.

Jay locked and doublelocked the door behind them.

"Jay, I'm dying to know how you came to be so flush."

"No, I haven't been robbing any banks. . . . It's your friends Marquand, Merlin and O'Brien have been making so much money since they let me in as a junior partner that the time has come to splurge a little. Another reason why we need to get married. Two can spend money more pleasantly than one."

Suddenly he turned to her. "Emily, it would be not only extravagant but silly for us to go out to a hotel. Let's stay right here. If those burglars come back, I want to get a look at them."

She looked at him with a tenderness she had never shown before. "Jay," she whispered, "it's taken me a long time to melt. I was terribly fond of young Tom Merlin. I know you like his brother Jake; he was twice the man Jake is and more. But now here you are, I'll take you for better or worse."

They shook hands rather solemnly.

"Emily, the funniest little suspicion has started to bud in my mind. Do you suppose this visitation could have come from Danny DeLong? I don't think he would do this to us personally but a lot of burglaries are planned at Sing Sing and executed by remote control. Remember how he was impressed by the value of your furnishings?"

"To tell the truth, it was the first time I paid any attention, I was so used to having them around."

"That was the only time he was here."

"Jay, anything is possible in this funny little world." She began to look thoughtful.

"What would be interesting would be to find a way of getting the stuff back. It was obviously a professional job. No fingerprints. Things carefully wrapped up."

"Give a dog a bad name," said Emily.

"It's not exactly that, but we do know Danny likes to talk big. He could have been boasting to some of his larcenous friends in jail about all the valuable antiques. Danny never forgets an address."

They started to yawn at almost exactly the same moment. "Now, Emily, if you hear any strange noises, don't only stay in bed but if necessary slide back under the bed."

Emily began to giggle. "Now wouldn't I look silly?"

Jay stifled her giggles with kisses. For the first time they were desperately happy together. Their tired old carcasses responded again and again.

Outside not a sound. The street was empty. They didn't even hear a mouse gnawing. The night was breathless quiet.

When they woke up, they had broken into a new world.

Emily took the first bath, then while he bathed and shaved, she put a firstrate breakfast together: cantaloupe, Italian coffee with hot milk, toasted English muffins with poached eggs. Jay declared it was the best breakfast he had ever eaten.

"Next time I'll have eggs Benedict."

"What are you planning for the morning, Emily?"

"I know you won't want me here. I'll go uptown to buy a dress." She blushed.

"I have to go to the office for a while. Suppose you meet me there at eleven thirty," Jay said in a rather peremptory tone.

"What for?"

"To get married, you goose. A lawyer's office is really a good place to get married. You have all the necessary data and witnesses at hand. My secretary, Mary Isbrandsen, will be so pleased—she's just one of the nicest people in the world. I know you'll like her. I may even get Jake Merlin over from Boston. We'll order lunch somewhere. The time in between we'll take the swag to the safe deposit vault to get that out of the way."

"Jay, I'll do everything just as you say. You can't imagine what a pleasure it is to have someone to plan my day for me. The state of mind won't last, but let's enjoy it while we can."

Mrs. Isbrandsen had set up some of those little brass merry-go-rounds that spin and tinkle from the heat of candles that the Swedes bring out for Christmas on the tops of the bookcases, and had managed to entangle Swedish and Italian colored ribbons around a seal of the city of Genoa.

"But Mary, when did the Swedes colonize Genoa?" asked Emily widening her eyes.

Mrs. Isbrandsen giggled and blushed. "Never," she said, "but it seems the nearest I'll come to a happy marriage."

Emily patted her hand indulgently. There were teardrops on her eyelashes, so blonde they looked almost white.

Mr. Abrams, the notary public, arrived early. He was obviously very much set up by the importance of the occasion and the importance of his clientele. Jay caught him carefully estimating the amount of champagne in a carton of wine bottles shoved under the desk. He kept crying out, "Imagine, a marriage without any previous divorces."

Jake Merlin burst in just in time to give the bride away. His happiness was volcanic. Mr. Abrams ran off the ceremonial words so fast that nobody heard them. Jake poured himself out the first glass. "Honeymoon in Maine," he announced blowing the bubbles off the champagne as if it were beer.

"I'll drive you up right now and then leave you to yourselves. The house will be empty all week. We have the boat at Newport for the races."

"Jake, do you suppose we could wait until after lunch? I have a royal, or at least a ducal, lunch ordered for us at La Potiniere at one thirty. Meanwhile, Emily and I have to go back to 13th Street to stow the remaining swag in a deposit vault."

Mr. Abrams almost fell in a swoon when it was explained to him that he was invited.

Jay had ordered a chauffeur-driven car; he and Emily set off in style. The chauffeur was sulky about all the heavy cartons he had to handle at the bank until Jay told him they were just married and these were their wedding presents.

"Marry in haste and repent at leisure," growled the chauffeur from under his visor.

"But we didn't marry in haste. I've been wooing the young lady for many years." Jay finally mollified him by buying him a bunch of carnations for his wife when he stopped off for flowers on the way to the restaurant. "Monsieur Petit will be horrified if we appear without flowers."

Lunch was impeccable but they hurried through it. Jake wanted to hit the road, and to tell the honest truth, Jay and Emily were getting a little tired of the company of Mr. Abrams and the office staff. He ordered a bottle of brandy and told them to sit there sipping it in honor of the bride. Mr. Abrams intoned a Jewish blessing and they left.

"Well," said Jake, "that was the most original wedding I ever attended."

The drive north was muggy and hot. It wasn't until they turned into the narrow harbor of Kennebunkport that the chill fog freshened their faces.

6

Dr. James D. Watson and the Golden Molecule

James D. Watson was a Brooklyn boy.

He belonged to the generation with heads where mathematical ideas circulated naturally as the daydreams of an earlier time.

At twentythree, he found himself invited to the Cavendish Laboratories of the University of Cambridge in England to help root out the mystery of DNA, deoxyribonucleic acid, the fundamental substance that controlled the shape of the genes that were the basic form of life—the Golden Molecule, Watson called it.

Watson wasn't the Cambridge type. The Cambridge idea of a scientist was a tight-lipped silent man in a dark suit with a gift for understatement. Watson was nothing if not noisy. He was determined that science should be fun.

He teamed up with a somewhat older Englishman named Francis Crick who worked at King's College London. He wrote he never had seen Francis in a modest mood—that went for Watson, too.

A sober Austrian chemist named Max Perutz who worked on X-ray refraction from hemoglobin crystals headed the laboratory. Sir Francis Bragg who presided over the institution had won a Nobel Prize in crystallography forty years before.

Crick and Watson both loved mountain climbing. They followed the girls, went to movies and concerts. Entertainment was abundant in London that winter.

Watson, who was boarding at Clare College, had trouble with the English food. He thought he was getting ulcers until he discovered that none of the Americans could digest the stringy meat. Eventually he moved over to a boarding house where a group of French girls ate, in London to learn English; the food agreed with him much better there.

Watson's discovery of the principle of the double helix was a continual race with Linus Pauling; another losing contender was Maurice Wilkins at King's College in London. Wilkins frustrated Francis Crick by modest understatements of important problems. Behind him was a spinster named Rosalind Franklin, a tall plain-faced Englishwoman with an incredibly accurate mind. Her understatements were even more modest. Crick and Watson credited her with contributing as much as anybody to the final outcome.

Inventing the double helix was like building a French hat. A great deal of collaboration from talented assistants.

Based at just the right angle the two antennae twisted according to the right impulses.

One first discovery was that the gene itself had sex. In the course of its development it broke up into sexual components.

Watson and Crick went to the Eagle pub and had a drink on that one.

A critical change of thinking had to be made when they discovered that the essential transmitter of the chain of life was DNA (deoxyribonucleic acid) and not RNA (ribonucleic acid). The acids were almost twins so more work was needed, but it was DNA that furnished the weird and complicated structure that transmitted heredity. After that, Linus Pauling conceded that Watson and Crick had won the race and it was to them that the Nobel Prize was awarded.

7

Christmas on the Moon

December 24, 1968, was one of the dates when history turns a corner. Ever since the discovery of atomic power, mankind had been tortured by the fear that science had unleashed forces beyond human ability to control.

August 6, 1946, augured ill.

The success of Project Apollo proved that the achievements of science could be directed with unbelievable accuracy. On December 24, 1968, three men, detached enough to make humorous cracks as they went along, proved that they could match and command the intricate energies and impulses technology had placed at their disposal.

Our thinking about the universe, our thinking about life on earth can never be the same since that moment when three men orbiting the moon paused from their routine to look back with tenderness over two hundred and forty thousand miles of space at the tiny blue earth which was their home. This was the day man proved his mastery of matter, the day he wiped out the unhappy prospects of Hiroshima.

On December 24, 1968, at 8:31 P.M., U. S. Central Standard Time, a voice from the control desk of the Houston Space Center reached the ears of uncounted millions of listeners on television and radio to announce that the Apollo 8 spacecraft, 85 hours and 39 minutes out of Cape Kennedy, was coming into the field of communication after its ninth revolution round the moon.

"We've got a picture here but . . . we've got a voice to go with it . . ." Bill Anders:

"How does the picture look Houston?"

"Loud and clear."

"Does everything look okay?"

"Rog. Very good."

"Welcome to the moon Houston."

A million viewers feel something somersault inside them, wonder, awe. There are moments of astonished awareness that don't come often. This is such a moment.

Houston is asking if the blob on the top left side of the picture is the earth.

Frank Borman's confident voice takes over.

"This is Apollo 8 coming to you live from the moon. . . . We showed you first a view of Earth as we've been watching it for the past sixteen hours. . . . Now we are switching so that we can show you the moon that we've been flying over at sixty miles altitude. Bill Anders, Jim Lovell and myself have spent the day before Christmas up here doing experiments, taking pictures and firing our spacecraft engines to maneuver around. . . . What we will do now is follow the trail we've been following all day and take you through to the lunar sunset. The moon is a different thing to each of us. . . ."

Borman calls it "a great expanse of nothing . . . clouds and clouds of pumice stone." Jim Lovell remarks on how pleasant the bright earth looks, the only color in the lonesomeness of space. Bill Anders tells how during the lunar sunrises and sunsets the black shadows pick out details of the terrain you couldn't see in the dazzle of sunlight.

Bill Anders describes what the viewers on earth should be seeing: the sky pitch black and the moon quite light, small bright impact craters dominating the lunar surface . . . "the contrast between the sky and the moon is a vivid dark line . . . the mountains coming up now are heavily impacted with numerous craters whose central peaks you can see . . . a vastness of black and white, absolutely no color . . . been bombarded through the eons with numerous small asteroids and meteoroids pockmarking the surface every

468

square inch. . . . The crater you see on the horizon is the Sea of Crises. Are you reading us Houston?"

"Loud and clear."

"We are now breaking the moon's sunrise or the spacecraft's sunset. . . . This is the Sea of Fertility and we're coming upon a large crater, the delta rim variety. Has strange circular tracks patterned round the middle of it. . . . We are now going over one of our future landing sites selected in this moon region called the Sea of Tranquility. . . . We are now approaching the lunar sunrise and for all the people back on earth the crew of Apollo 8 has a message that we would like to send to you."

Bill Anders starts reading the first chapter of Genesis which Borman typed out on fireproof paper before they left: *"In the beginning God created the heaven and the earth. And the earth was without form, and void; and darkness was upon the face of the deep. And the spirit of God moved upon the face of the waters. And God said let there be light . . ."*

Jim Lovell's voice chimes in . . . *"And God called the light Day and the darkness he called Night . . ."*

Frank Borman: . . . *"And God called the dry land Earth and the gathering together of the waters He called Seas: and God saw that it was good. . . .* And from the crew of Apollo 8 we pause with good night, good luck, a Merry Christmas and God bless you all on the good earth."

It is not often that a great moment in history finds the right words to express it. This time it did.

The critical event in the Apollo program was when the men in the spacecraft out of communication and behind the moon felt the thrust of the rocket engines that were to snap them out of the moon's orbit into their path towards the earth. Nobody had ever tried it before. Would all systems function? They did.

At twelve twenty Christmas afternoon, Houston reported that Honeysuckle Station in Australia had a radio signal. Seconds later came Frank Borman's voice:

"Apollo 8. Over."

"Hello, Apollo 8. Loud and clear."

"Roger. Please be informed there is a Santa Claus."

What Frank Borman was saying was that the chief problem of

space travel, how to come back, was solved. A Christmas present to the world. From that moment a manned landing on the moon was assured.

The Apollo program was only eight years old. It was authorized by Congress, at President Kennedy's urging, in May 1961. The repercussions of the Russian breakthrough with their first Sputnik in 1957 had given a great boost to rocketry in America. N.A.S.A. was set up soon after to put American space exploration on a civilian basis.

The Vanguard experiments, the Explorer probes, the Mercury projects, the Gemini manned orbital missions brought answers to hundreds of questions. Men could live and function in the artificial environment of a spacecraft. In spite of the encumbrance of space suits they could perform the complicated maneuvers in the Gemini Agena program. They could come back to earth undamaged physically and mentally. Electronic guidance of space vehicles could be refined to an incredible degree. Crews could keep in touch with Earth stations by voice and picture across astronomical distances. On Christmas Day 1968 the successful boosting of Apollo 8 out of lunar orbit proved that men could, without drastic danger to themselves, fly at a low altitude round the moon's irregular globe and when the time was right shoot out of its gravitational field towards the appointed "window" in the earth's atmosphere to splash down on schedule into the Pacific Ocean. That was what gave such significance to Frank Borman's homespun phrase: "Please be informed there is a Santa Claus."

How was it possible to accomplish so much so soon?
Planning.
The meshing-in of a thousand techniques in industries great and small operating in every state in the Union. The type of planning and management that brought the new art of computers into industry.

When the technicians reviewed the performance of Apollo 8 they discovered that the combined Saturn rocket and Apollo spacecraft had attained 99.9999% efficiency. Out of something like five million separate parts there were only five minor malfunctions. This hardly-hoped-for perfection speeded the program.

The Apollo 9 and 10 missions followed in quick succession, rehearsals to test the capabilities of men and machines to accomplish a descent to the moon's inhospitable face.

Impossible obstacles were toppled along the way. Finding men willing to take a chance in space was no problem at all. Scores of testpilots and military and naval flyers were ready to volunteer. It was a question of picking the men who seemed physically and mentally best qualified and putting them into training. One episode casts an amusing light on the kind of men who emerged as trained astronauts. To hold off the nausea that had bothered two of the Apollo 9 people, it was decided to let the Apollo 10 crew do as much stunt flying as they wanted to, barrel rolls and the like, in the week before the launching date, to keep their stomachs in tune.

Producing the hardware needed for building an industrial machine geared into an enterprise men had hardly dreamed of before was more complicated. The planners could draw on the experience of the industrial coordination which had been the cornerstone of victory in the 1941–45 war.

Competition spurs the inventive faculty. The Manhattan Project had been driven to continual shortcuts by the knowledge that the Germans were experimenting with heavy water. In the race to the moon, innovators were prodded by the need to compete with the great industrial complex and the Russian brains at the Kremlin's command.

Science is a sport as well as a discipline. Inventors, engineers, researchers, metallurgists, computer programmers, welders, seamstresses cutting out space suits caught fire with the race to the moon. People tended to do just a little more than was expected of them. It was fun to work at top capacity in the service of so rare an adventure.

The hardware would never have been produced without the knowledge supplied by modern research. The Apollo program had at its disposal the greatest array of banks for the storage and processing of data ever assembled in the world. A new art, computers were the field for the young. The average age of the engineers engaged in computer work at Cape Kennedy was twentythree.

An investigator at Cape Kennedy could in an instant bring under his magnifying glass any event he needed to scrutinize in the chain of supply. Management, from being a hit-or-miss proposition, was approaching an exact science. In a matter of seconds the history of a faulty valve could be traced to the ores from which it was forged.

The innumerable varieties of novel materials produced by thousands of different contractors in virtually every state in the Union could never have been collected at the time or the place where they were needed without the refinement of management which computers made possible.

Christmas 1968 seemed to inaugurate a period when the most fruitful human effort converged on space exploration. Already the technology developed for the accomplishment of the Apollo program could be relied on as a permanent achievement available for the solution of a hundred different scientific problems.

What good will it do? people ask. "Couldn't the money be better spent on earth? Is it worth all that expenditure and effort to coop a man up in a spacesuit so that he can take a few steps in that desert?"

The answer is not fame or fortune. The answer is not that men are impelled to the moon, like the first man to climb to the top of Everest "just because it is there." The answer is not: "We do this for national glory," or to prove that some system of political-economic organization works better than some other system.

The answer is that by his very nature, man has to know.

In our century we have seen everything that is hideous in man come to the fore: obsessed leaders butchering helpless populations, the cowardice of the led, the shoddy selfinterest, the easy hatreds that any buffoon can arouse who bellows out the slogans, public derision of everything mankind has learned through the centuries to consider decent and true; but now, all at once, like the blue and white stippled bright earth the astronauts saw rise above the rim of the moon's grisly skeleton there emerges a fresh assertion of man's spirit.

We live in a time when scientism has been foisted as a nonreligion on most of the human race. People have been taught to grovel before the word science. We mustn't forget that science is just Latin for knowledge. The passion for knowledge constantly brushes aside the established dogmas of the day to seek the reality

beyond. Each smallest addition to human knowledge makes it clear
that nobody knows very much about anything. Your first cry when
you studied a photograph of a lunar crater brought back by Apollo
10 was "I didn't know it was like that."

The literary imagination has been pretty good in forecasting
discoveries, but not all the science fiction in the paperbacks could
have forecasted the astonishment, the awe you felt when you first
saw the photograph of the lovely living earth rising above the dead
horizon of the moon.

We know a great deal about certain aspects of reality. About
other aspects we know almost nothing. The most experienced
astronomers' view of the universe is as full of gaps and mysteries as
the medieval world maps where the engraver filled in the blank
spaces with stormlashed galleons and elegantly delineated sea mon-
sters. Our present ignorance of the universe is intolerable to the
best minds. There are many things we need to know about our own
solar system exploration may still uncover. Some key to more precise
knowledge may lie within the radius of the first faltering steps the
astronauts of Apollo 11 made on the lunar surface.

When President Kennedy lightheartedly named 1970 as a
target date for a lunar landing, none of the experimenters with
rocketry had the faintest idea of how it could be done. No spacecraft large enough for the trip had yet been developed. When it was
invented, how could the men aboard be kept alive? How could they
be brought back?

Throughout history the human spirit has advanced unevenly.
The best brains and the most ardent imaginations tend to face one
challenge at a time, leaving other sectors to stagnation and degener-
acy on the eternal battlefield where man struggles to dominate the
evil within him and the impartial pressures of his material environment.

The most ignorant layman bused through the installations at
Cape Kennedy couldn't help but be stirred by the feeling that
knowledge was being expanded dizzily fast all around him. After
this, nothing in the universe will look the same to him.

Some astonished awareness of the great implications must
account for the emotion people show on the packed viewing stands

as they follow the countdown on each lunar flight. The families on the beaches, the groups with field glasses and telescopes along the shores of the Indian River wait tense with excitement as the minutes tick away. "This is like pioneering in the old days," fathers tell their children. "You are going to see something no man has ever seen before."

With each successive launching the tension has risen. Apollo 11 was the climax. All the rest were practice heats. Through the long apprehension of the countdown a myriad anxious eyes watched the gleaming white pencil wrapped in its dainty plume of steam on the launching pad six miles away.

"Two minutes, thirtysix seconds and counting . . . all systems go." Ears throbbed in anticipation, hearts beat a tattoo. Suppose something went wrong. "Thirty seconds and counting." Now the fire. Red and yellow flames. The great white pencil lifted itself slowly out of its billow of brown smoke. An enormous rumbling roar filled the sky. Faster, higher. The flaming rocket curves into the clouds. Frantic throats answer the jet engines' roar only to be hushed when the quiet workaday voices of the spacecraft's crew take over the radio. Worldwide, uncounted millions of television viewers joined in a prayer for the men in that golden bullet. In every one of them the need to know, the smouldering spirit of adventure, buried deep down under the routine of every day, flared for a moment like the rocket engine into soaring flame.